BARBARA LIVINGSTON'S

Saratoga

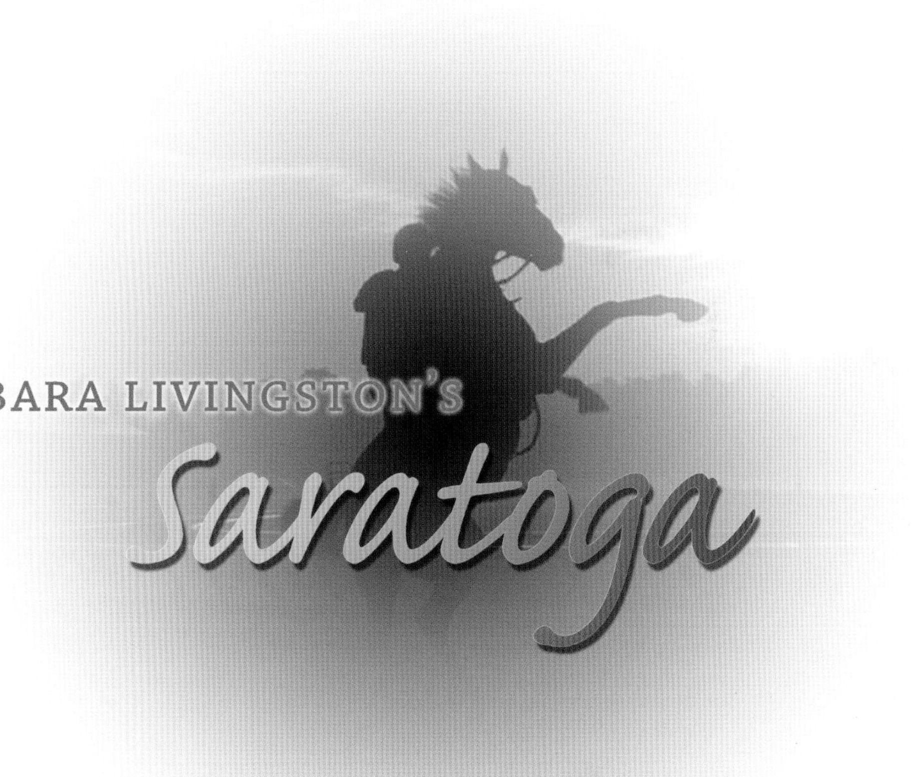

Library of Congress Control Number: 2005920843

ISBN 10: 1-58150-129-3
ISBN 13: 978-1-58150-129-2

Printed in China
First Edition: 2005

Distributed to the trade by
National Book Network
4720-A Boston Way, Lanham, MD 20706
1.800.462.6420

ECLIPSE PRESS

a division of The Blood-Horse, Inc.
PUBLISHERS SINCE 1916

BARBARA LIVINGSTON'S

Saratoga

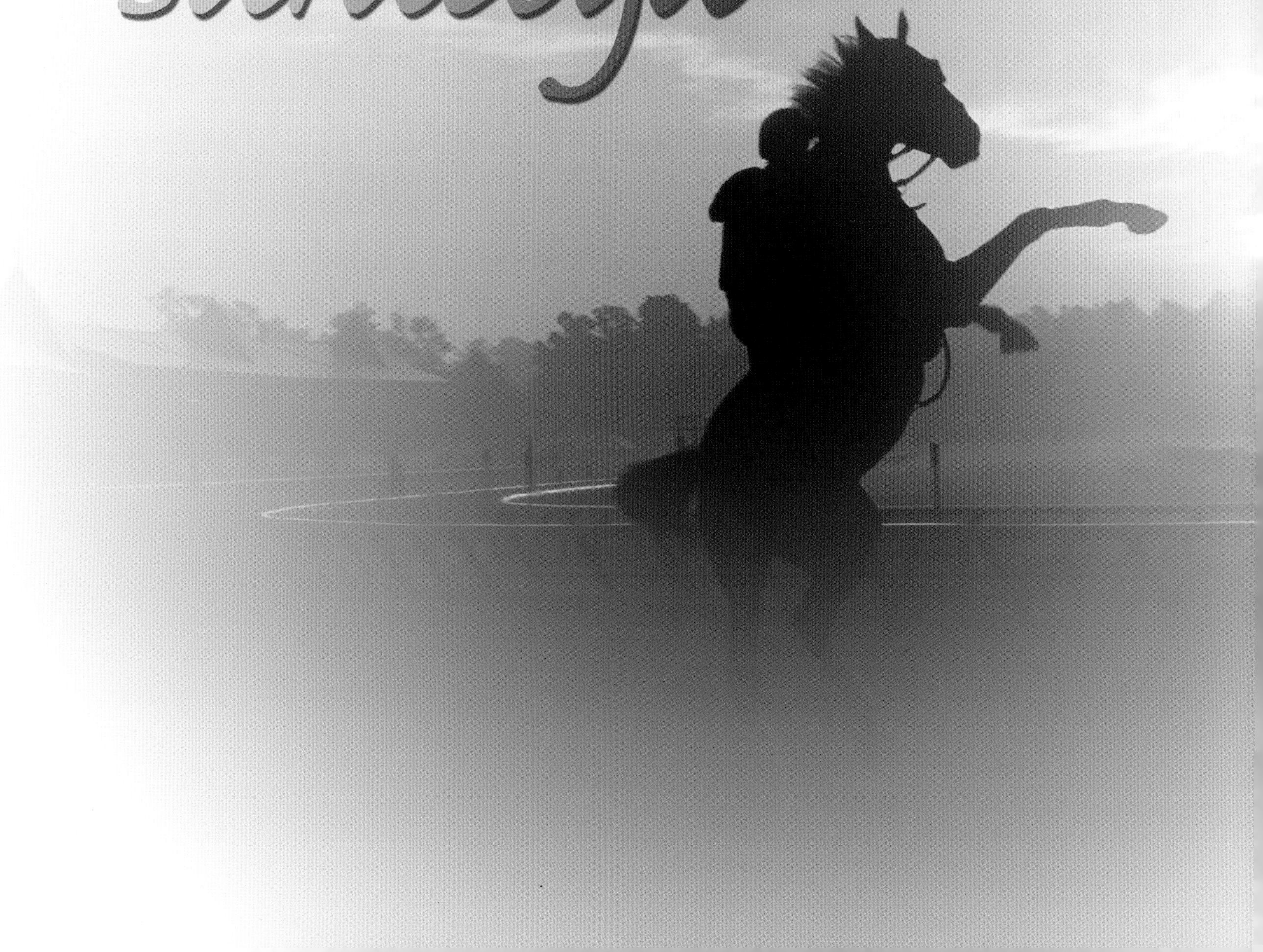

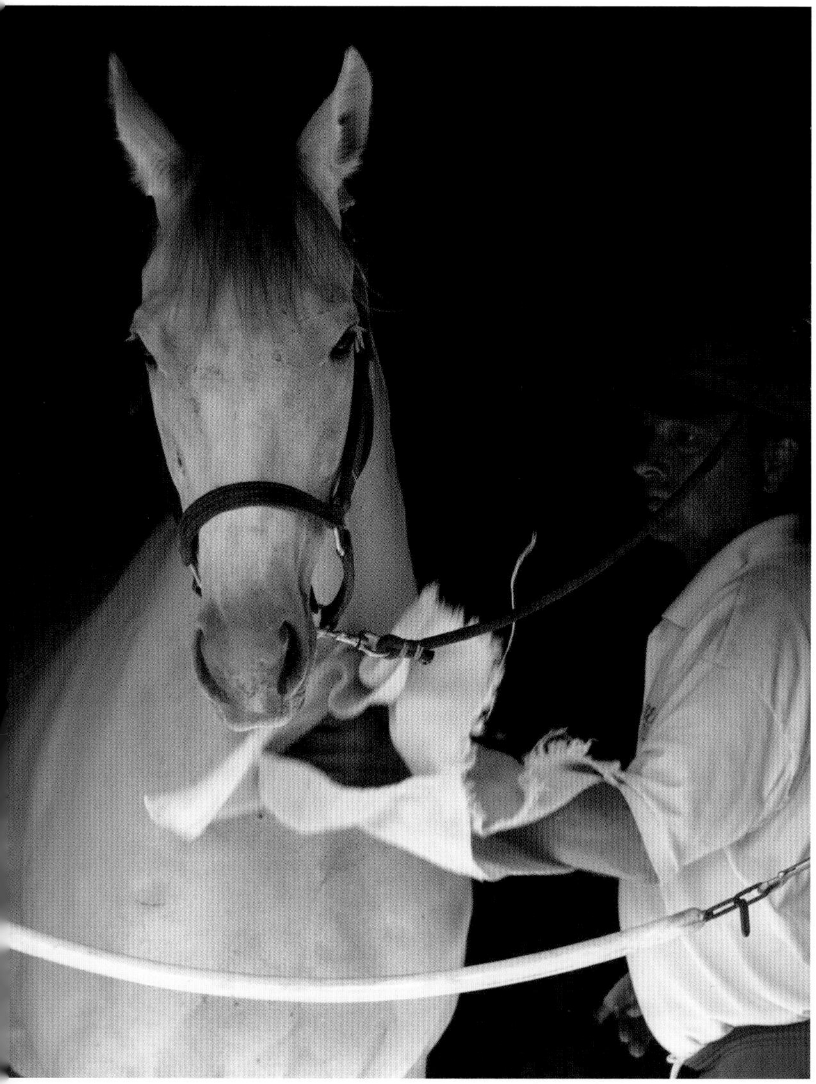

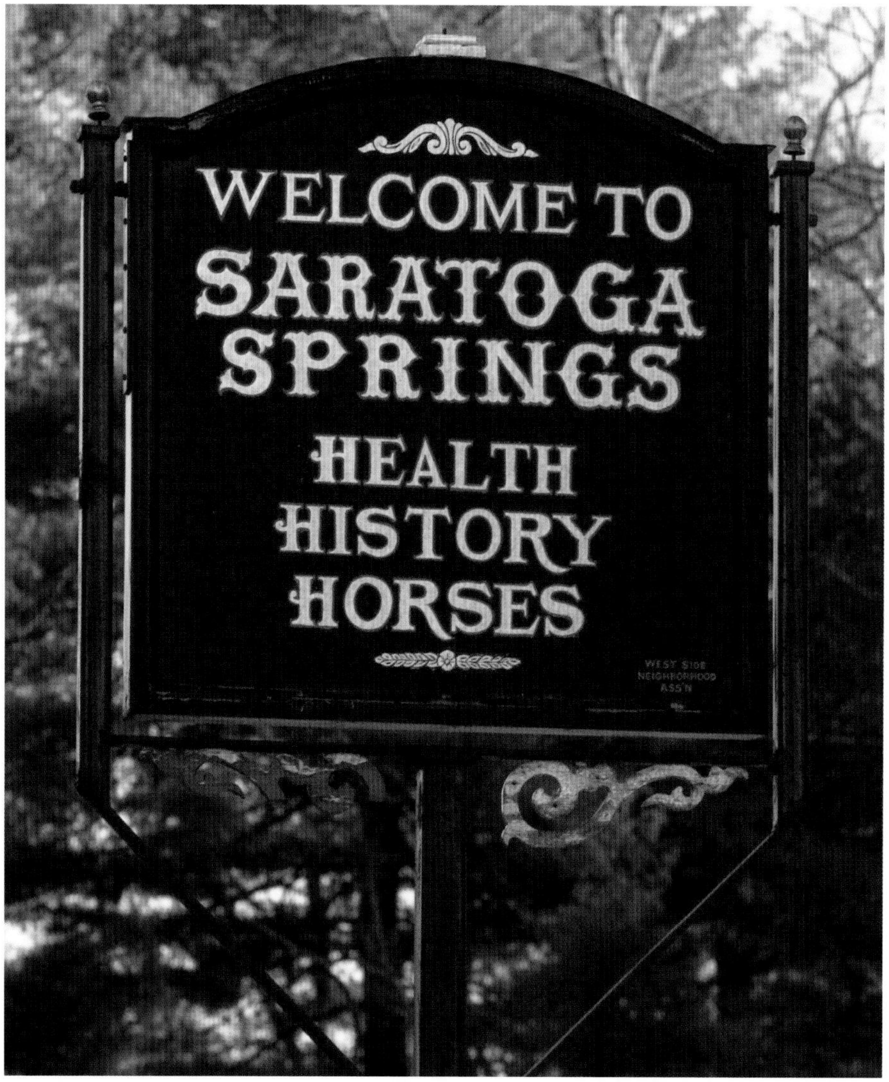
WELCOME TO
SARATOGA
SPRINGS
HEALTH
HISTORY
HORSES
WEST SIDE
NEIGHBORHOOD
ASS'N

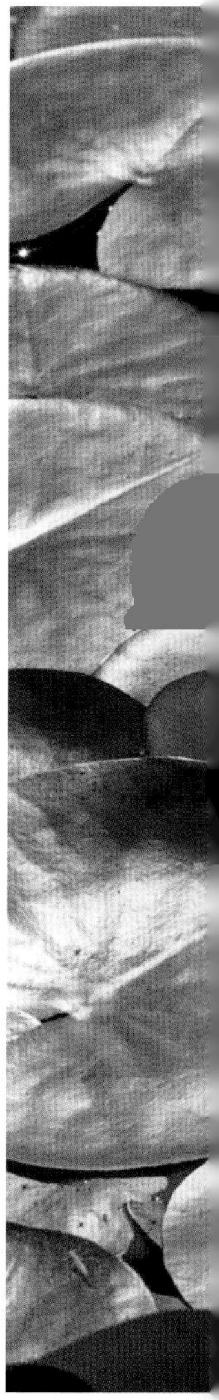

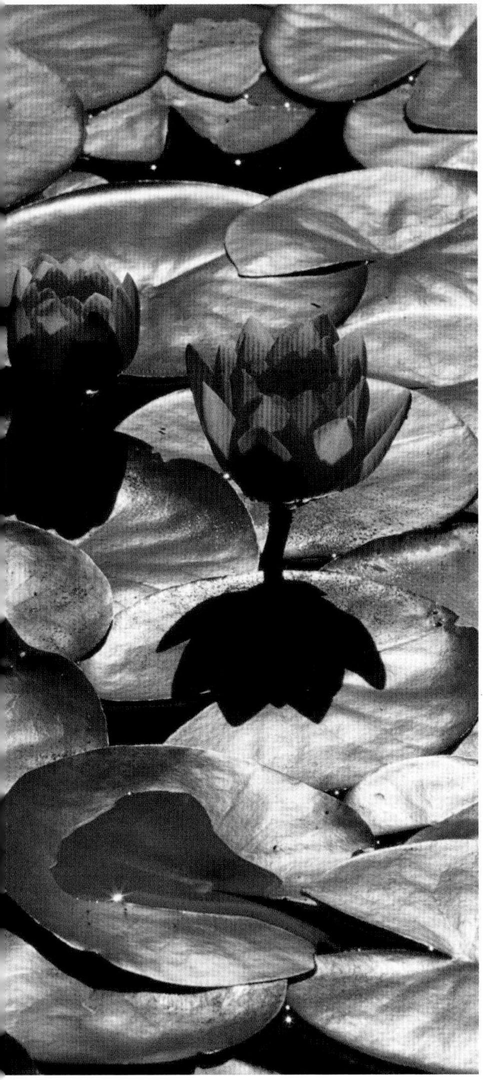

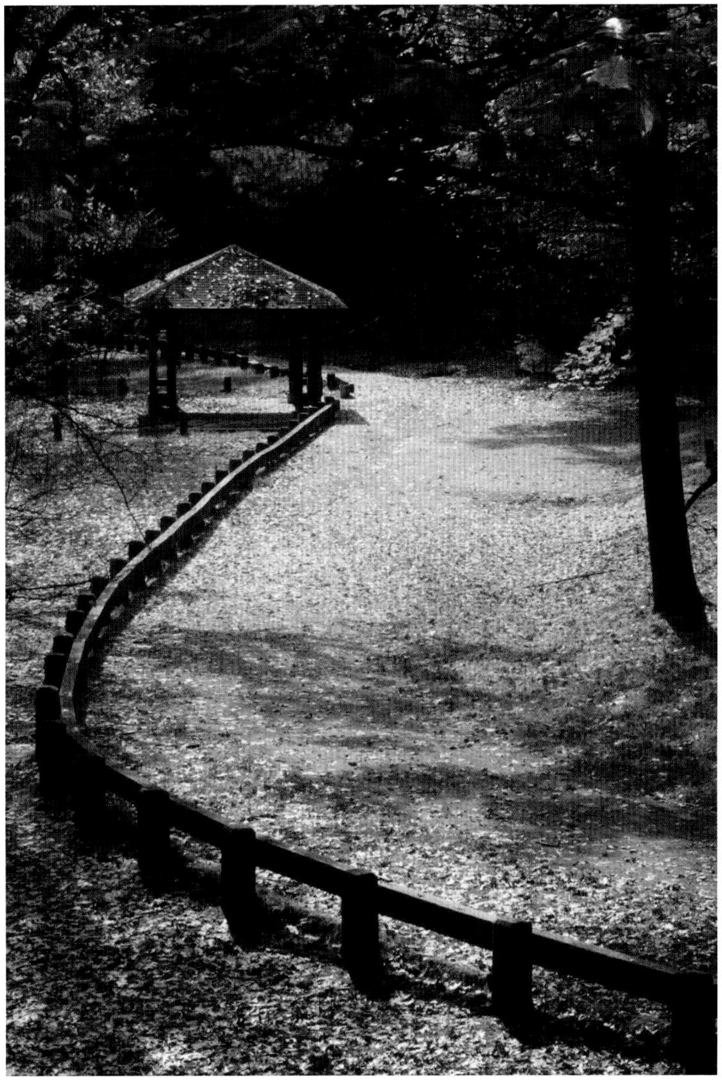

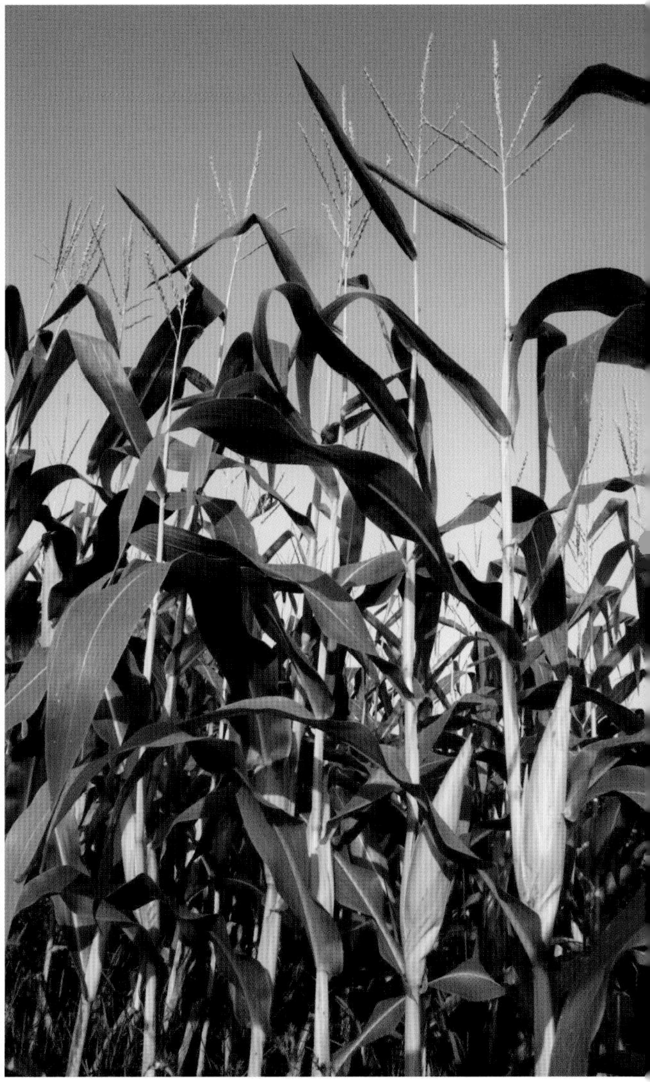

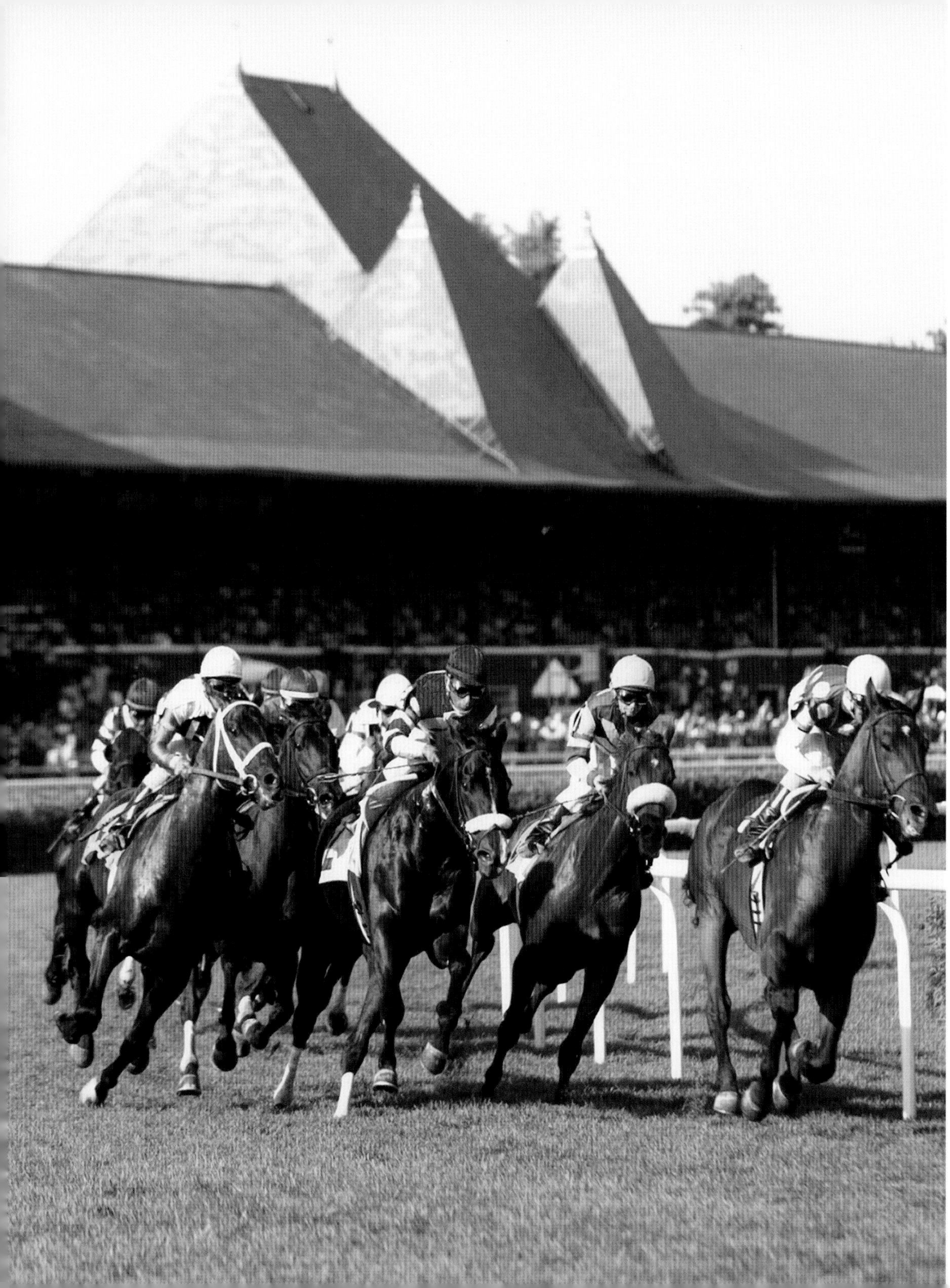

It is a city rich in tradition, a beloved vacation resort, and home to more than 25,000 people. Yet, for me, Saratoga Springs, New York, is much more. It is hallowed ground.

I first remember visiting Saratoga Race Course, the historic racing oval on Union Avenue, when I was eleven. The track was a natural place for parents to take a horse-crazy daughter, and mine took me there often during my teen years.

It was a magical time in Saratoga's history, a time when Secretariat, Ruffian, Forego, and Affirmed and Alydar wrote the headlines.

Saratoga was a wonderland. Morning visits meant horses working out through brilliant golden light or lazy white fog. Afternoons meant the races, and I pored over the racing program, learning names, bloodlines, racing colors, and the art of wagering.

Betting, however, wasn't the draw. It was the majesty of the Thoroughbred and the beauty of the historical track. I was so devoted to horse racing that I knew nearly every Kentucky Derby winner's name by heart. Saratoga's racing past was filled with titans of the sport. Man o' War ran here; so did Exterminator and "the gray ghost" Native Dancer.

Toting an Instamatic camera to the track, I learned I could preserve my heroes forever. Those early photos were pitiful perhaps, but by the age of thirteen I had decided upon my profession: horse racing photography. More than thirty years later, that's still what I do, whether chasing Cigar back to his barn in the morning or dodging raindrops during Birdstone's Travers. Photographing racehorses is, in the words of the old classic movie, a magnificent obsession. And Saratoga is still a wonderland.

From my reverence for the racetrack grew a deep love for the area. After all, racing is conducted only in the summer, and the city holds year-round treasures. Driving up Union Avenue is stunning proof of that, with aging mansions sporting expansive porches and overflowing flower boxes.

I have read historical books, about racing and the region, many purchased at the priceless Lyrical Ballad Bookstore on Phila Street. I have spent countless hours there perusing its vast collections of antiquarian books. The proprietors of the shop share my love for this city's history.

Most locals seem to as well. Art exhibits at my favorite coffee shop, Uncommon Grounds, and photo lab, Image, often feature Saratoga-related landmarks. A popular downtown store, deJonghe Original Jewelry, creates custom works featuring Saratoga themes.

The Adirondack Trust Company, a long-standing local bank whose main branch towers over Broadway, is known for its philanthropy. The post office's lobby sports moody, touching 1930s murals of area scenes. Many local businesses sport "Saratoga" in their names.

Pride is everywhere.

The area's emphatic four seasons — happy spring, green summer, brilliant autumn, and stark winter — offer a beautifully varied photographer's palette.

While many areas of Saratoga County inspire me to bring along my camera, hoping to preserve the moment, some locations feel truly magical. The racetrack, of course, is one.

Another is Yaddo, the artists' retreat. While photographing in the rose gardens, I sense the appreciation and benevolence of philanthropist Katrina Trask, who more than a hundred years ago decided this land would be an artists' haven.

I've visited Congress Park and the Saratoga Spa State Park more times than I can count. I've driven through the gates of historic Greenridge Cemetery, nestled just off of Broadway, in the rain and snow. The beautiful aging headstones, imposing mausoleums, and carved angels would catch any photographer's eye, but Greenridge especially moves me. My best friend lies buried there.

Saratoga Battlefield is inspirational and haunting. I admit, I am most inspired by scenes not exactly historical. I love photographing the wild deer that, just before sunset, wander out from the golden thickets to browse. And I am moved when imagining the field back in 1777 when Americans — fighting for their independence — scored their first major victory over the British.

Walking through the heart of downtown Saratoga always brings me joy. Century-old buildings watch over the passersby, while old-time clocks and streetlights promote the other-era feel. There are musicians, and horse-drawn carriages, and frequent street festivals, from Victorian street walks to grand First Night celebrations.

I've lived elsewhere for short periods of time. Yet Saratoga always beckons, and I always return.

It is home.

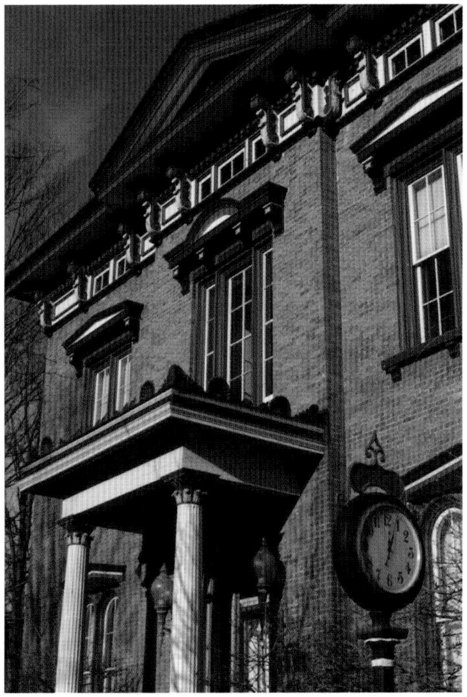

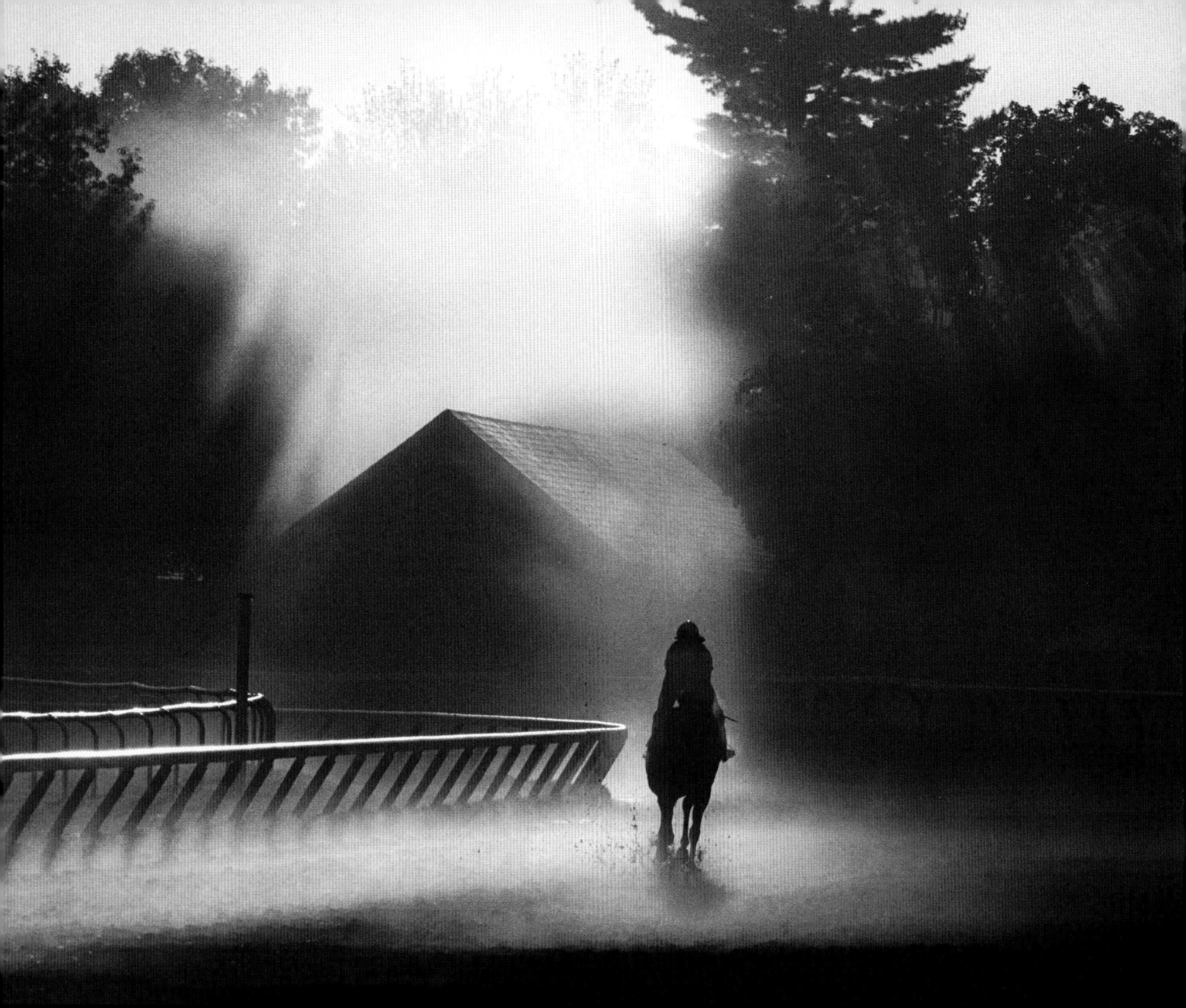

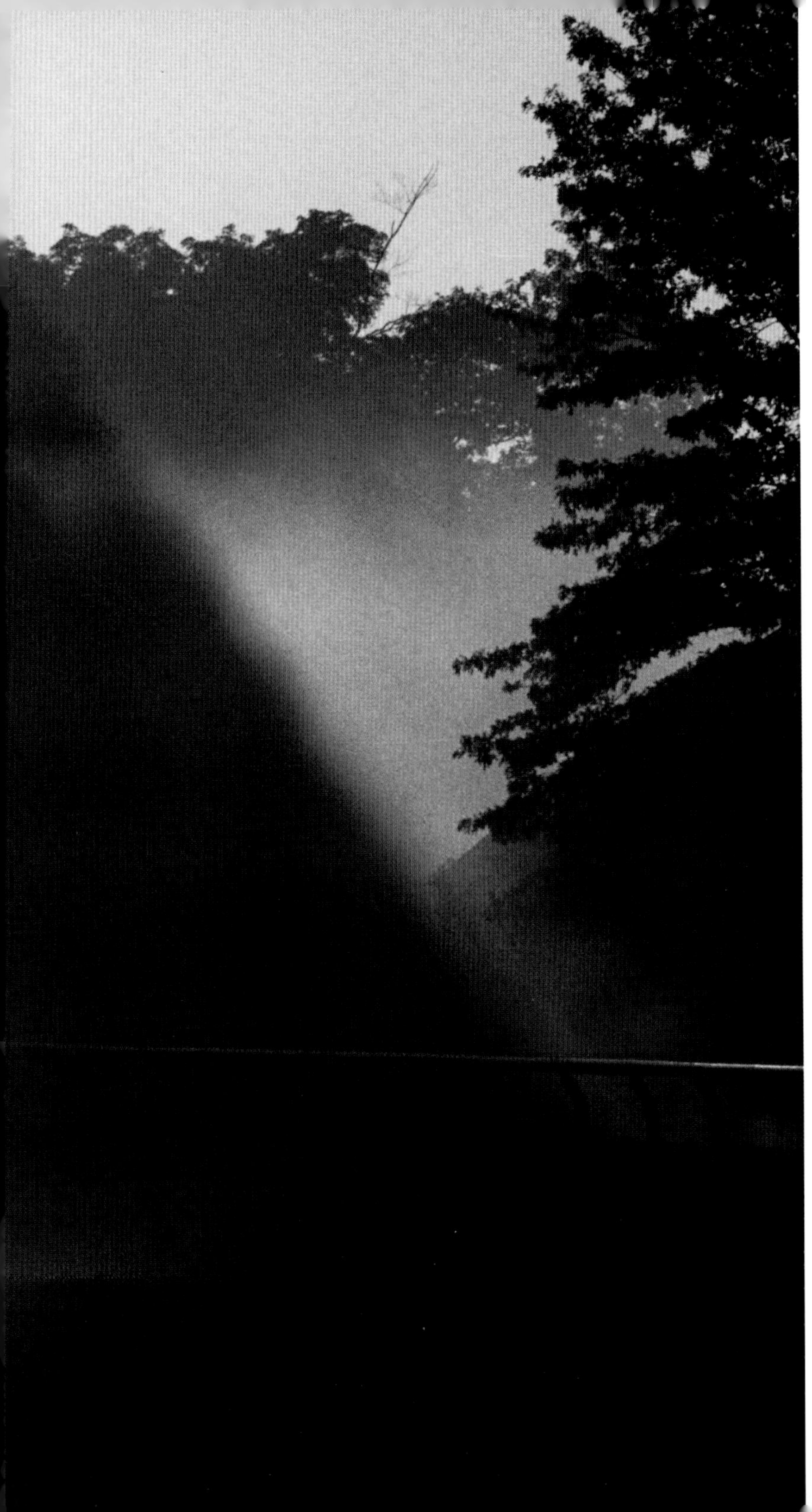

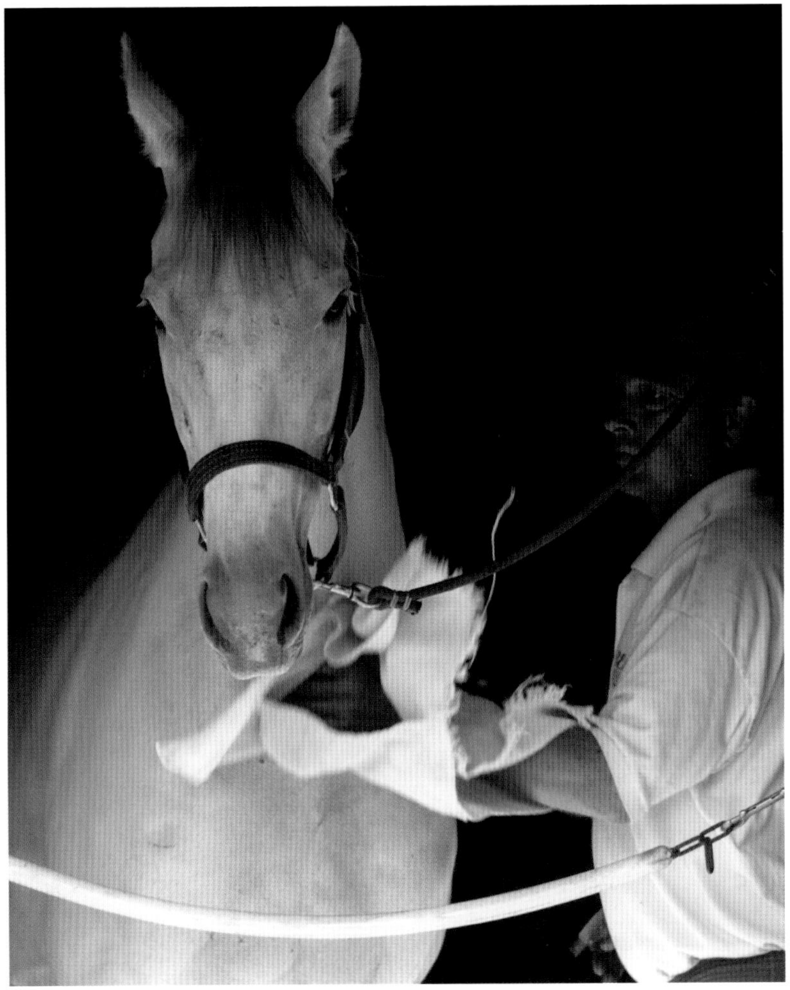

Saratoga Race Course

The sun has not yet risen over Saratoga Race Course, but the glory of impending dawn paints the sky lavender. Fog wanders the infield in wisps, slipping over the inside rail and onto the track. While the town lies silent, most occupants asleep, the track awakens.

The aged Saratoga grandstand keeps silent vigil as another morning unfolds. The sound of hoof beats echoes up the stairs, through the stands, reverberating off wooden walls and ceilings more than a century old. Man o' War's hoof beats resounded here, and Native Dancer's, and Secretariat's. Now it is their descendants' turn to continue the written history of the track.

Every year around mid-July, the pilgrimage begins anew as oversized horse vans, with grooms eagerly peering from side windows, trek up the Northway. Their cargo — Thoroughbred racehorses — converges from seemingly everywhere. The owners of these racehorses carry the same dreams of horse owners for more than a century: to win a race at Saratoga.

Saratoga Race Course provides a remarkably rich, varied palette for the photographer's lens. On sunny mornings, the first light bathes countless scenes a brilliant gold. When the fog rolls in, the world is monochromatic, with shrouded forms slipping through the viewscape in surreal fashion.

Hall of Fame trainers Allen Jerkens and Bill Mott head trackward with morning sets, as Jerry Bailey and Edgar Prado zoom by on exercising horses. Angel Cordero Jr., a true Saratoga legend, gallops horses many mornings, as another Spa City legend, Marylou Whitney, visits her latest batch of racehorses.

The modern day is forgotten for those who wander amidst the ancient barns, watching horses being bathed through clouds of rising steam and grooms performing their morning ritual. It is a quiet world — a world away from the afternoons.

During the afternoons, the racetrack comes alive with sound, excitement, and hope.

Saratoga's beautiful wooden grandstand, so quietly reflective in the morning, now teems with the buzzing, swelling crowd, and revels in the happy tension of the day. As each race unfolds, and another field of horses sweeps into the hallowed homestretch, the tremendous roar of the crowd drowns the sound of hoofbeats. The horses and jockeys drive to the finish wire, and as they sweep beneath it, they, too, become another paragraph of Saratoga's history.

The jockeys' brilliant silks, the bugle call, the seemingly always-uncertain weather, the drama of each exciting race …

How grand racing at Saratoga is!

MORNING FOG (PREVIOUS, LEFT)

WITH ANTICIPATION (PREVIOUS, RIGHT) being groomed by Dave Holstein.

ARTAX, champion sprinter, greets sunrise on the Oklahoma track.

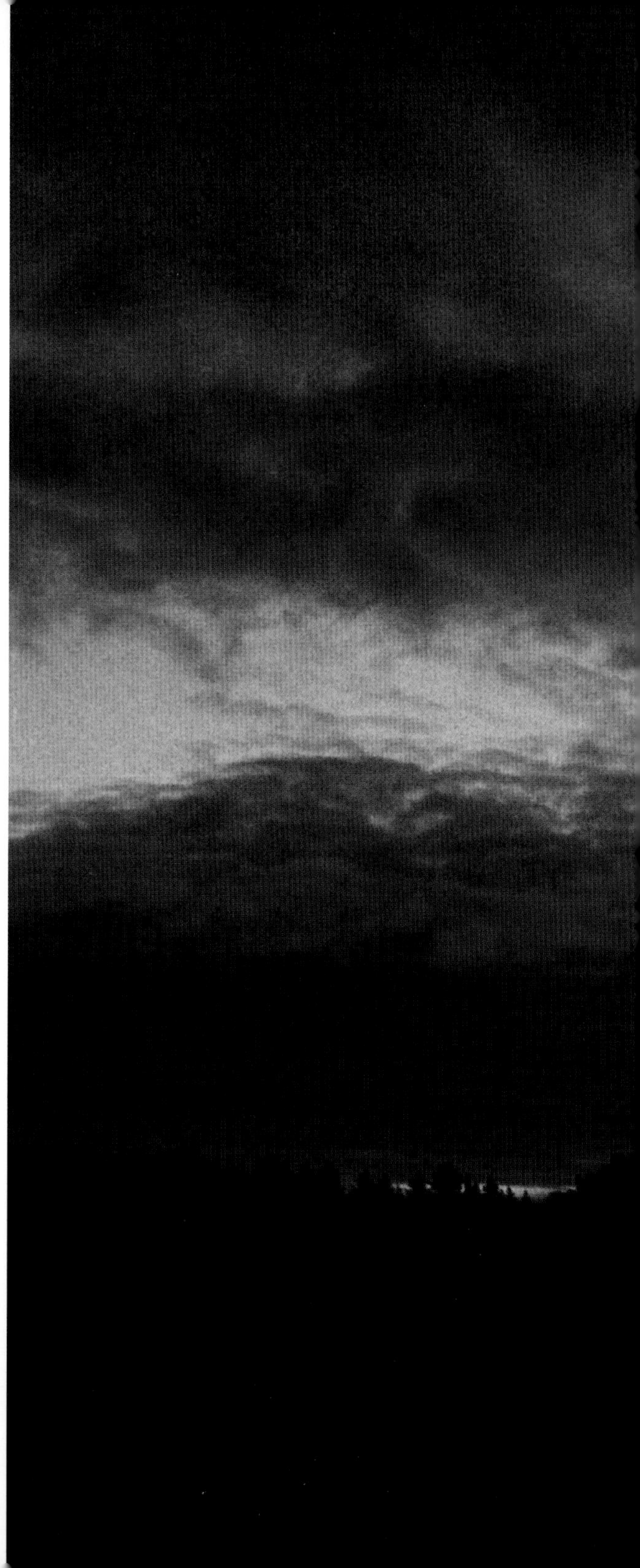

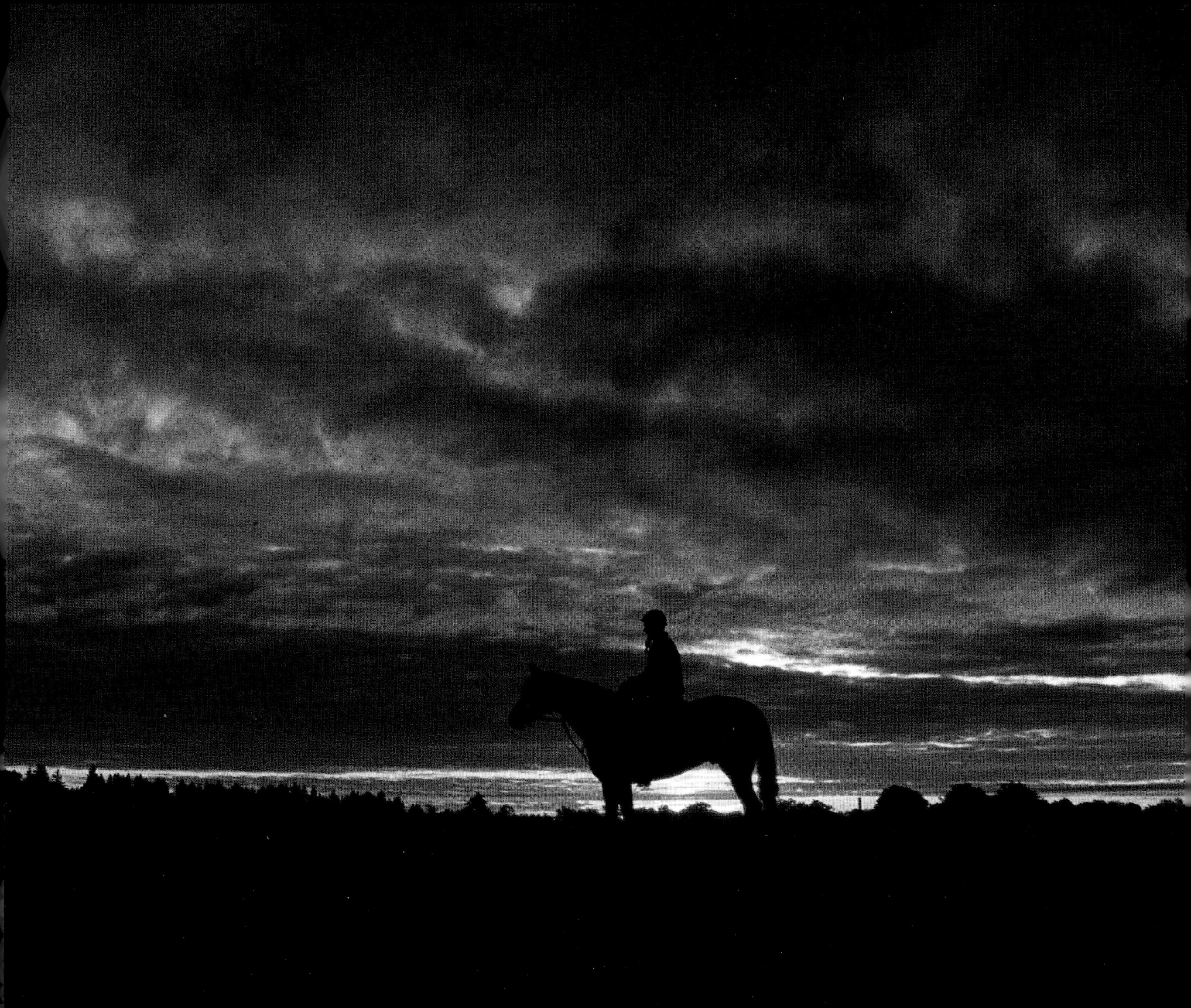

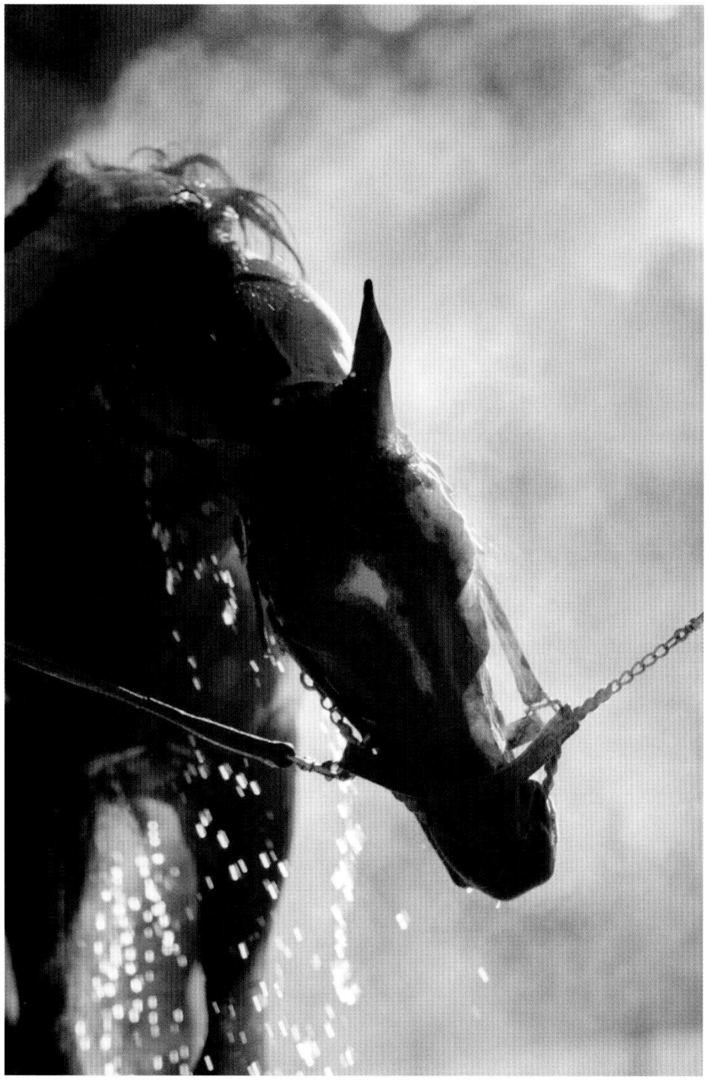

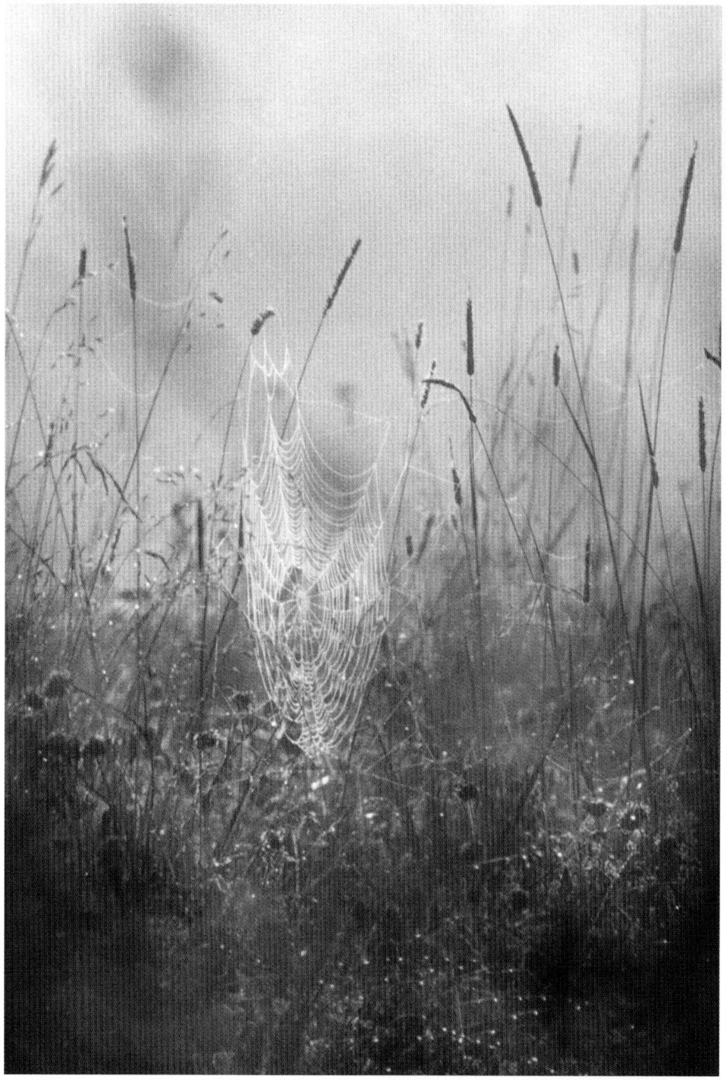

CIGAR (ABOVE), two-time Horse of the Year, gets a bath at Greentree Stable, adjacent to the racetrack and Yaddo.

A BILL MOTT-TRAINEE (RIGHT) gallops at beautiful Stonerside Stable, formerly Greentree Stable.

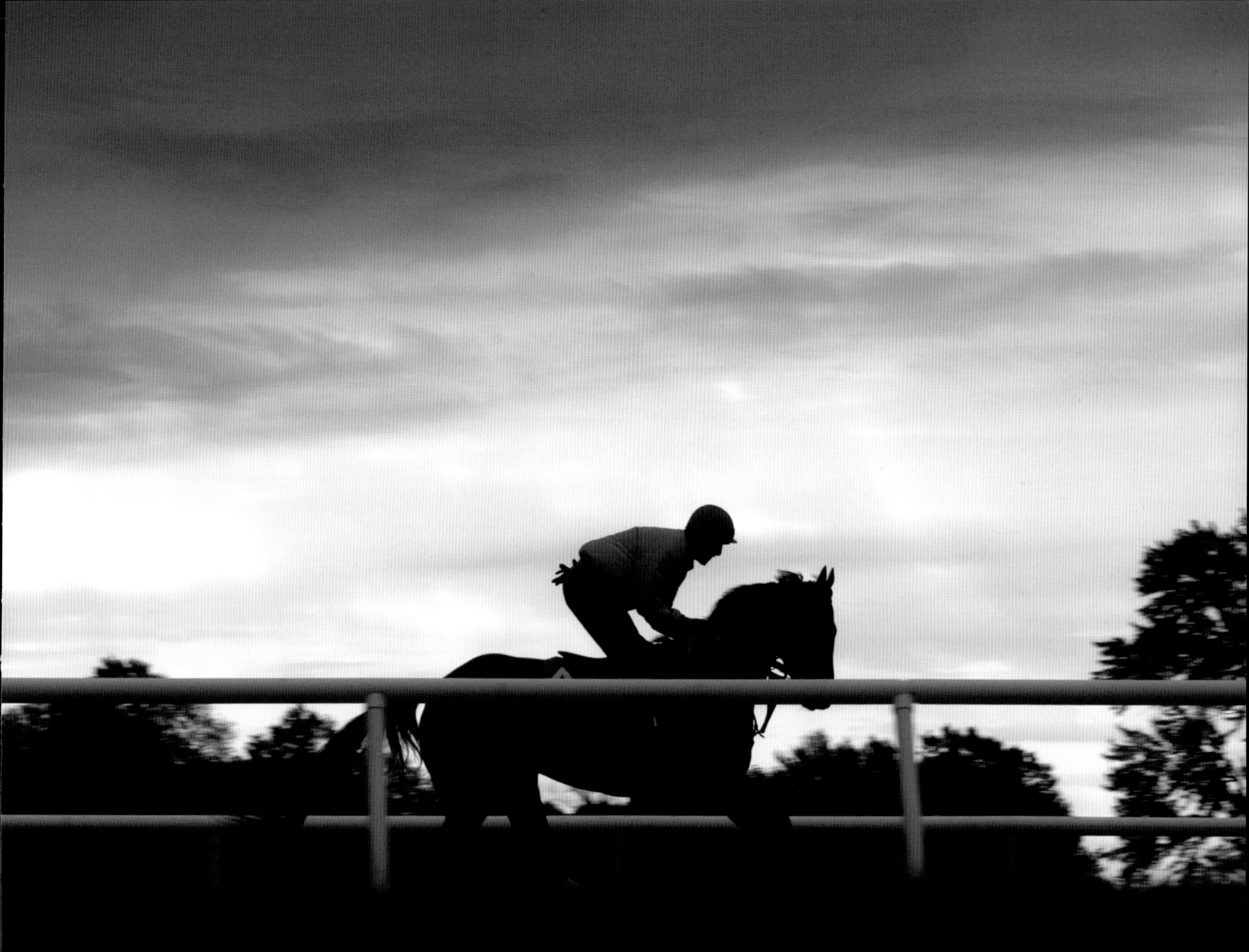

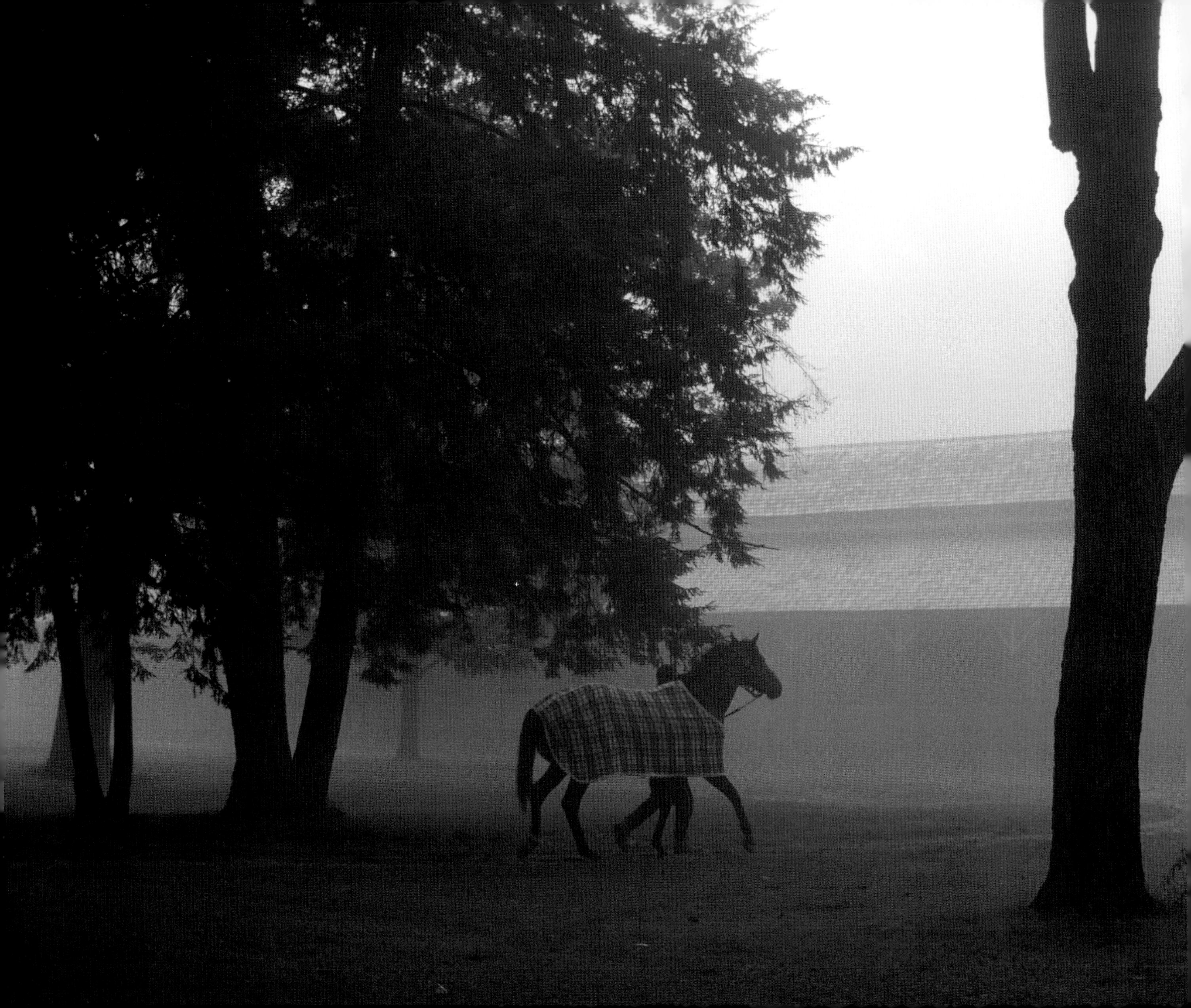

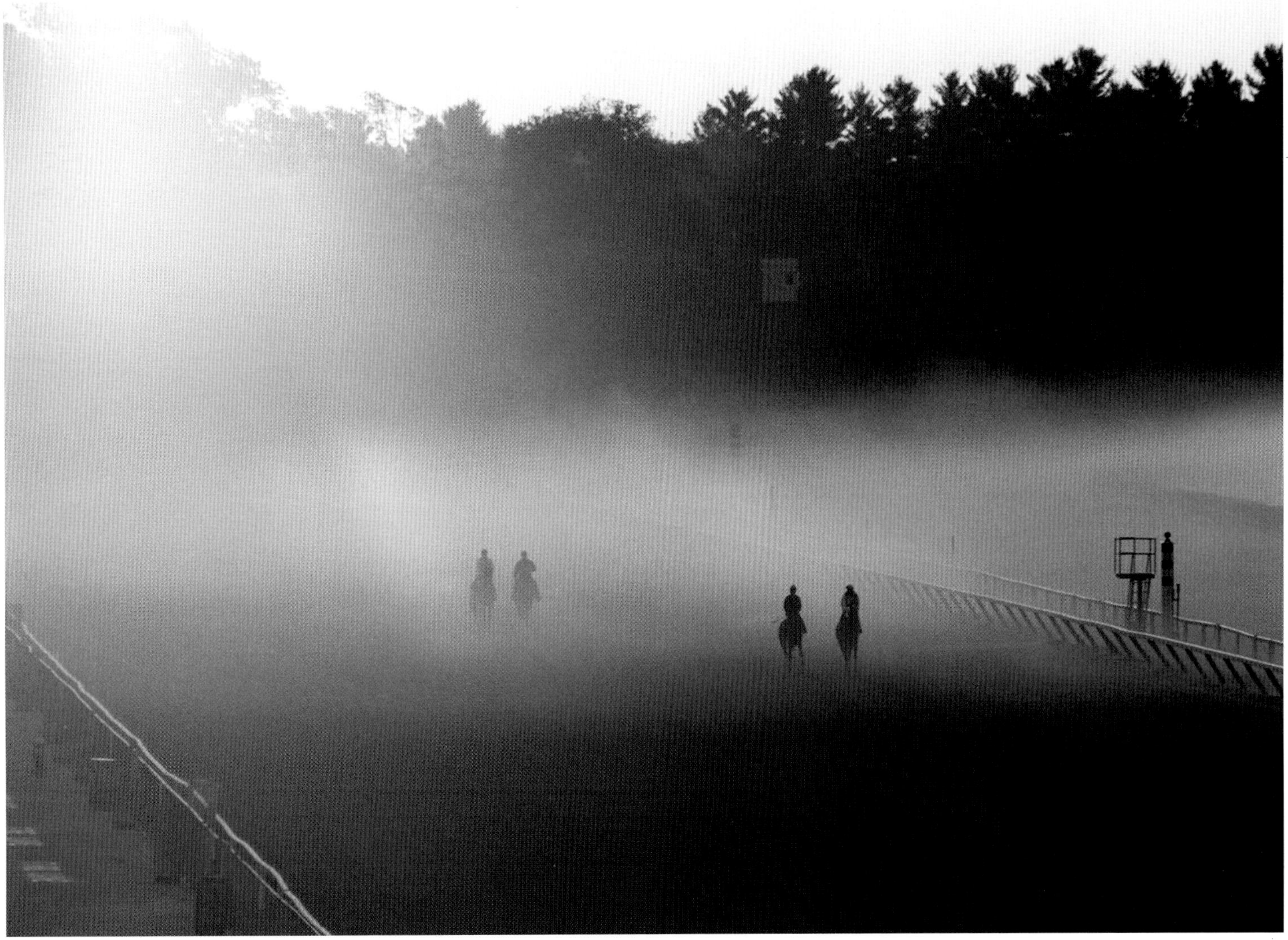

COOLING OUT (LEFT), Clare Court.

SCHULHOFER SET (ABOVE) emerging from the fog.

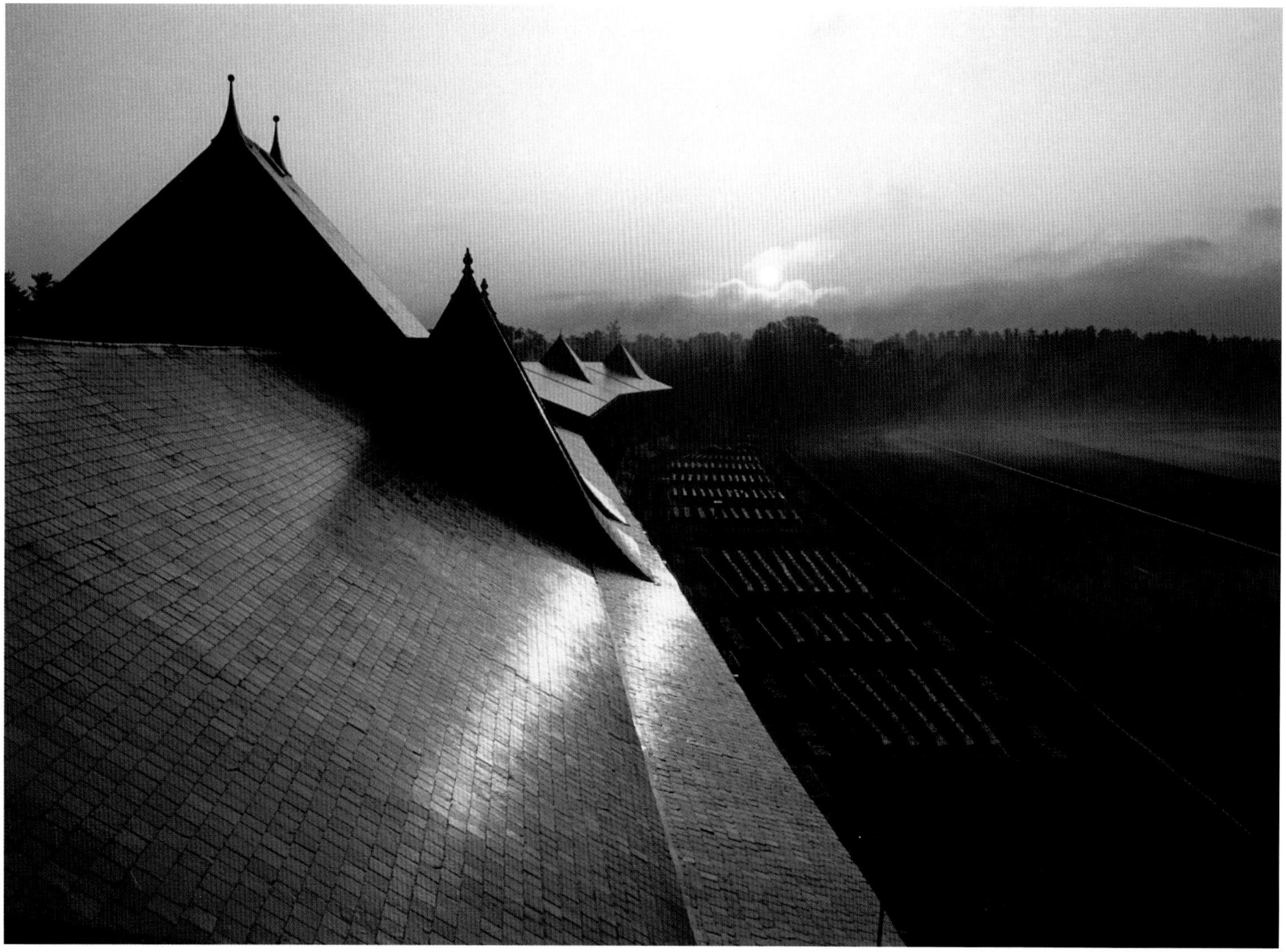

 SARATOGA SUNRISE

DAWN AT THE LUKAS BARN (RIGHT)

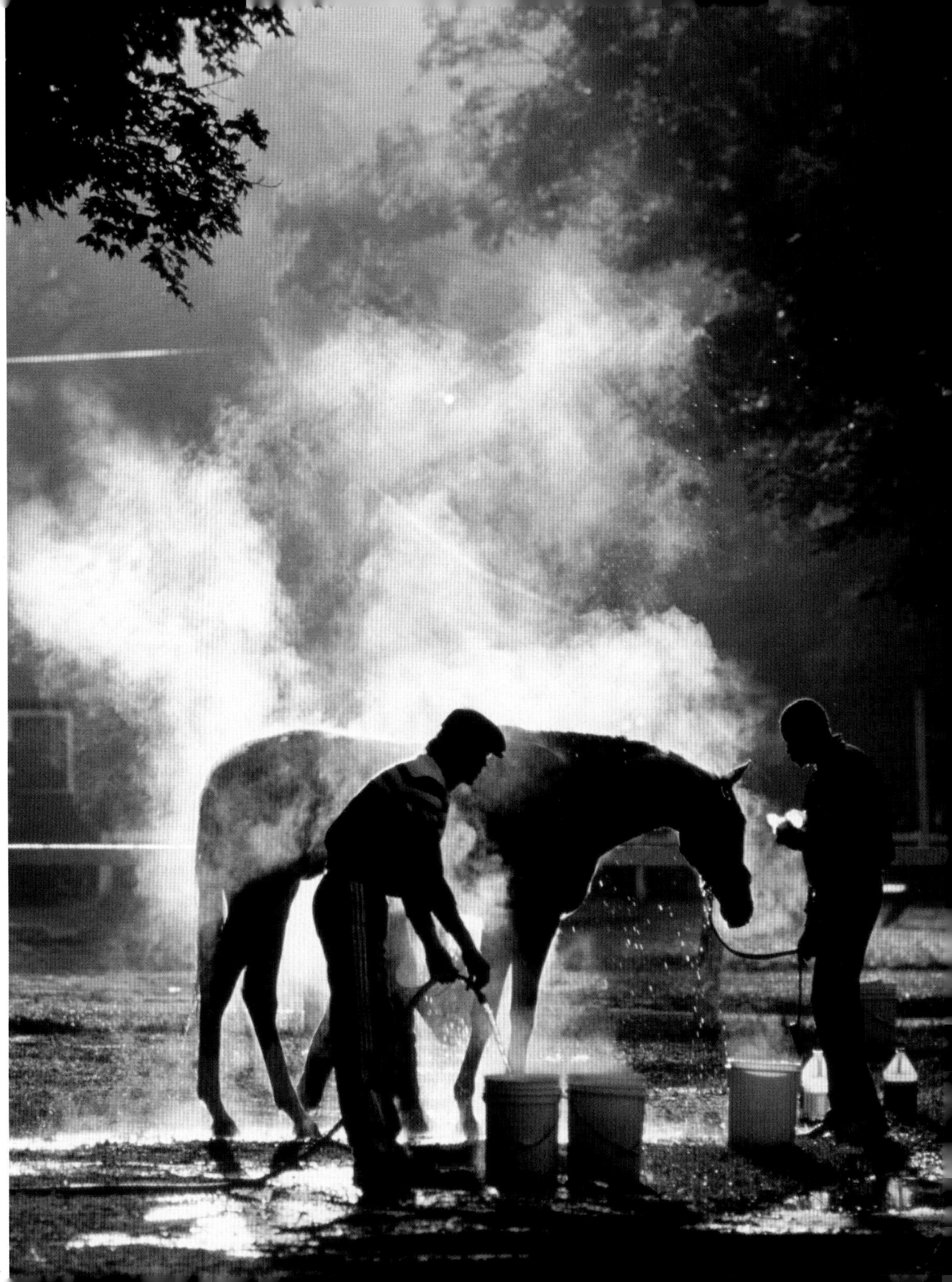

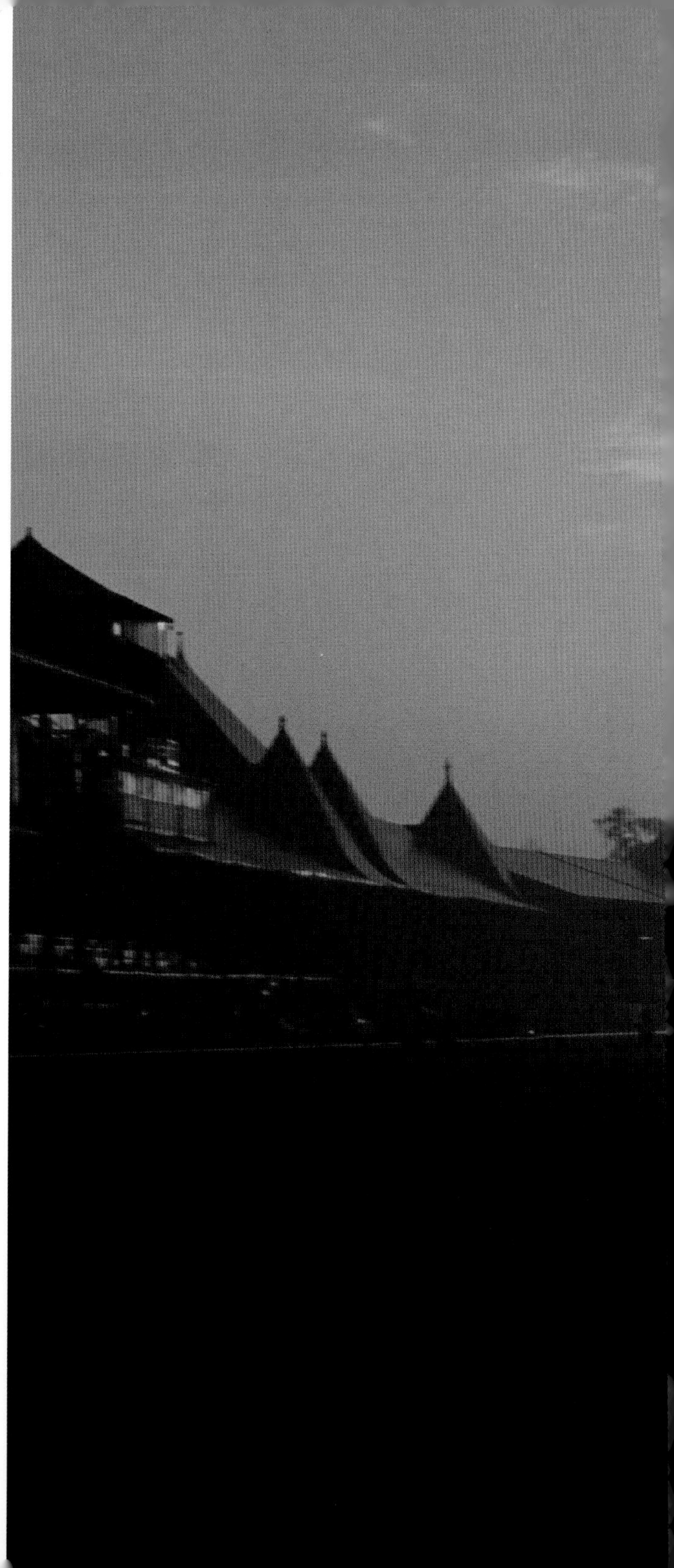

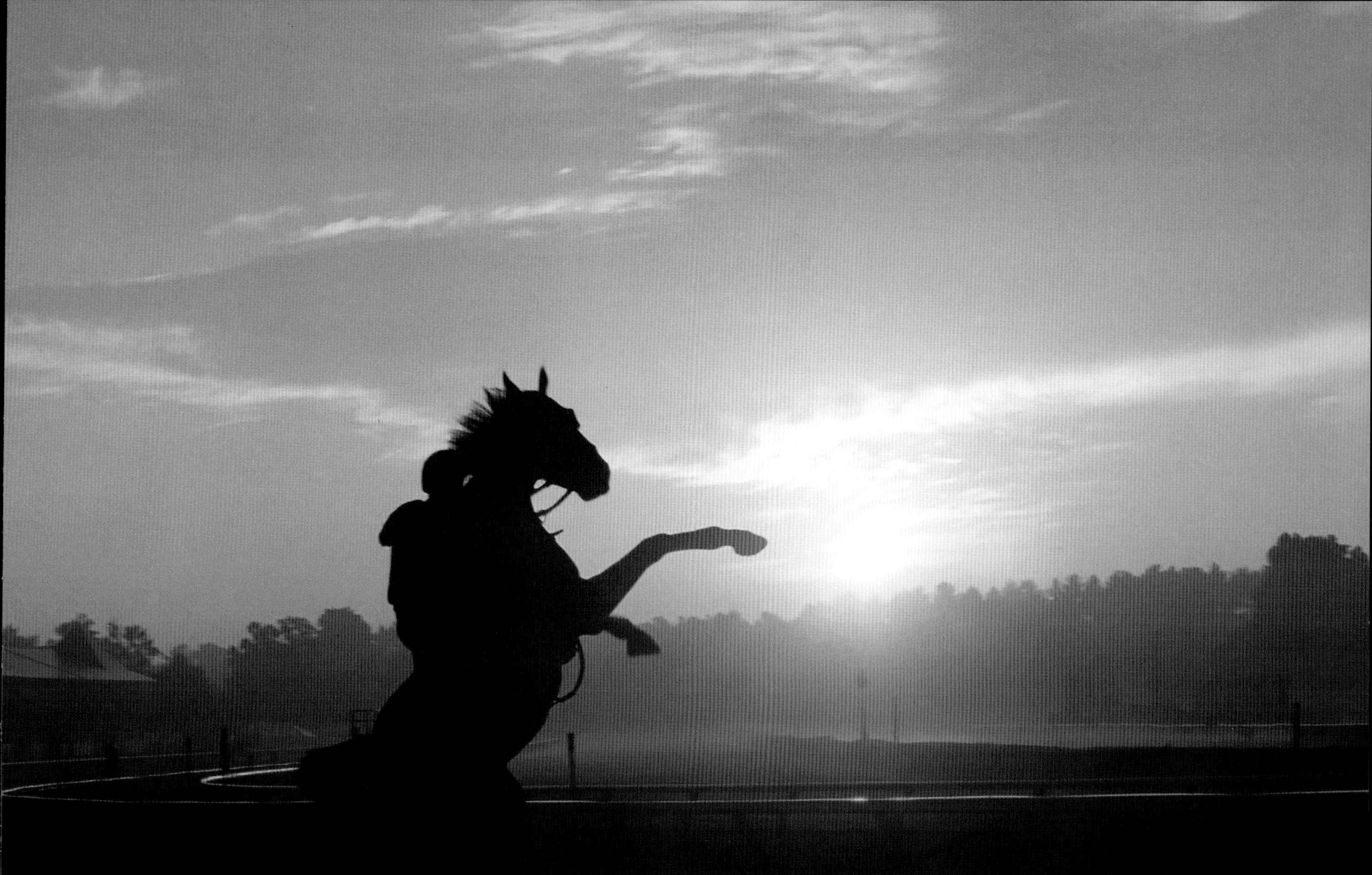

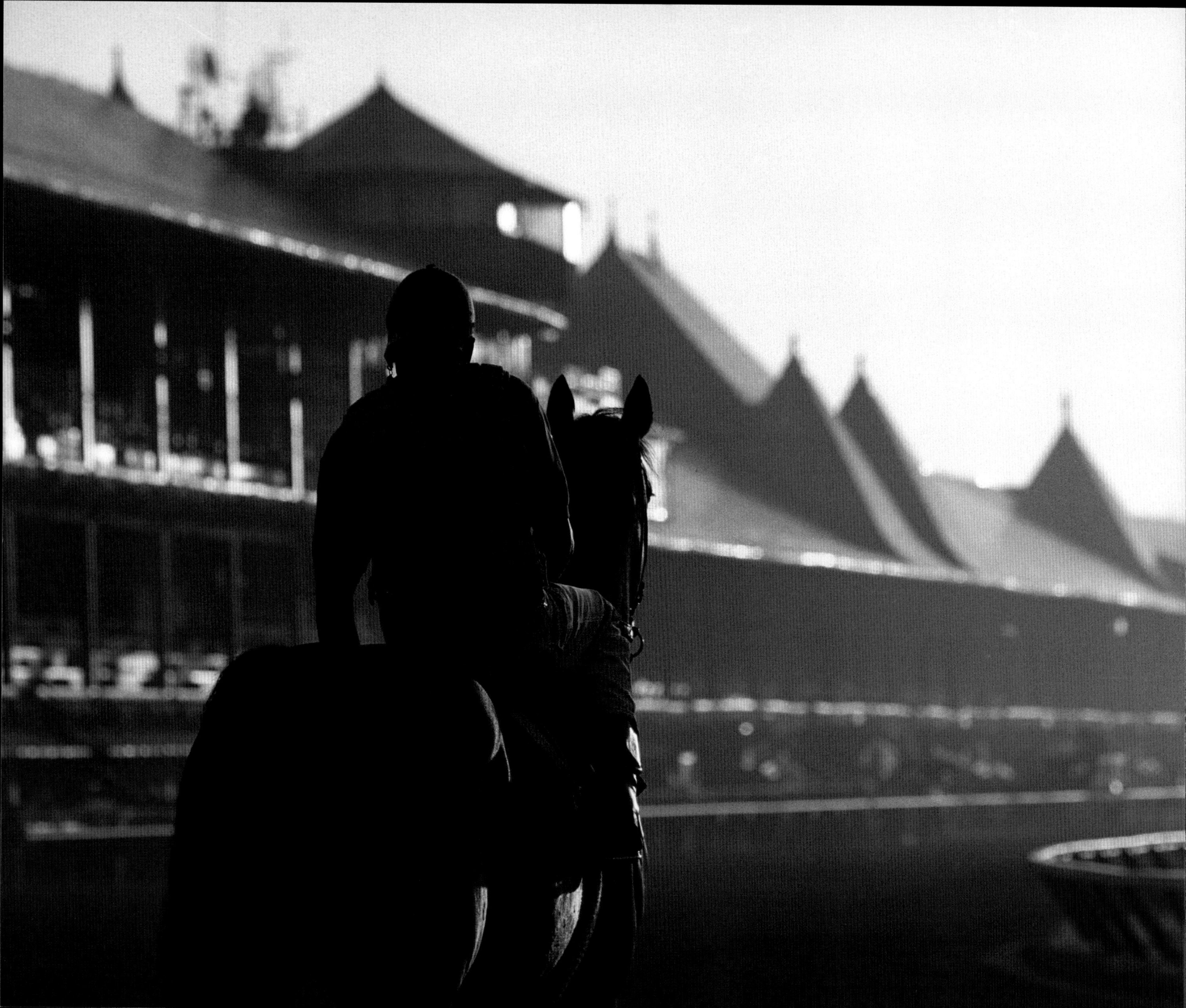

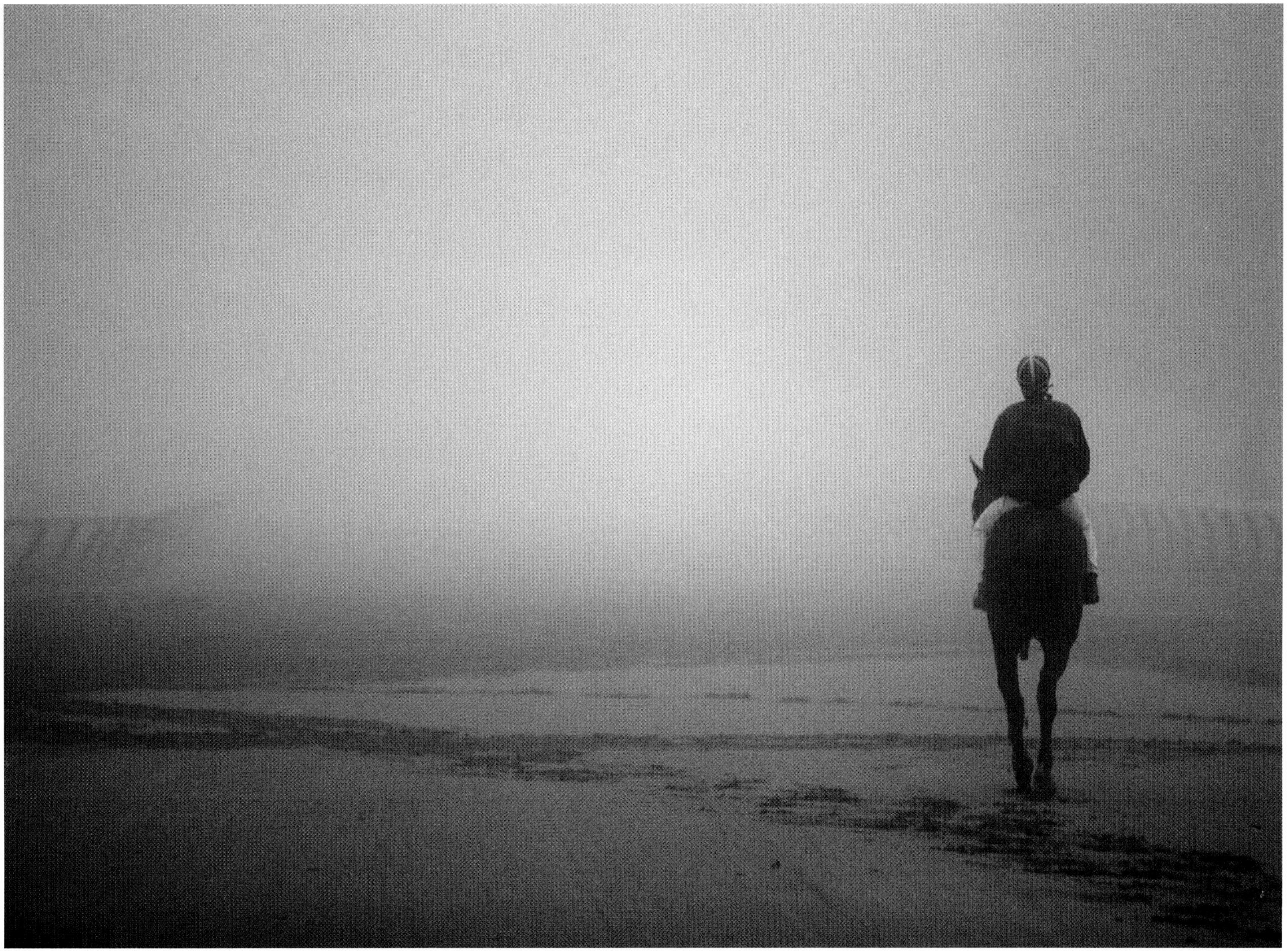

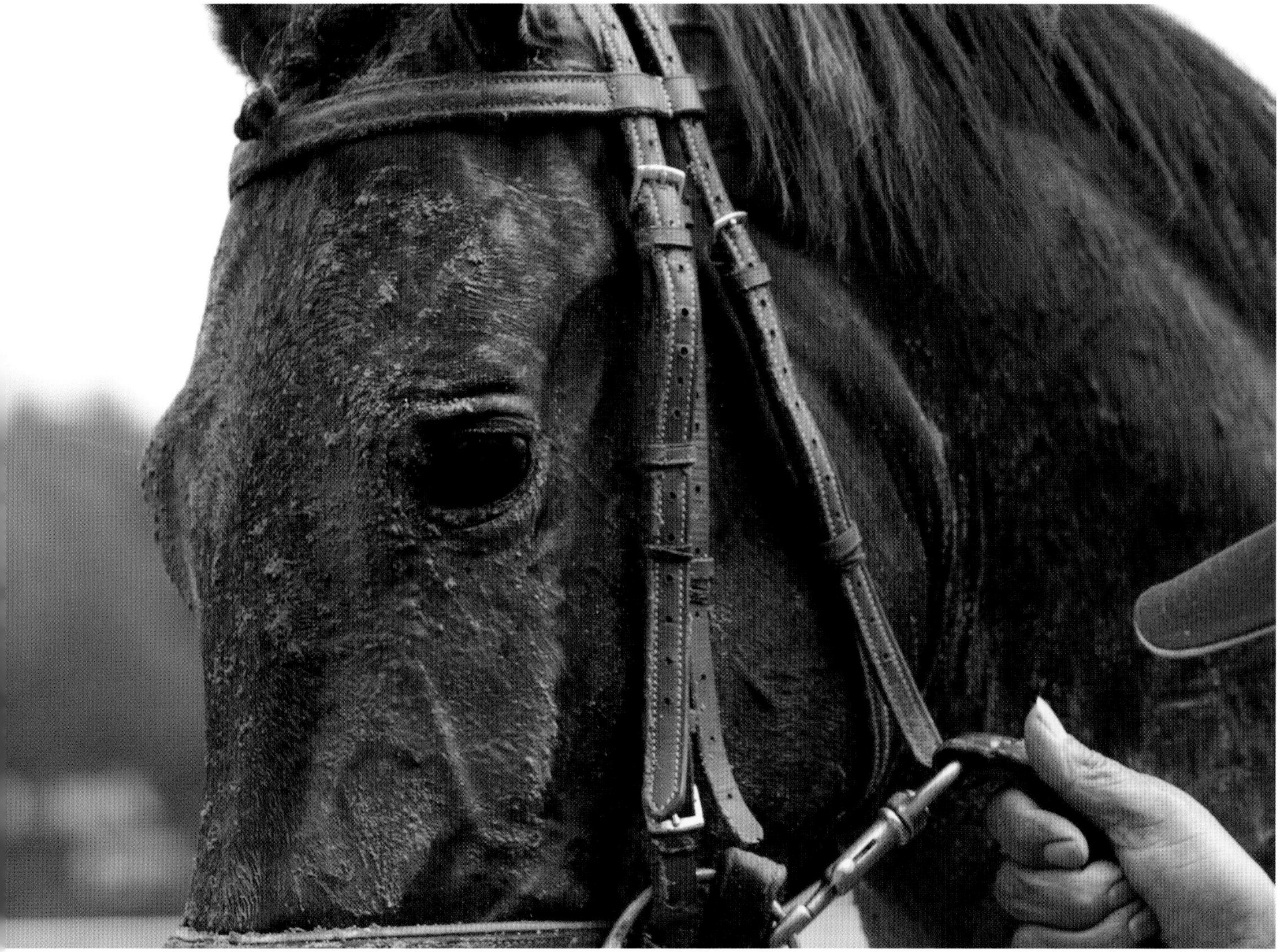

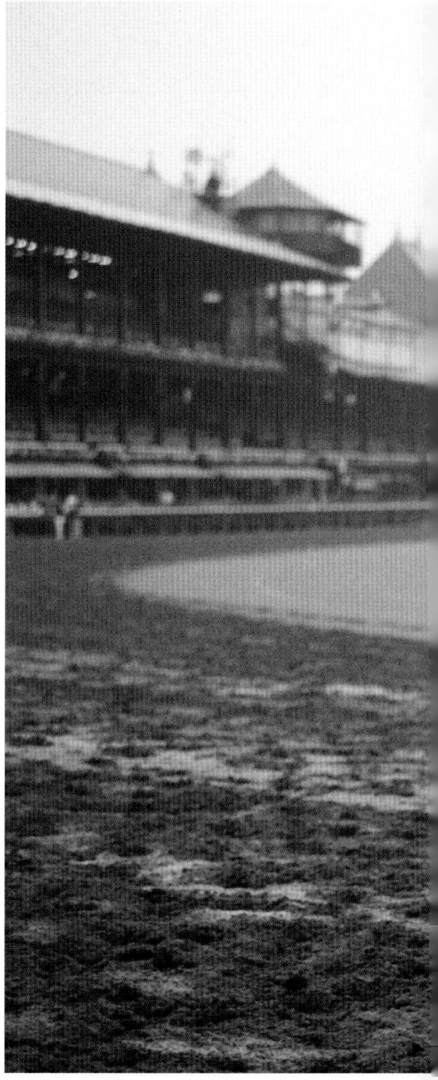

GANDER (CENTER), the wonderful New York-bred champion.

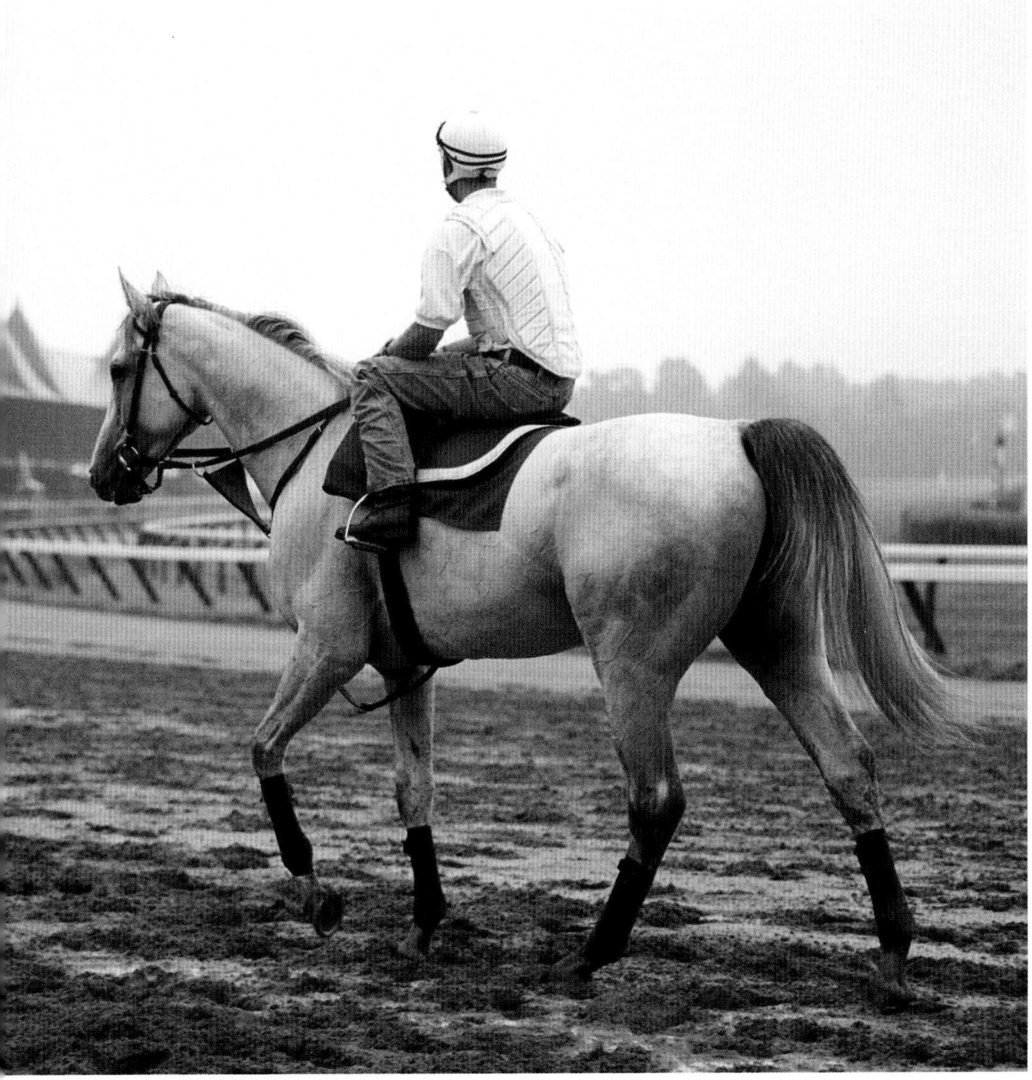

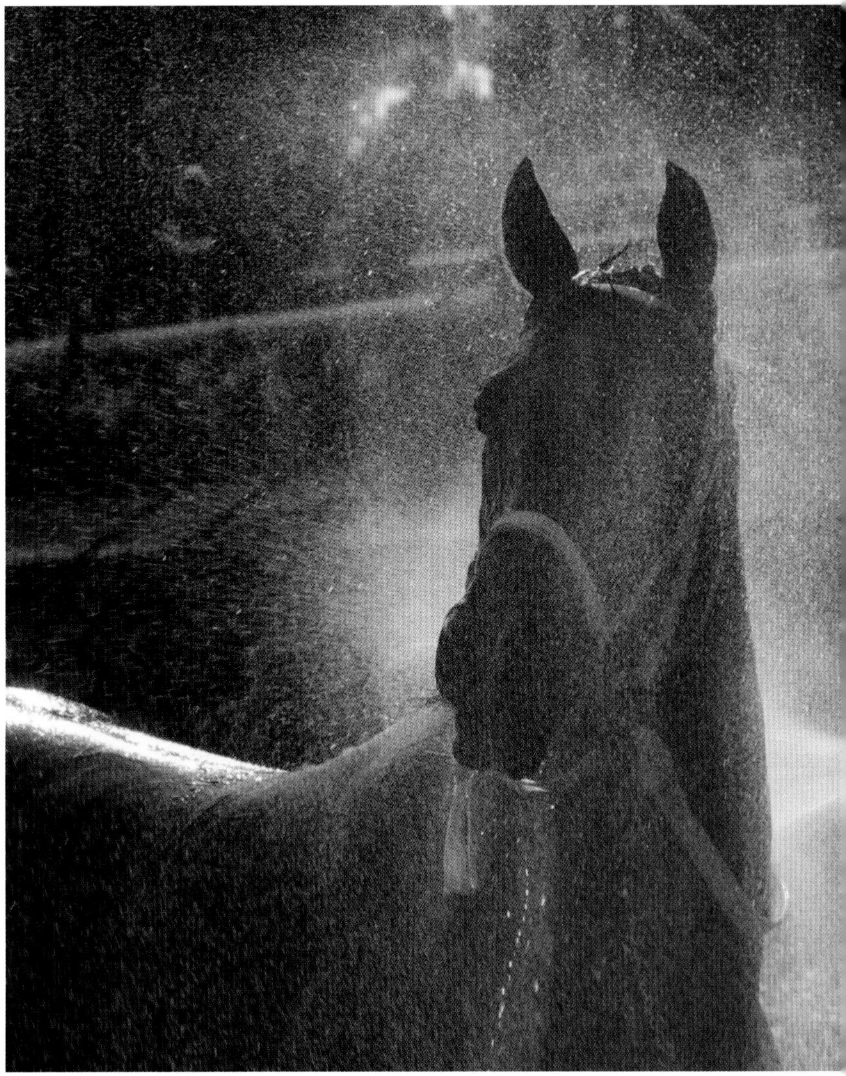

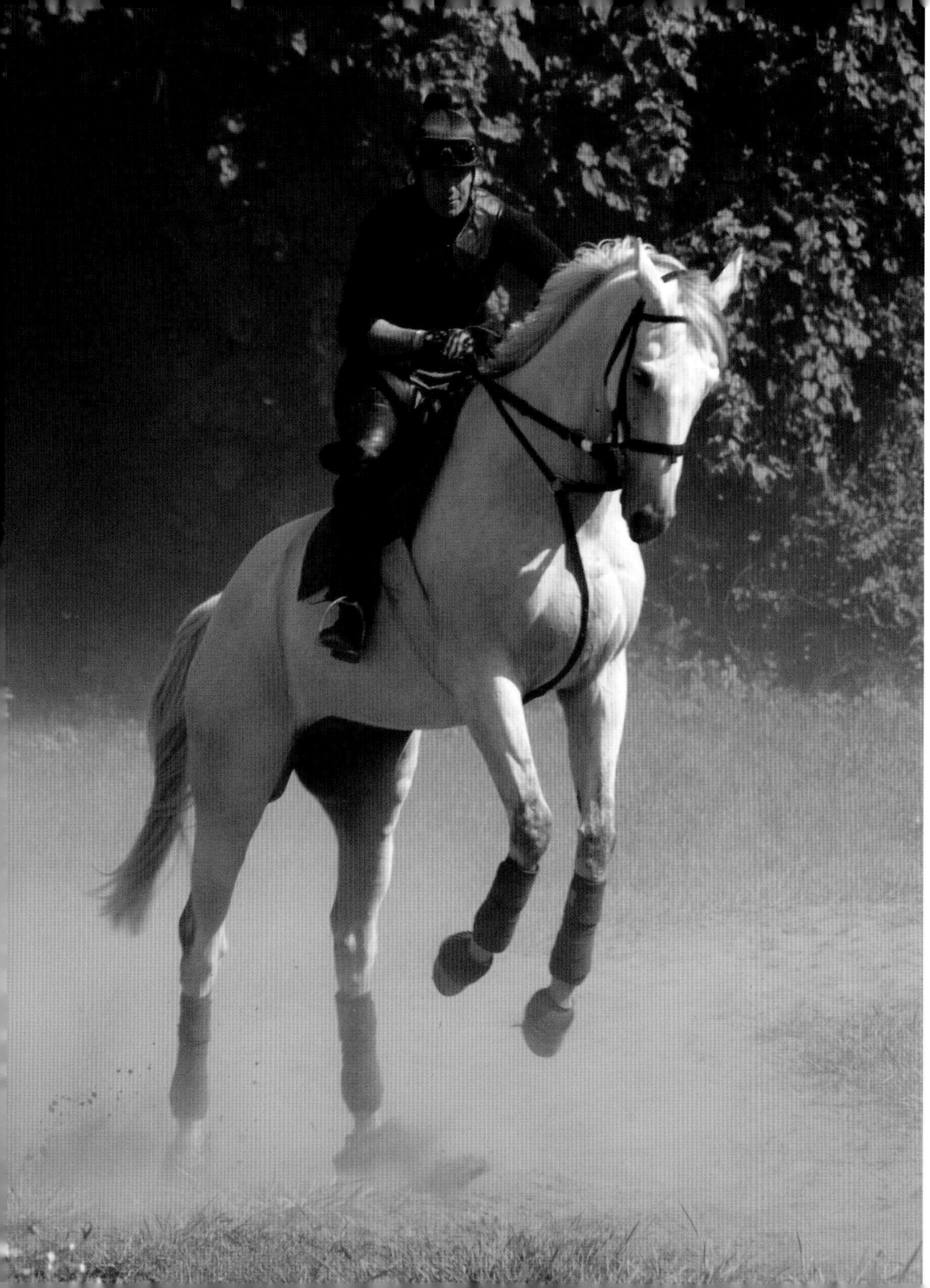

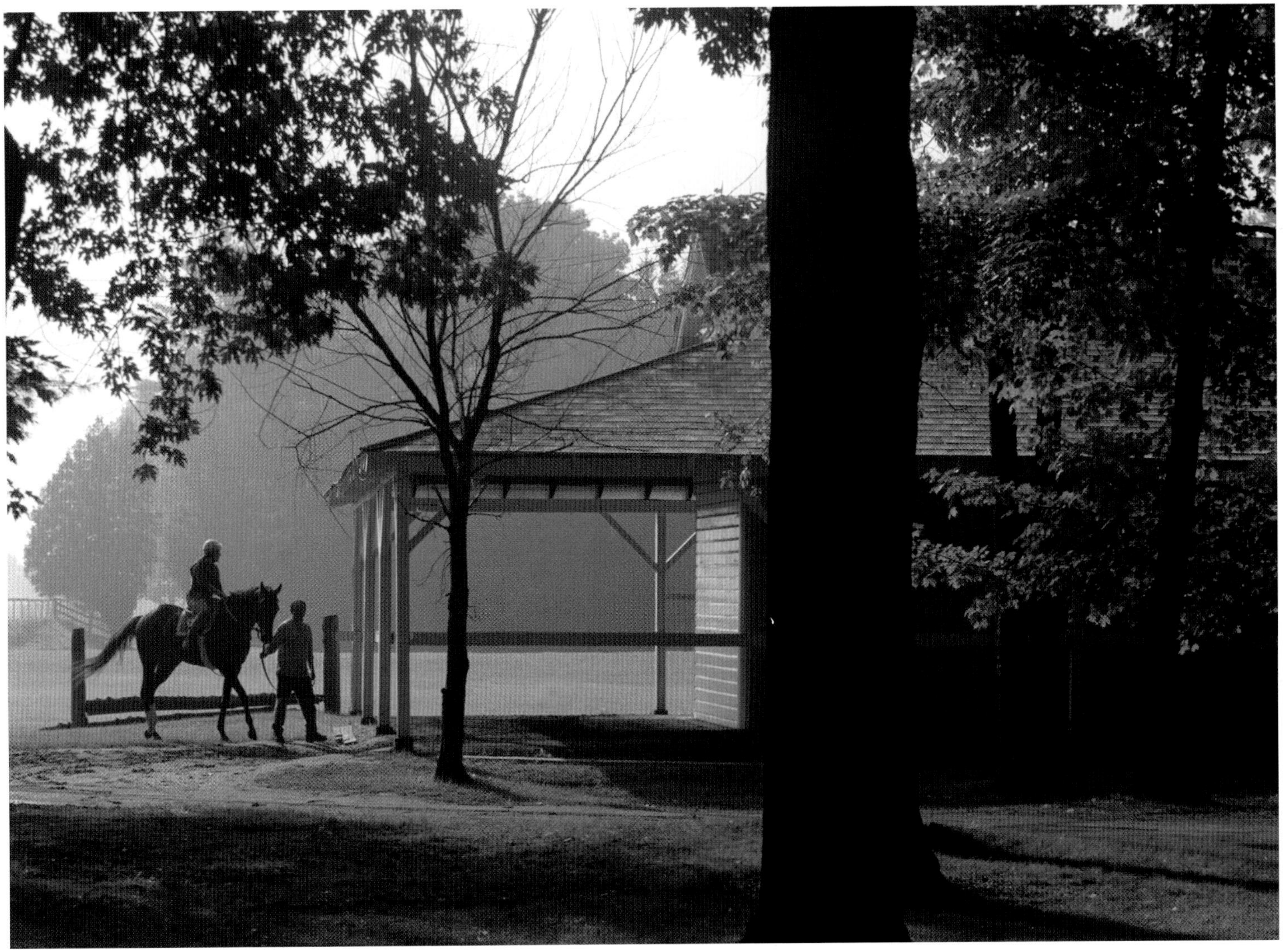

WITH ANTICIPATION (LEFT), the beloved turf specialist, with Jennifer Young.

GREENTREE STABLE (ABOVE) on a crisp autumn morning.

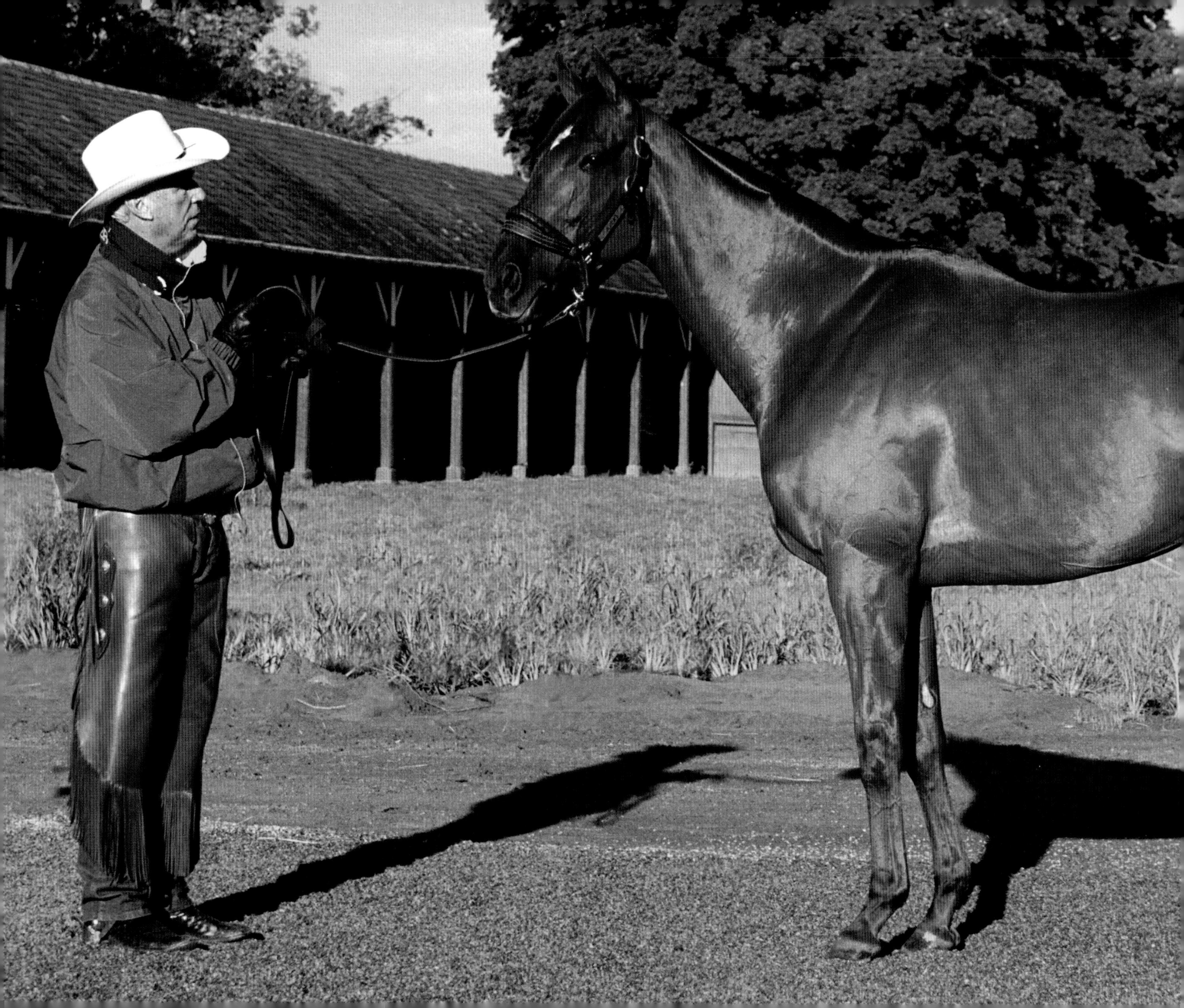

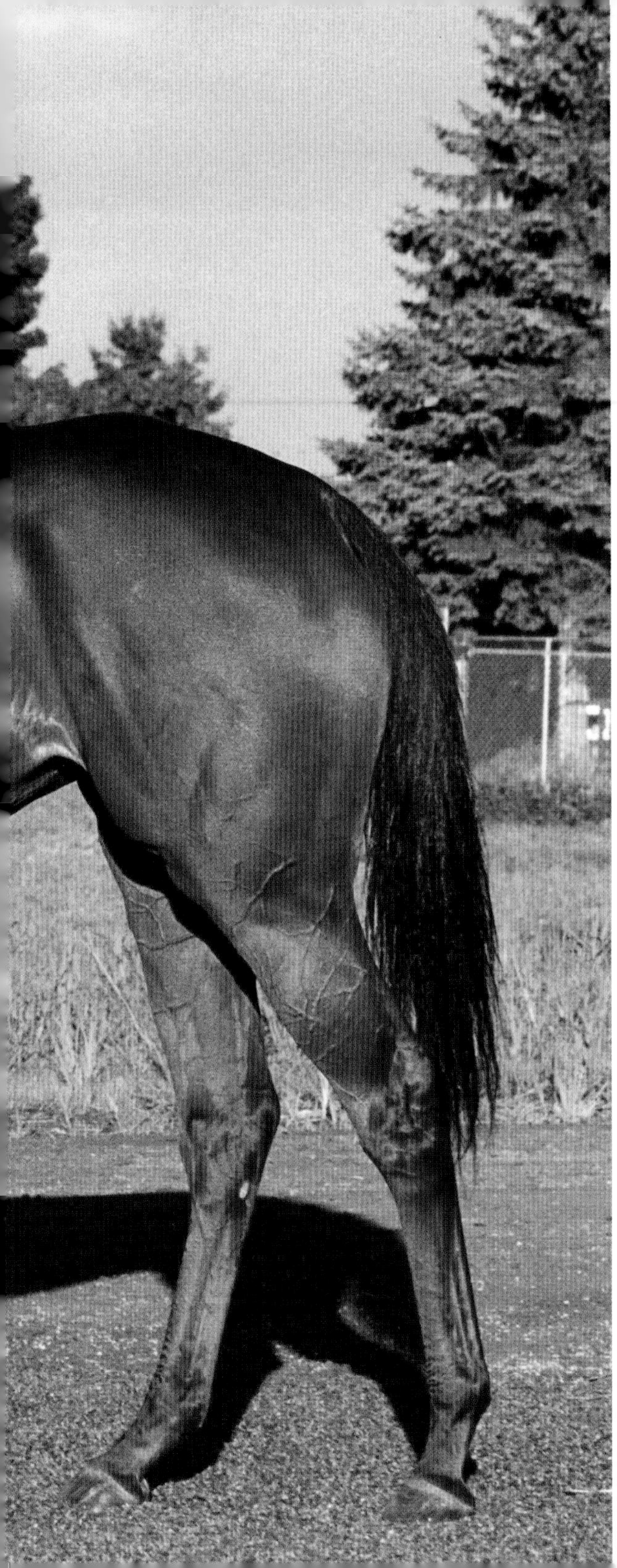

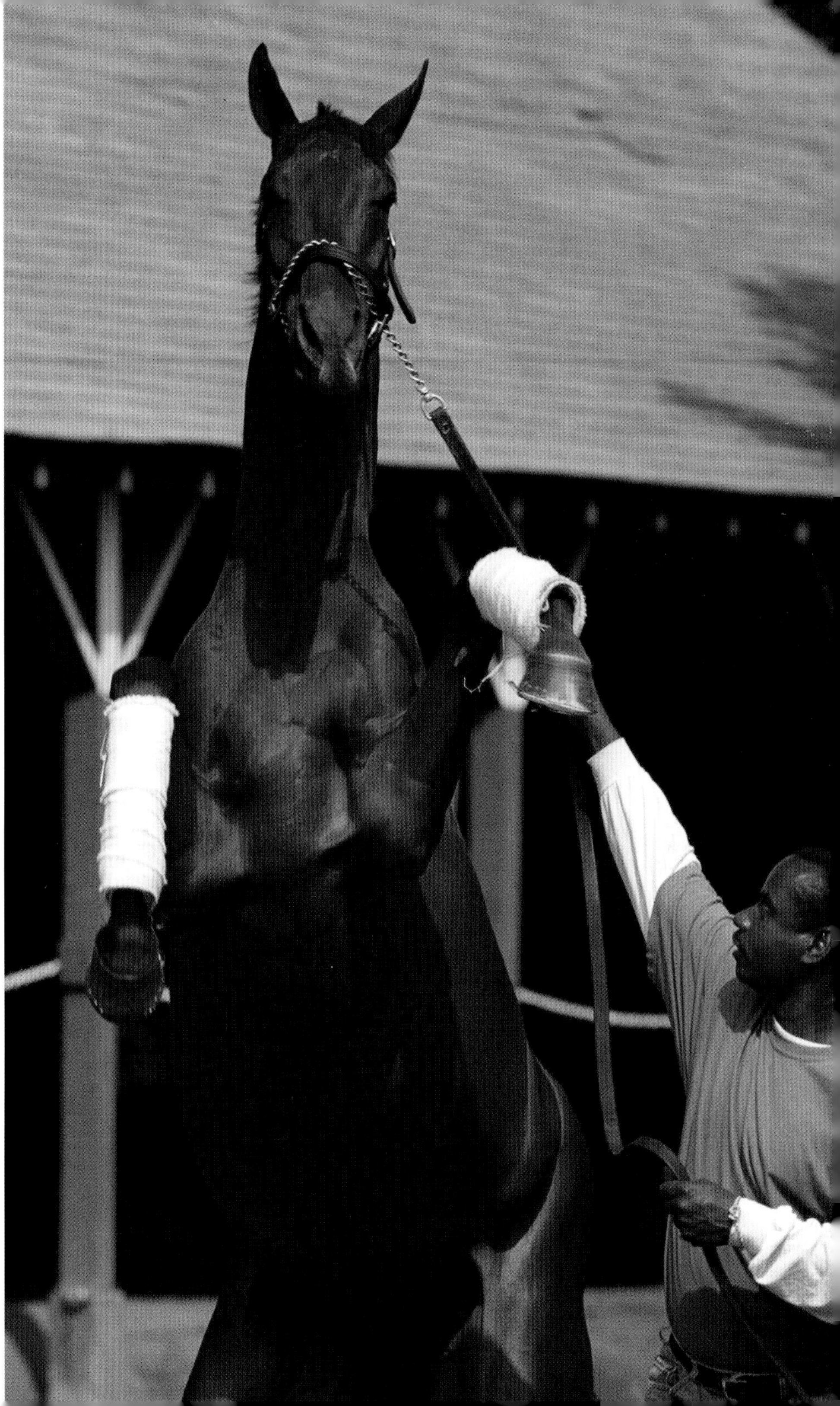

AZERI (PREVIOUS, LEFT), champion mare, with trainer Wayne Lukas at Saratoga.

FUNNY CIDE (PREVIOUS, RIGHT), beloved Kentucky Derby and Preakness winner born in Saratoga Springs, having fun with Raunie Hart.

SAYING HELLO — Electrified and Kirkwood Ranger touch noses at trainer Todd Pletcher's barn.

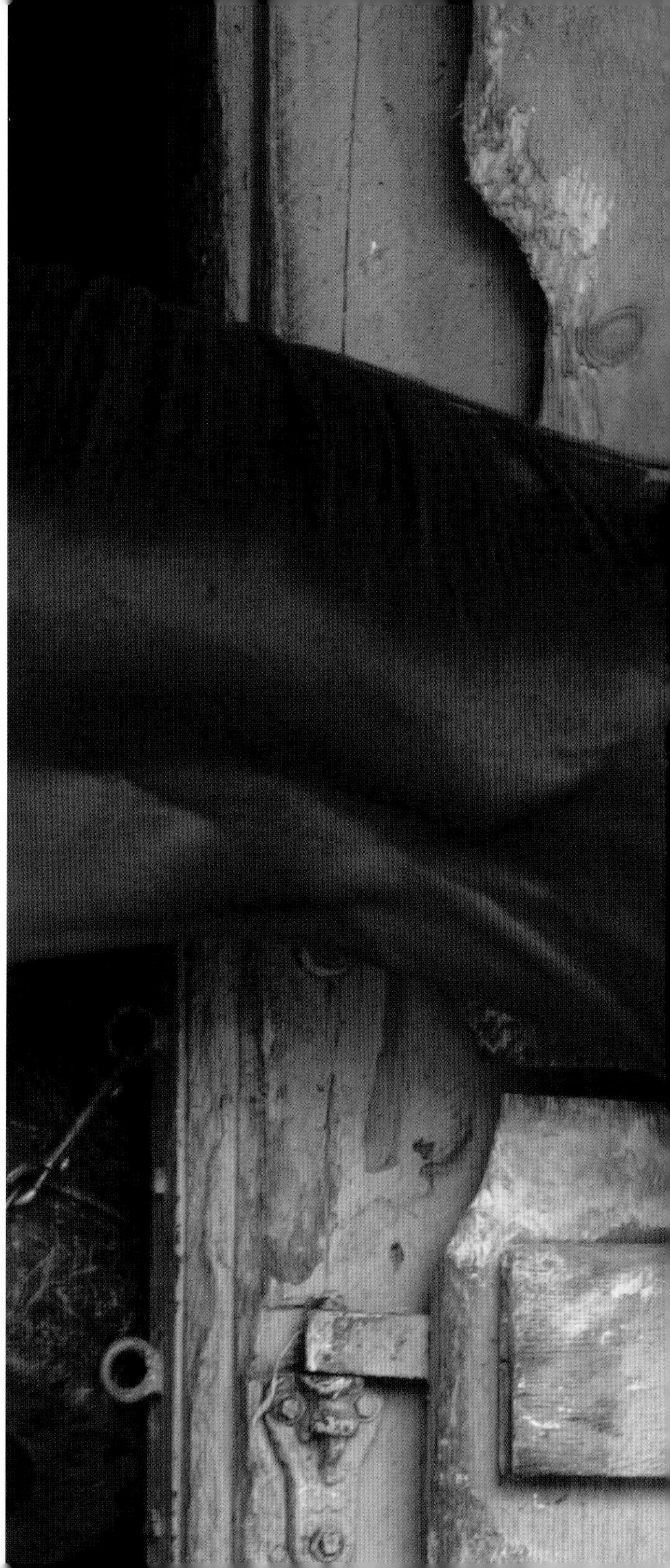

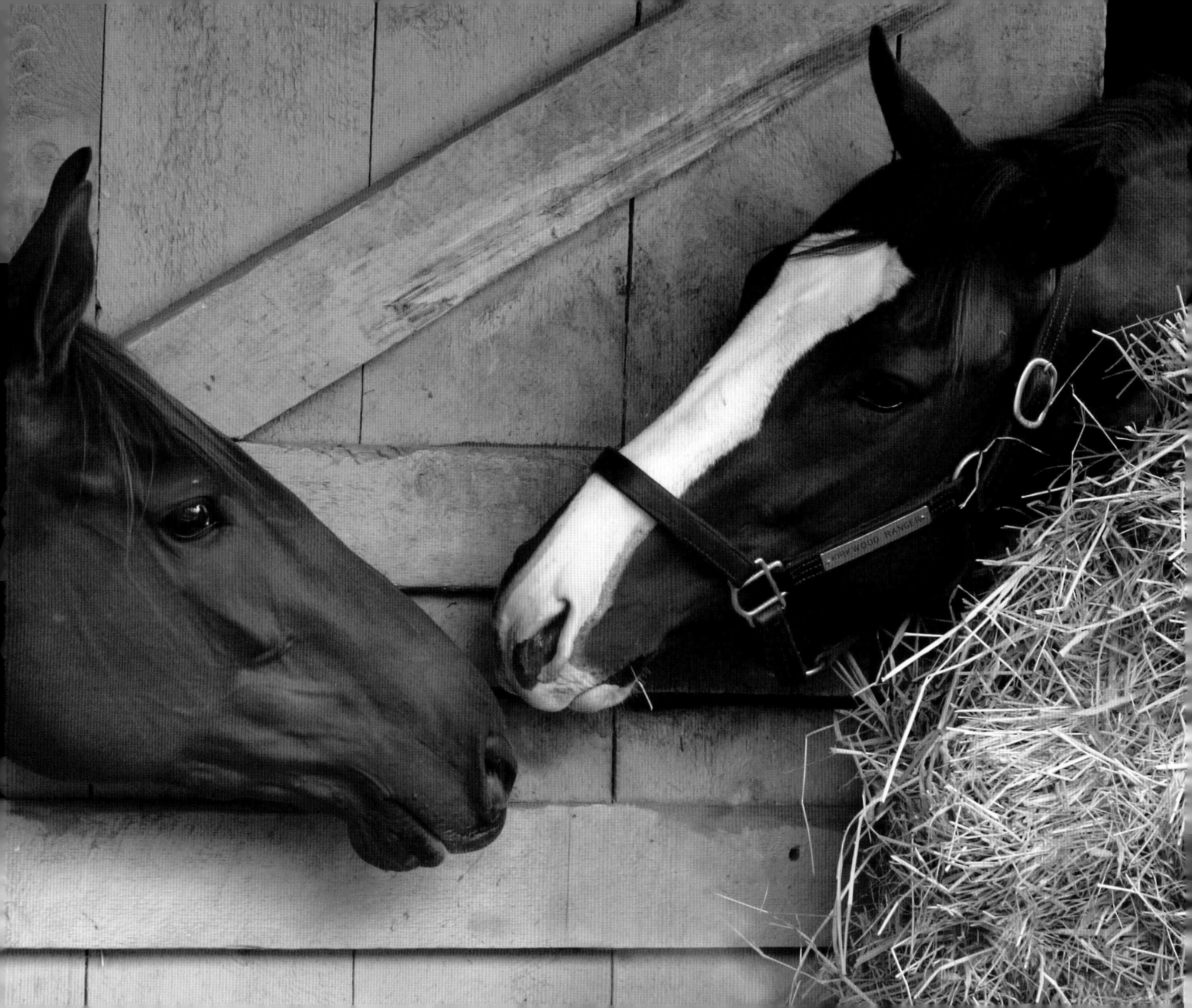
RANGER

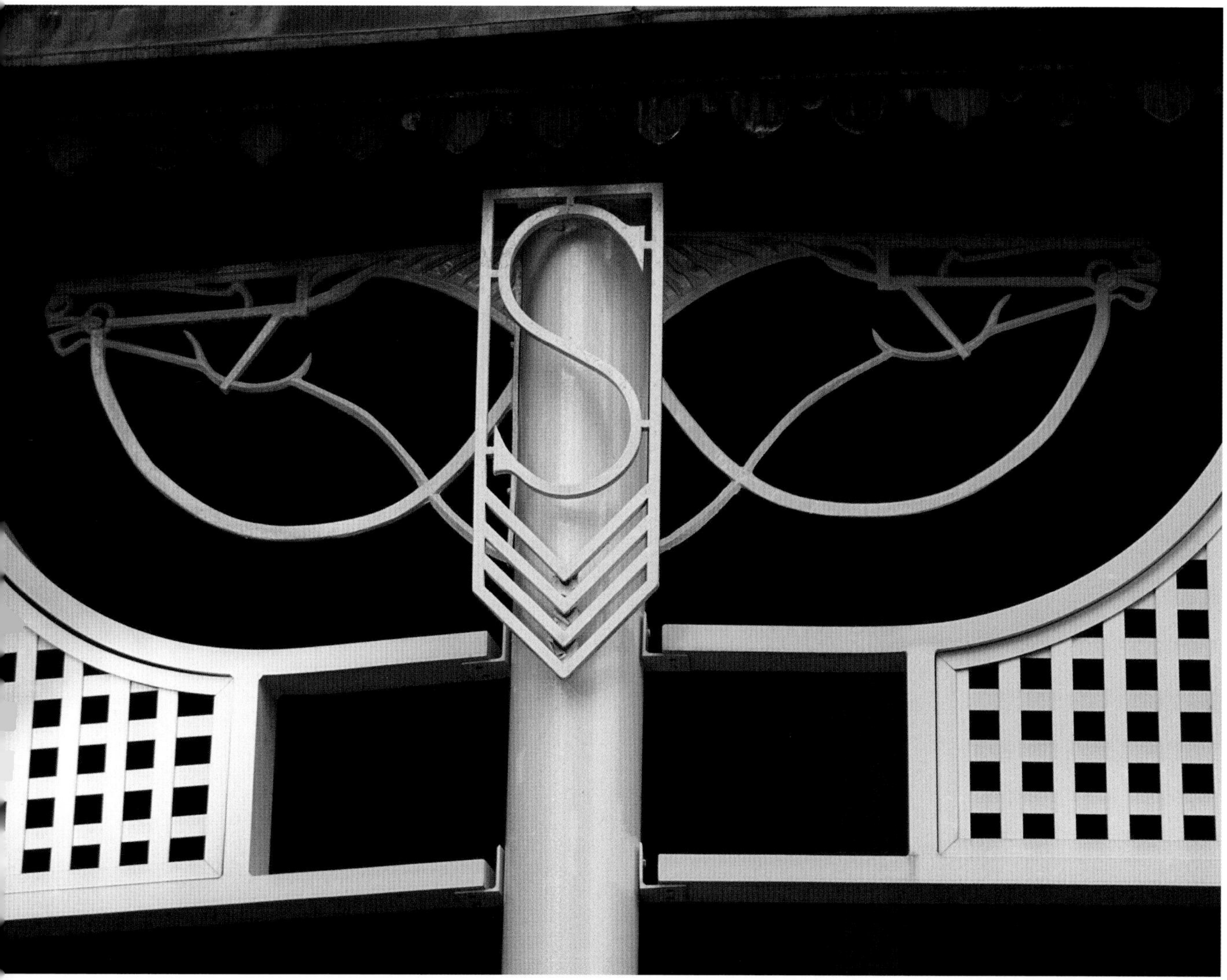

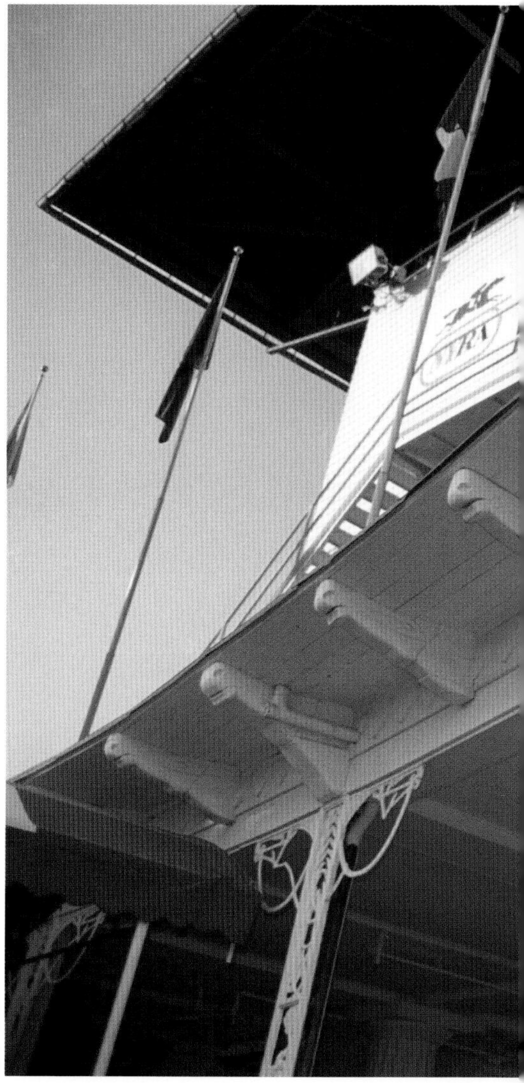

WOODEN HORSE HEADS (RIGHT) AND METAL WORK, in the clubhouse, are some of the many equine-related touches around the track.

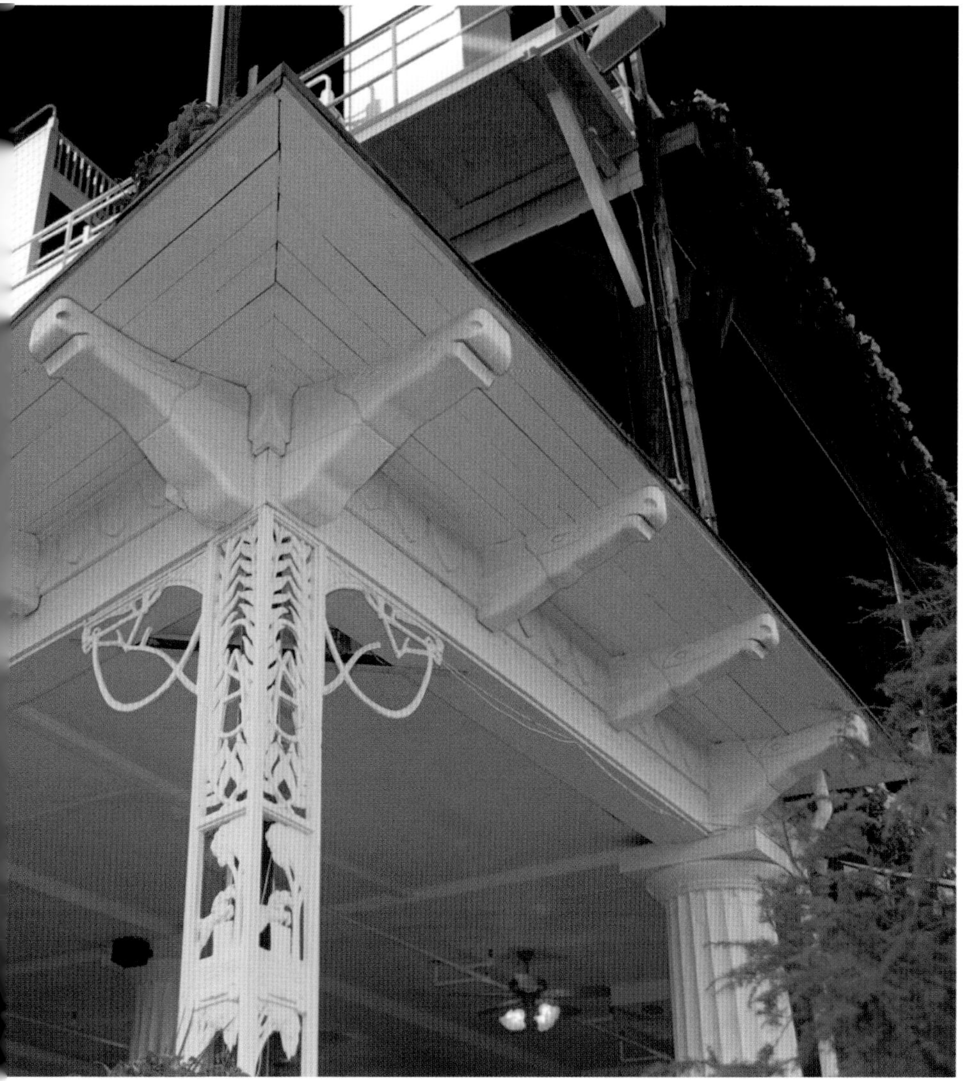

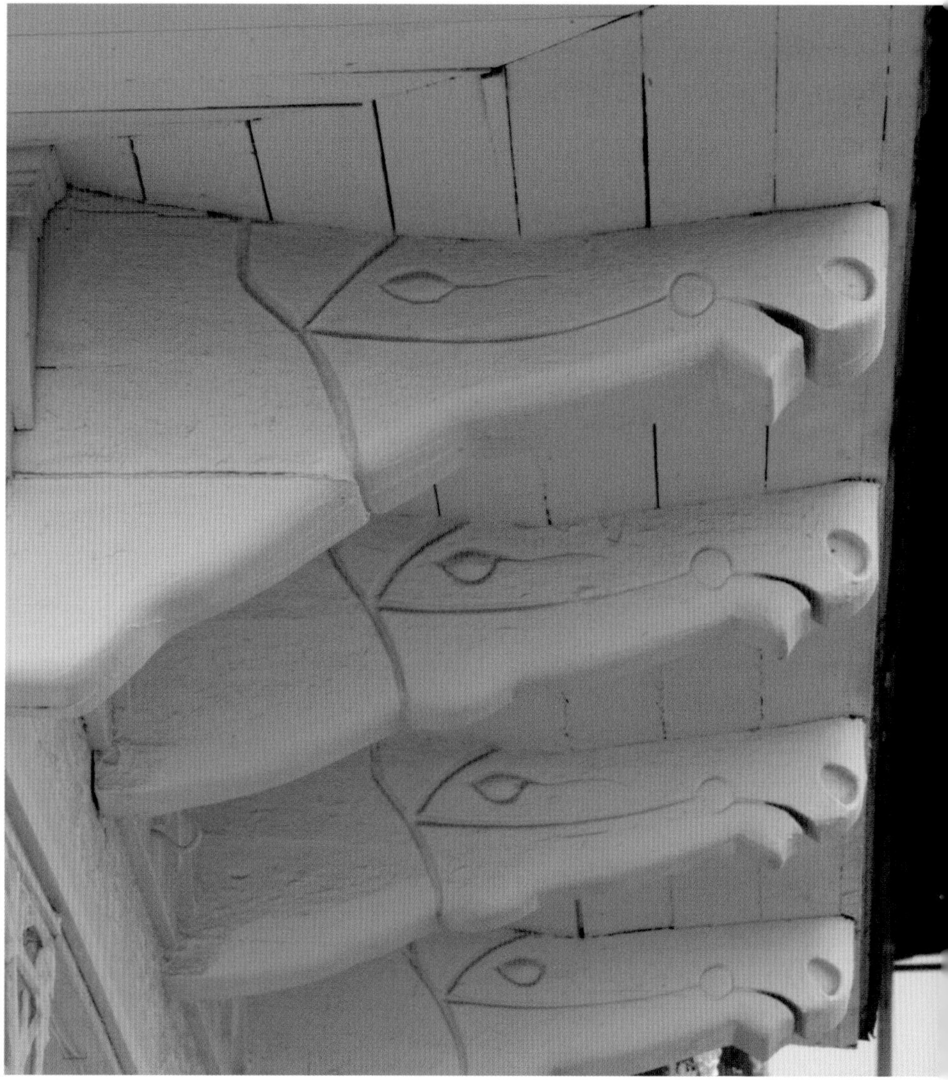

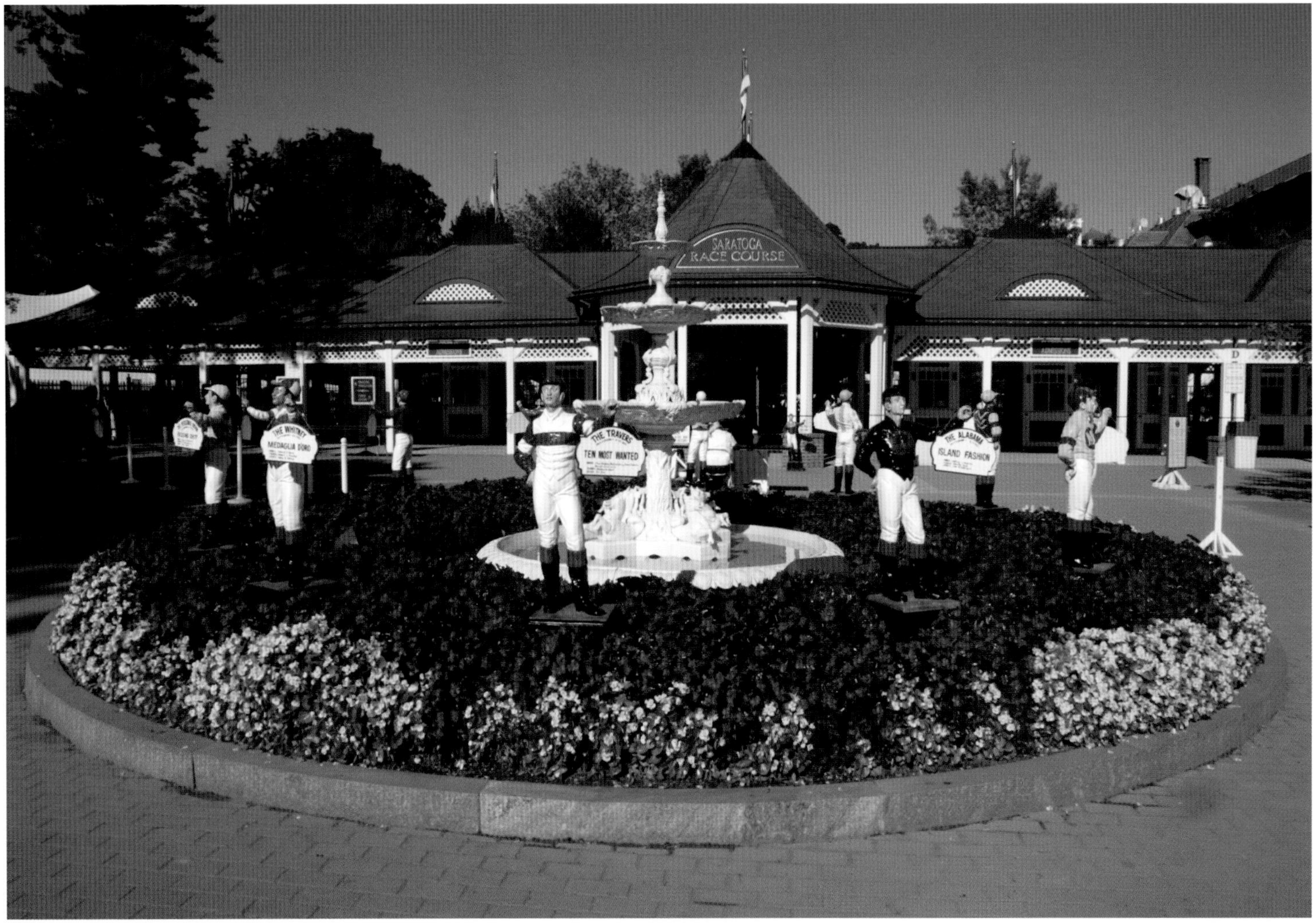

CLUBHOUSE ENTRY (ABOVE) — Lawn jockeys, representing the previous year's grade I winners, encircle an historic fountain.

TRAVERS CANOE (RIGHT) — The colors of the 2004 Travers winner, Marylou Whitney Stables' Birdstone, grace the infield canoe.

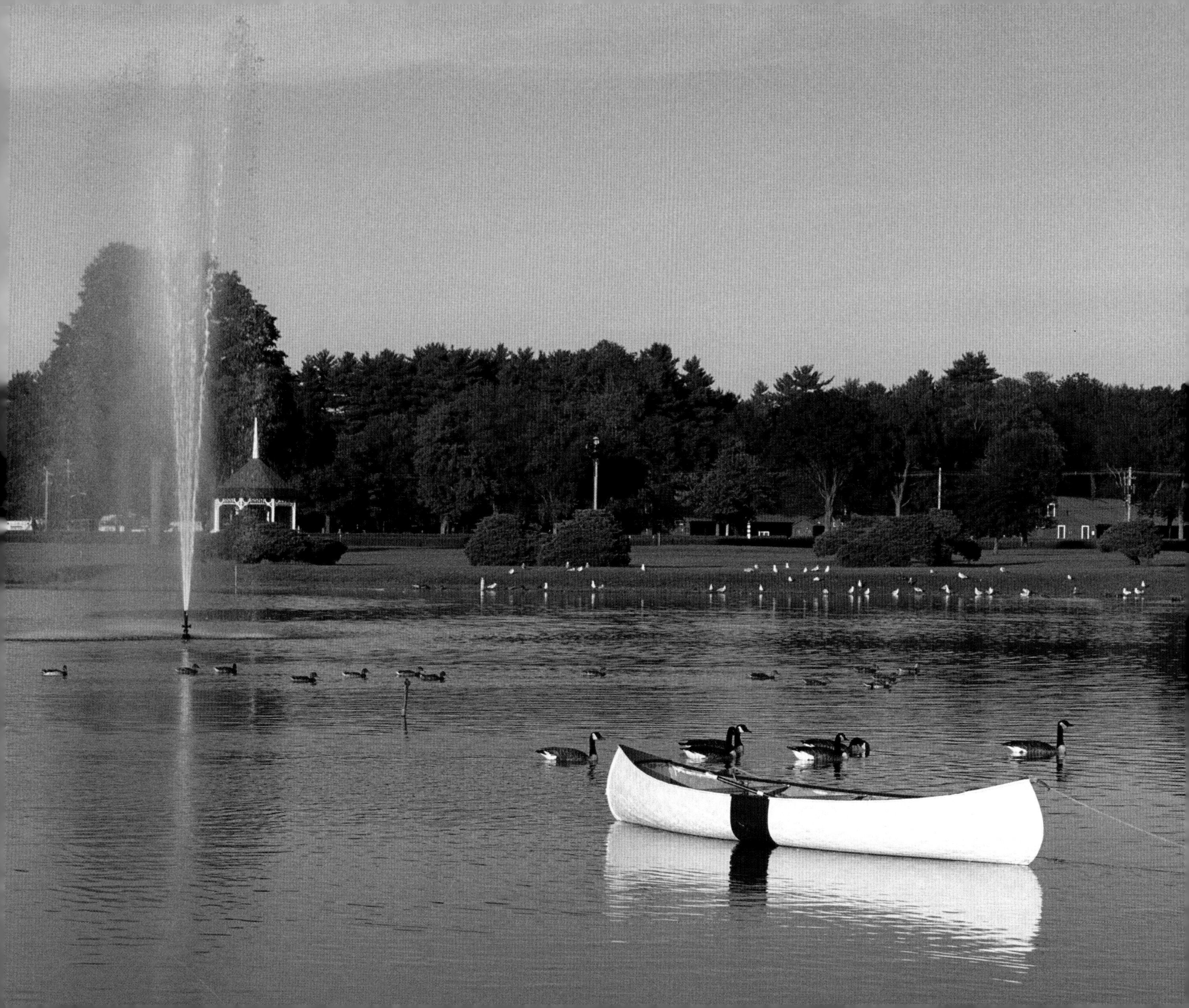

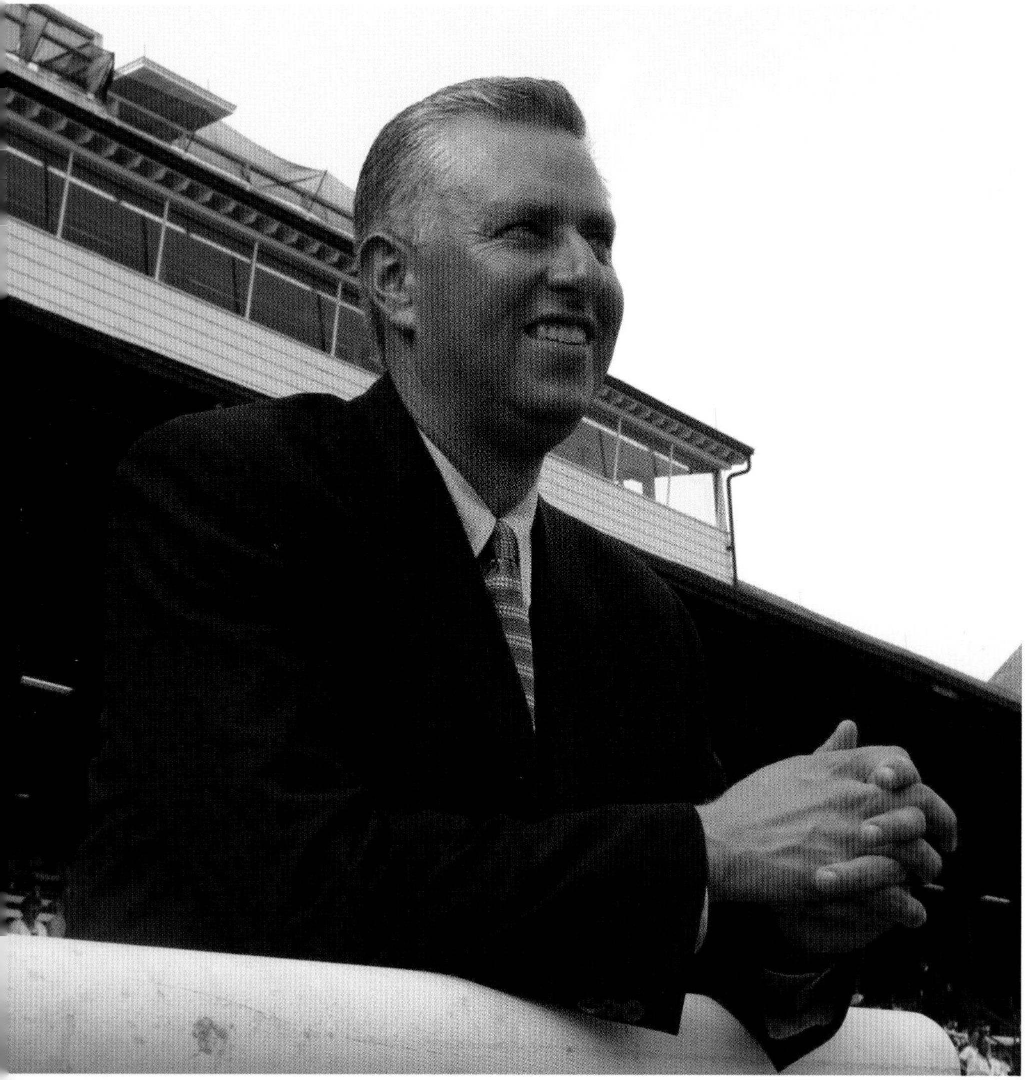

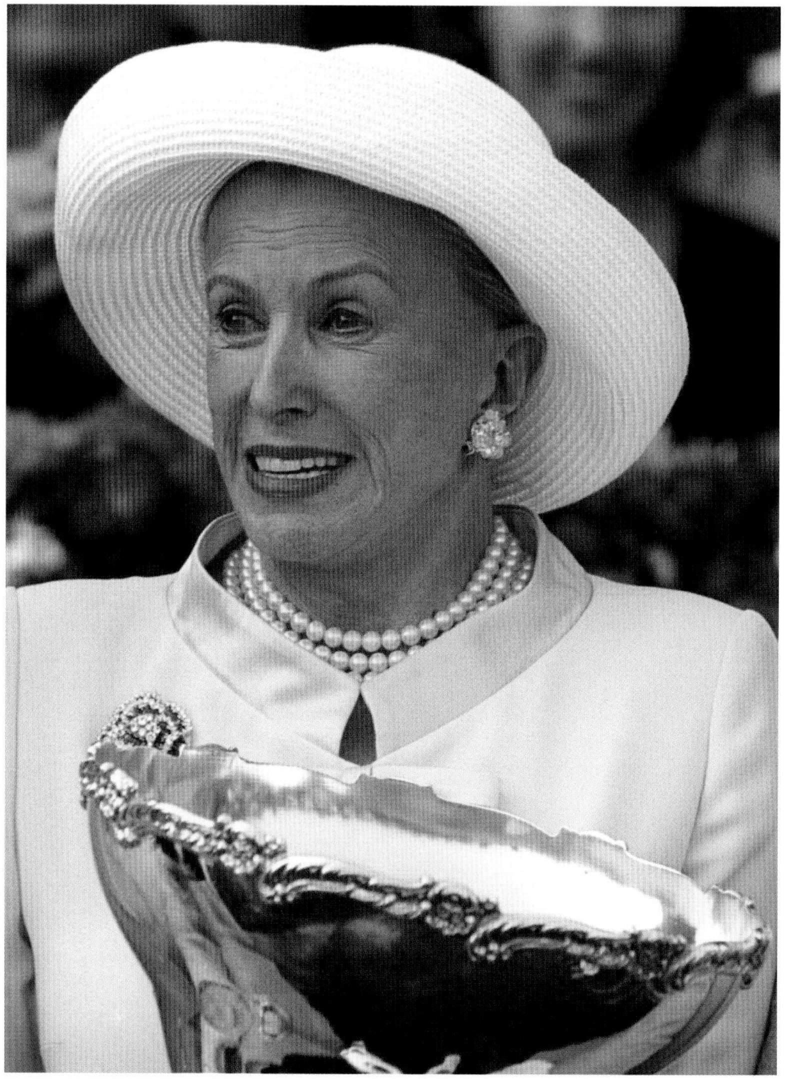

34 **SARATOGA PERSONALITIES (LEFT TO RIGHT)** — Trainer Todd Pletcher, owner Marylou Whitney, and trainers Allen Jerkens (shown with grade I winner Wagon Limit) and Nick Zito are perennial Saratoga favorites.

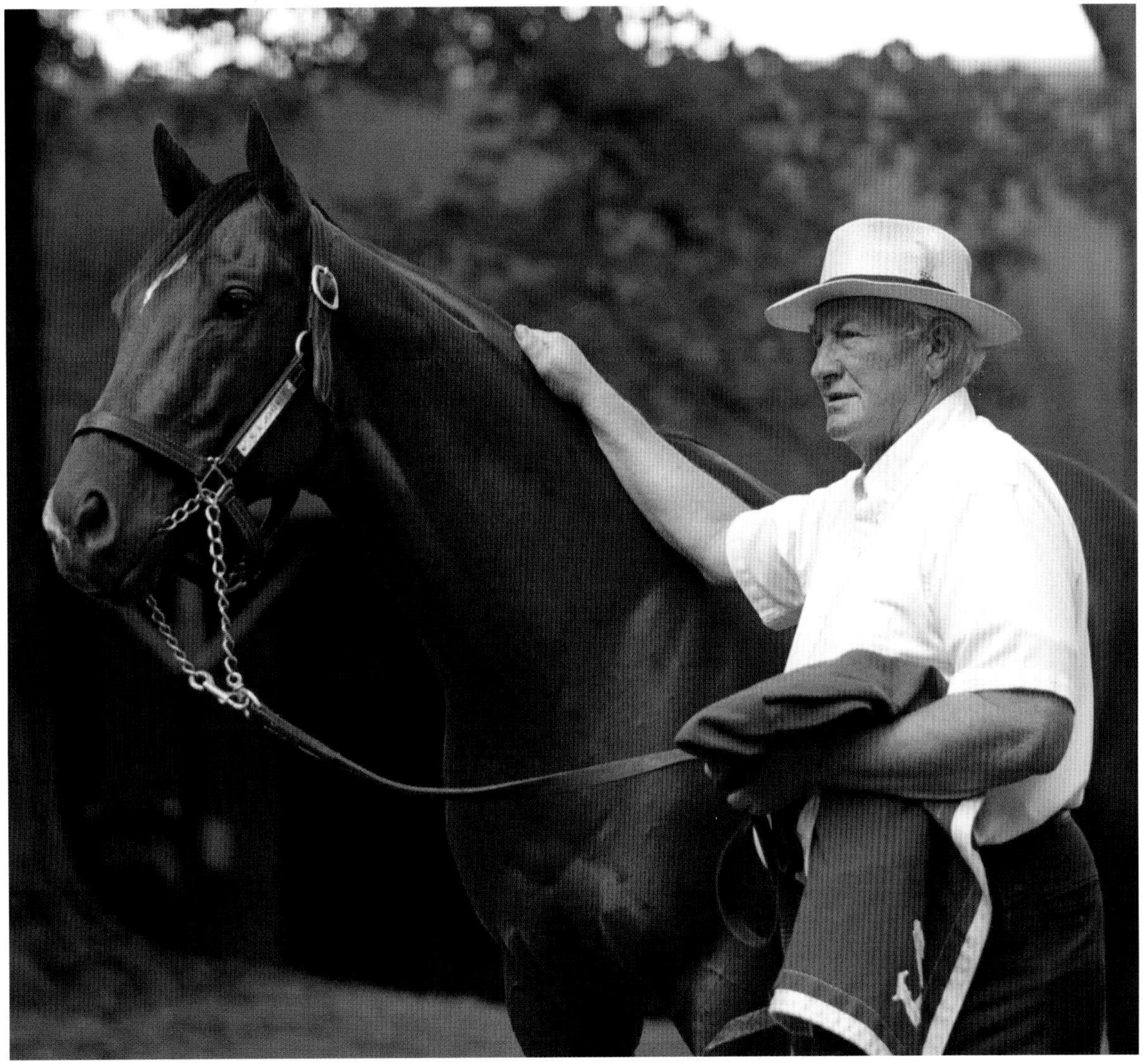

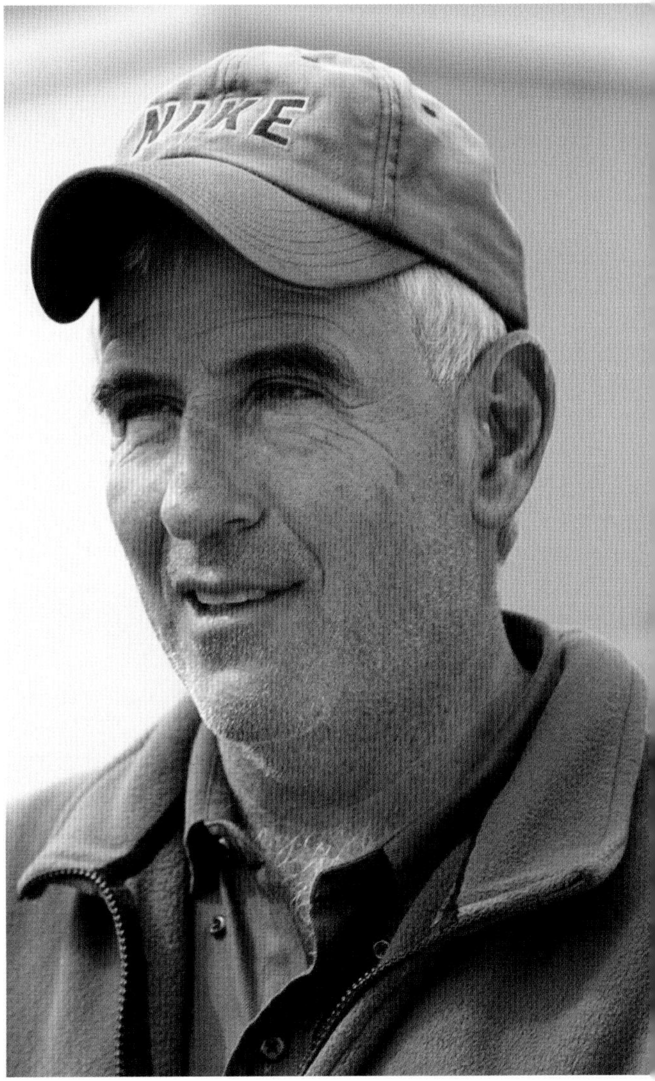
NIKE

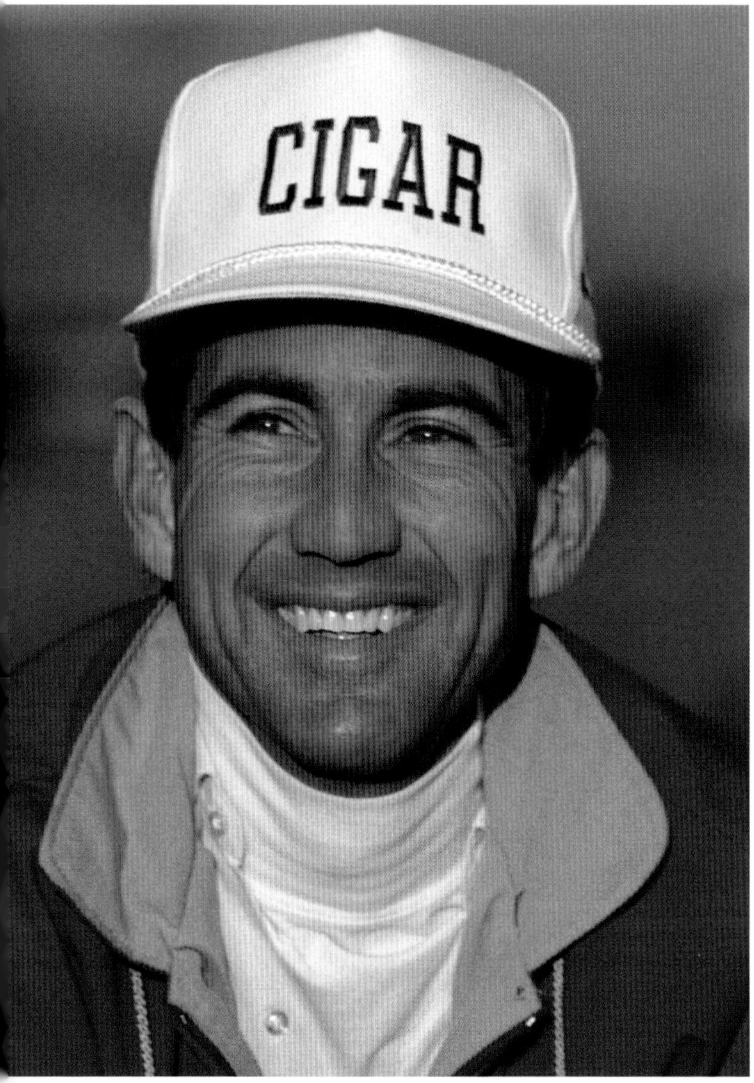

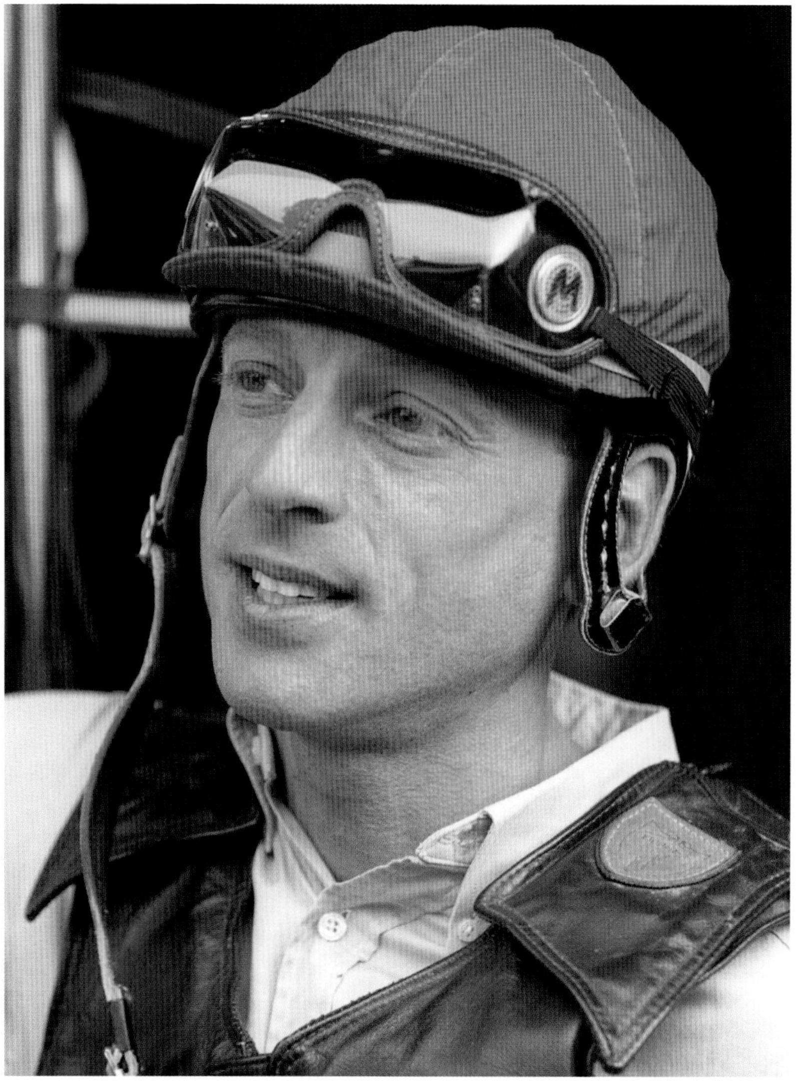

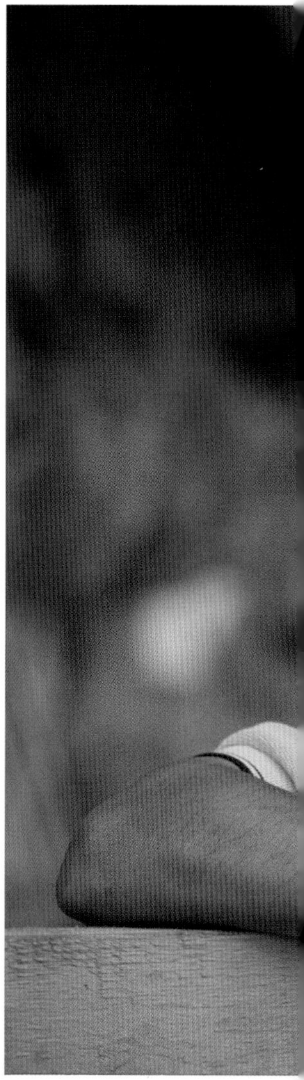

JOCKEYS (LEFT TO RIGHT) — Jerry Bailey, Richard Migliore, Edgar Prado, and John Velazquez are tremendous fan favorites.

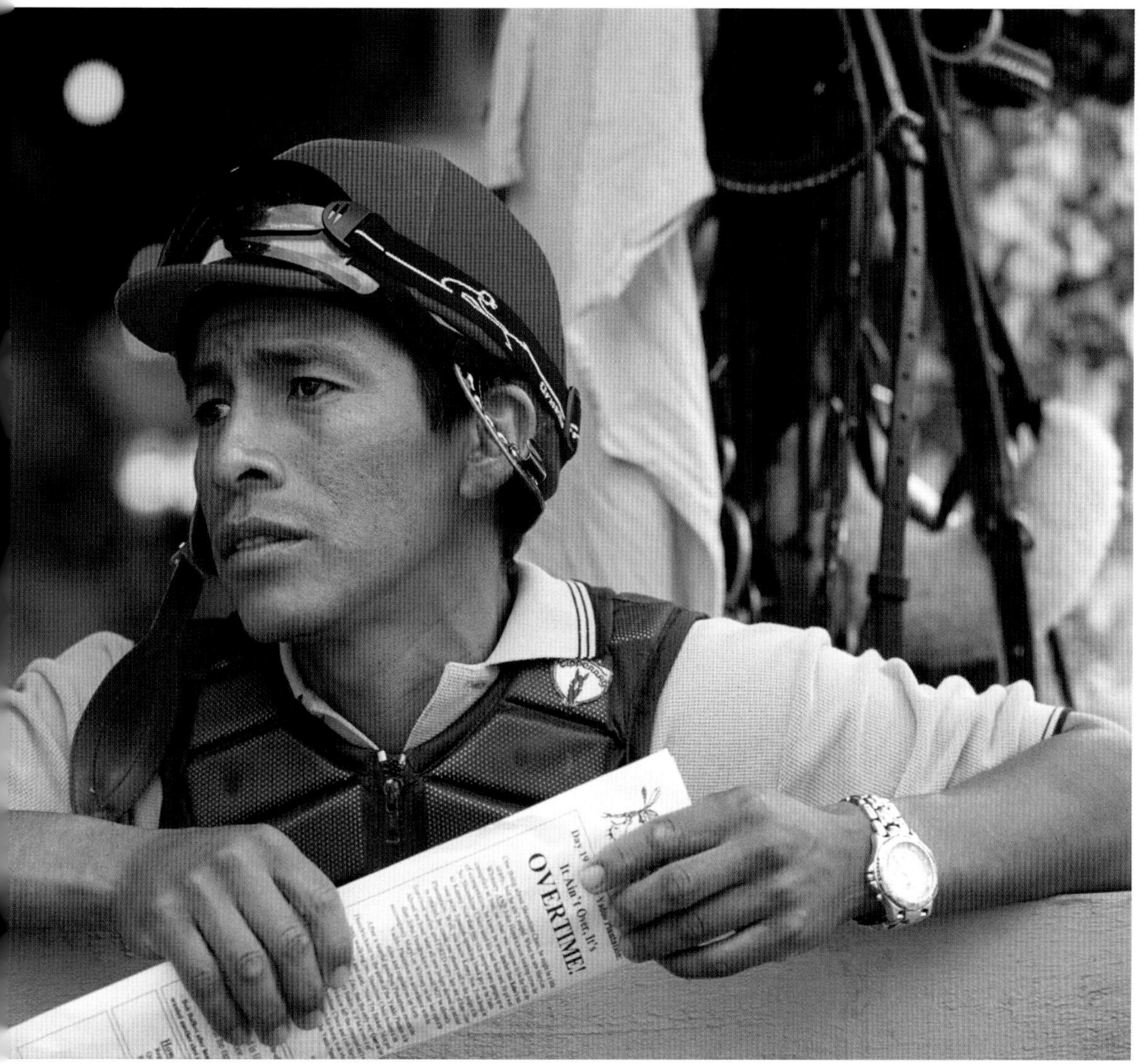
It Ain't Over, It's
OVERTIME!

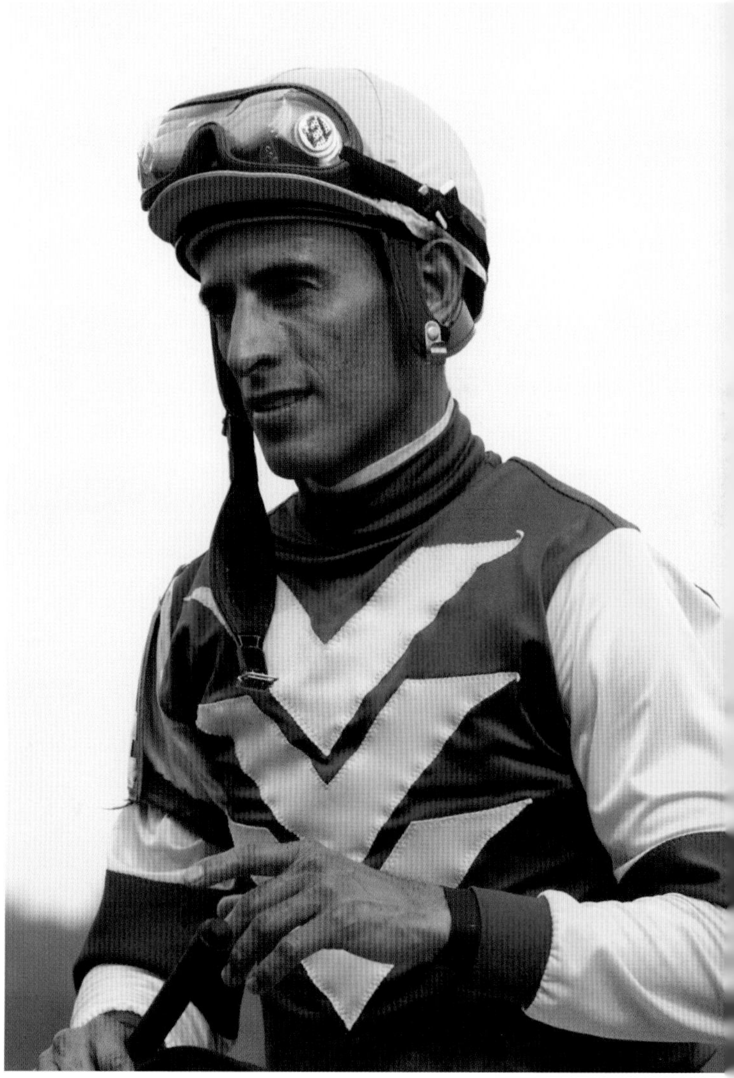

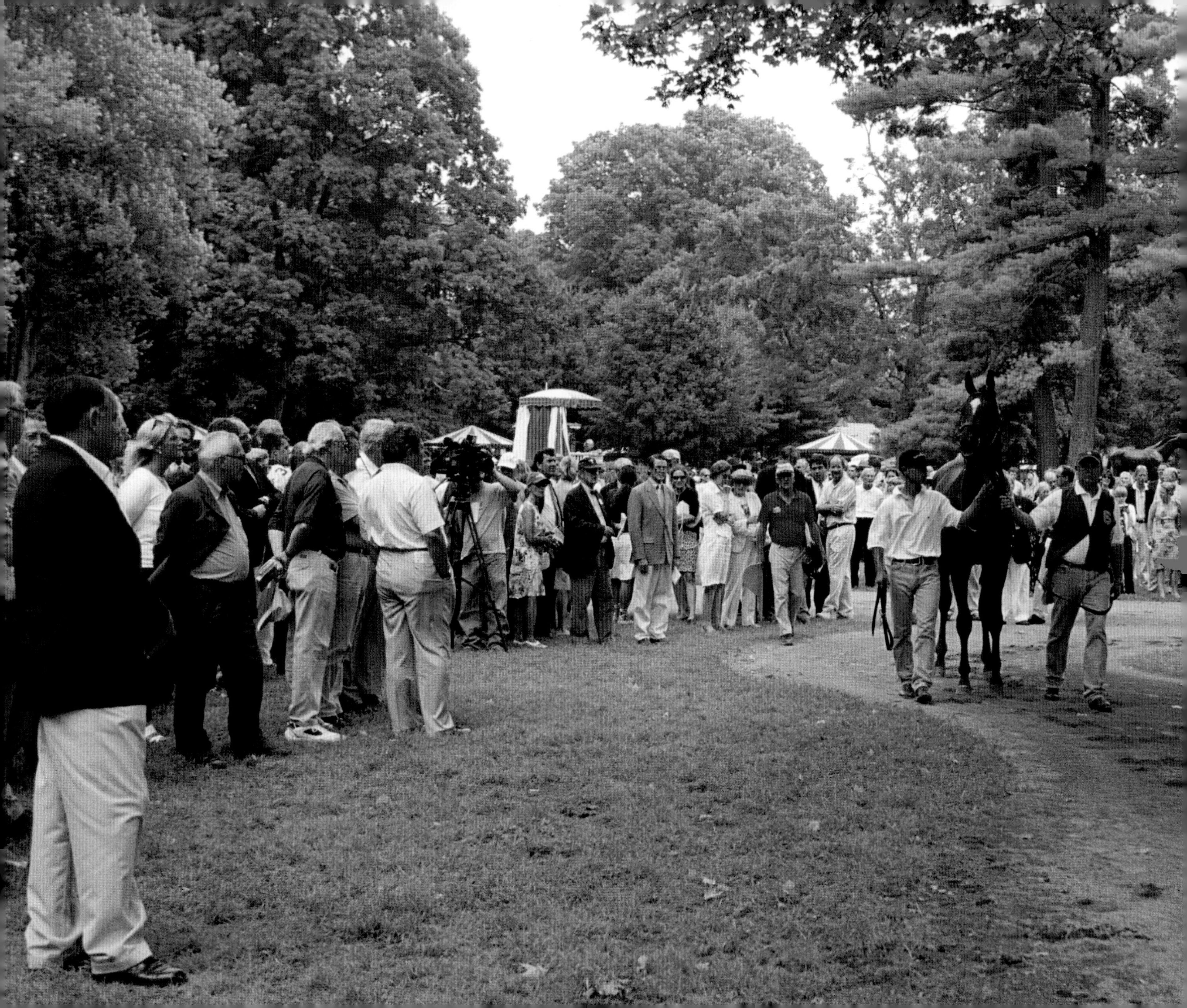

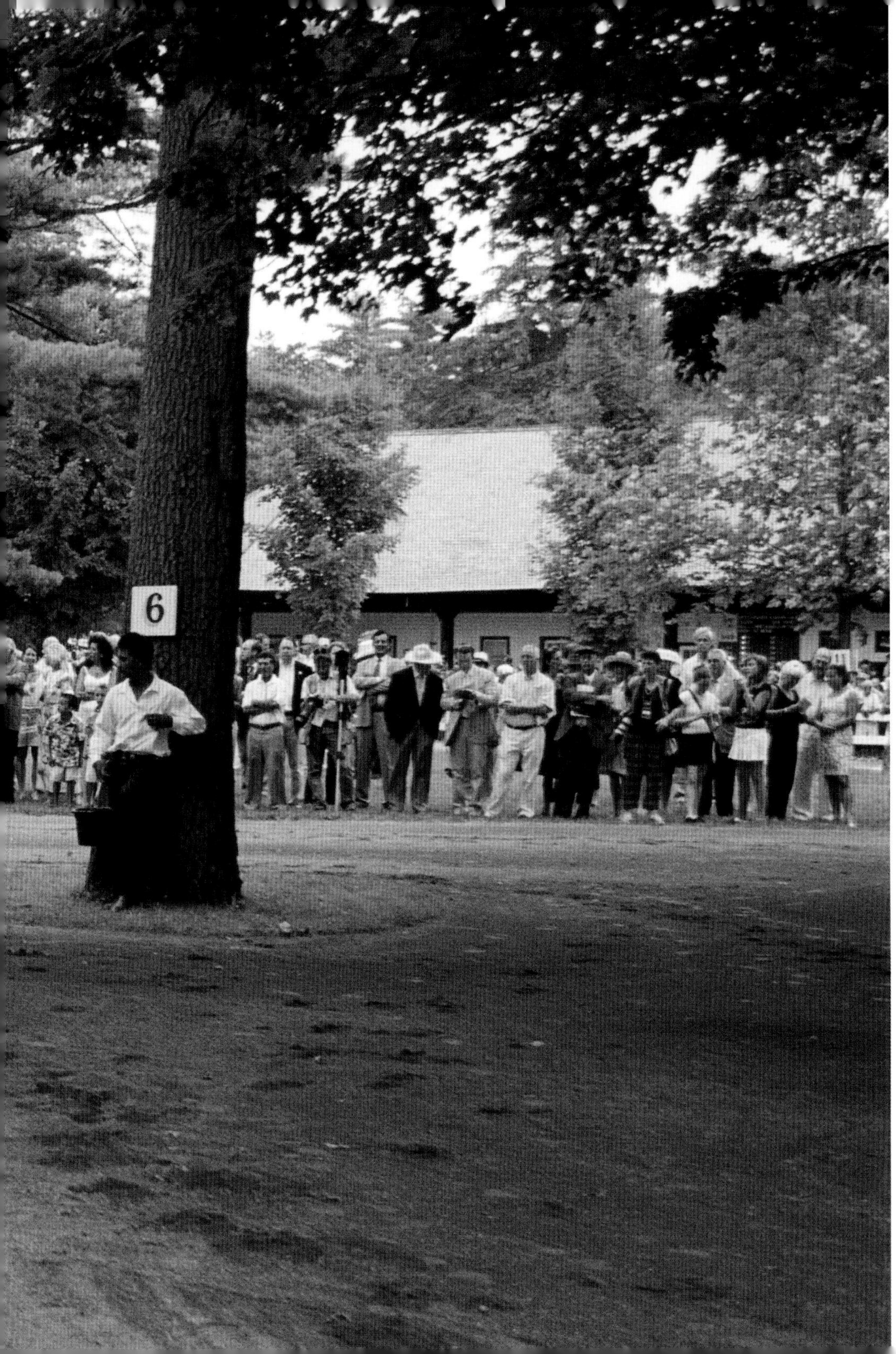

EMPIRE MAKER, the 2003 Belmont Stakes winner, in the paddock before that year's Jim Dandy Stakes, with trainer Robert Frankel in left foreground.

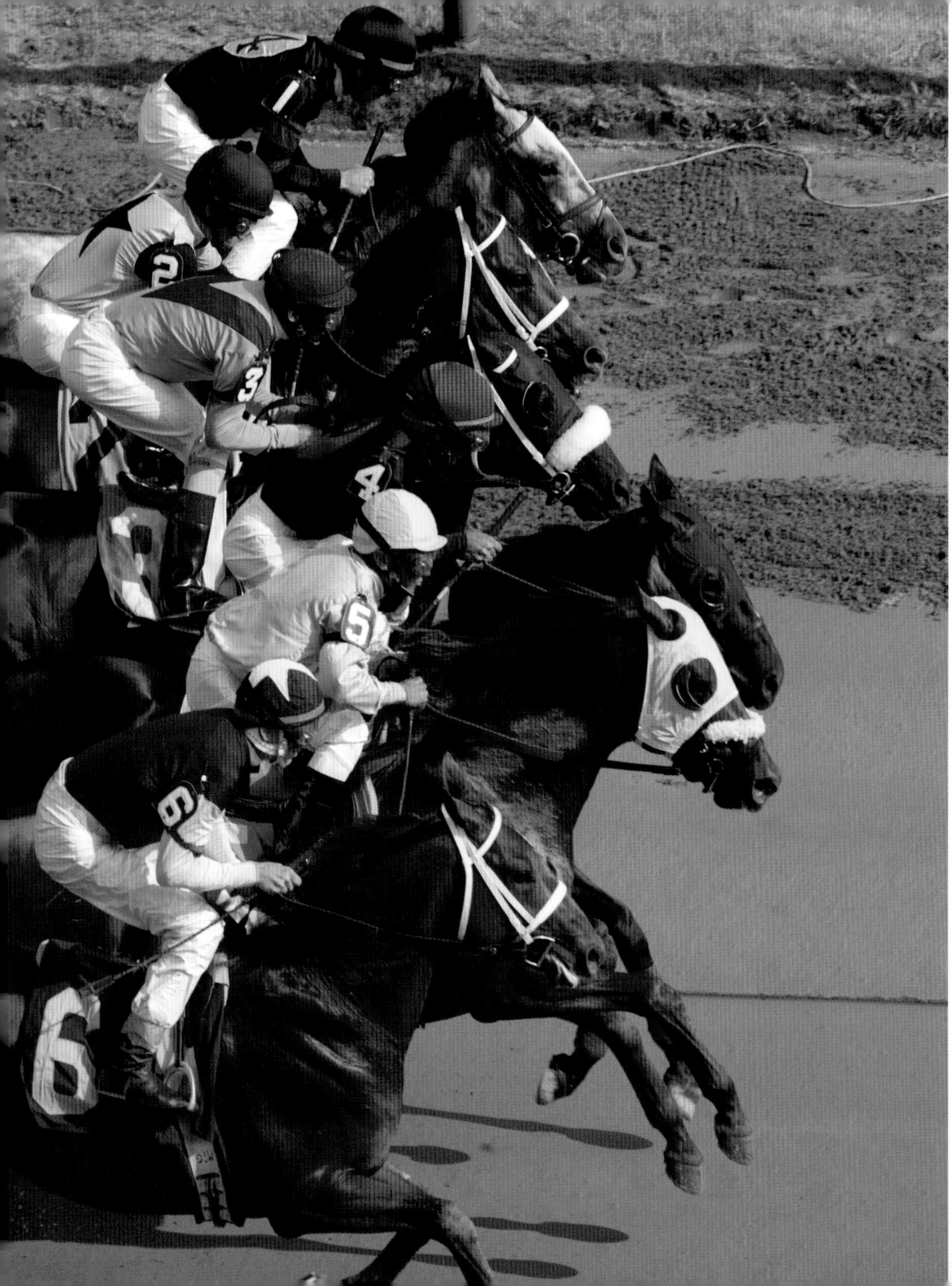
2
3
4
5
6
6

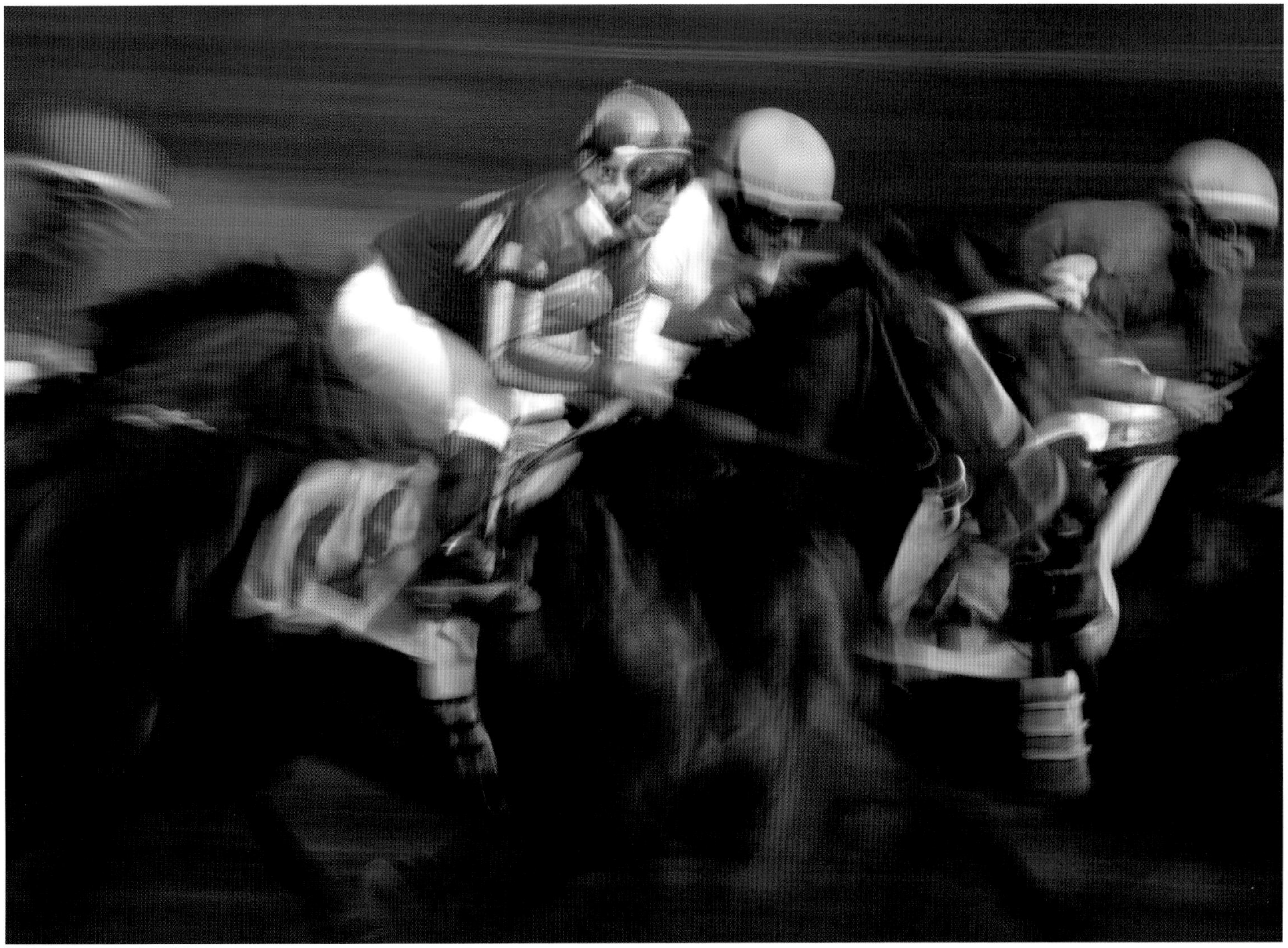

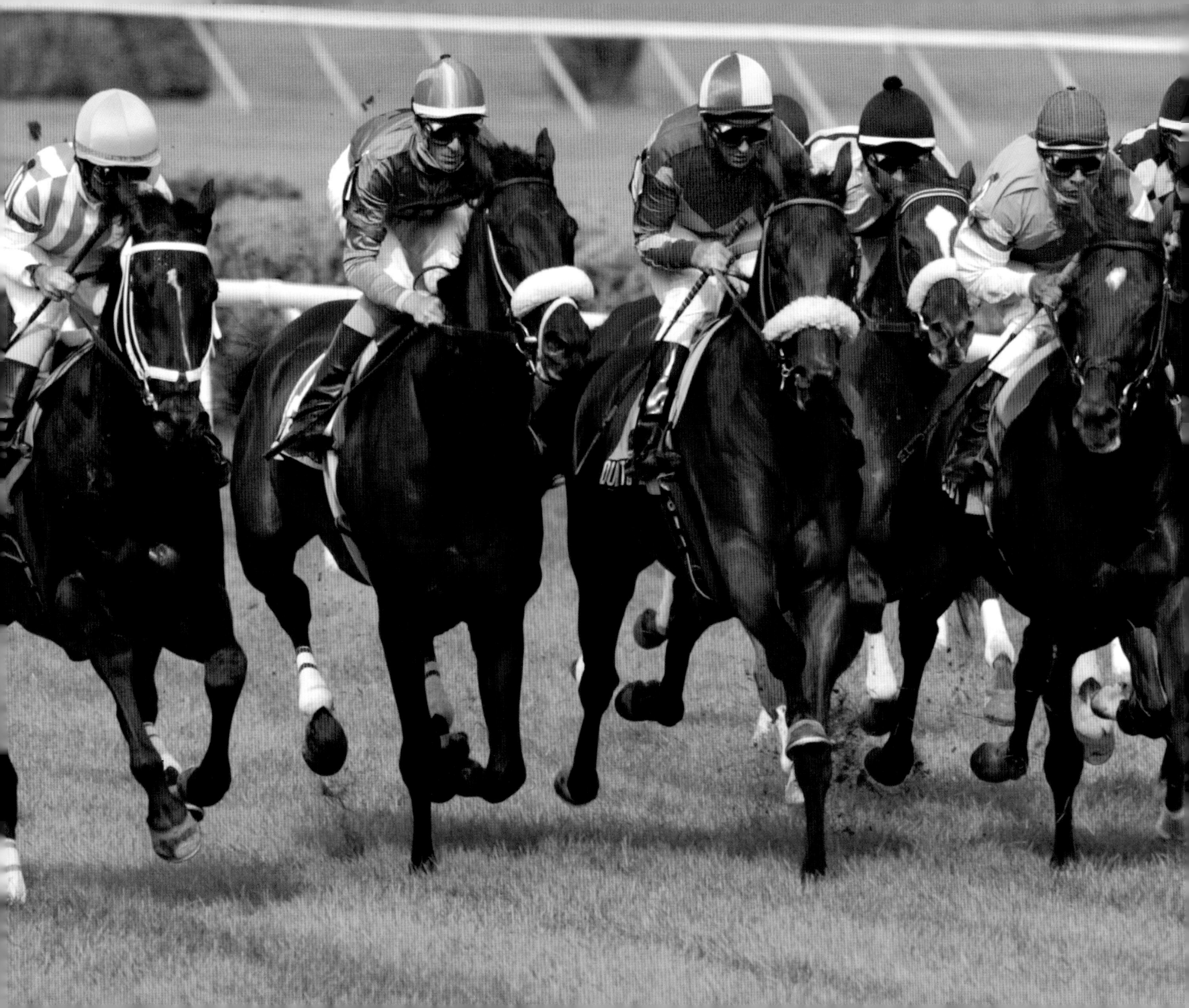

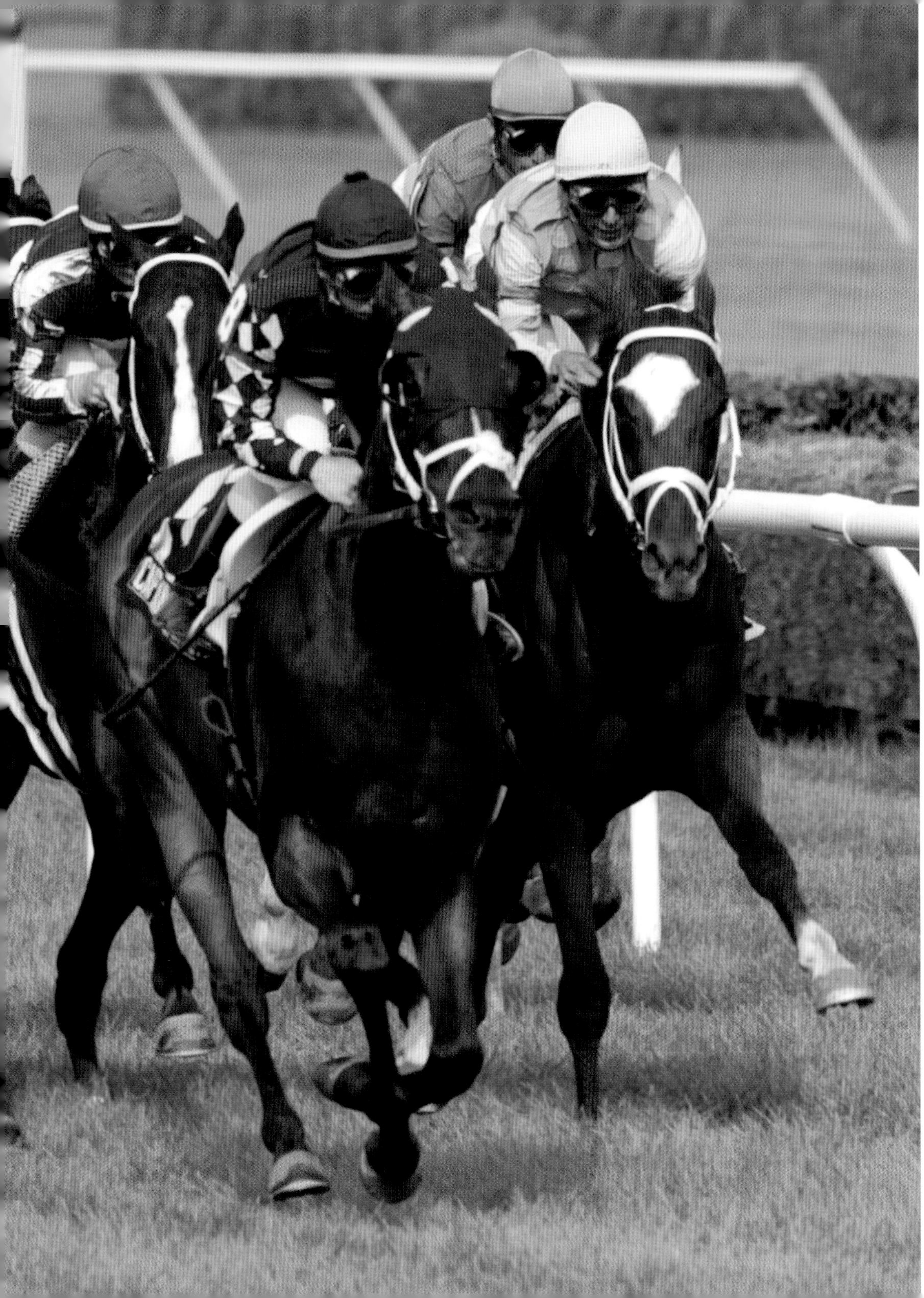

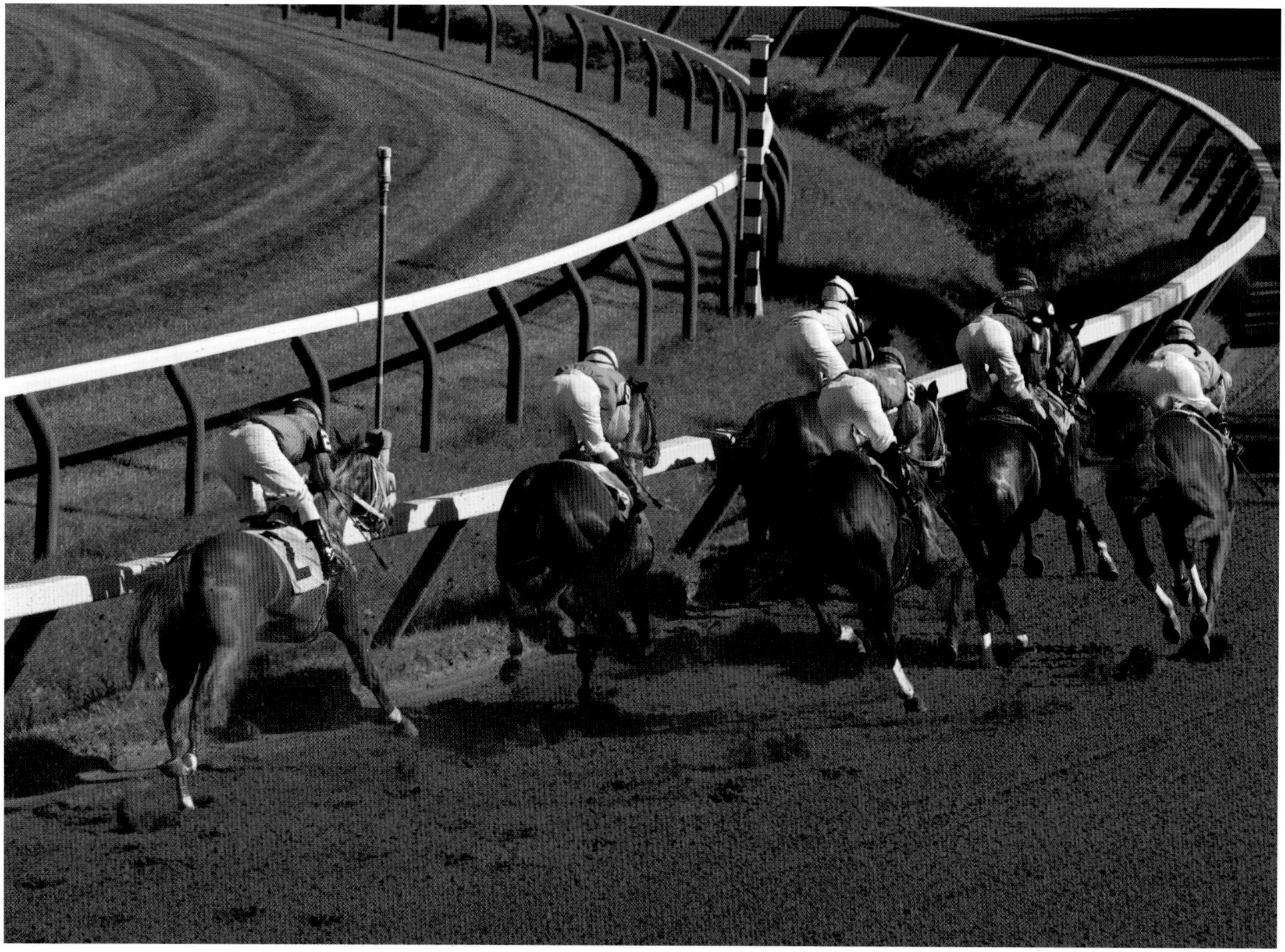

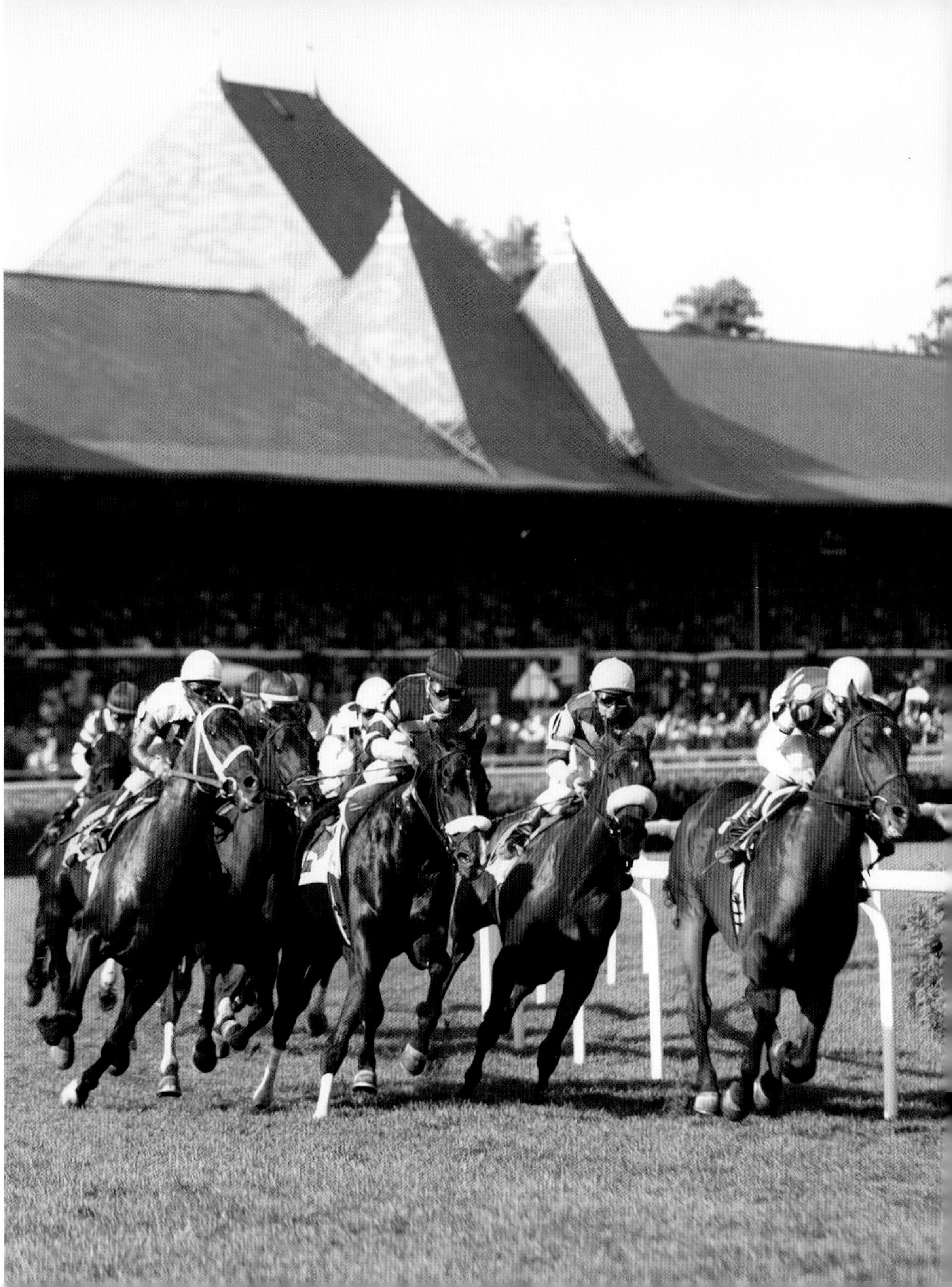

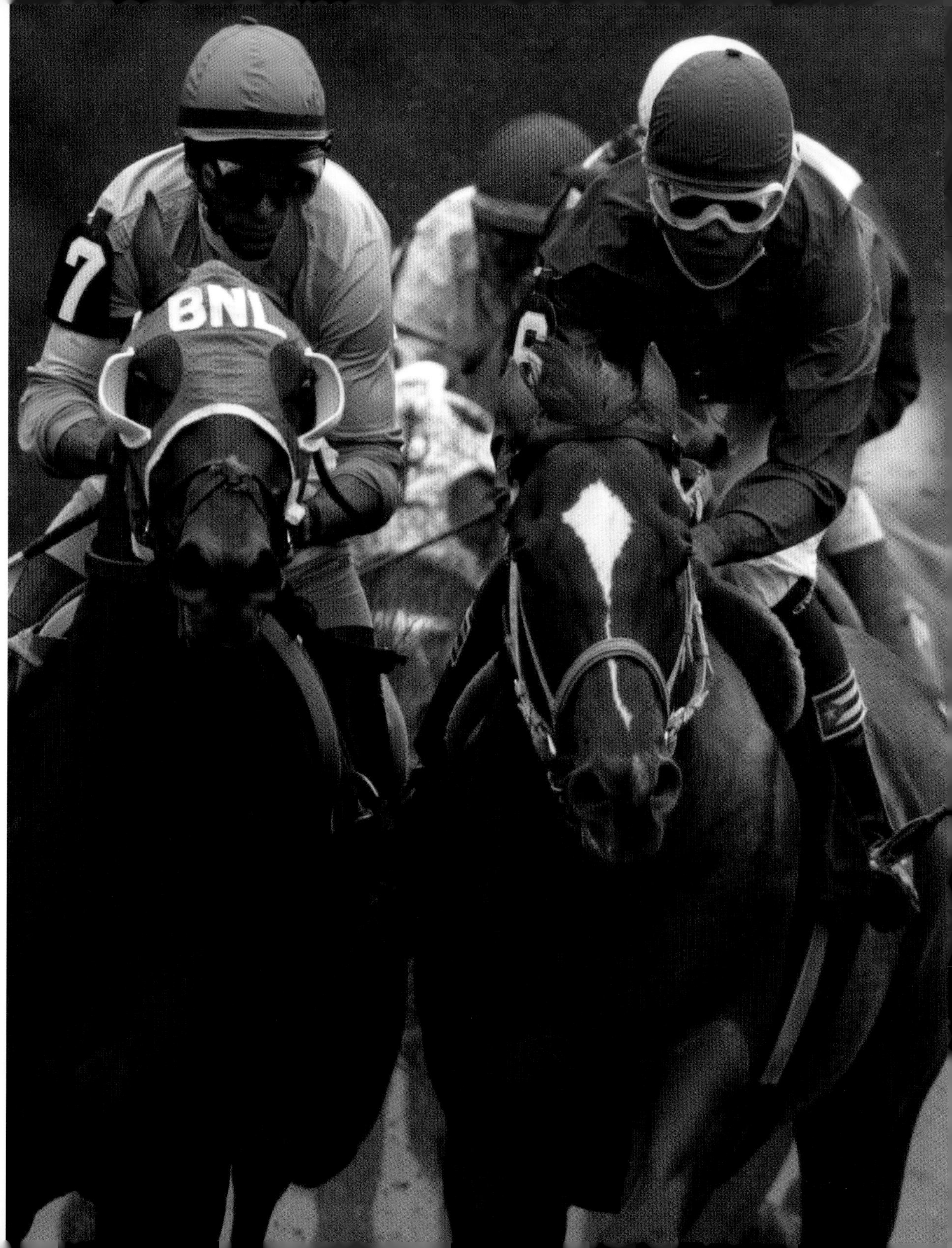
7
BNL

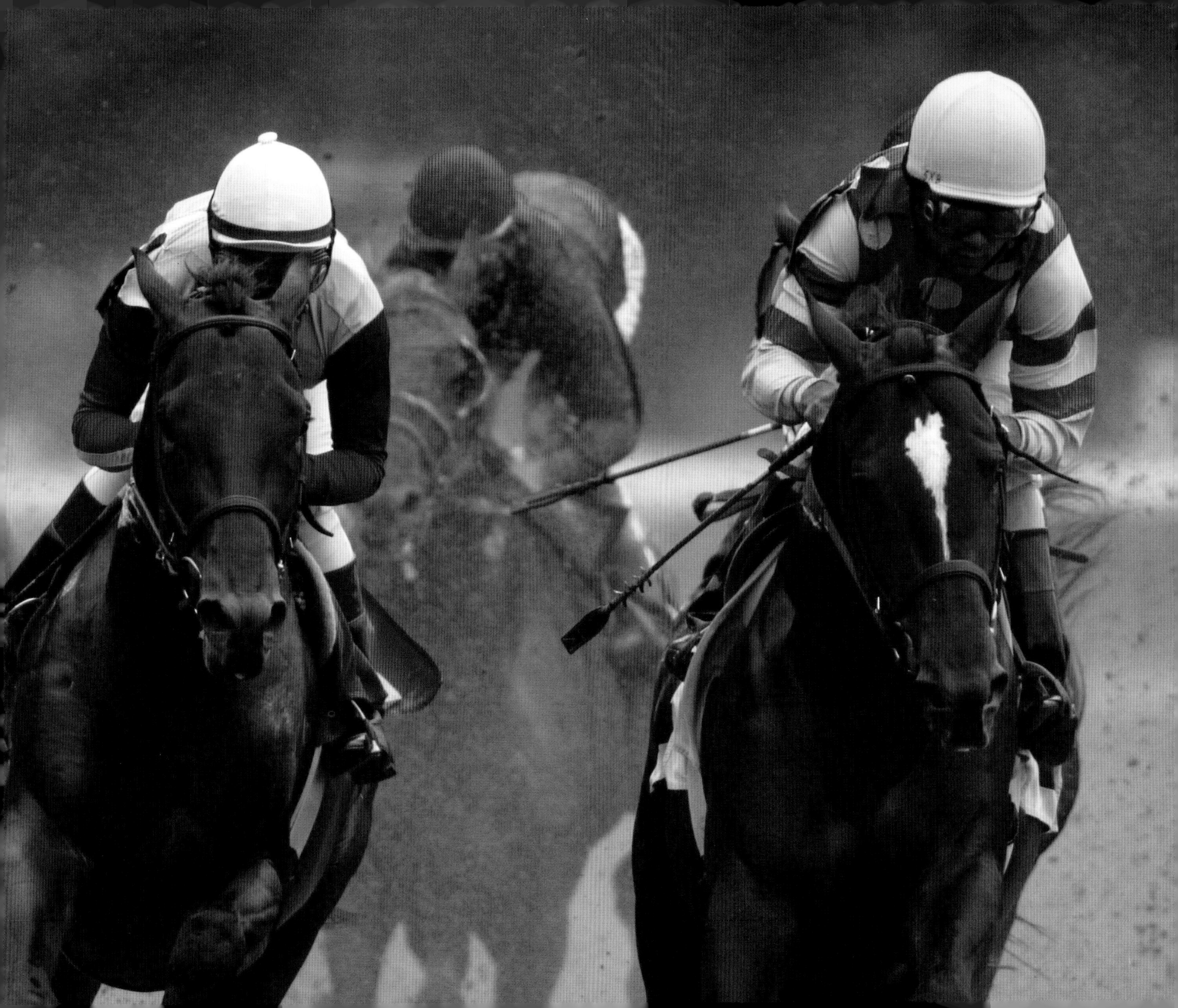

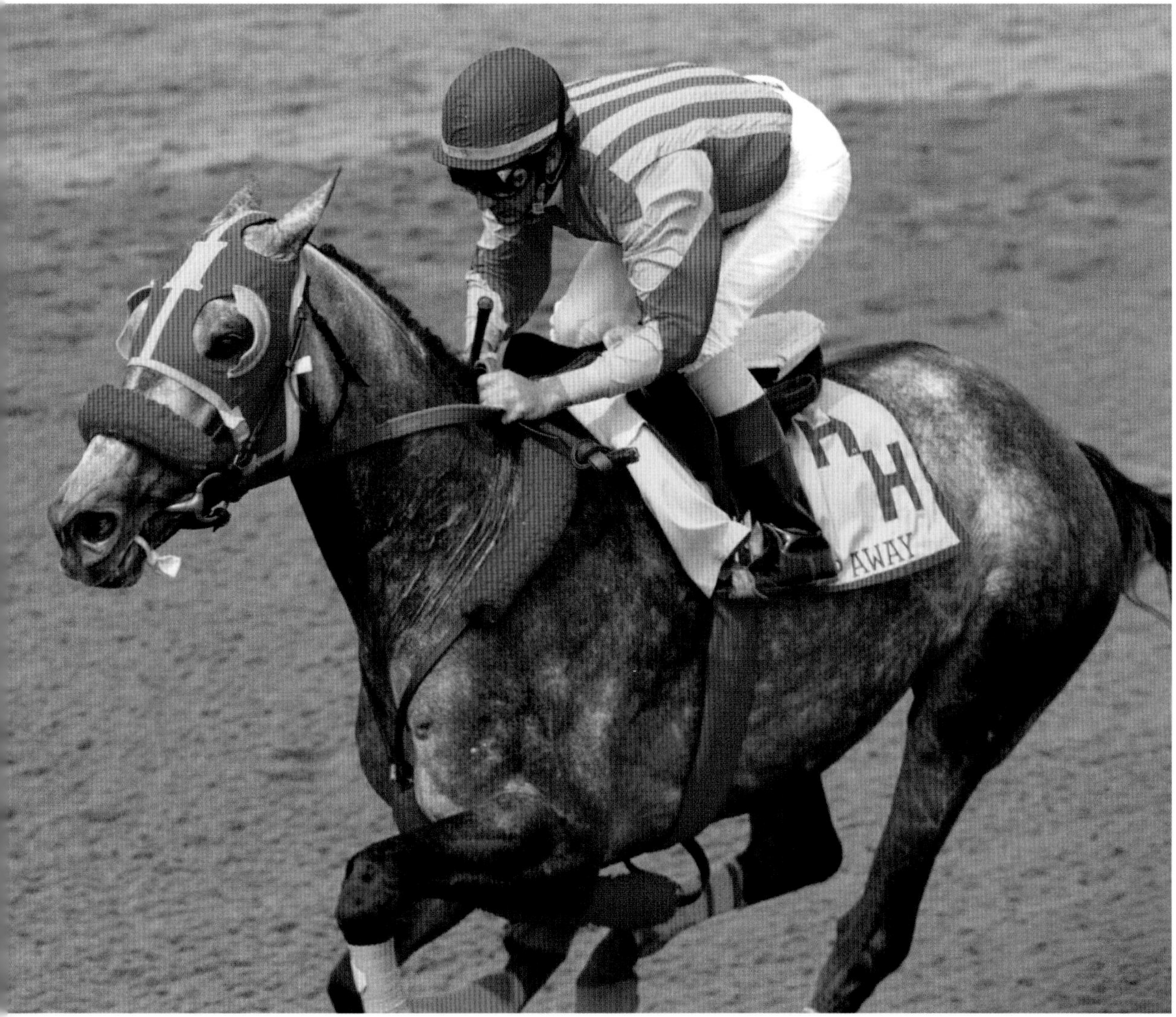

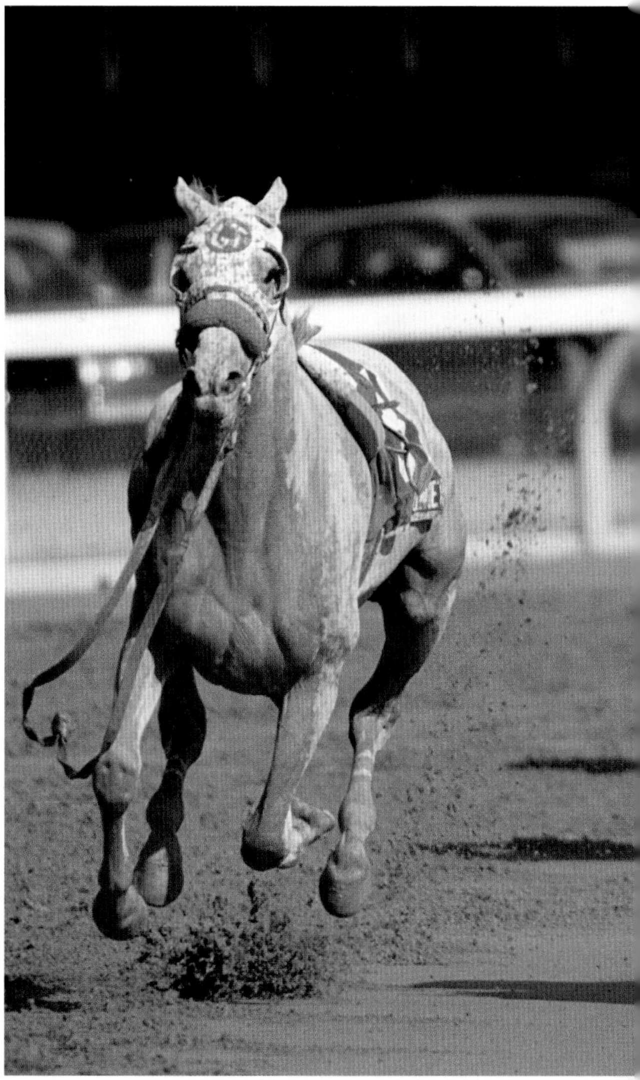

SKIP AWAY AND JERRY BAILEY (ABOVE) during a 1998 public workout.

A RIDERLESS GANDER (CENTER) in the 2002 Saratoga Breeders' Cup Handicap.

YOU (RIGHT, ON RAIL) narrowly beating Carson Hollow in the 2002 Test Stakes.

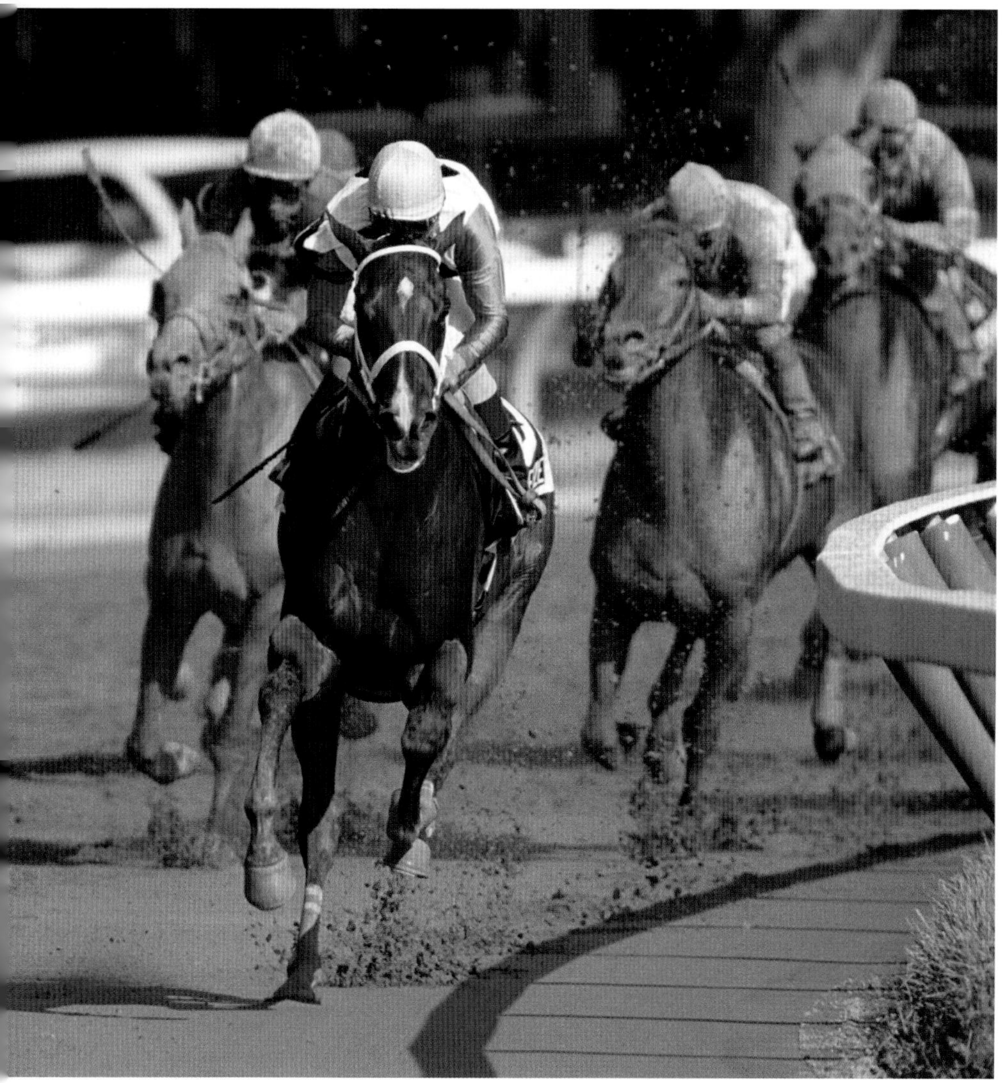

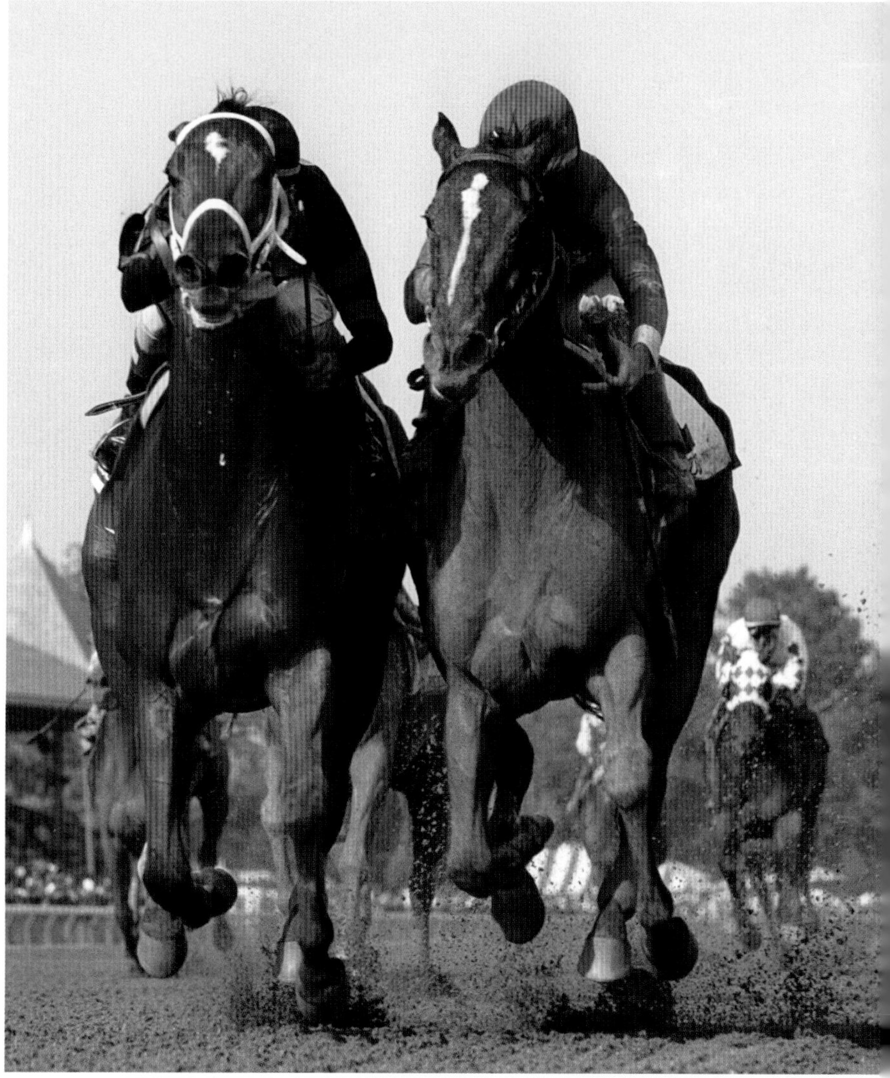

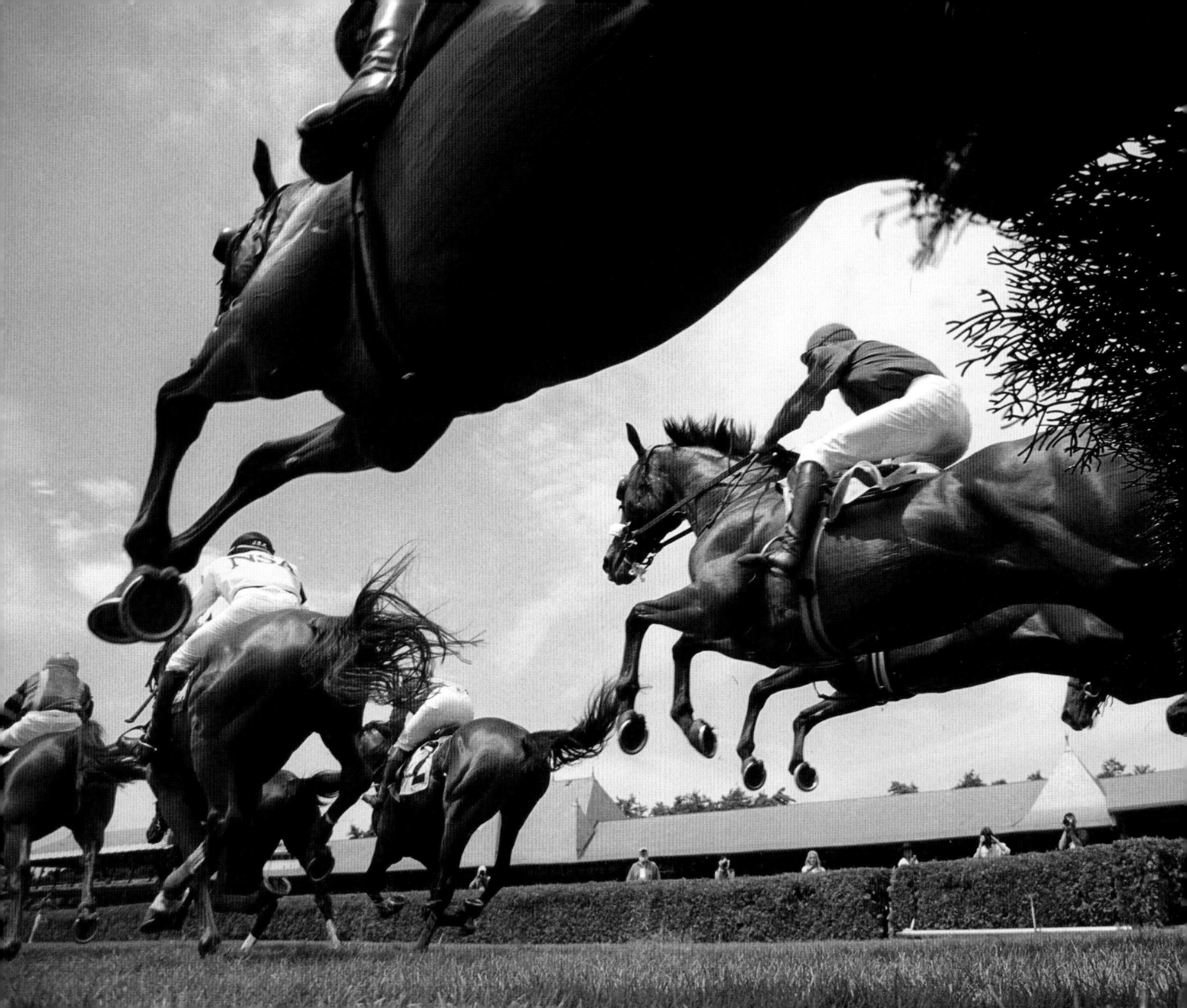

UP AND OVER! — Steeplechase racing has been part of the Saratoga racing scene since 1864.

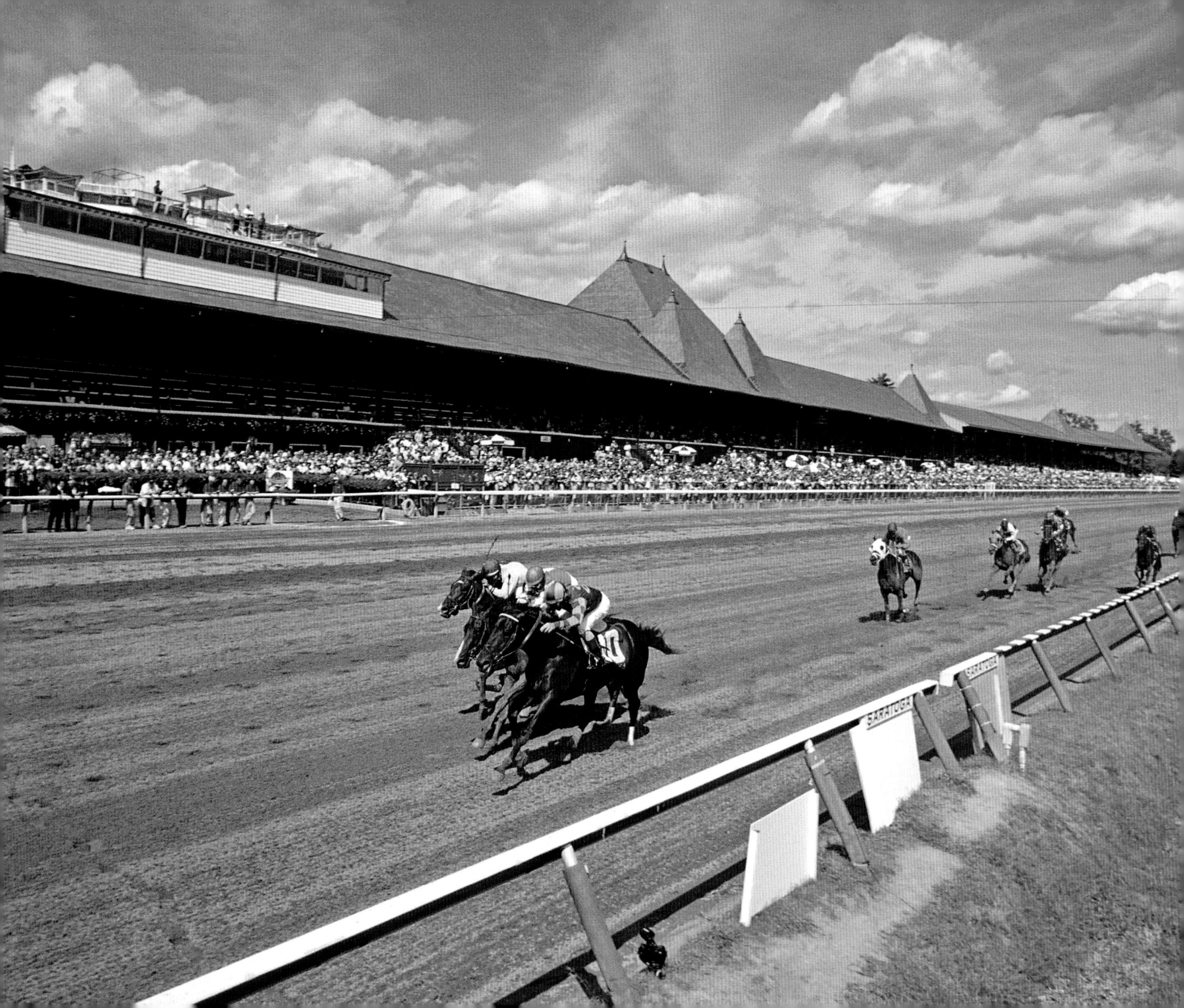
SARATOGA
SARATOGA

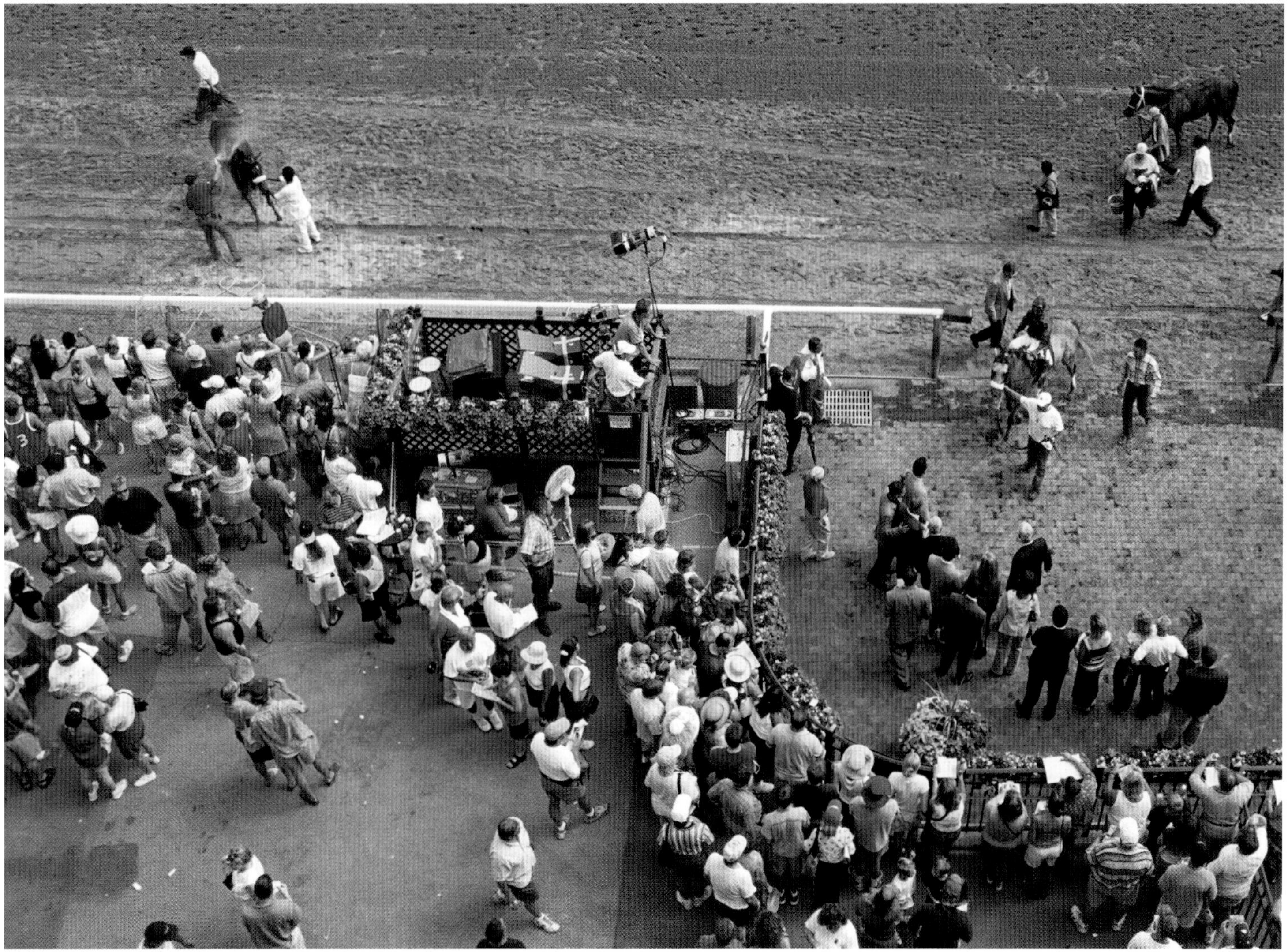

APPROACHING THE FINISH (LEFT)

VISITING THE WINNER'S CIRCLE (ABOVE)

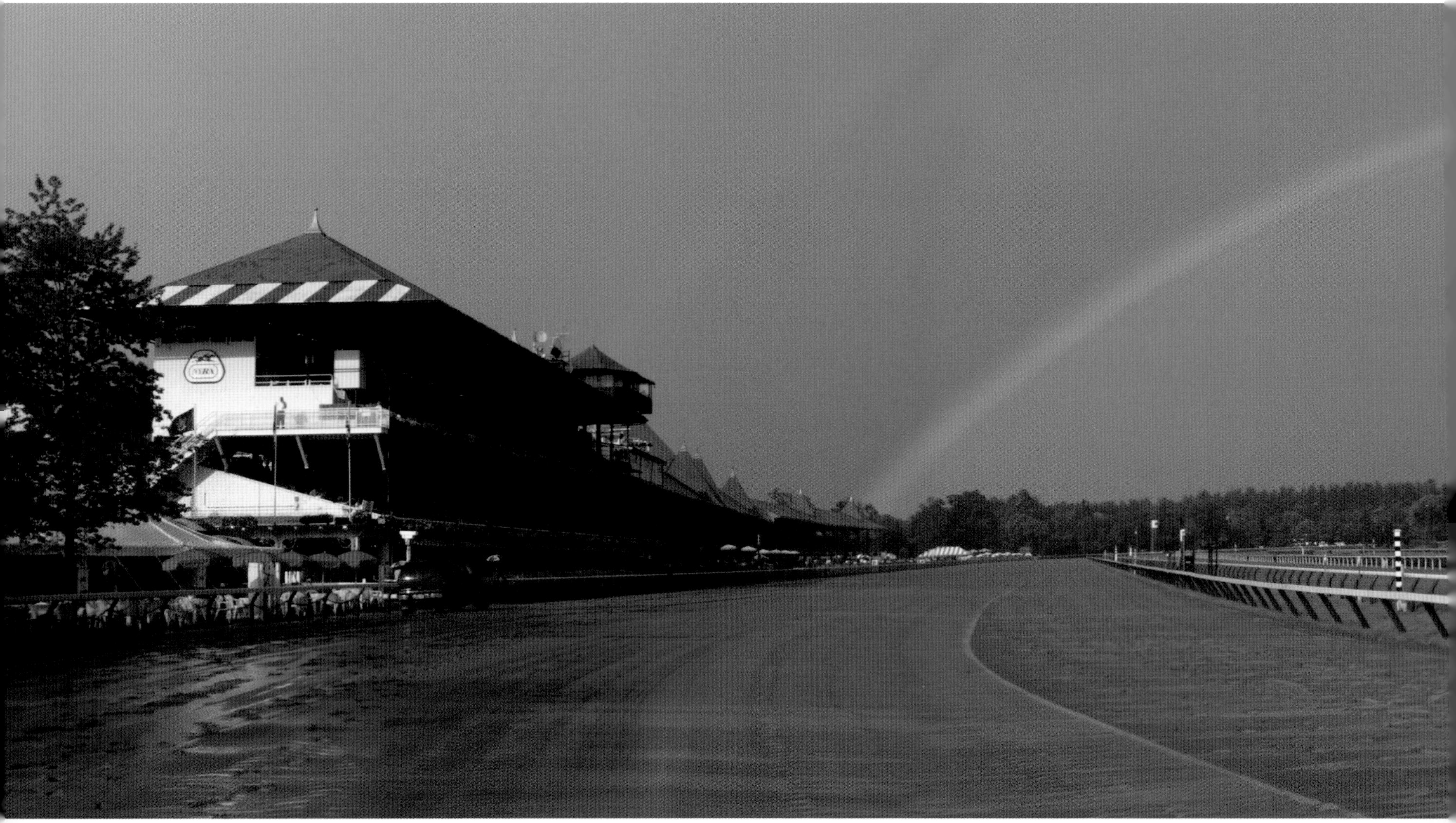

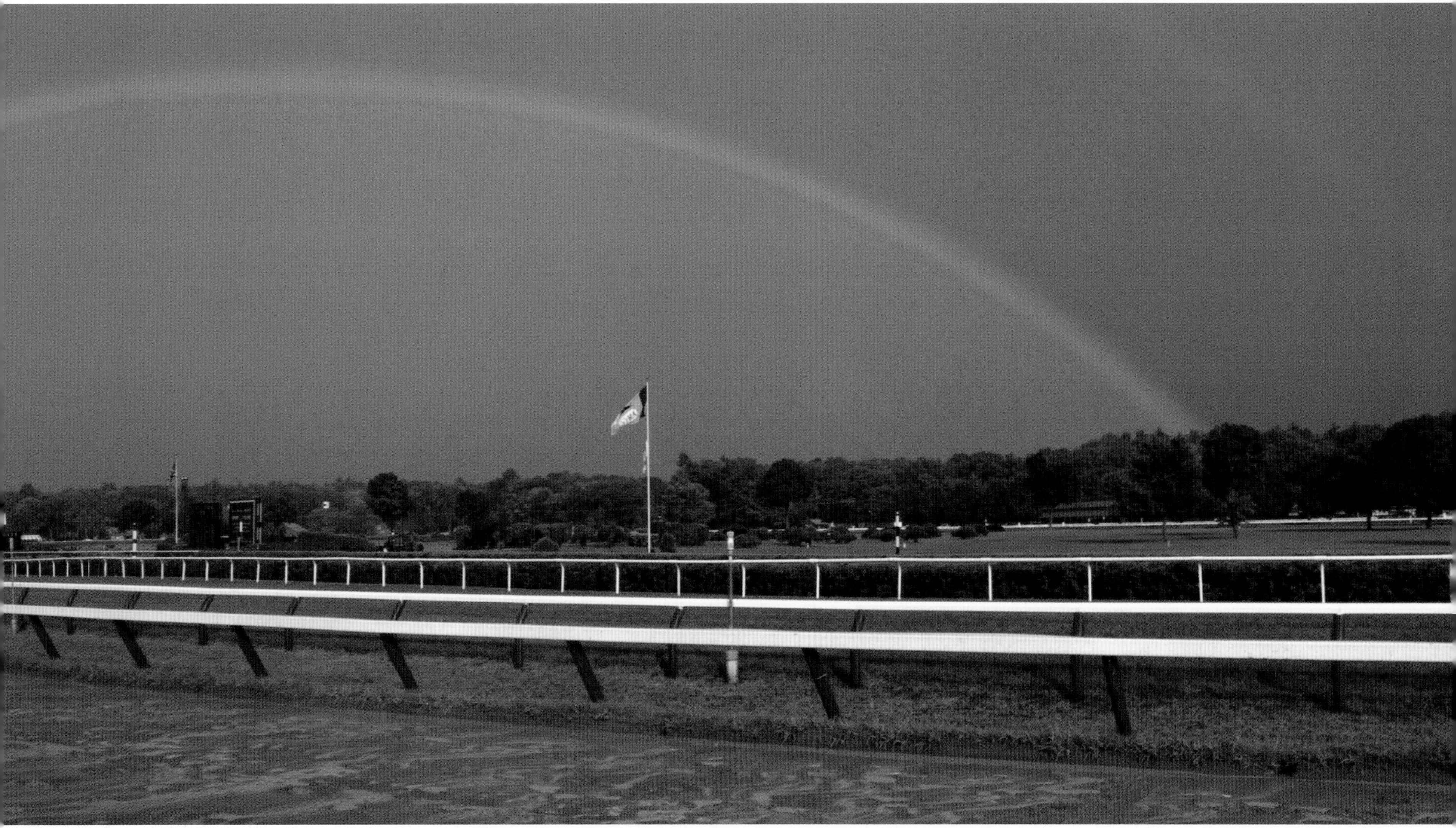

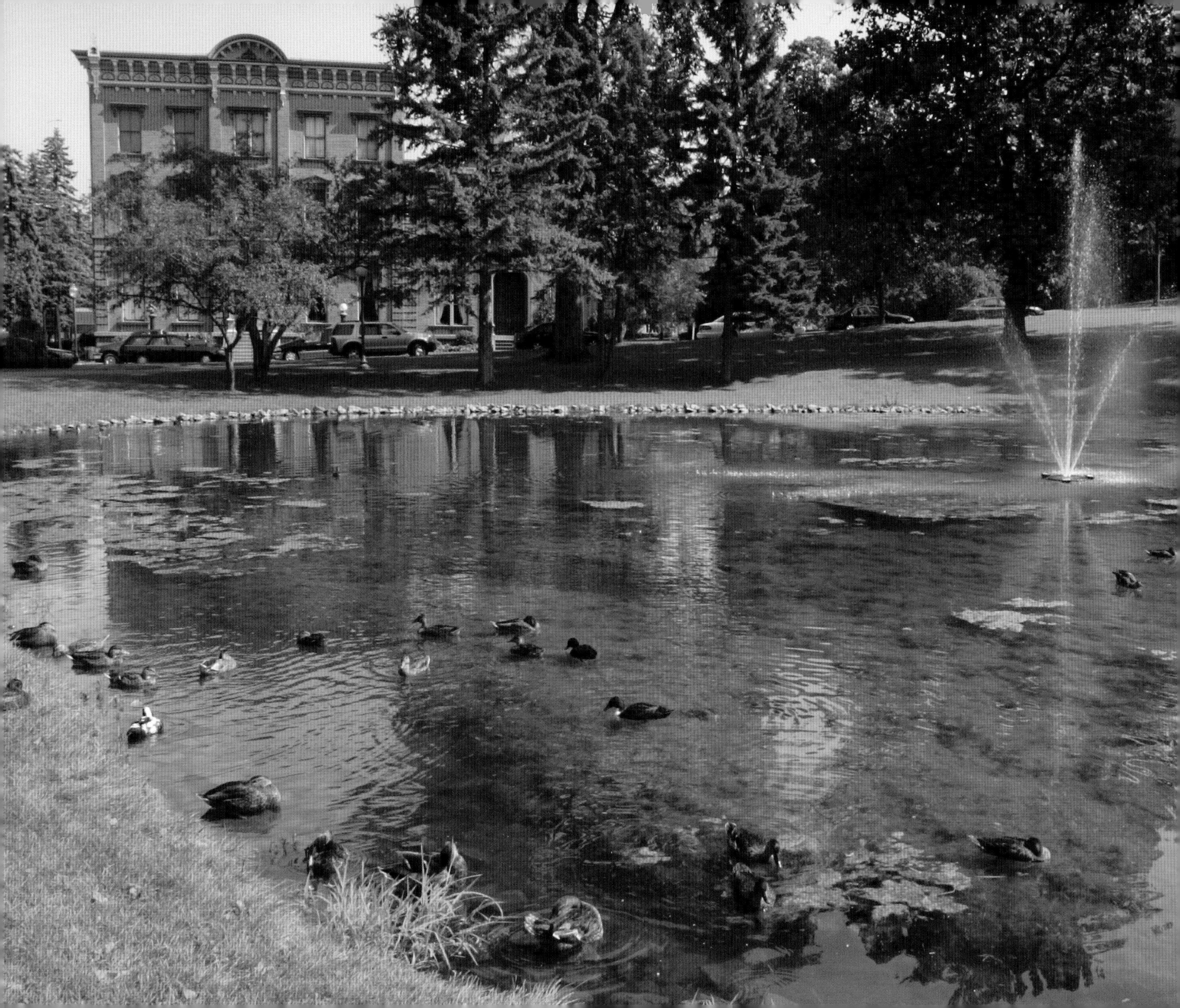

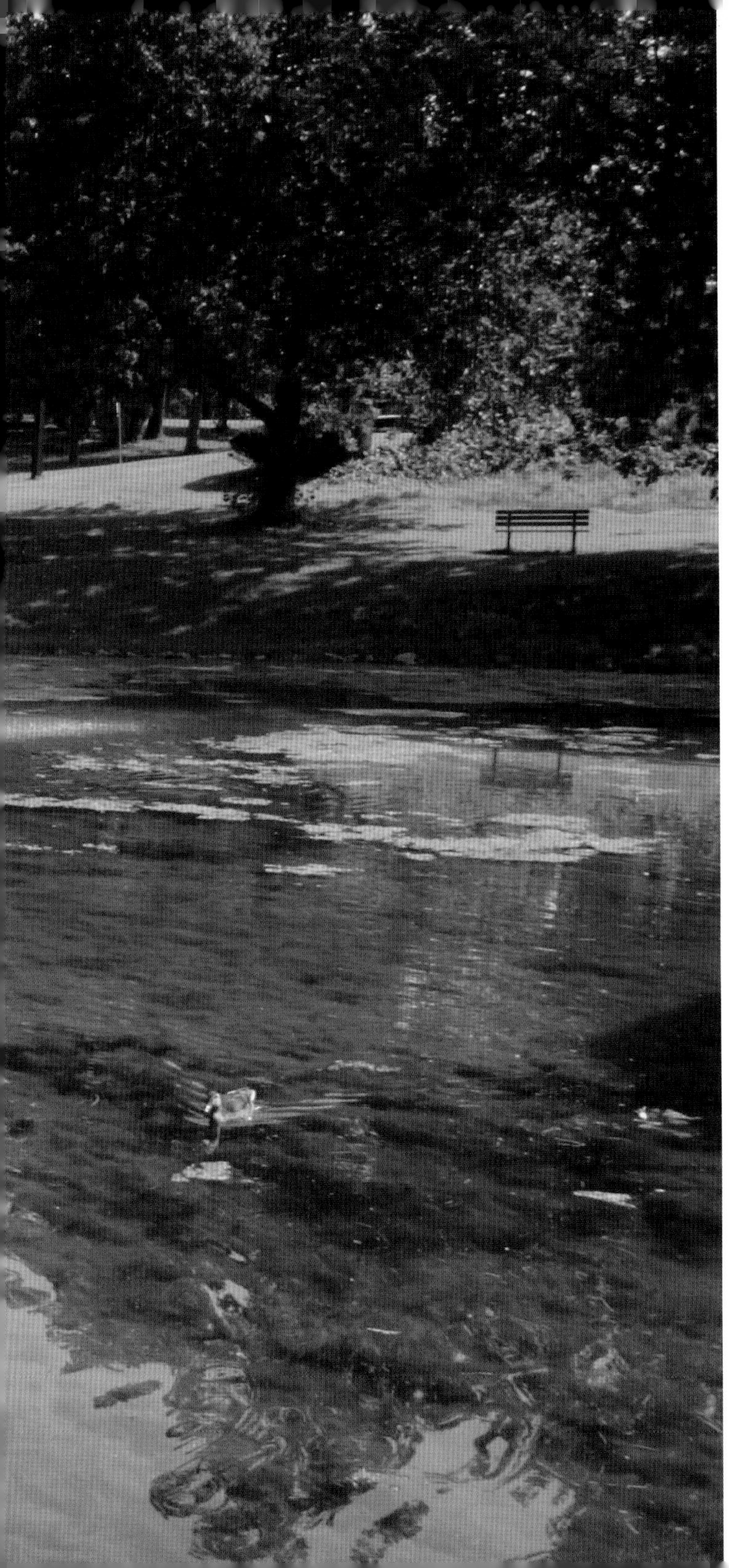

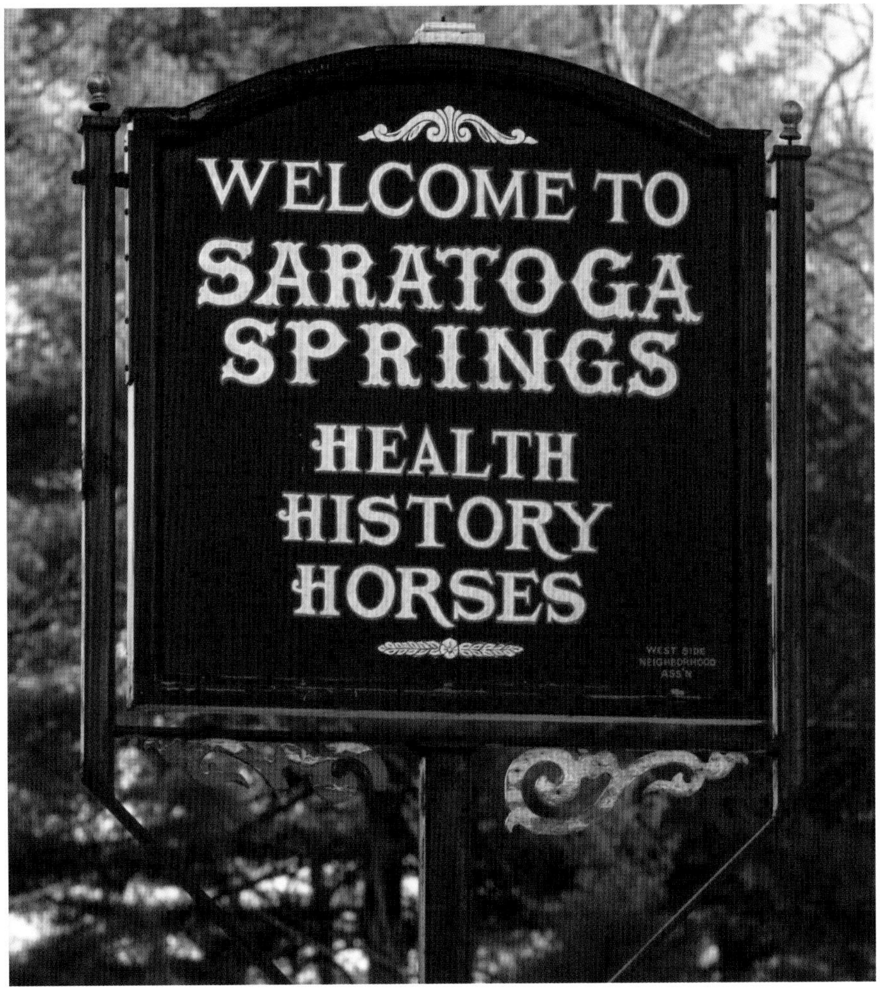

The City of Saratoga Springs

Walking through Saratoga Springs, visitors can easily envision the scene a century ago, when horse carriages provided transportation and society reigned supreme. Tradition forms a most graceful backdrop here in a city known worldwide for its charms.

So much so, in fact, that Walt Disney World in Florida recently created an expansive Saratoga Springs Spa & Resort, complete with a High Rock Spring pool and Congress Park section. In Utah a new city named Saratoga Springs is taking root.

Yet Saratoga Springs, New York, is one of a kind.

Diamond Jim Brady and Lillian Russell dazzled here during the opulent days of the late 1800s and early twentieth century, as did those with names such as Whitney, Sanford, and Vanderbilt. Socialites, actors, writers, and businessmen have long flocked to Saratoga's various entertainments — the track, the spas, the springs, and the casinos.

Natural springs, due to a fault line beneath the city, began attracting visitors in the late eighteenth century. Saratoga became the place to "take the cure," and the famous converged — from near and far — to be pampered at bathhouses and mineral springs.

Nowadays, Congress Park, nestled in the heart of downtown, perhaps most strongly captures that old-time feeling. Summer days are idyllic there. Families picnic near ponds as enchanting calliope music lures children to the century-old carousel. Aging fountains and statues view the ever-changing scene. Waters course ceaselessly from the park's Congress Spring.

Natural springs, so important to Saratoga's development, still dot the city landscape, and bathhouses — both old and modern — still pamper.

Victorian buildings are everywhere throughout the city. Some 900 buildings are listed on the National Register of Historic Places. Grand homes line Union Avenue and North Broadway, their oversized porches festooned with flower beds. Bountiful flower plantings grace city roadsides, splashing the city with vibrant colors.

Broadway has changed. Many tremendous hotels have long since yielded to progress, and downtown now offers Starbucks and Borders. Yet venerable landmarks like the Adelphi Hotel, town hall, and post office stand tall. The city still charms.

Some mourn the loss of Saratoga's "glory days" — those of Diamond Jim and Lillian, and sweeping hotels a quarter-mile long.

Yet a walk down Broadway just before sunset, the traffic deep in shadow and the last light blazing along the historic rooflines, affirms that the beauty of "now" is still remarkable.

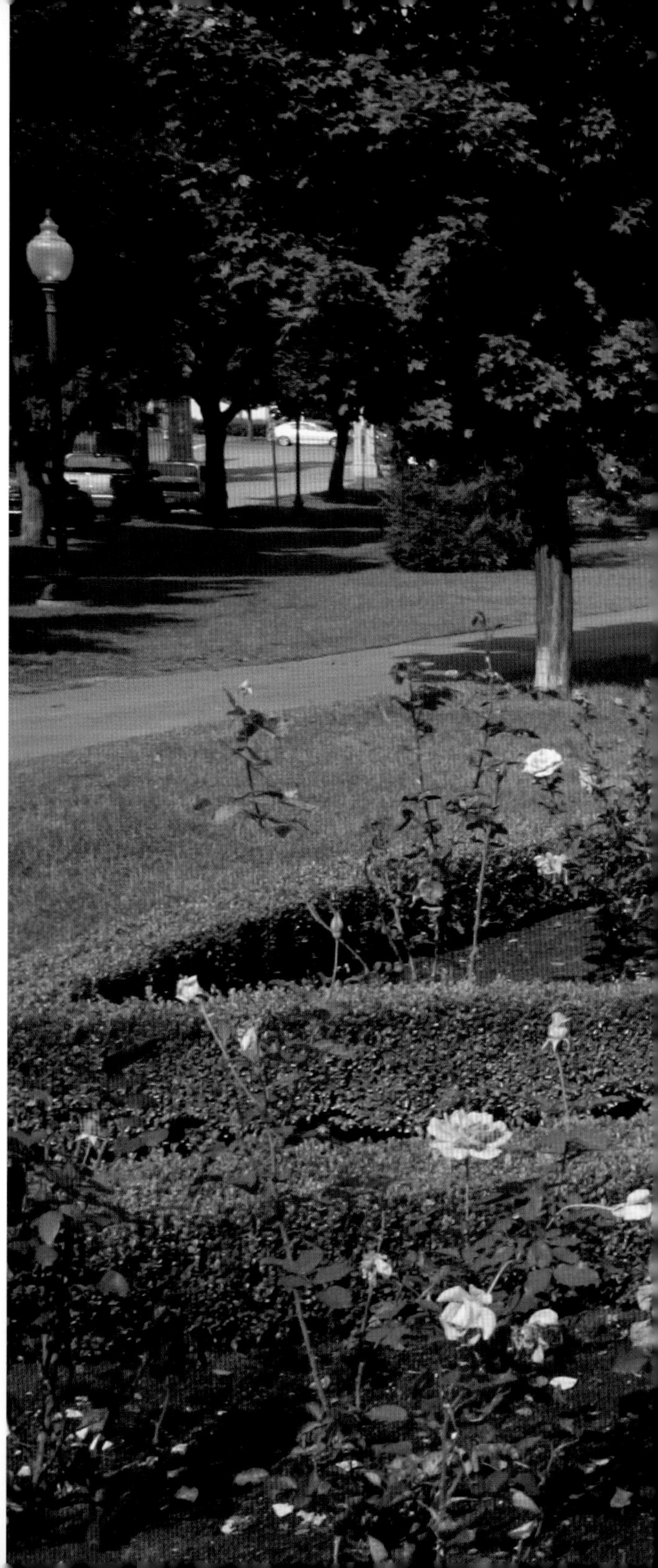

CONGRESS PARK, WITH CANFIELD CASINO (PREVIOUS)

THE MORRISSEY FOUNTAIN

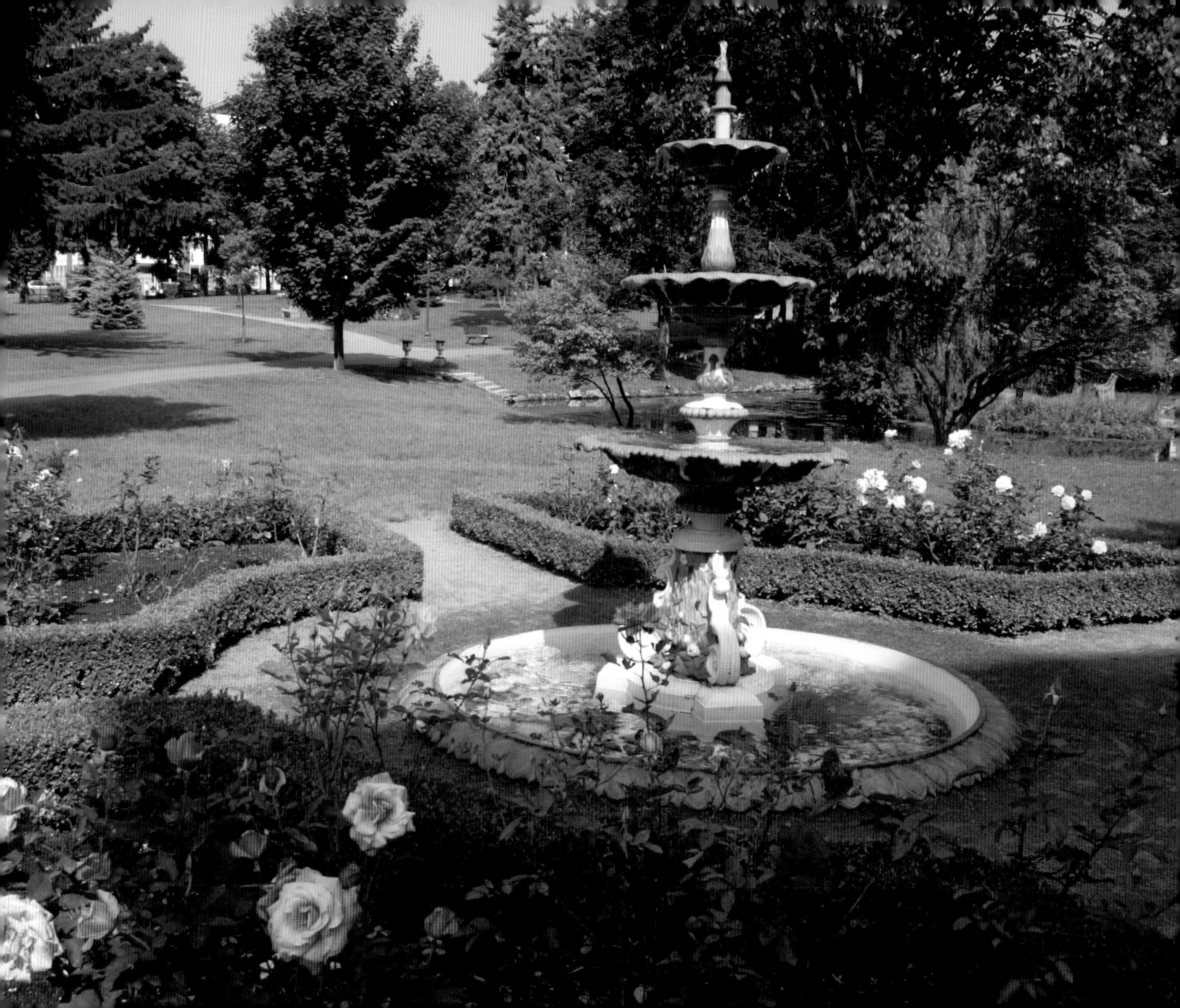

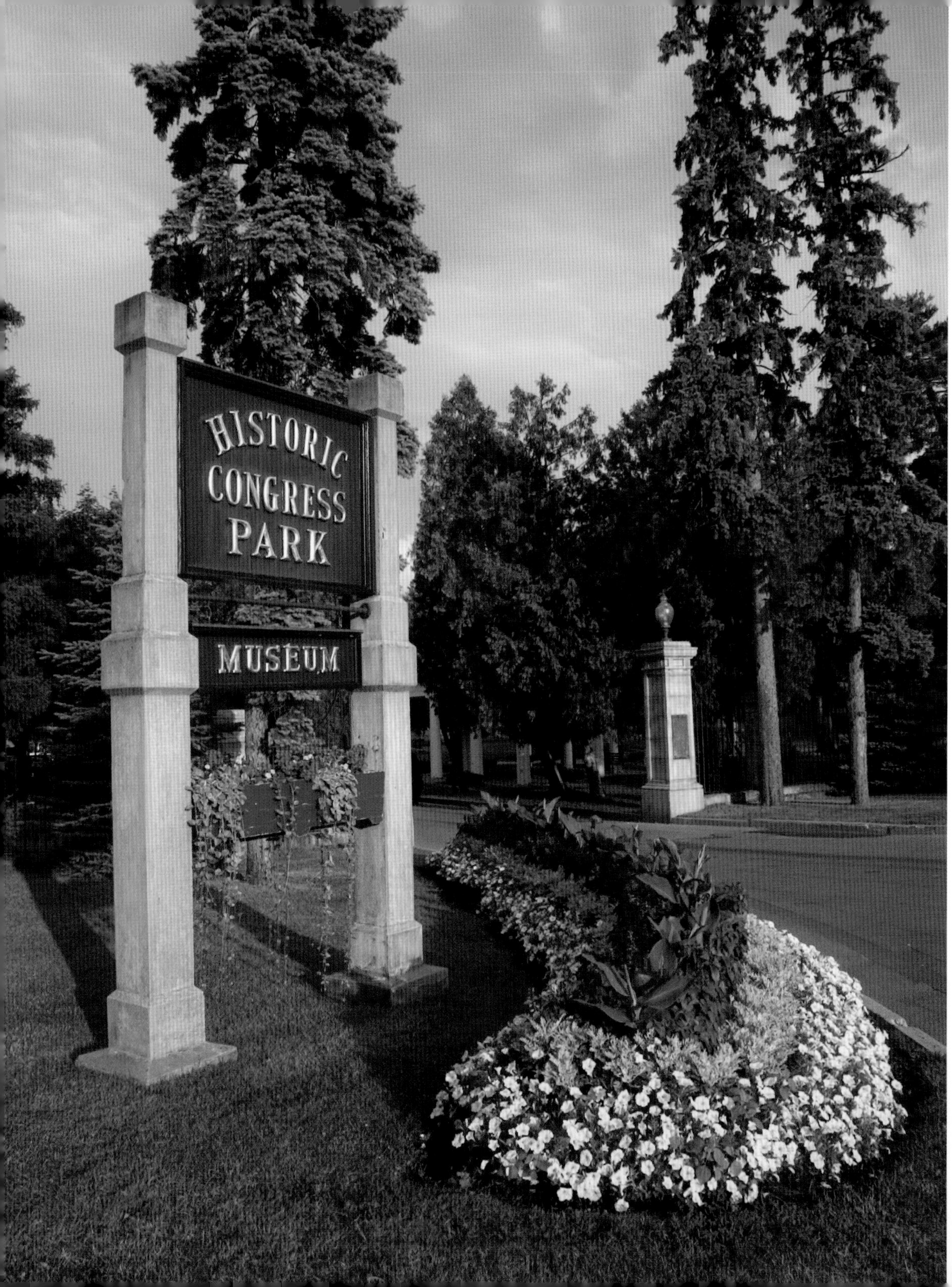
HISTORIC
CONGRESS
PARK
MUSEUM

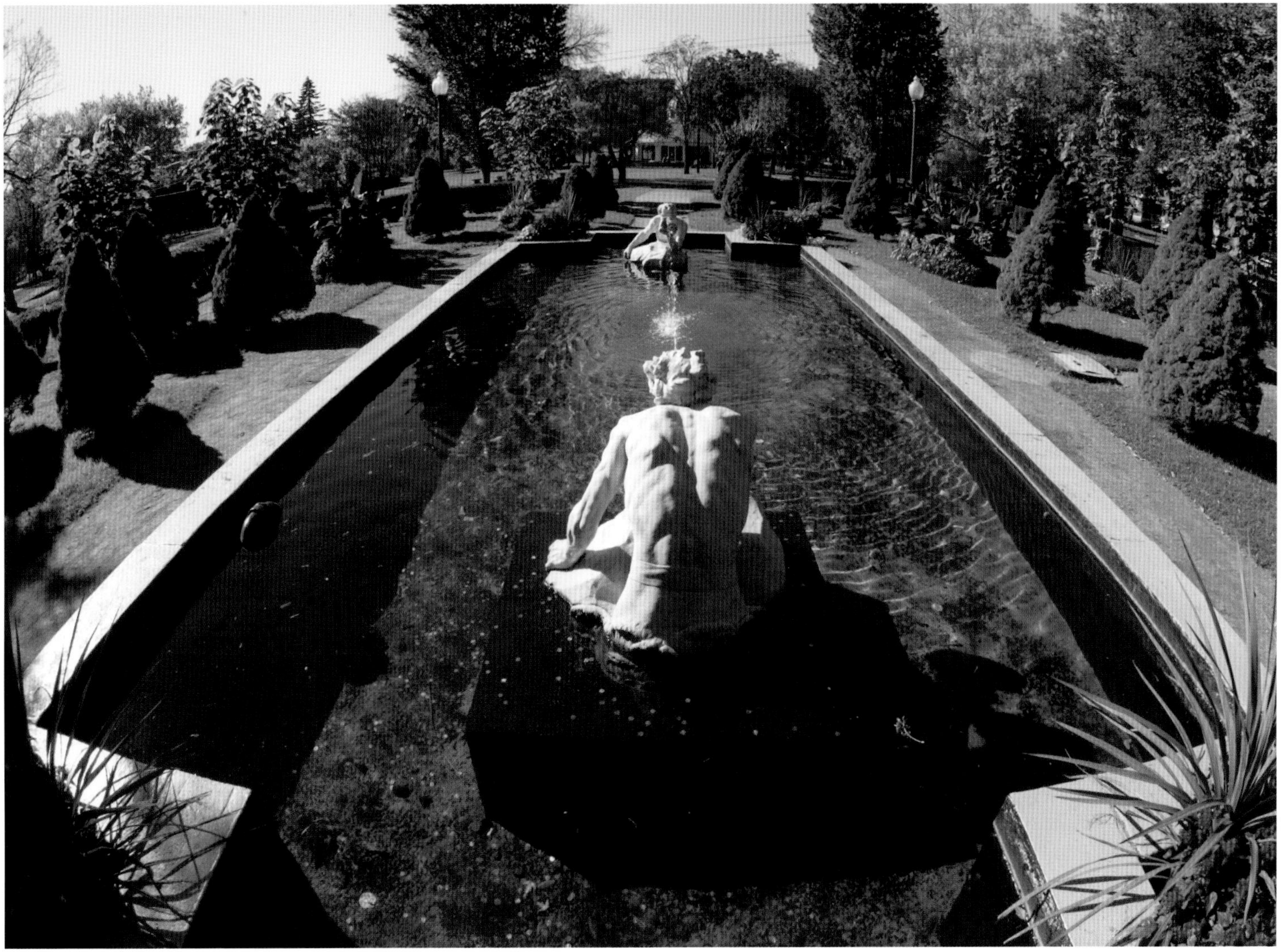

CONGRESS PARK ENTRANCE (LEFT)

SPIT & SPAT FOUNTAIN (ABOVE), located in the park's Italian Gardens.

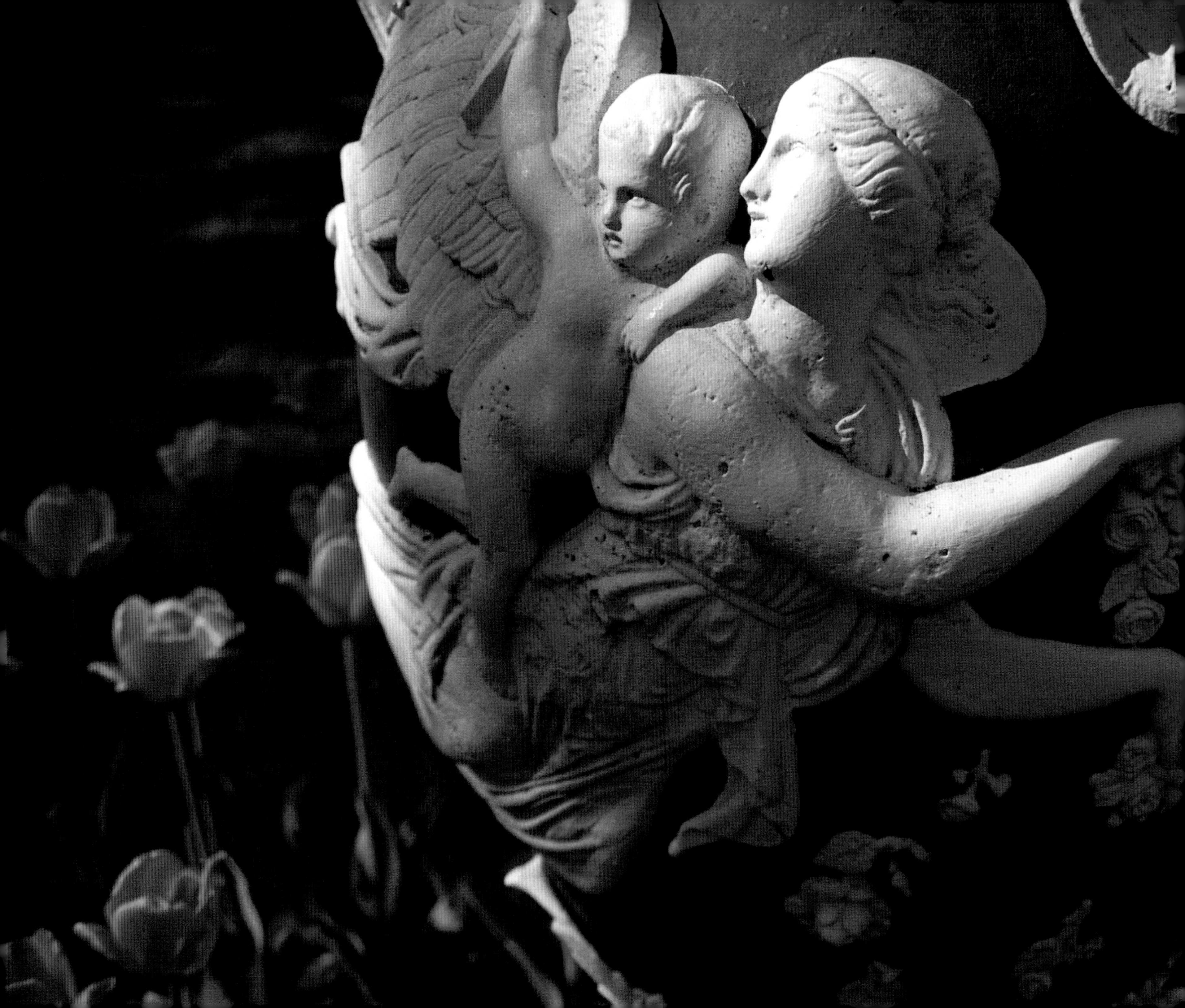

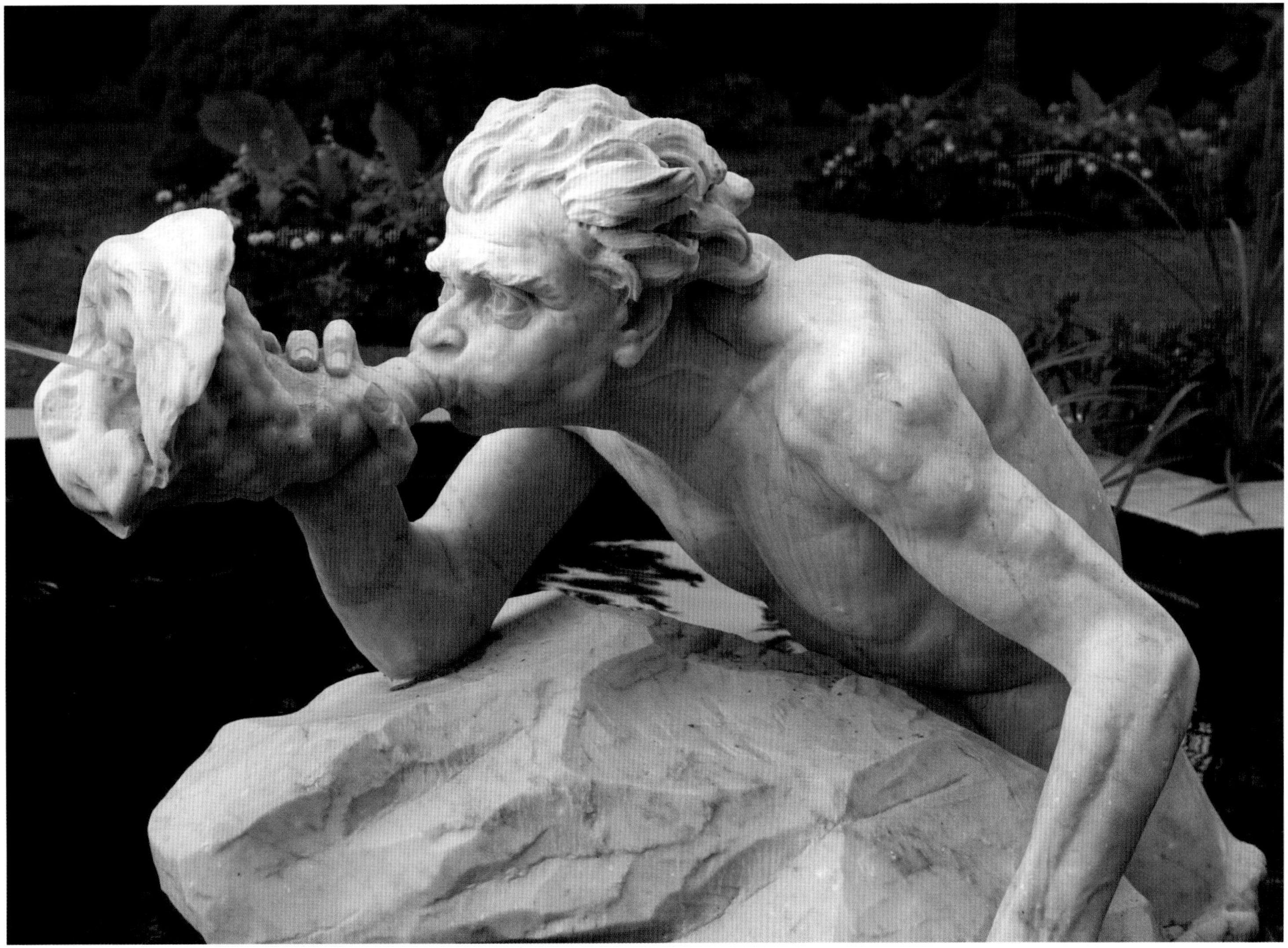

NIGHT & DAY CAST-IRON VASES (DETAIL, LEFT), created in the early 1800s by sculptor Albert Thorvaldsen.

SPIT & SPAT (DETAIL, ABOVE), beloved Triton statues sculpted from Italian Carrara marble.

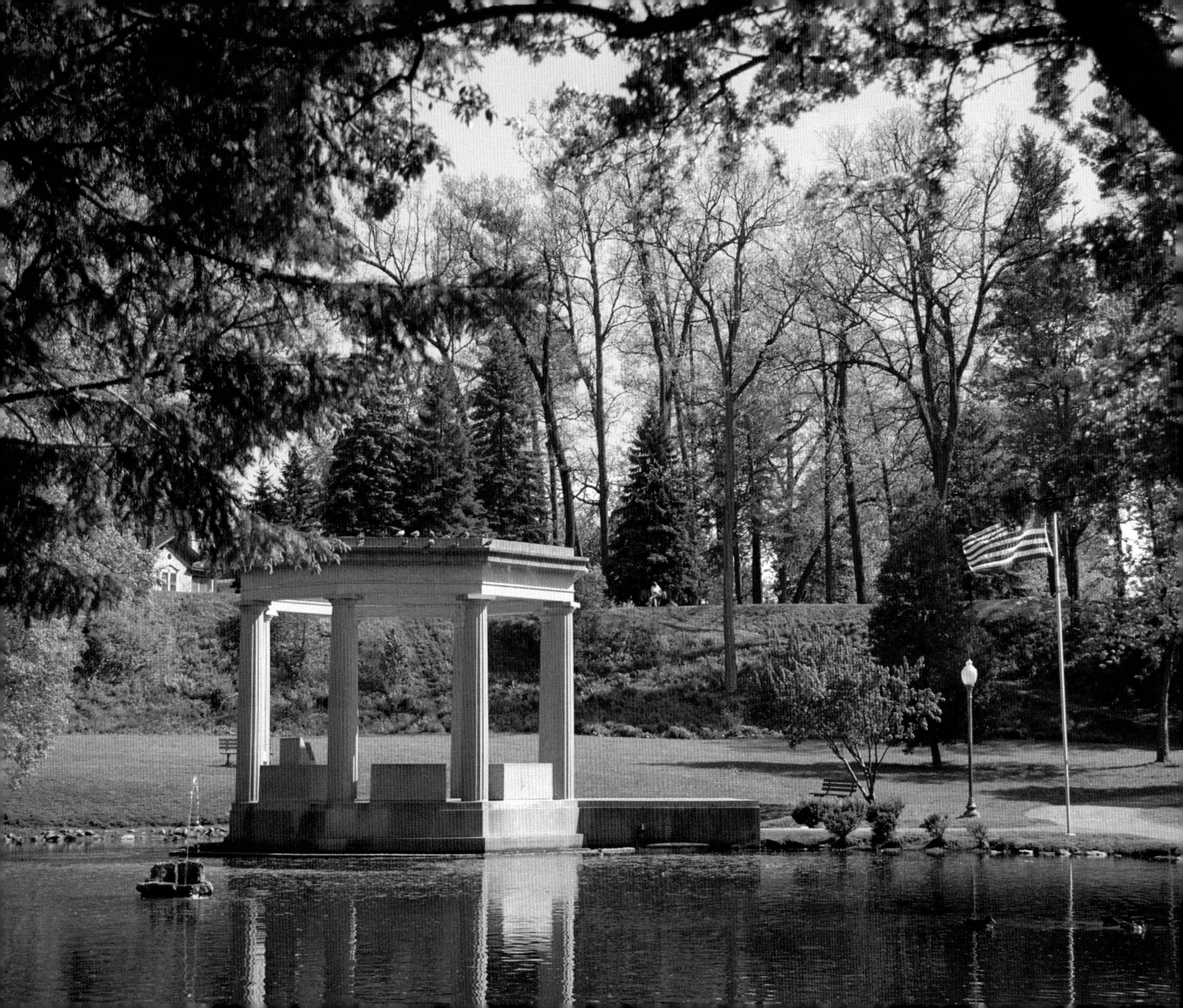

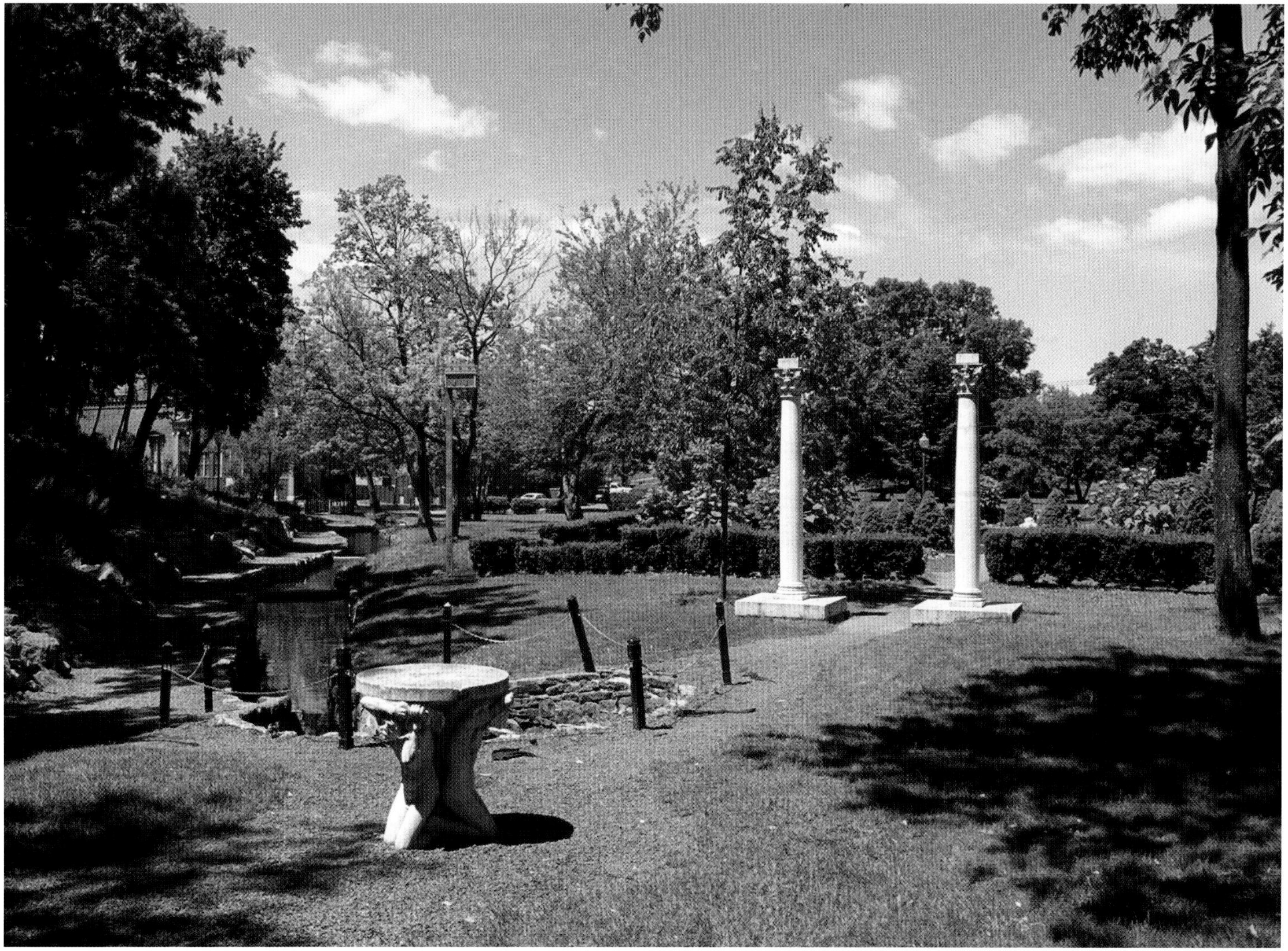

THE WAR MEMORIAL (LEFT) plays host to a variety of summer concerts.

THE ITALIAN GARDENS (ABOVE), added to the park in 1902.

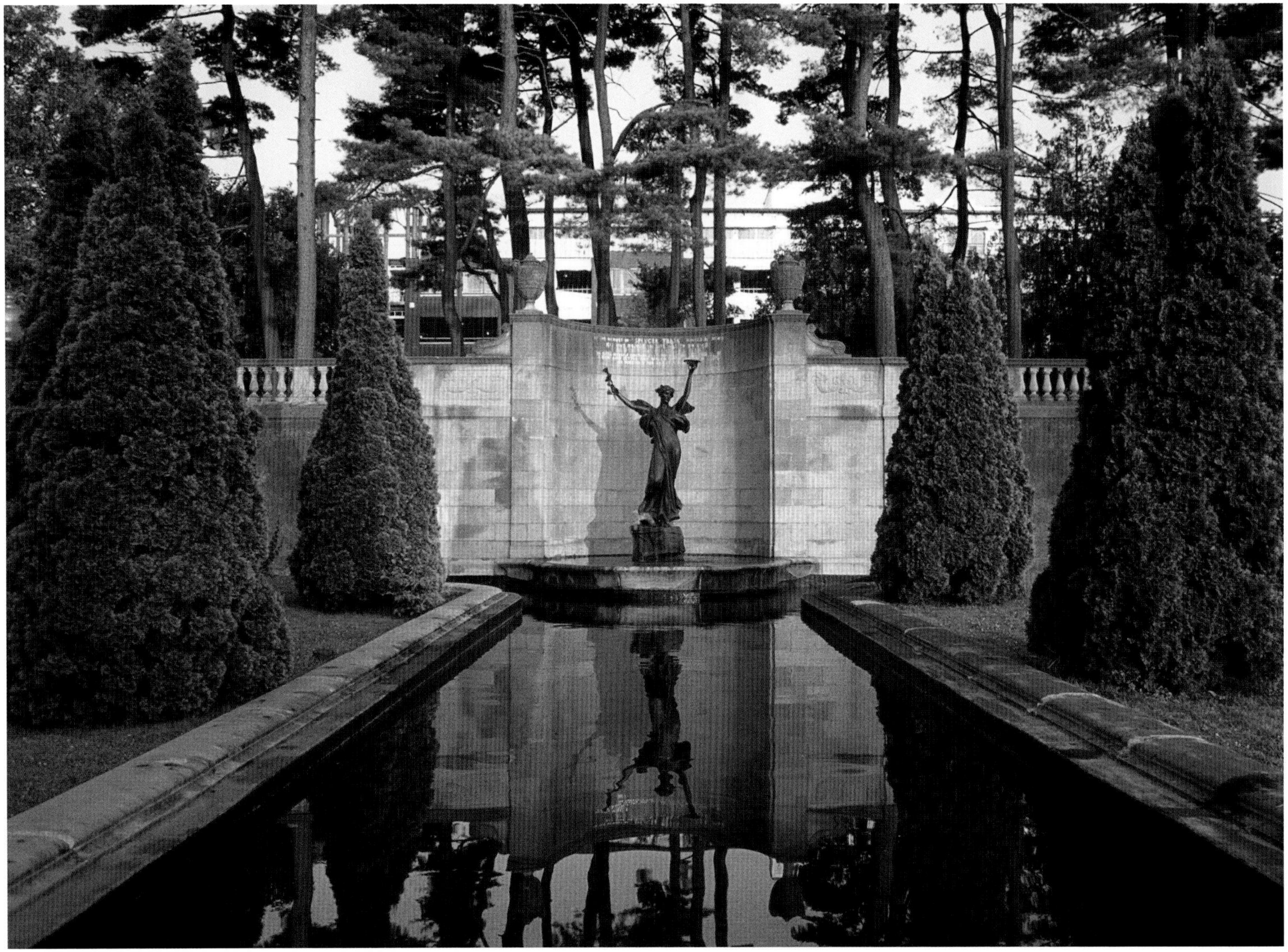

THE SPIRIT OF LIFE, unveiled in 1915, was fashioned as a tribute to philanthropist Spencer Trask by sculptor Daniel Chester French. French is most famous for his statue of Abraham Lincoln, centerpiece of the Lincoln Memorial.

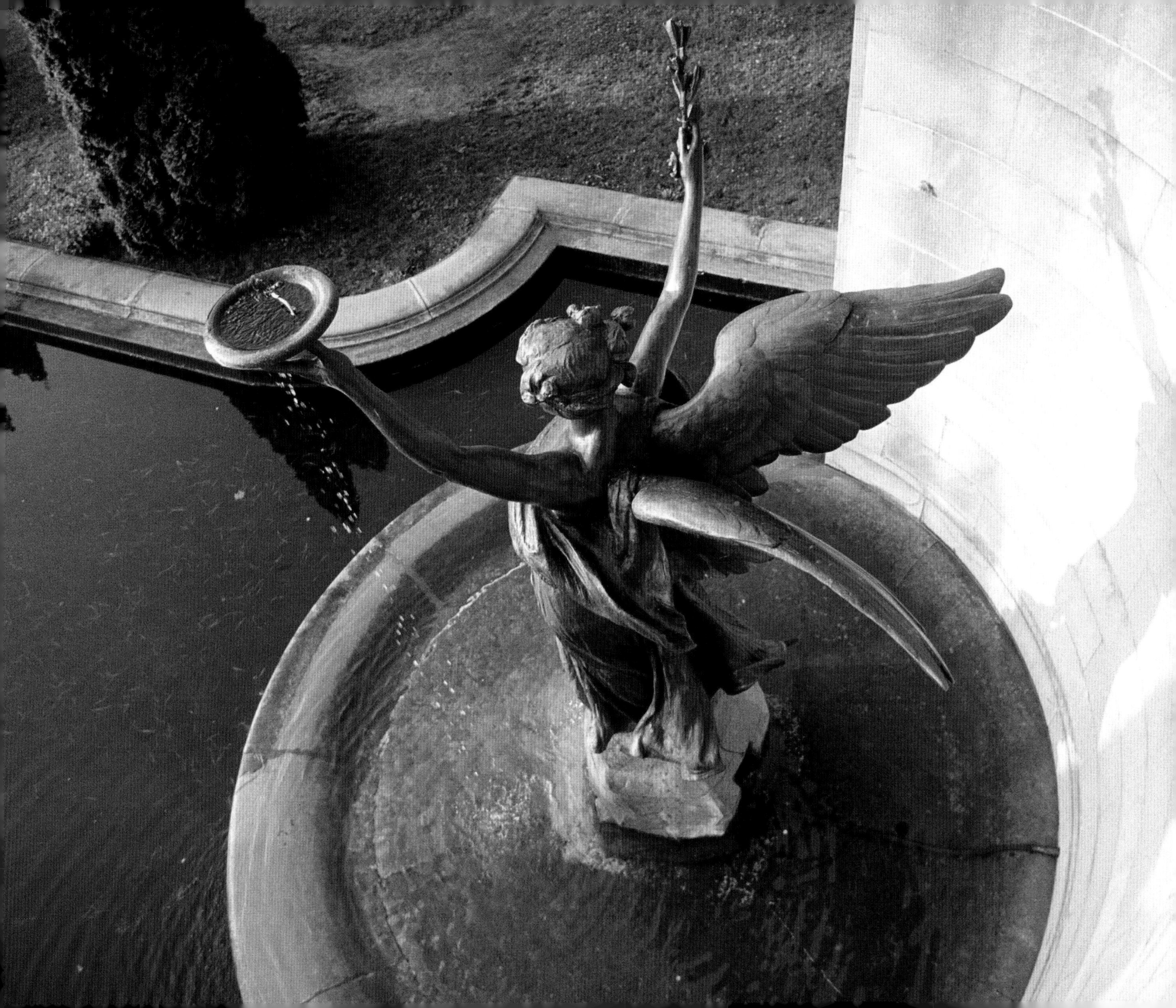

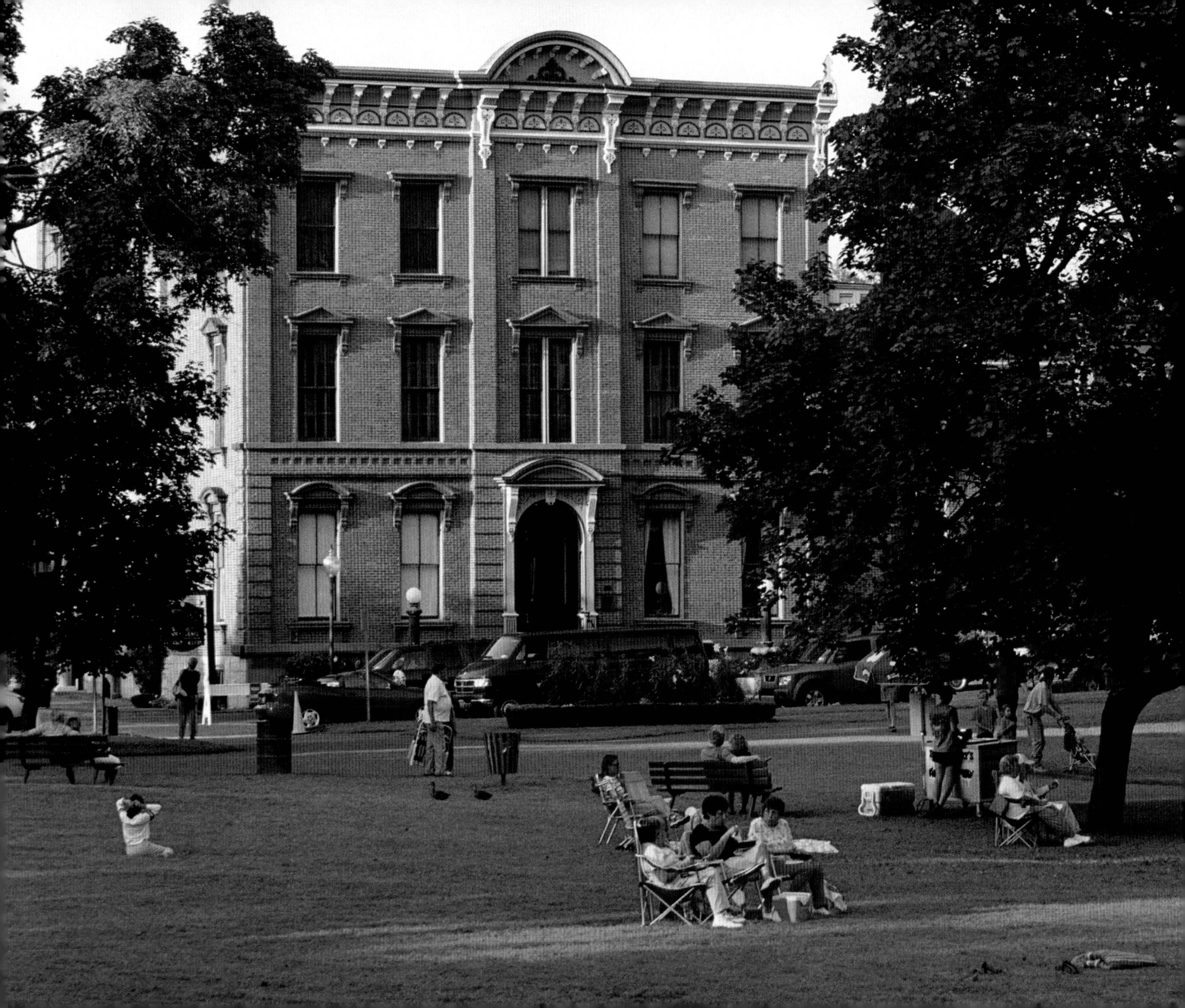

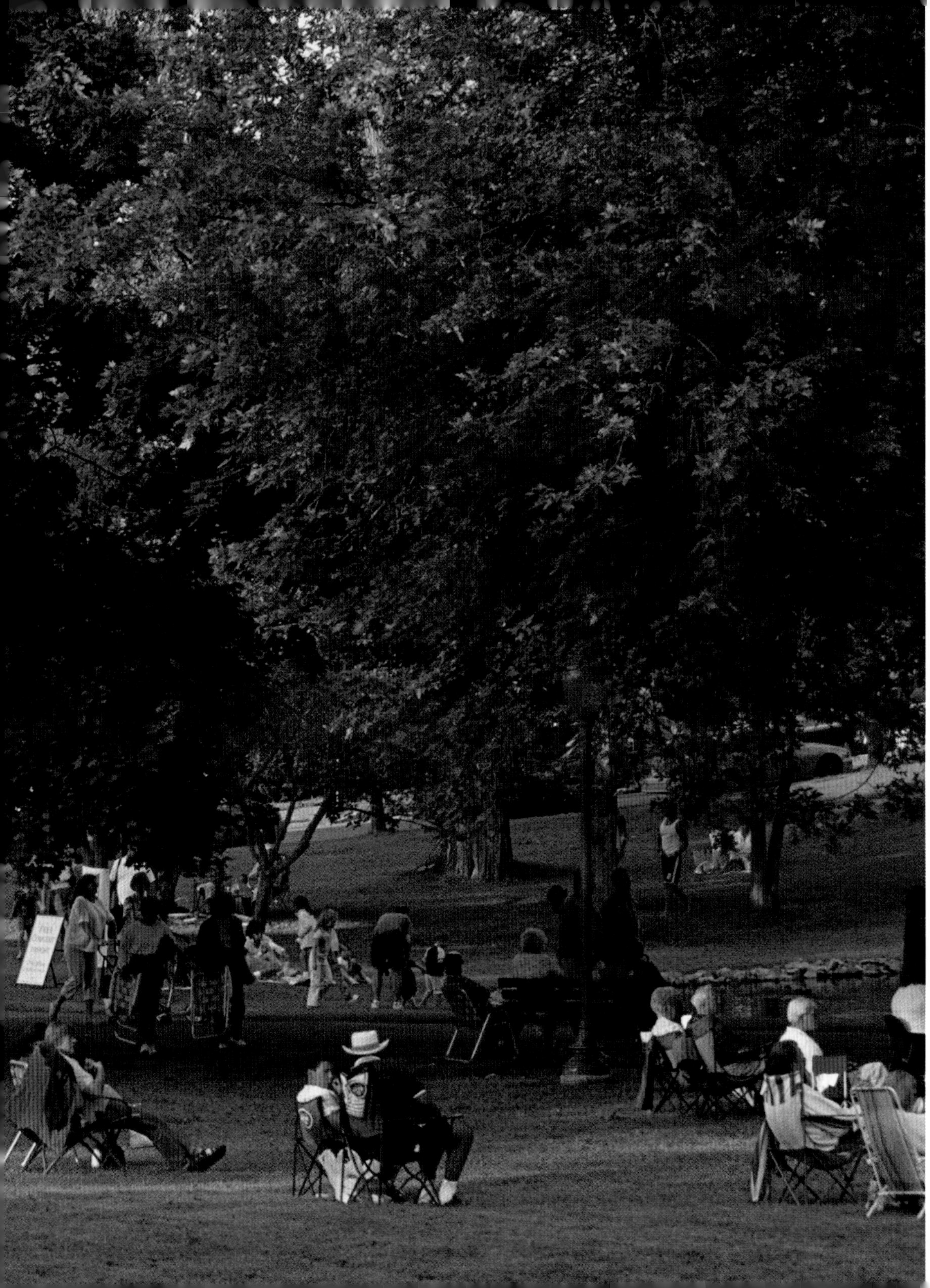

A LATE AFTERNOON CONCERT IN CONGRESS PARK

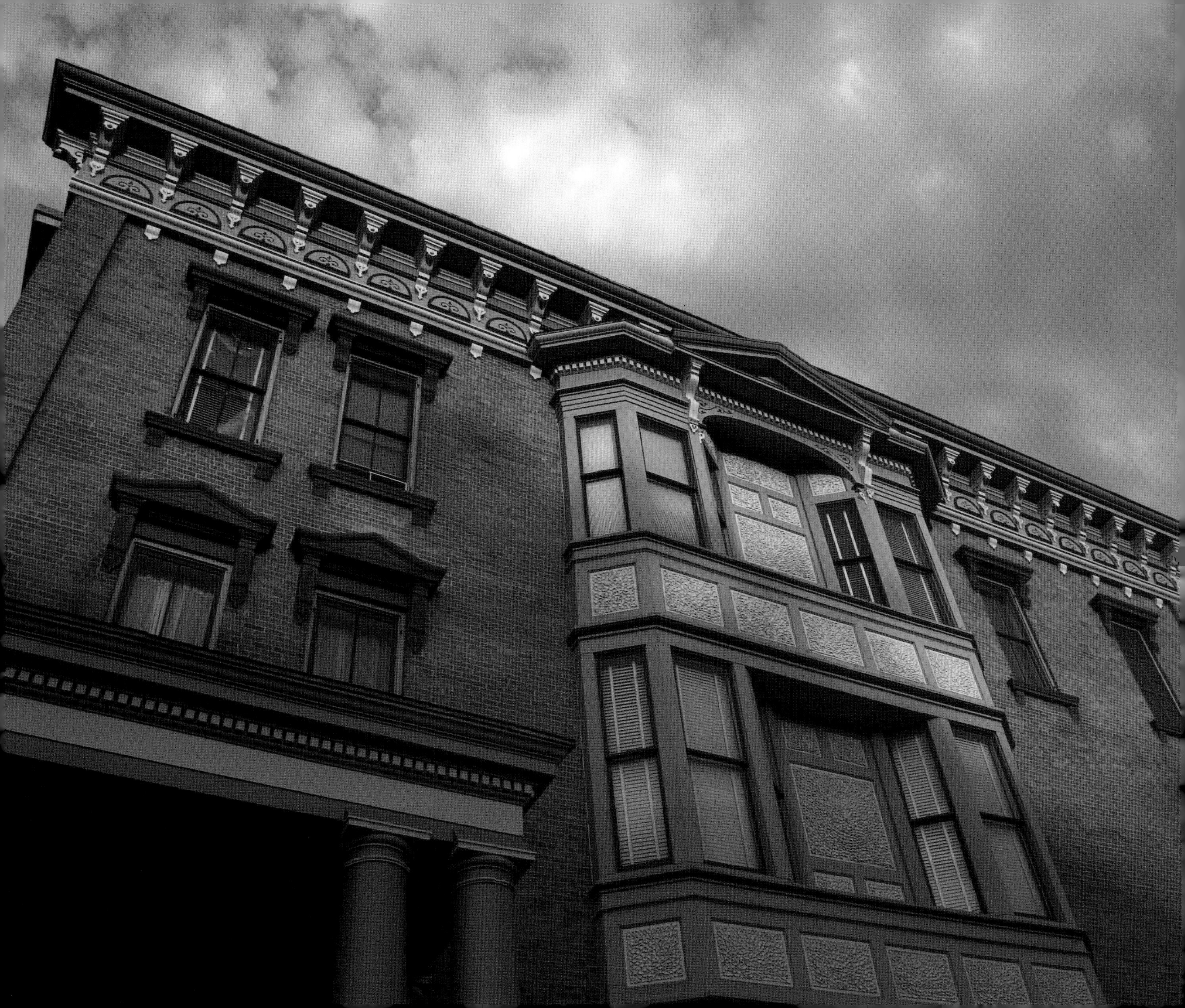

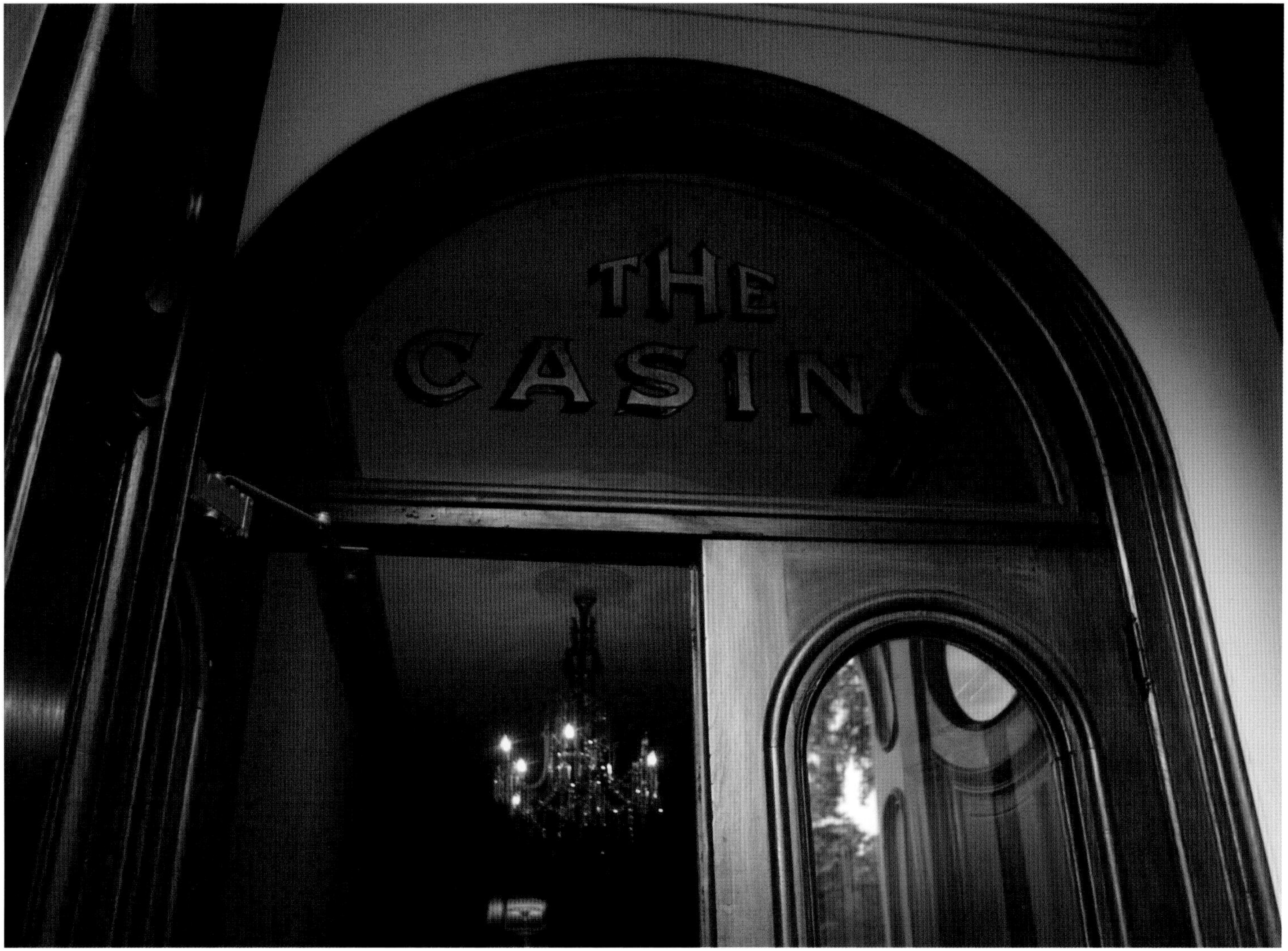

CANFIELD CASINO, built in 1870, entertained many of the world's biggest "high rollers" before anti-gambling legislation closed it in 1907. The building now houses the Historical Society of Saratoga Springs museum.

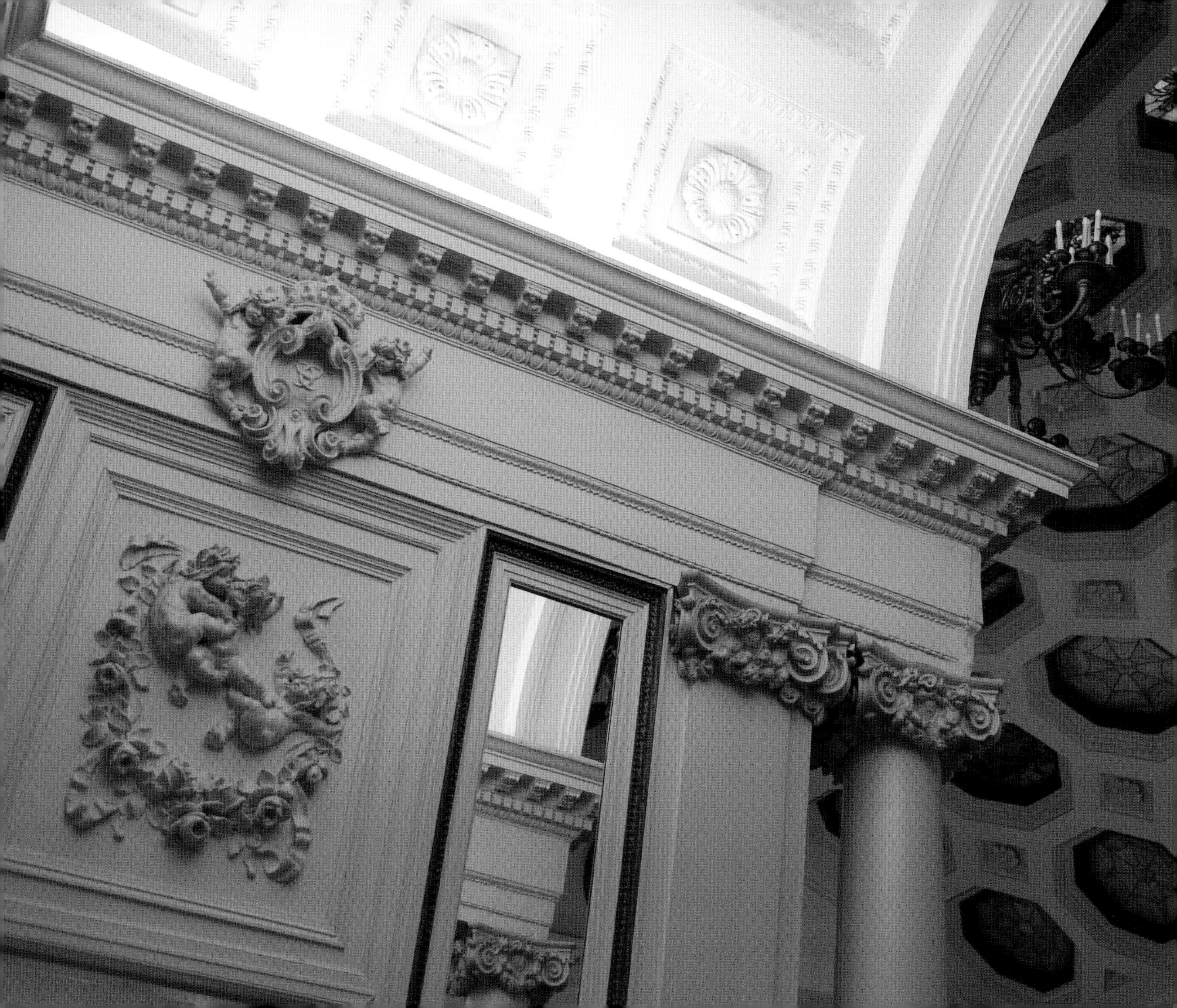

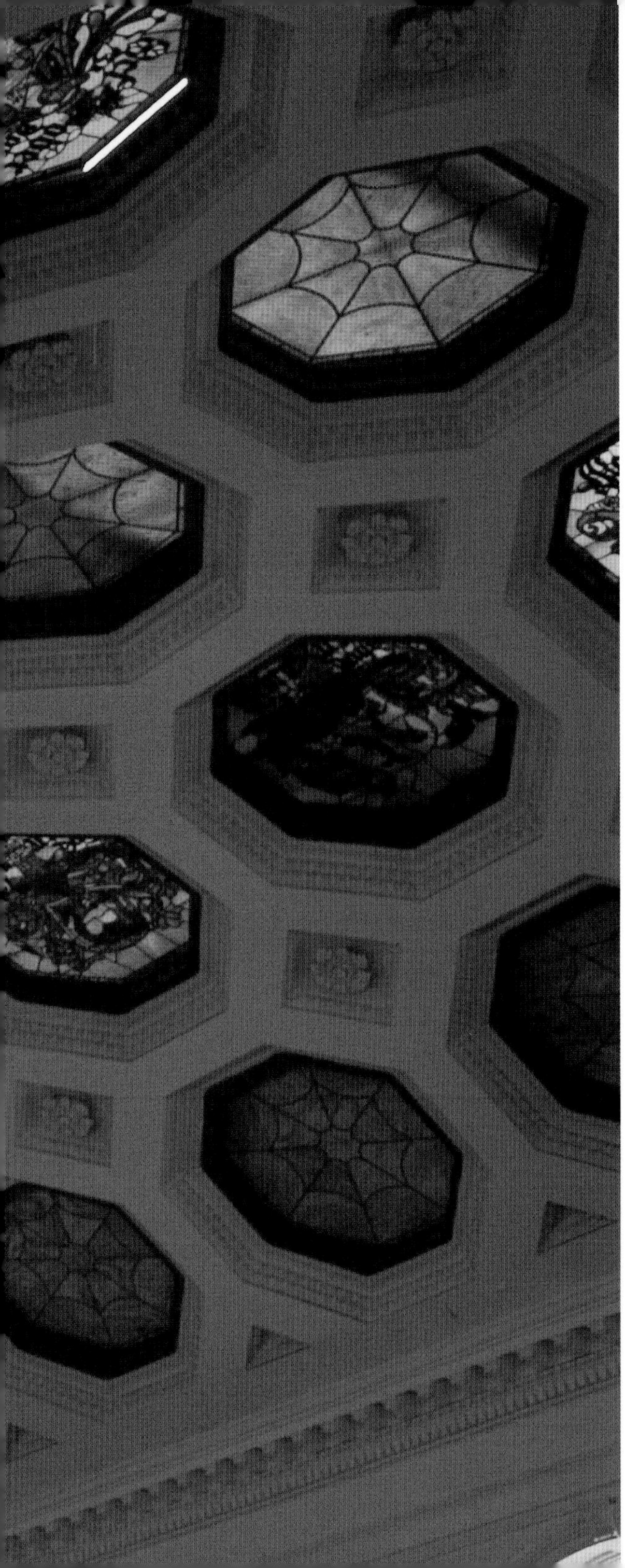

THE CASINO'S OPULENT BALLROOM (DETAIL), now used for weddings and other social events, such as the annual Whitney Ball.

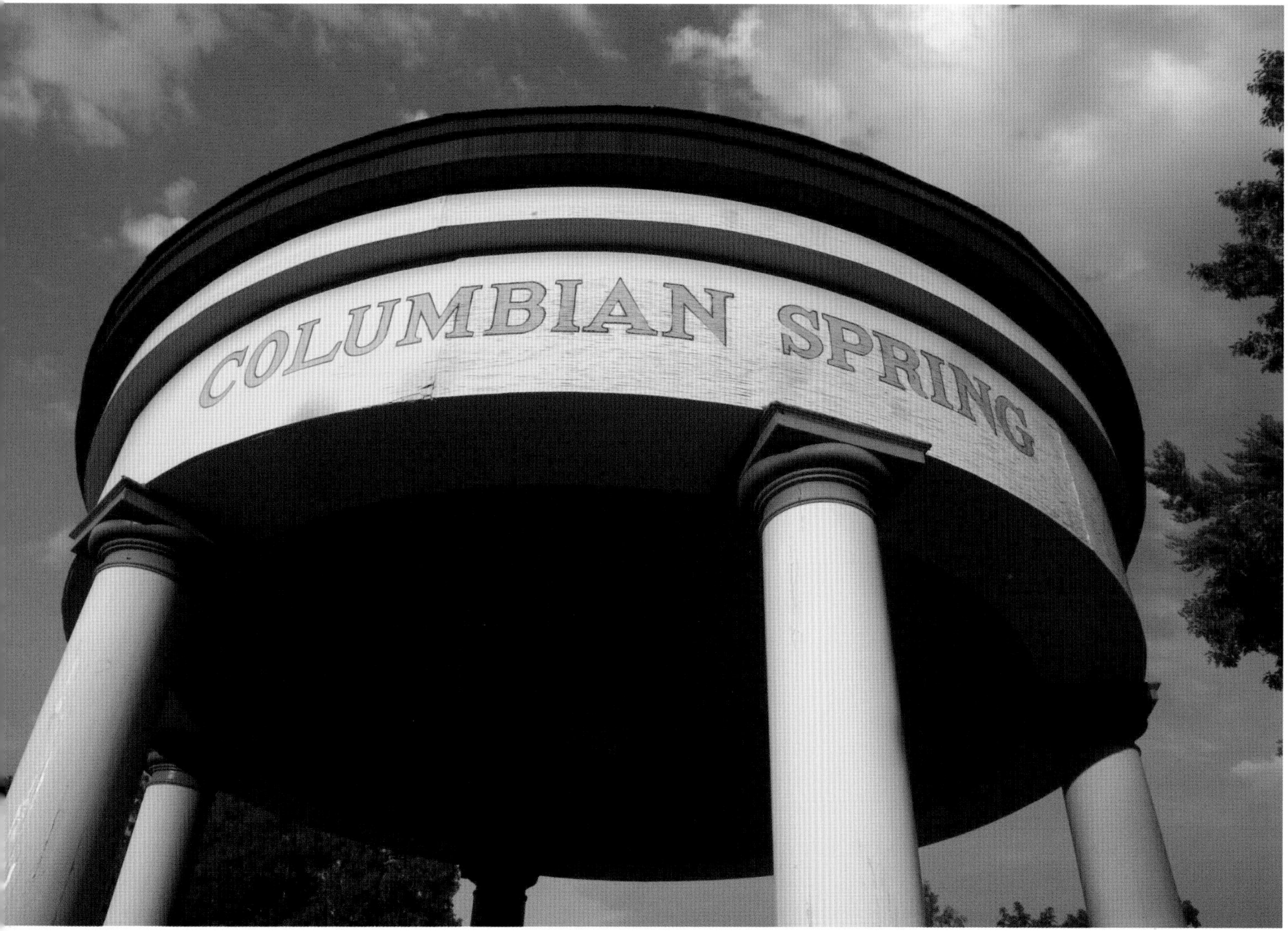

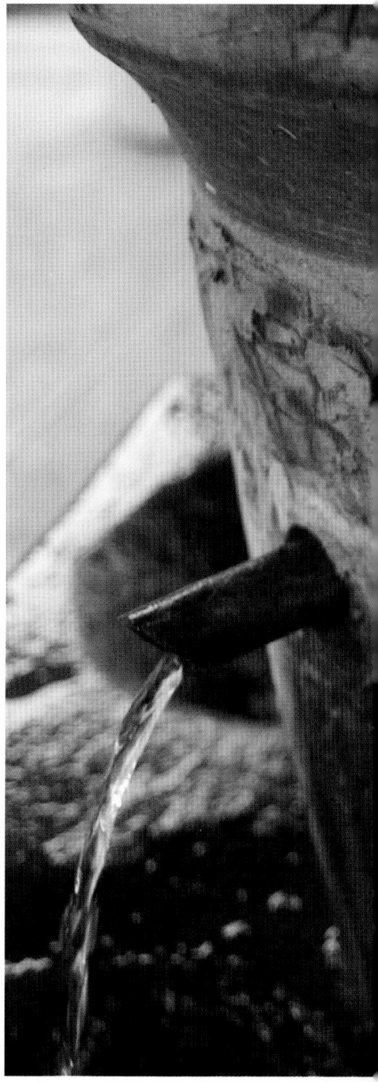

CONGRESS PARK CONTAINS THREE SPRINGS — the Columbian, Congress, and Deer Park.

Congress Spring (center), discovered in 1792, still features the waters that helped make Saratoga world famous.

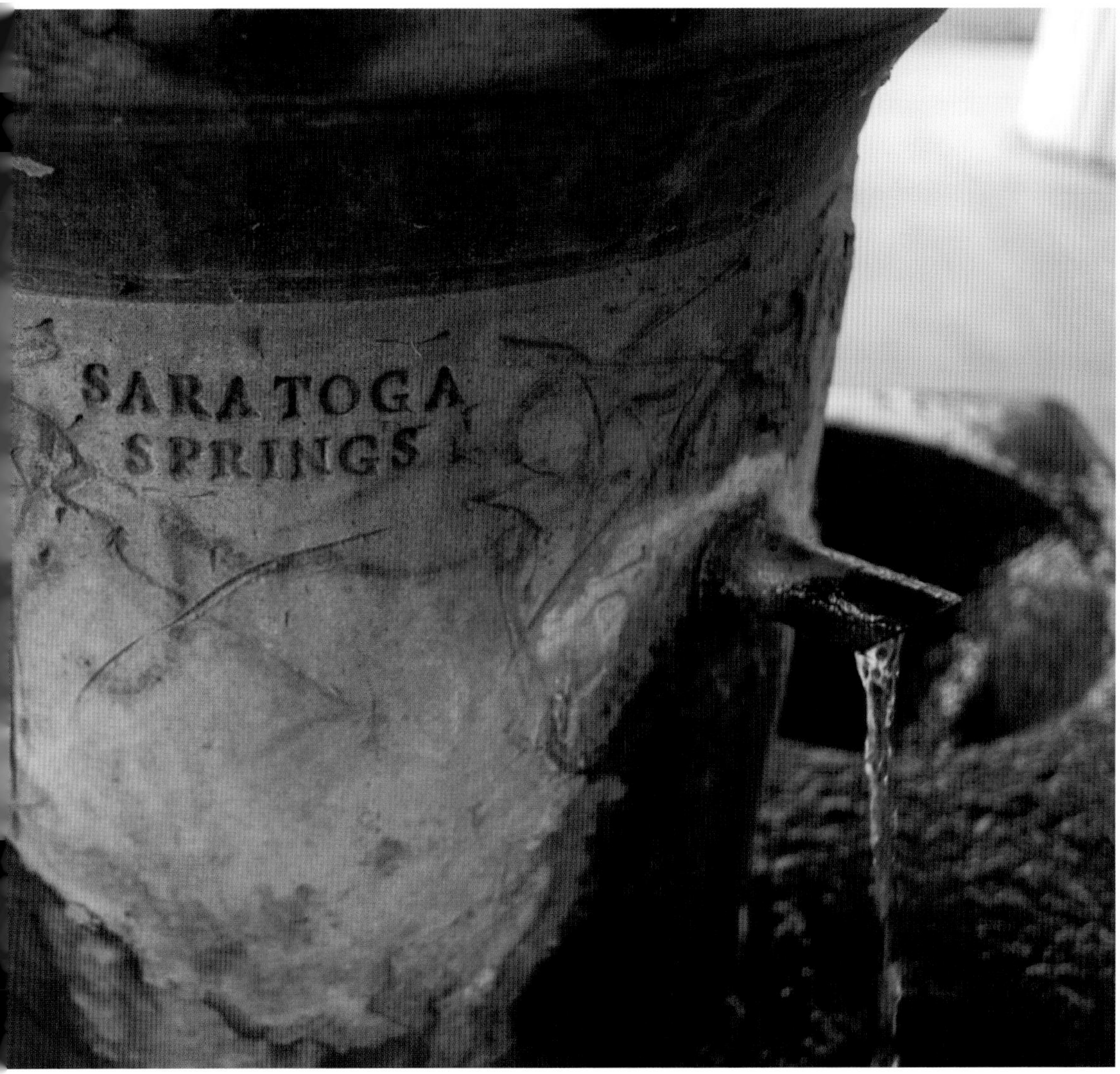
SARATOGA
SPRINGS
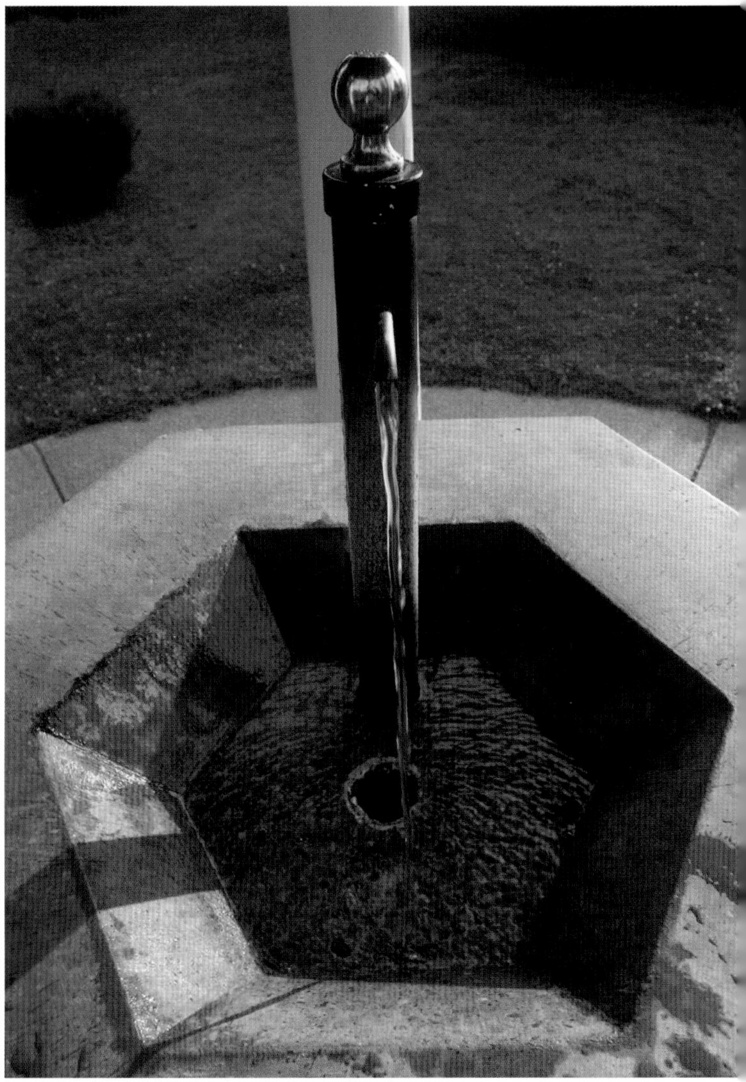

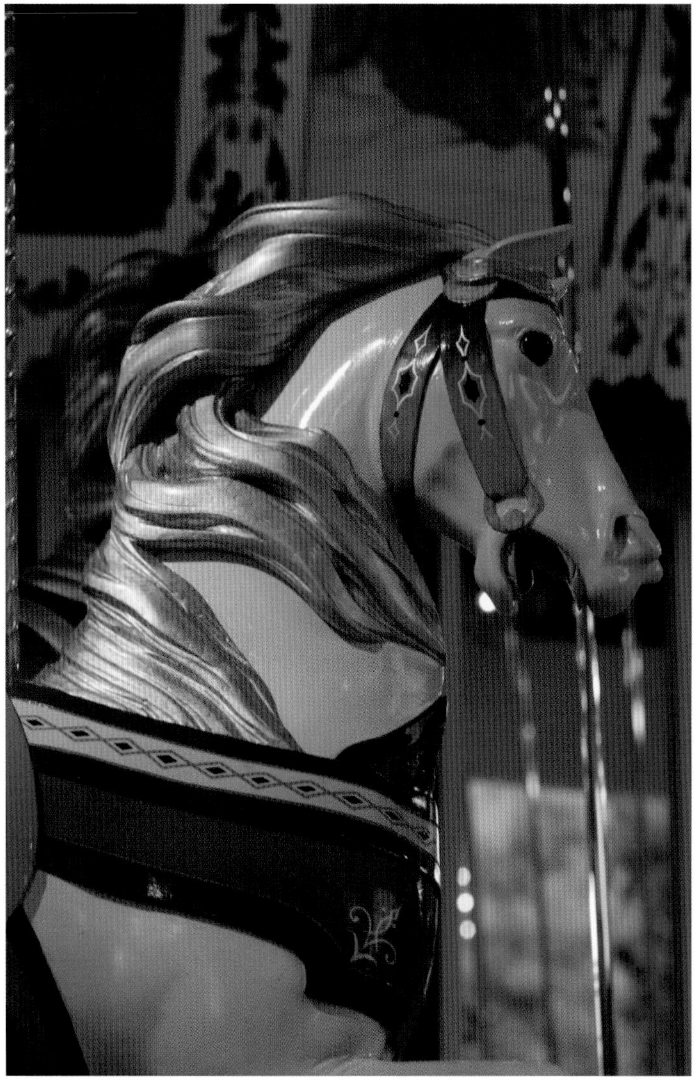

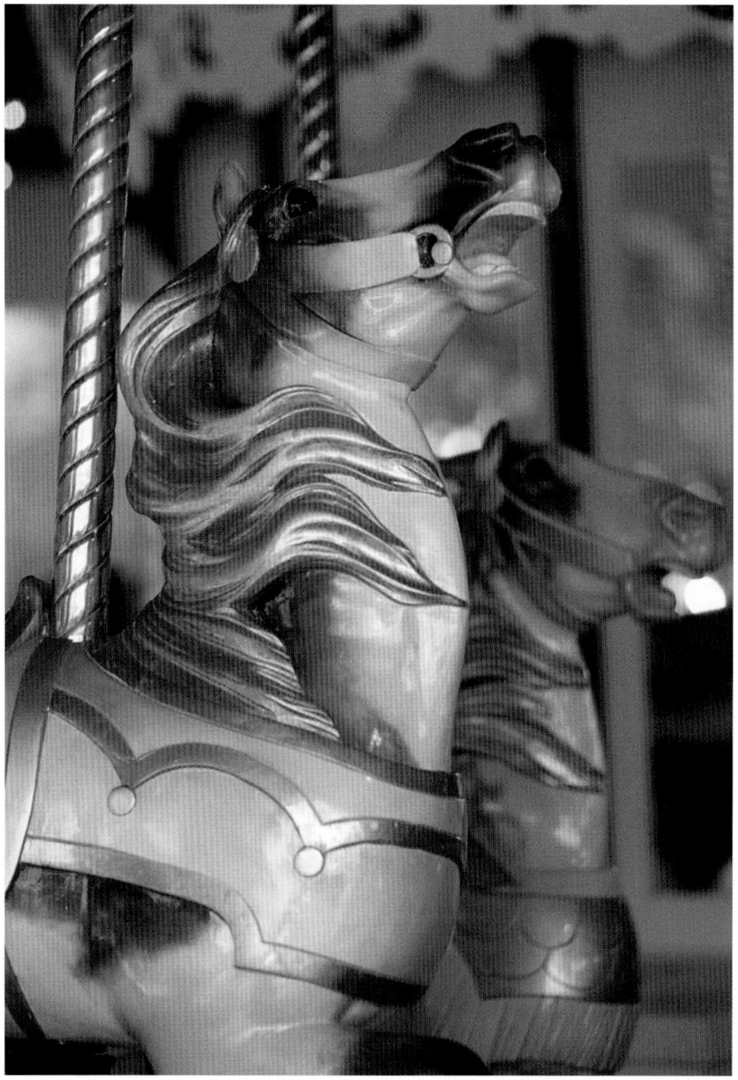

THE CONGRESS PARK CAROUSEL, crafted by master carver Marcus C. Illions approximately a century ago. Installed in Congress Park in 2002, this is Illions' only remaining two-row carousel.

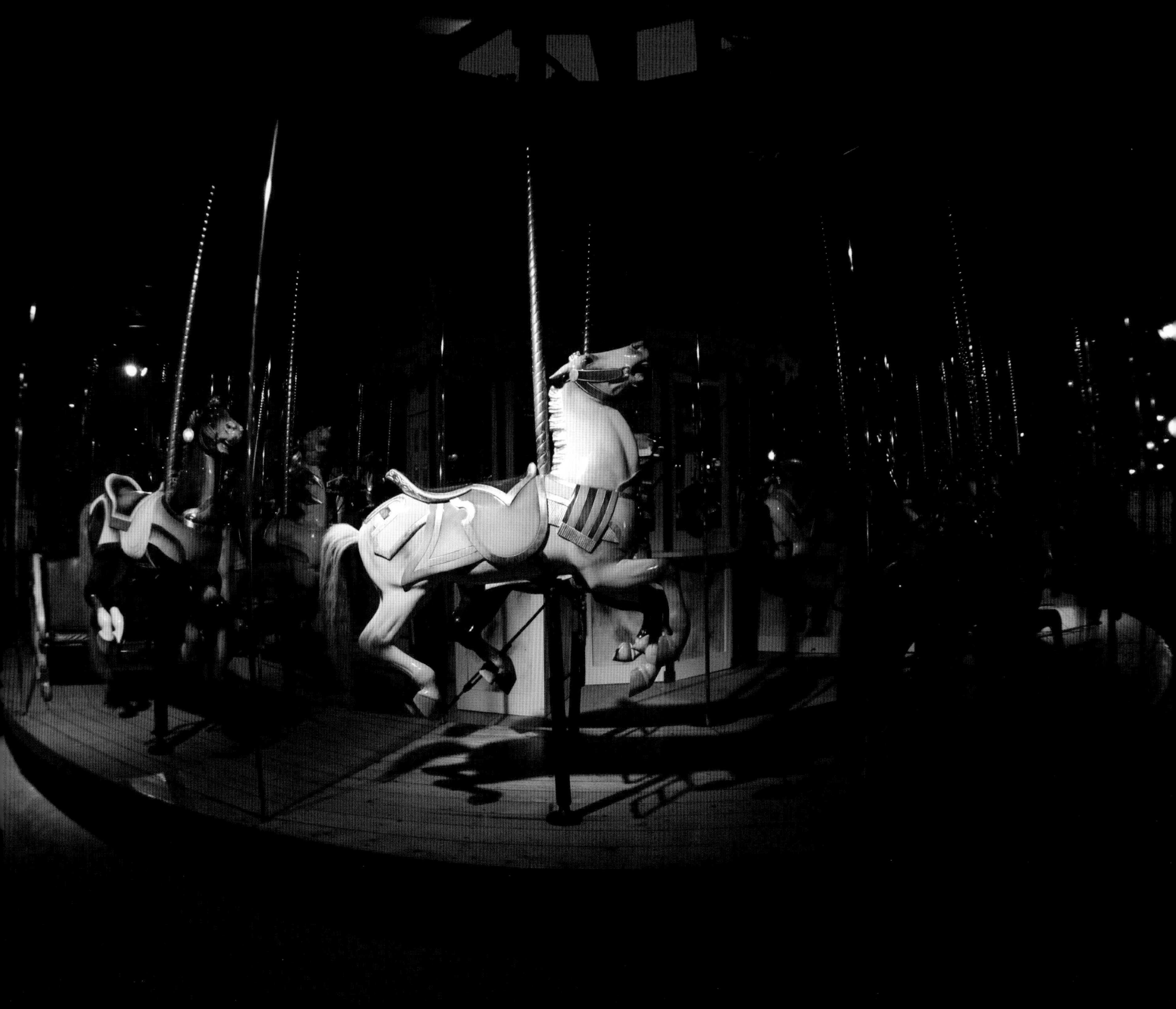

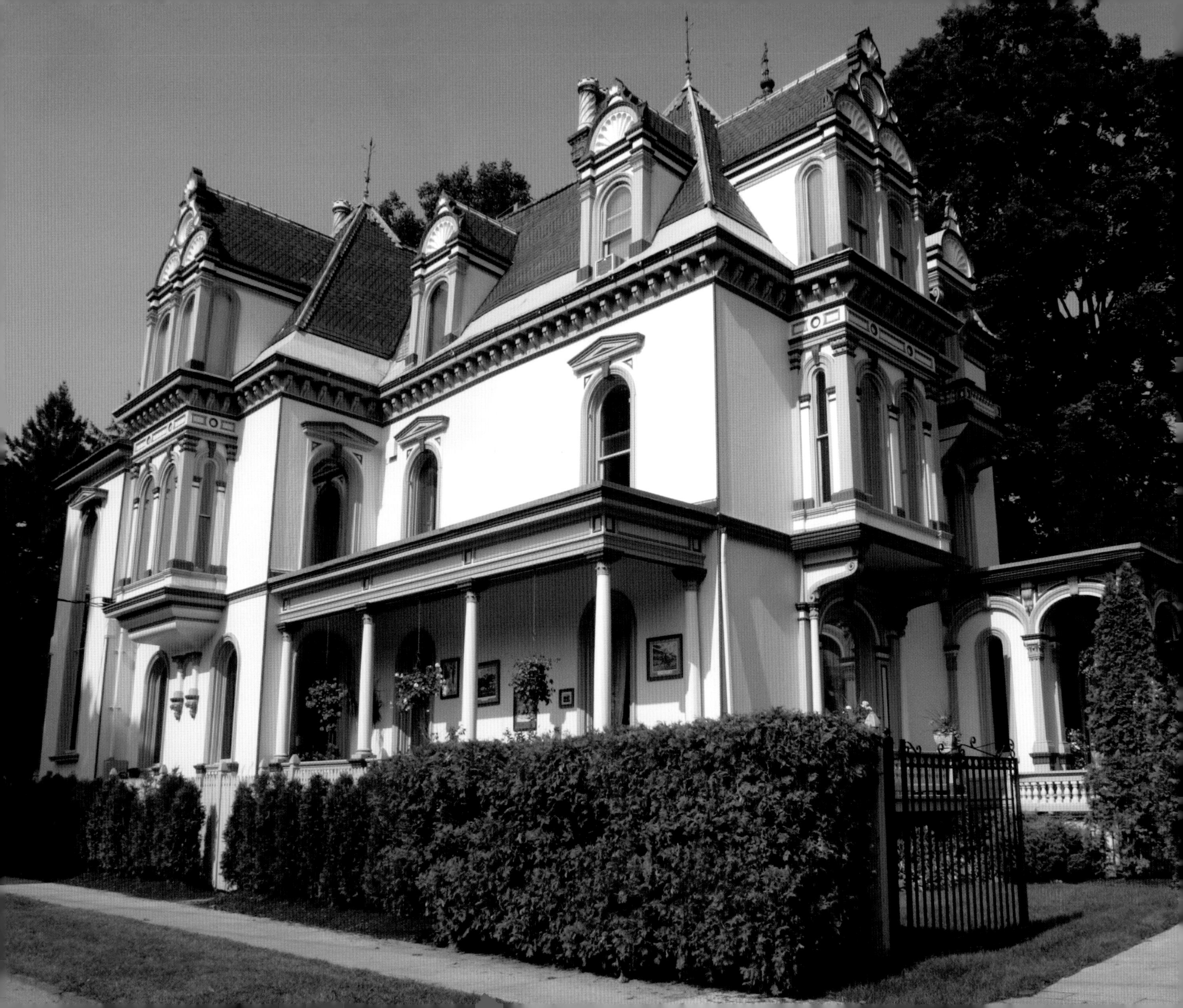

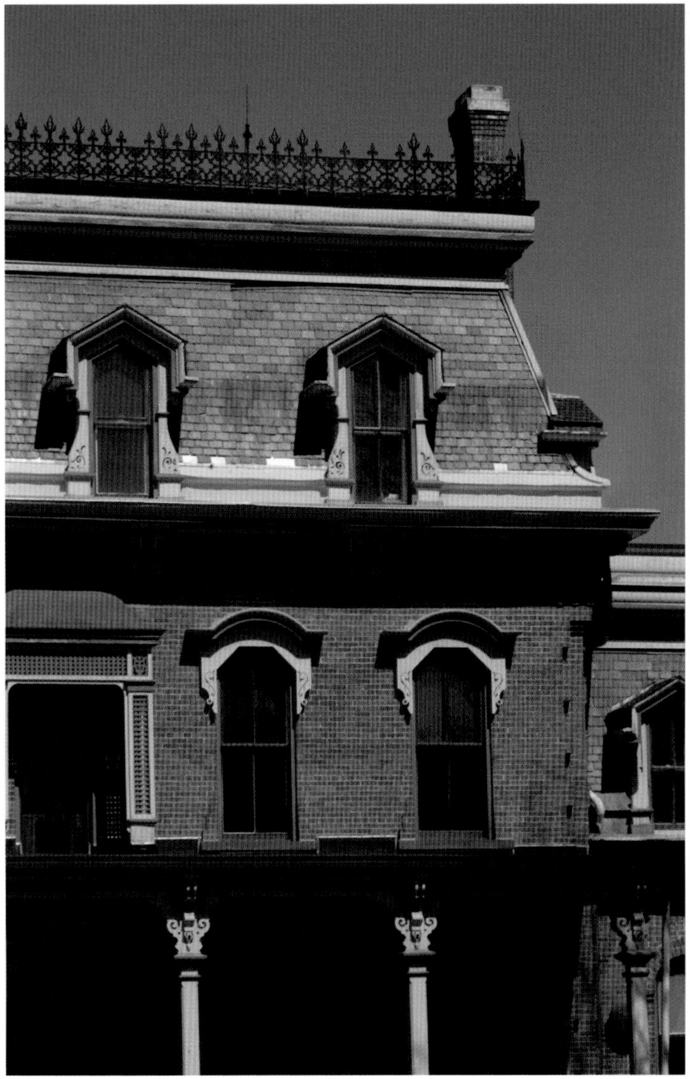

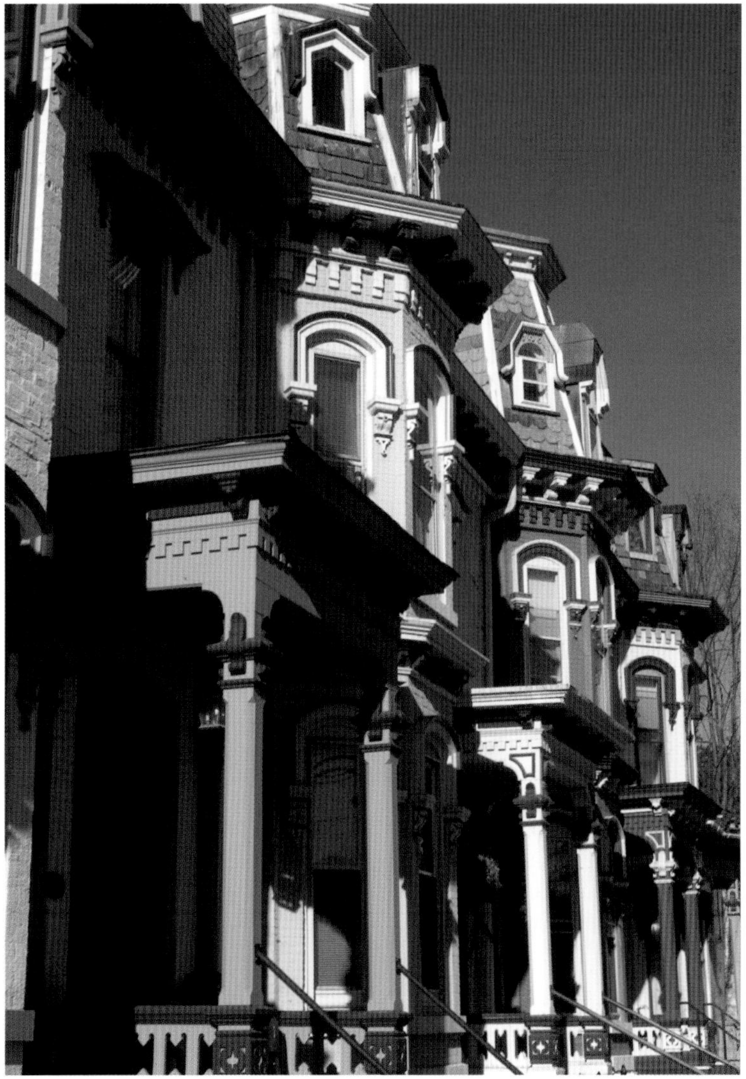

THE BATCHELLER MANSION INN (LEFT), designed in 1873 in the high Victorian Gothic style, was the first American private home to be patented. U.S. President Ulysses S. Grant stayed here.

SARATOGA SPRINGS ARCHITECTURE (ABOVE)

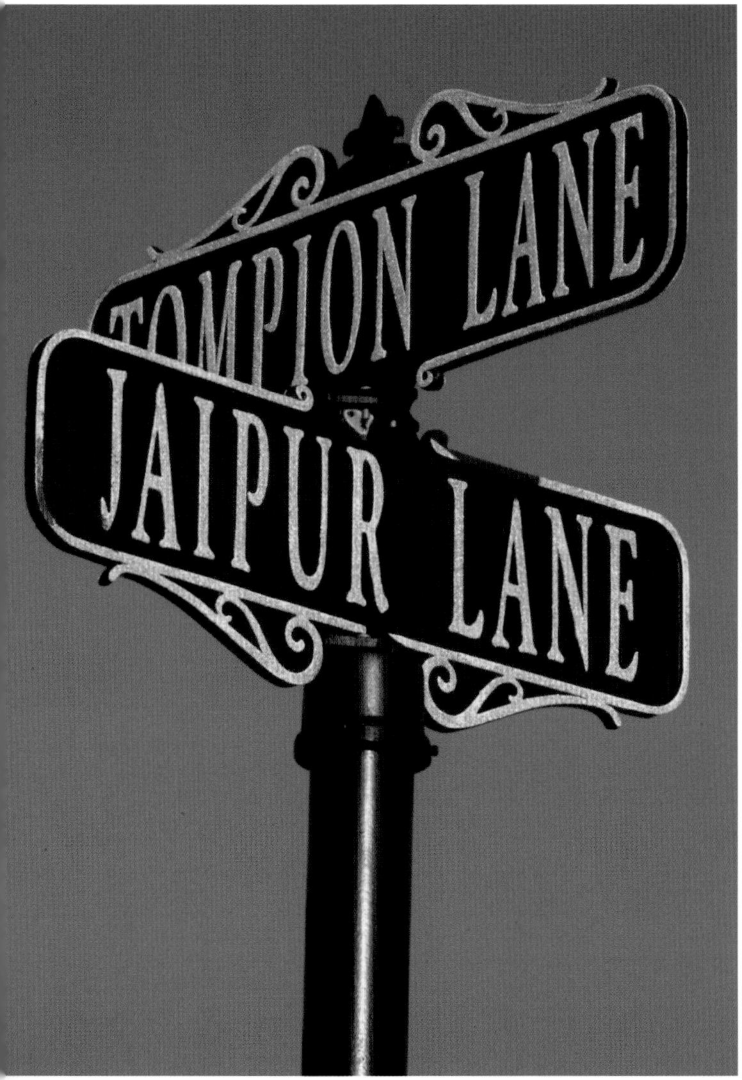

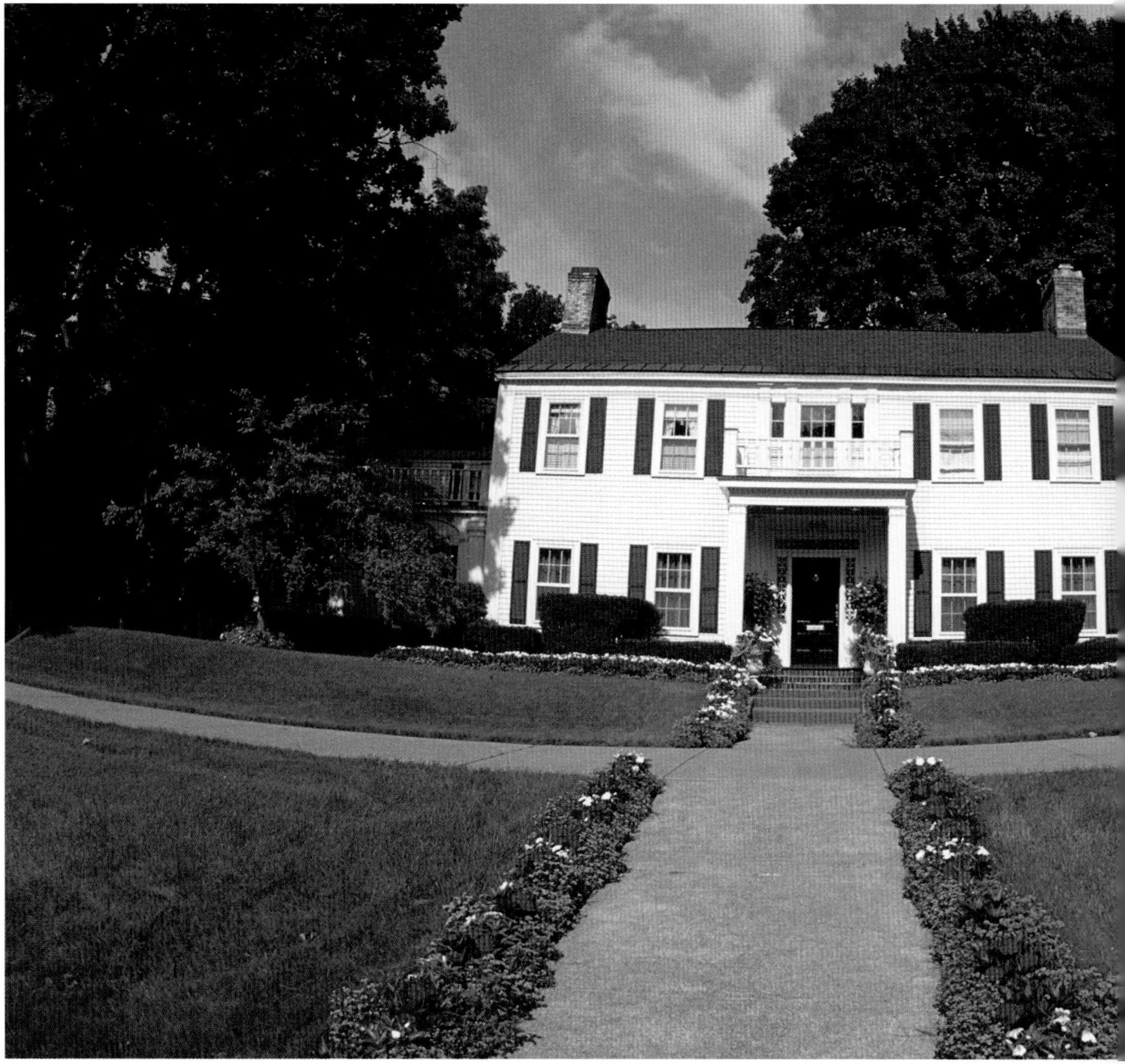

THE STATELY HOMES OF NORTH BROADWAY feature a wide variety of architectural styles. Saratoga Springs also plays upon its horse racing heritage with street signs sporting the names of Travers Stakes winners.

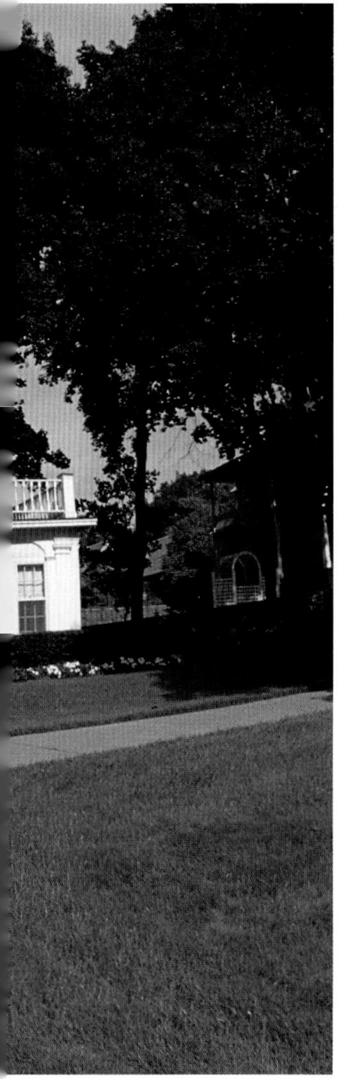

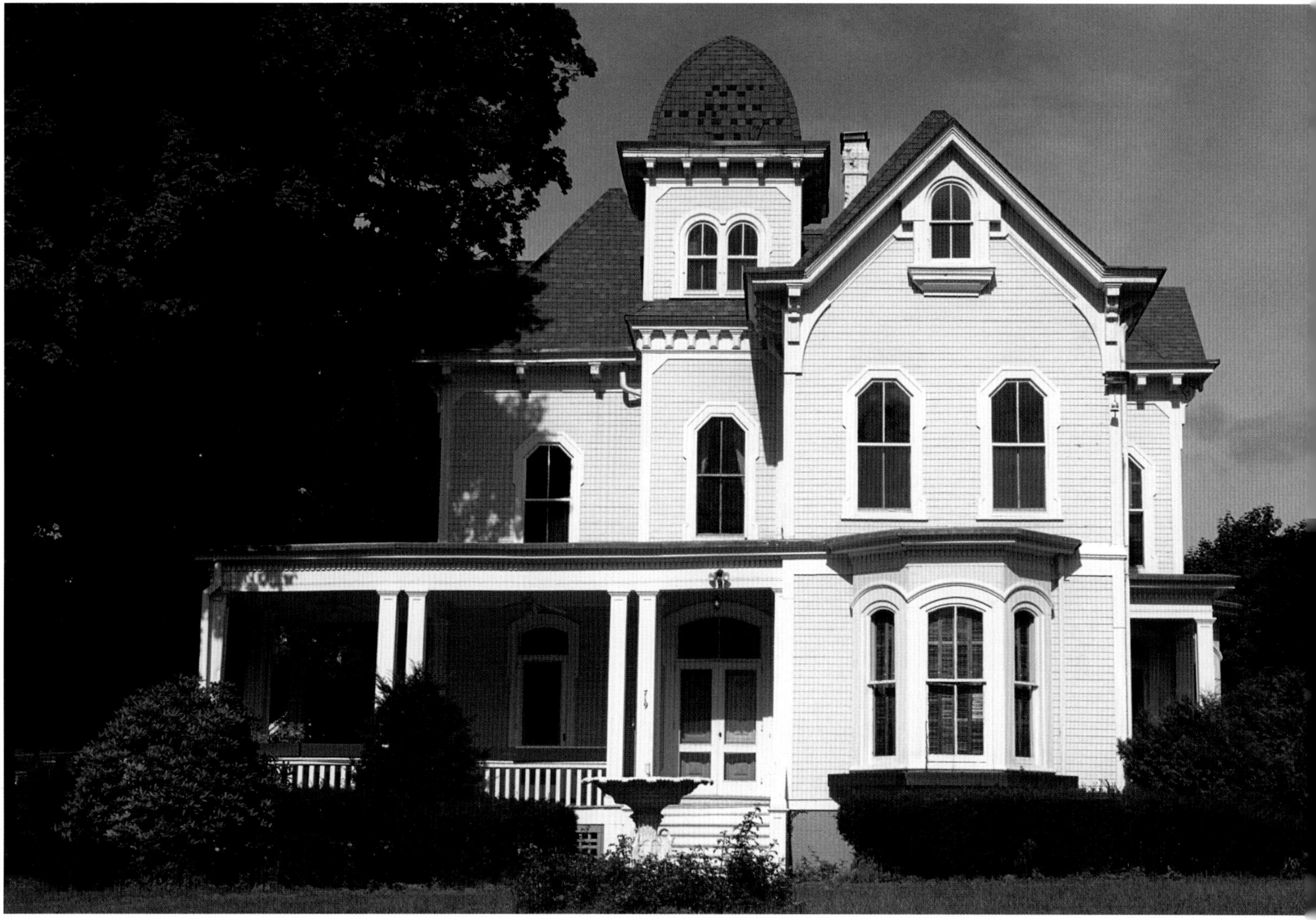

82 NORTH BROADWAY HOME

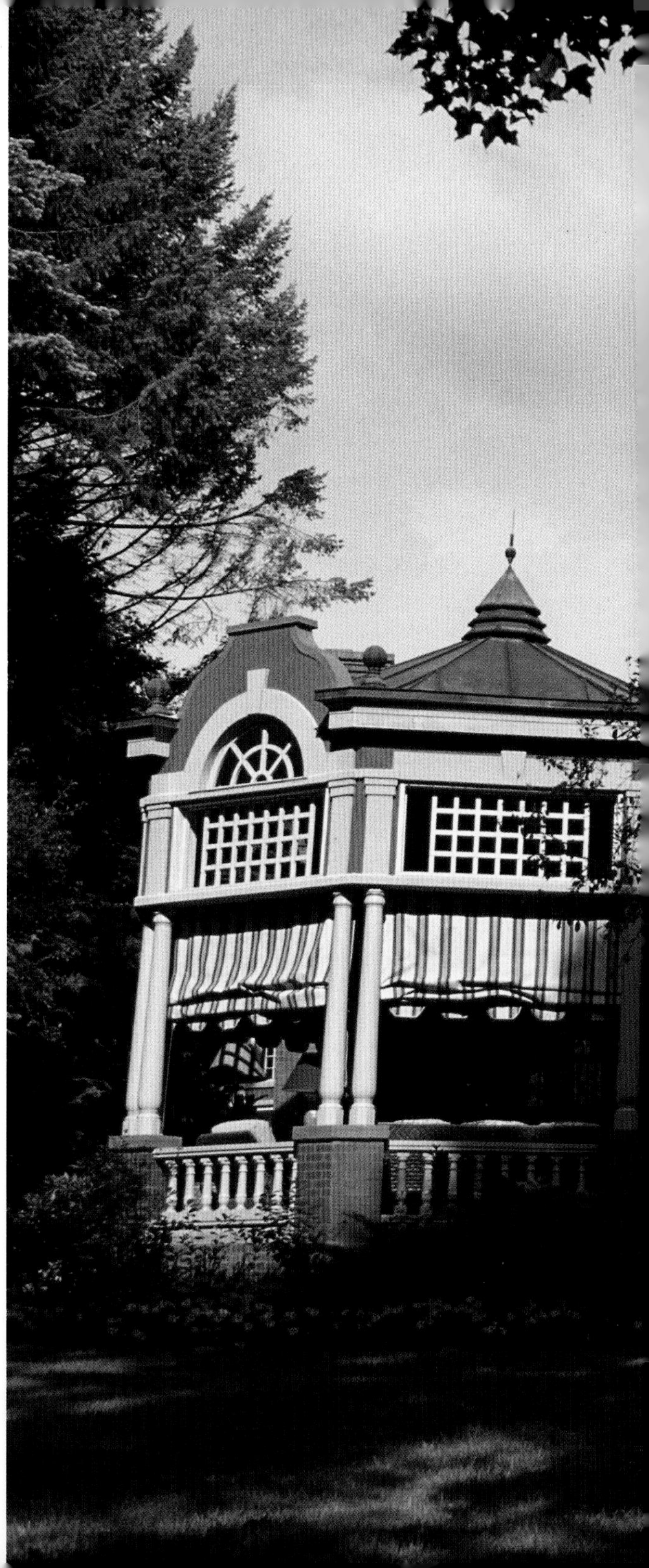

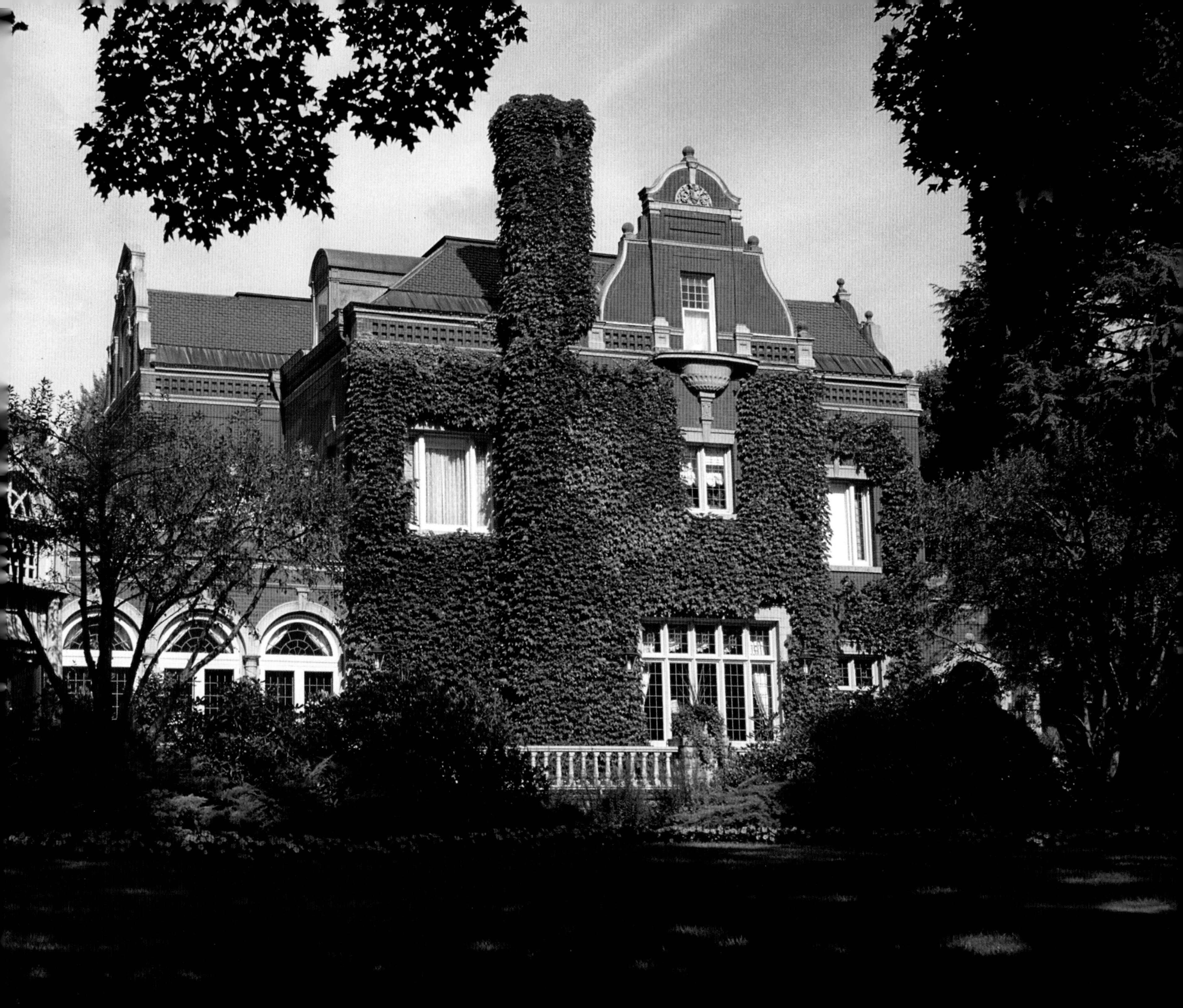

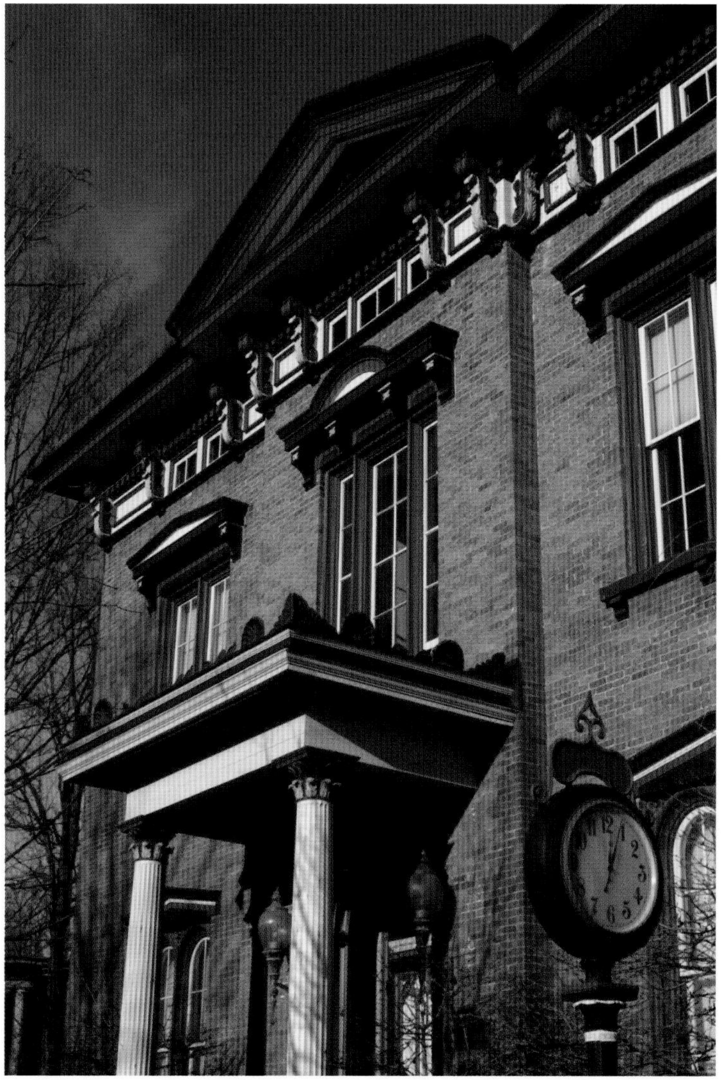

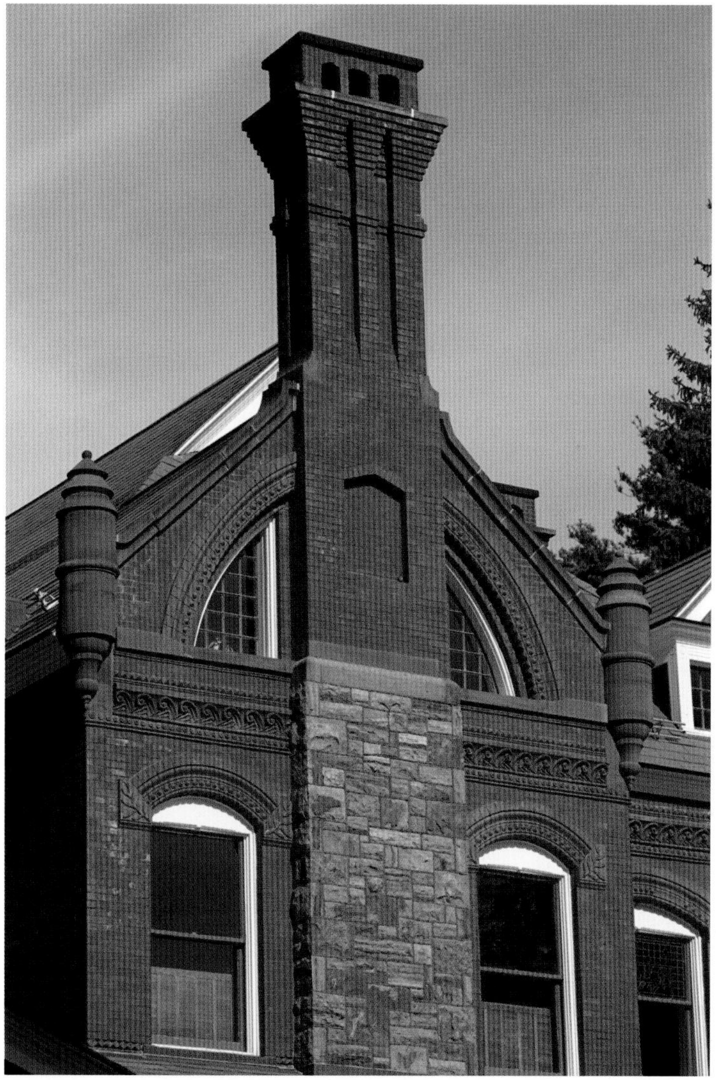

CITY BUILDINGS, including the Union Gables Bed & Breakfast on Union Avenue (right). Union Gables, built in 1901, is a classic example of the Queen Anne style.

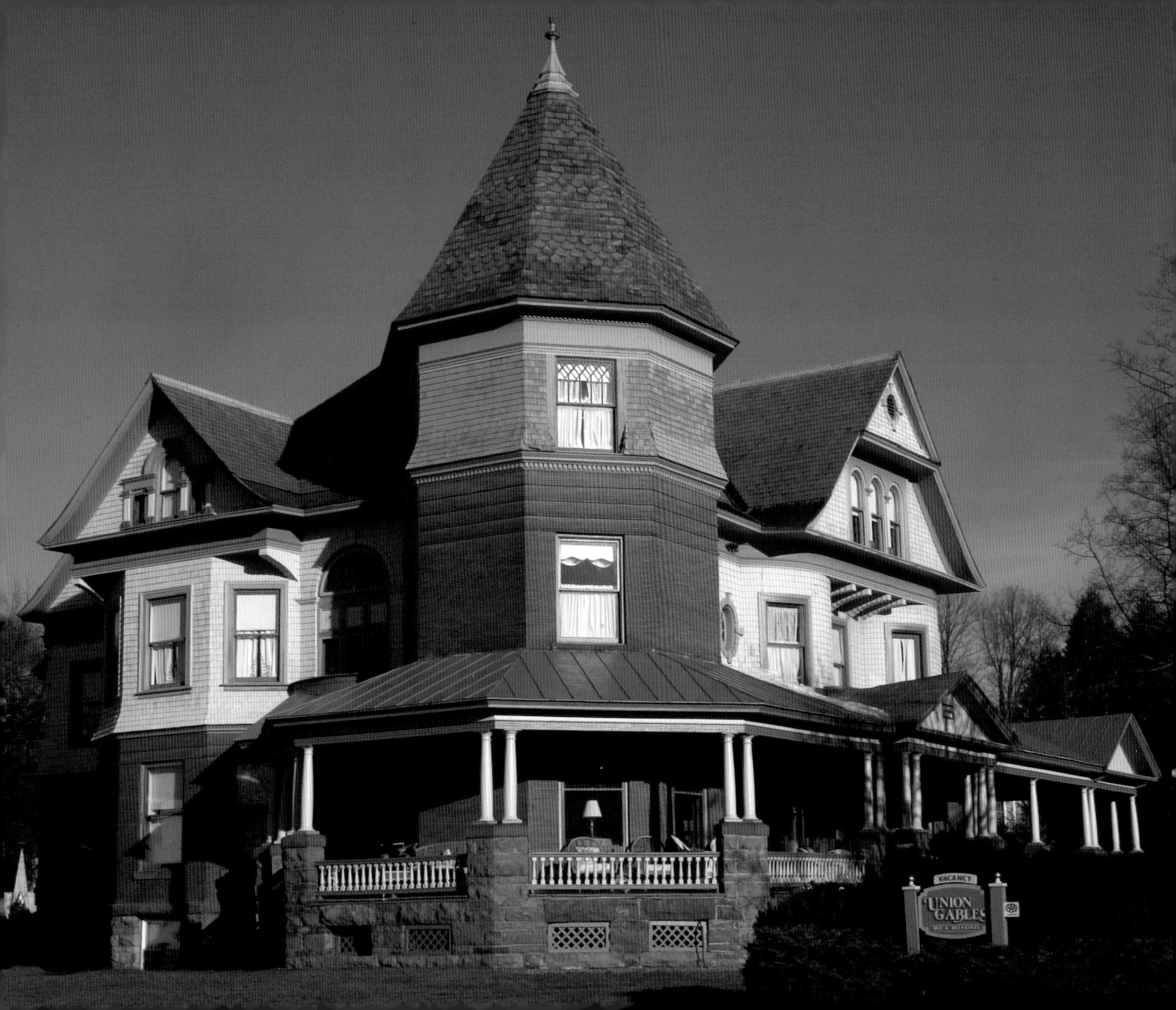
VACANCY
UNION GABLES

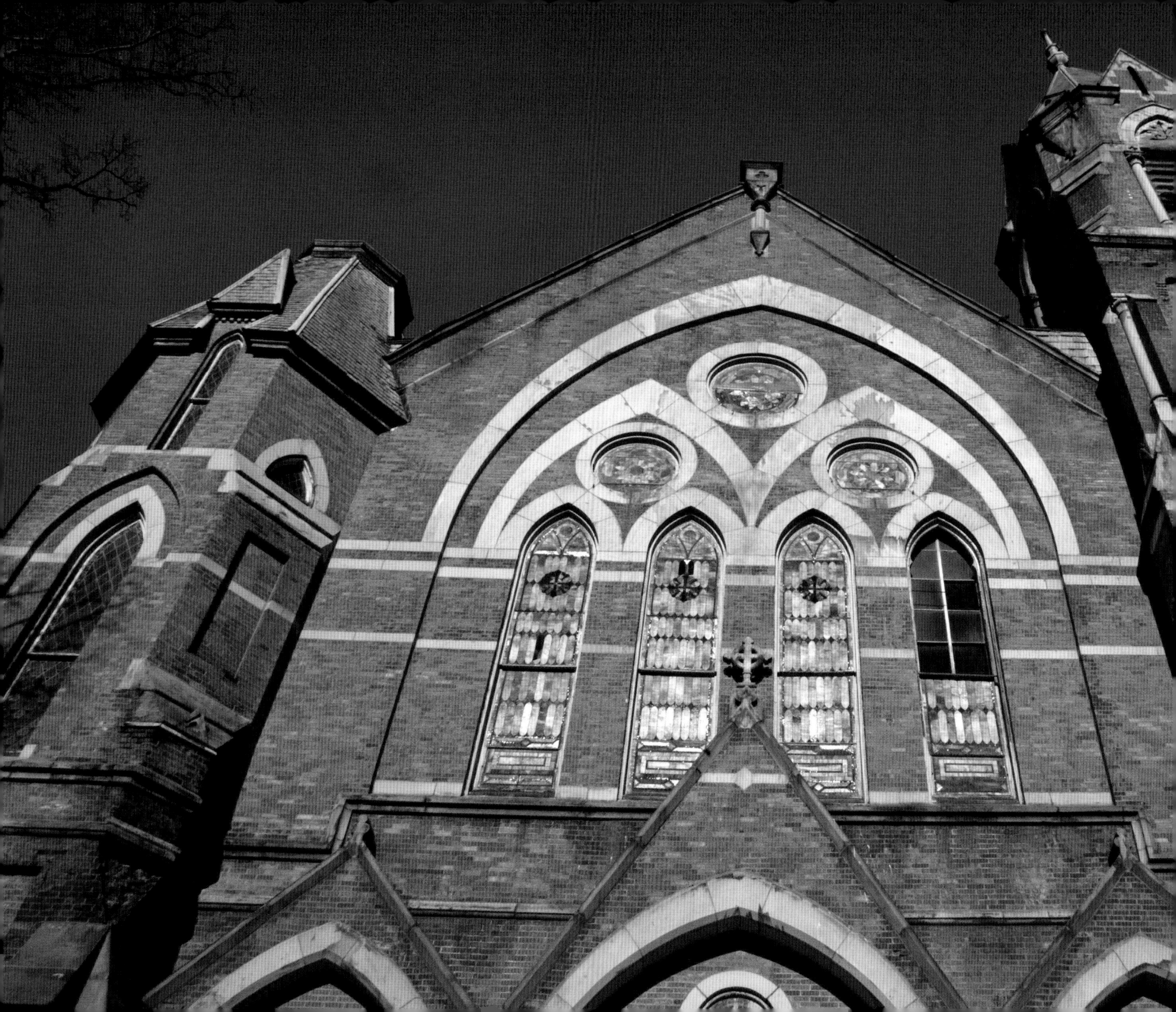

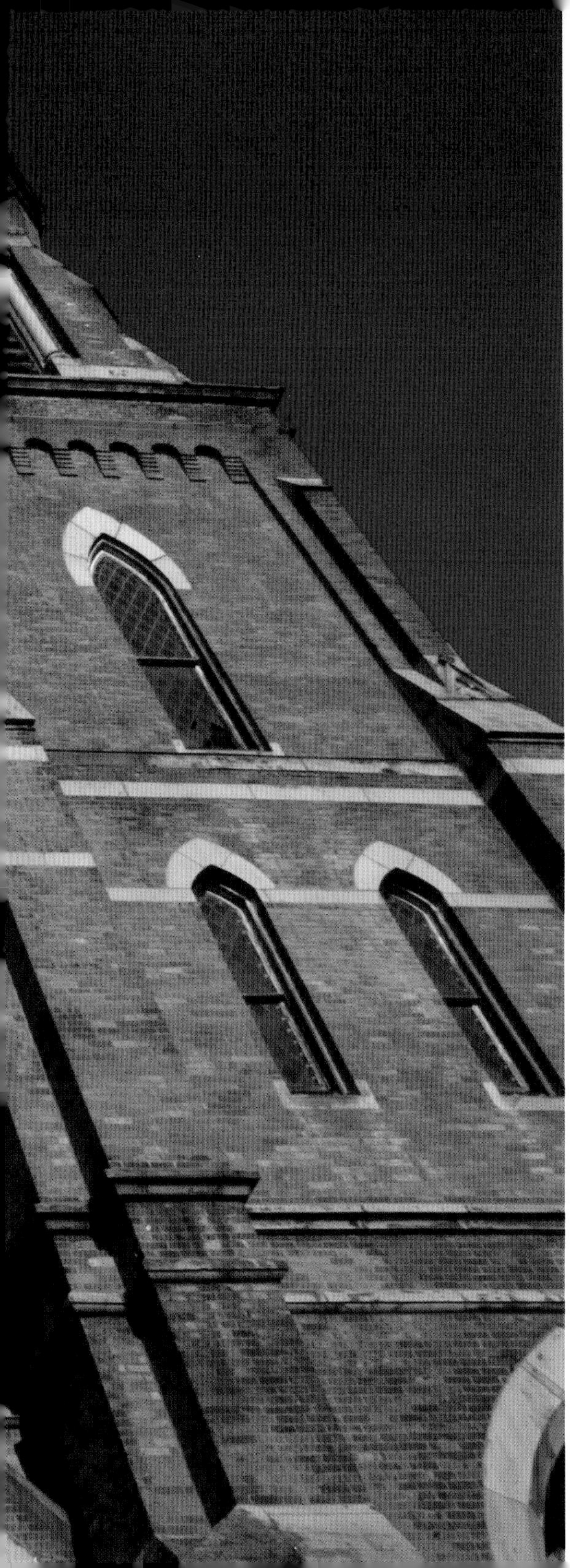

A SARATOGA SPRINGS CHURCH, currently under renovation, is one of many beautiful, historical area churches.

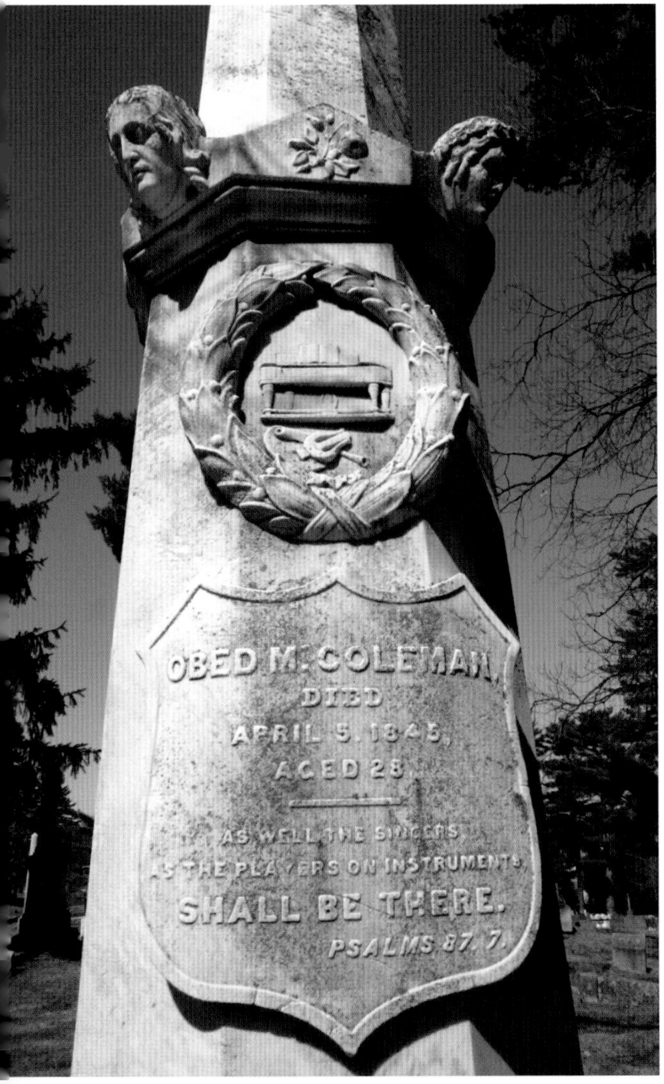

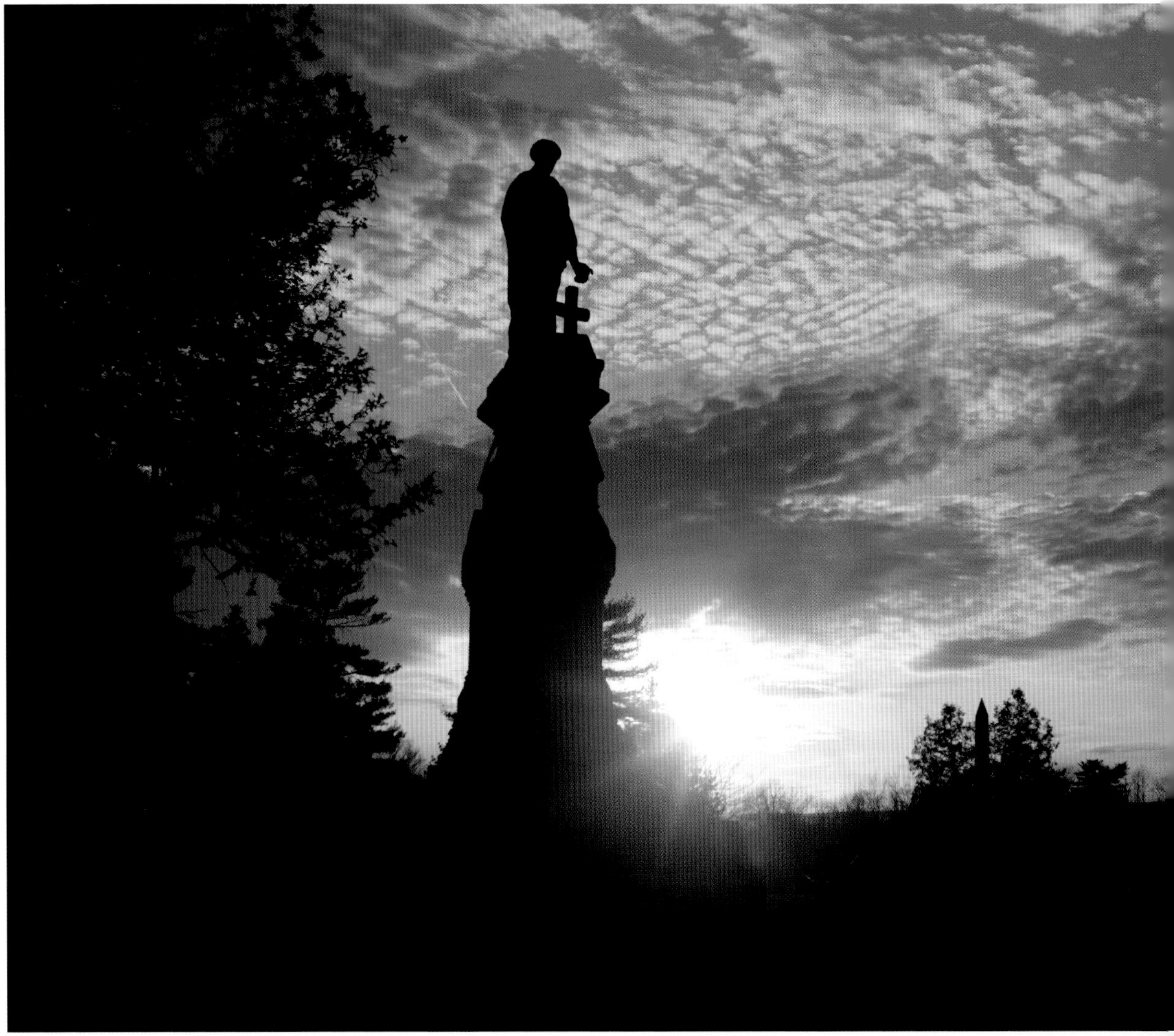

GREENRIDGE CEMETERY has been a final resting spot for both the famous and lesser-known. Among the many interesting monuments are those for famed pianist Obed Coleman (above), who died at sea in 1845 and whose stone is marked with a piano, and Willoby S. McMillan (second from right), an engineer who "was killed by his Engine" in 1853.

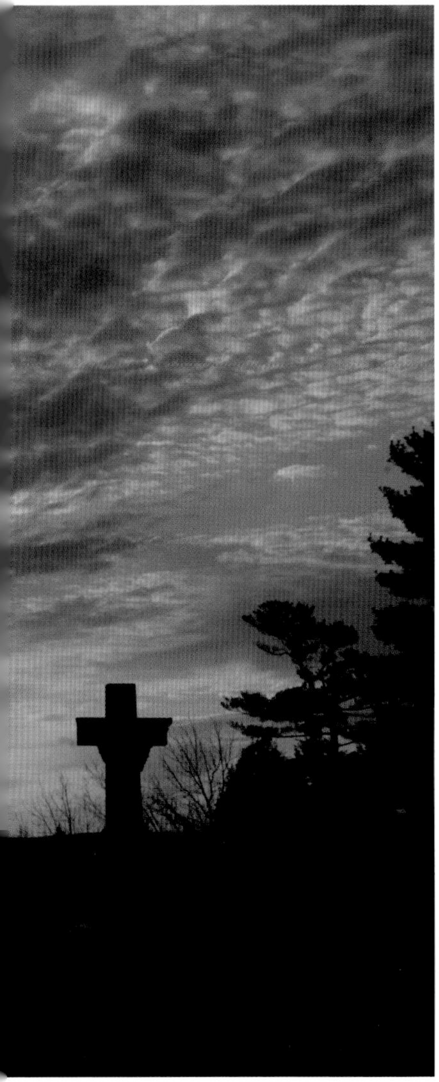

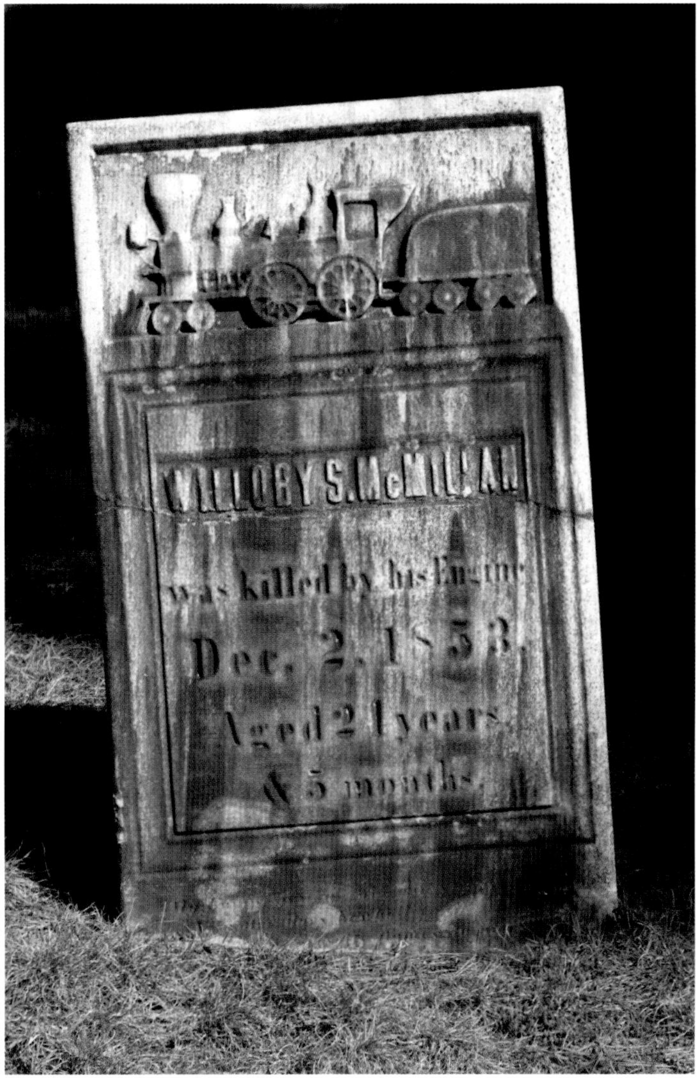
was killed by his Engine
Dec. 2. 1853.
Aged 24 years
& 5 months

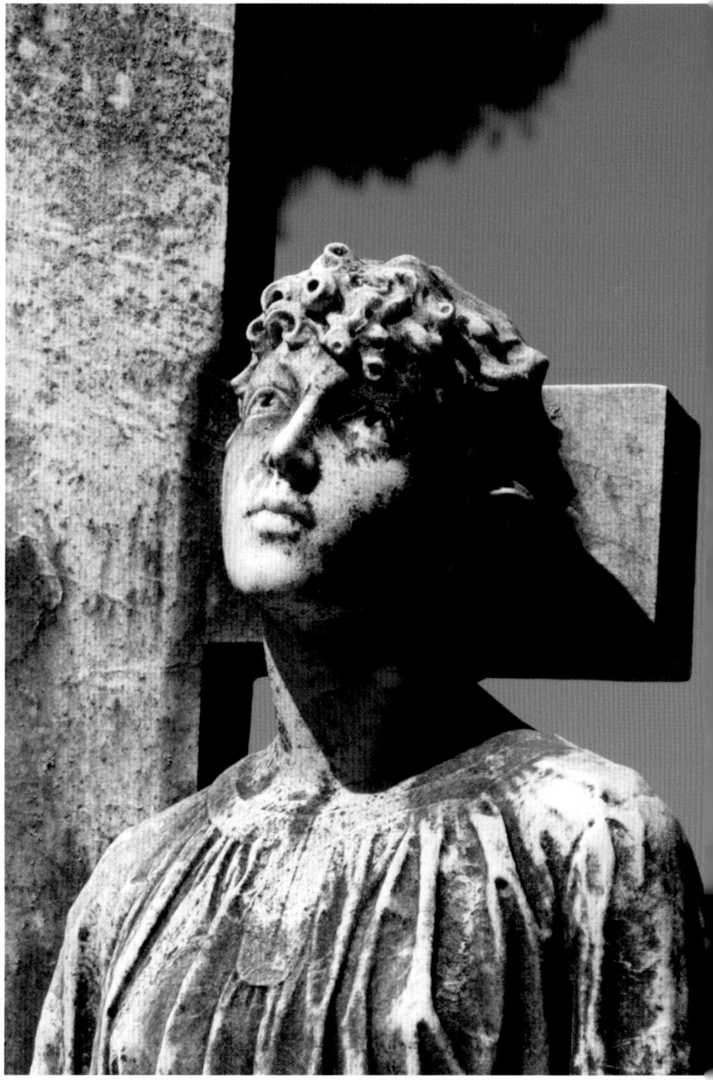

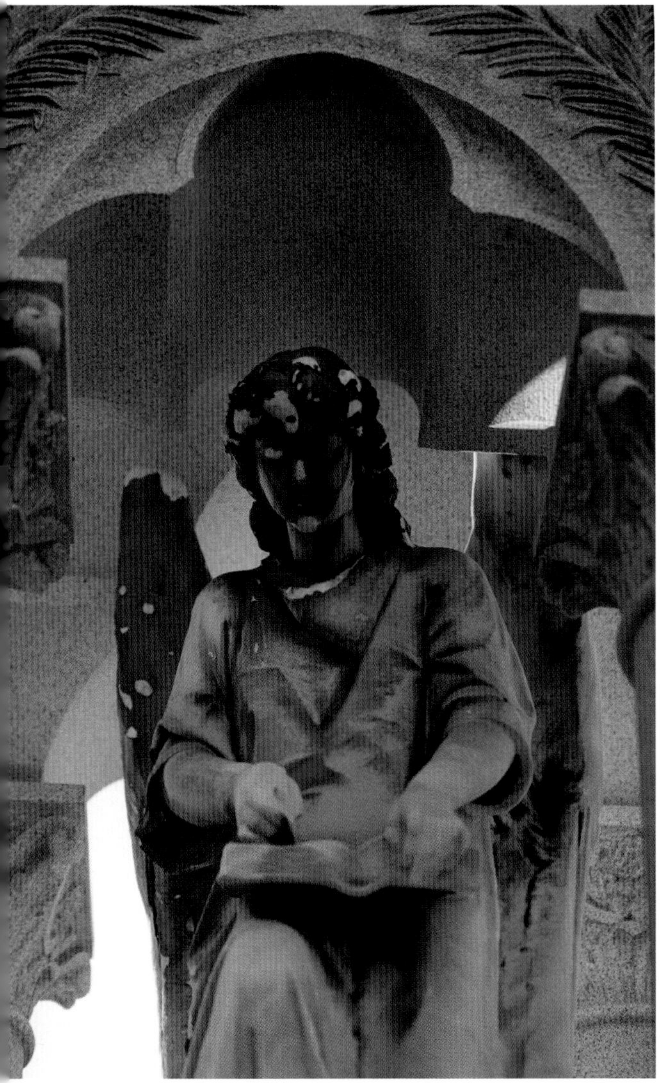

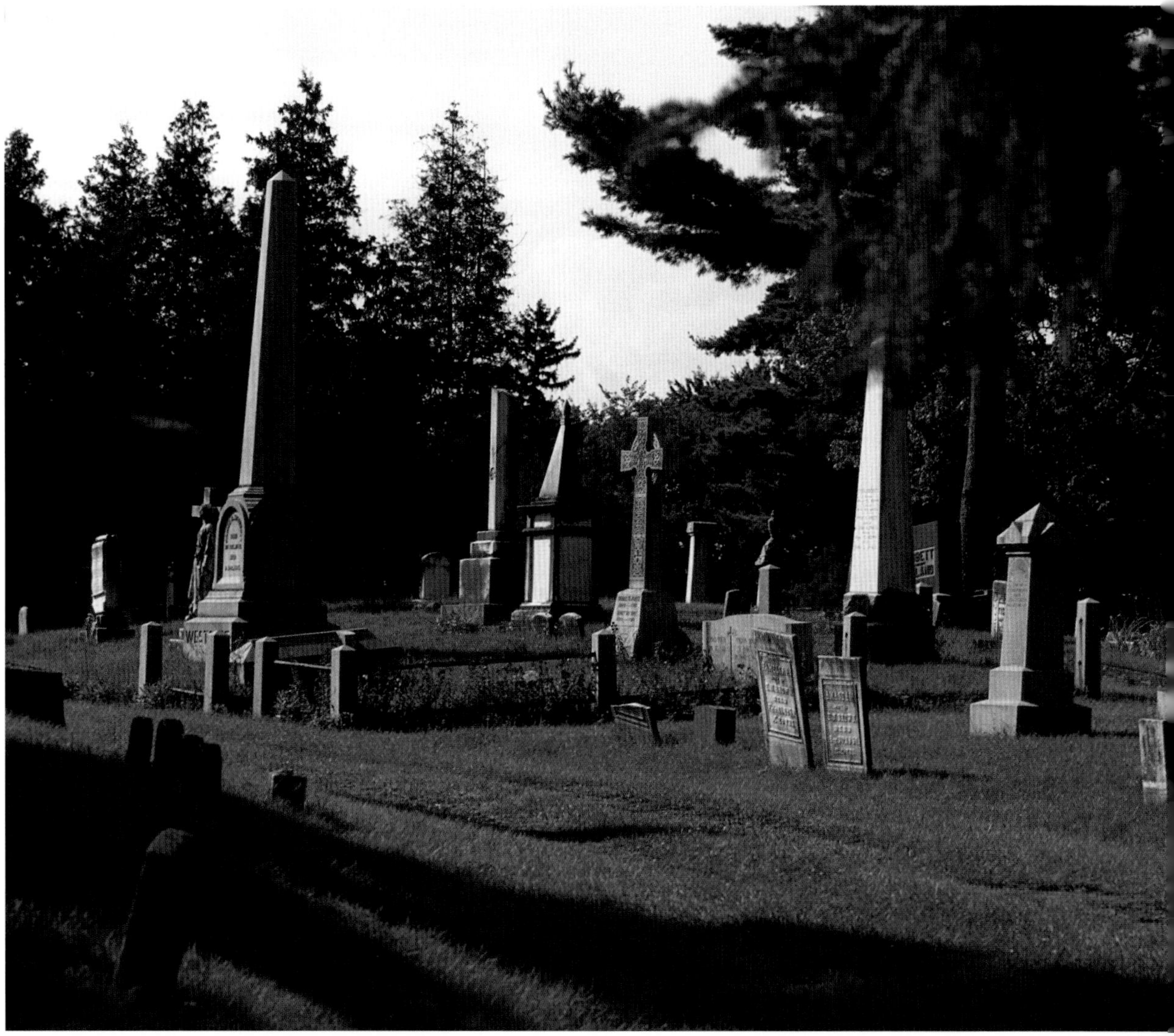

IN GREENRIDGE CEMETERY lie five U.S. Congressmen as well as three-time Academy Award-winning producer/screenwriter Charles Brackett and horseman/businessman/movie producer Cornelius Vanderbilt Whitney.

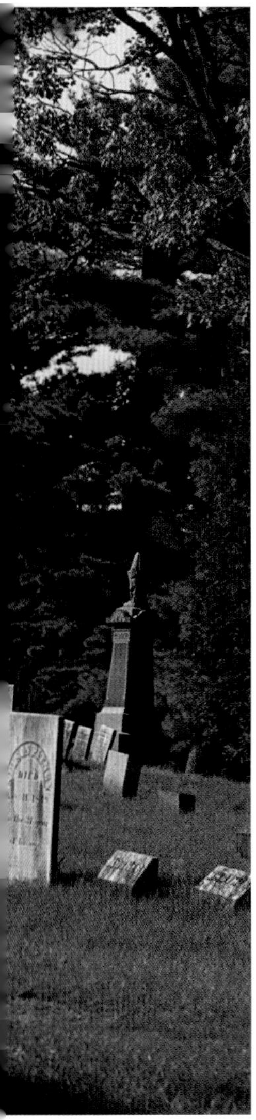

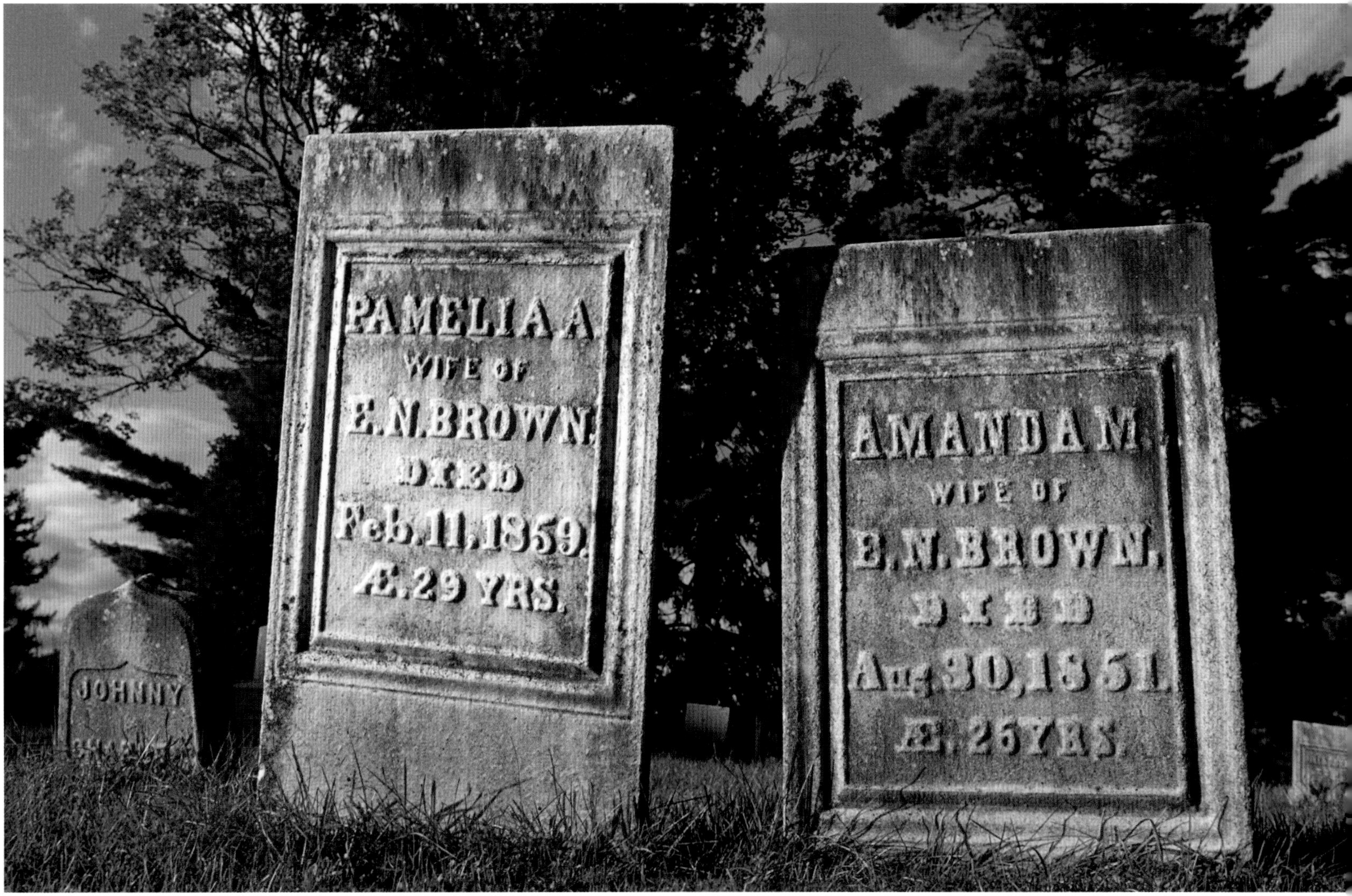
PAMELIA A.
WIFE OF
E.N. BROWN.
DIED
Feb. 11. 1859.
Æ. 29 YRS.
JOHNNY
AMANDA M.
WIFE OF
E.N. BROWN.
DIED
Aug. 30, 1851.
Æ. 25YRS.

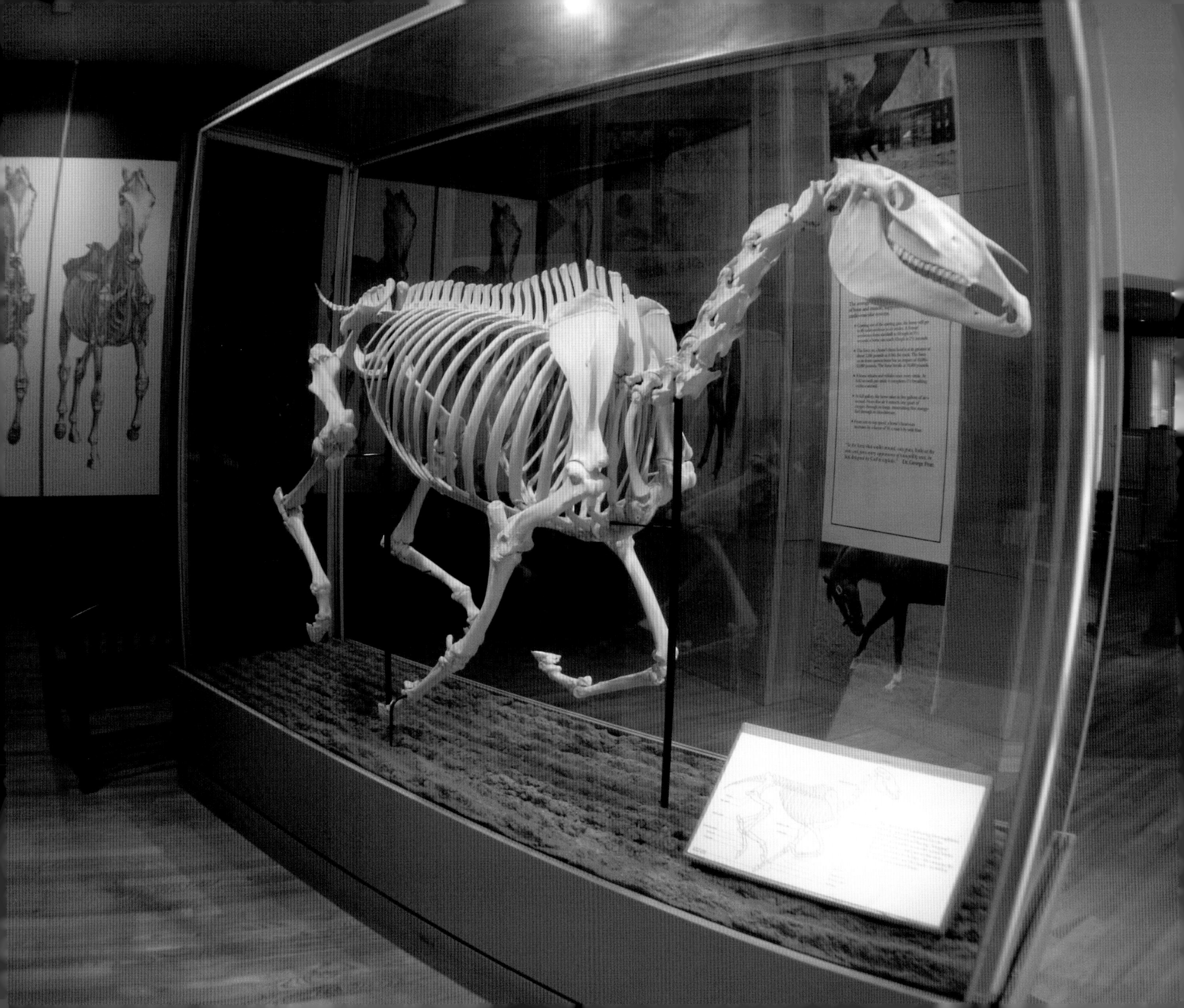

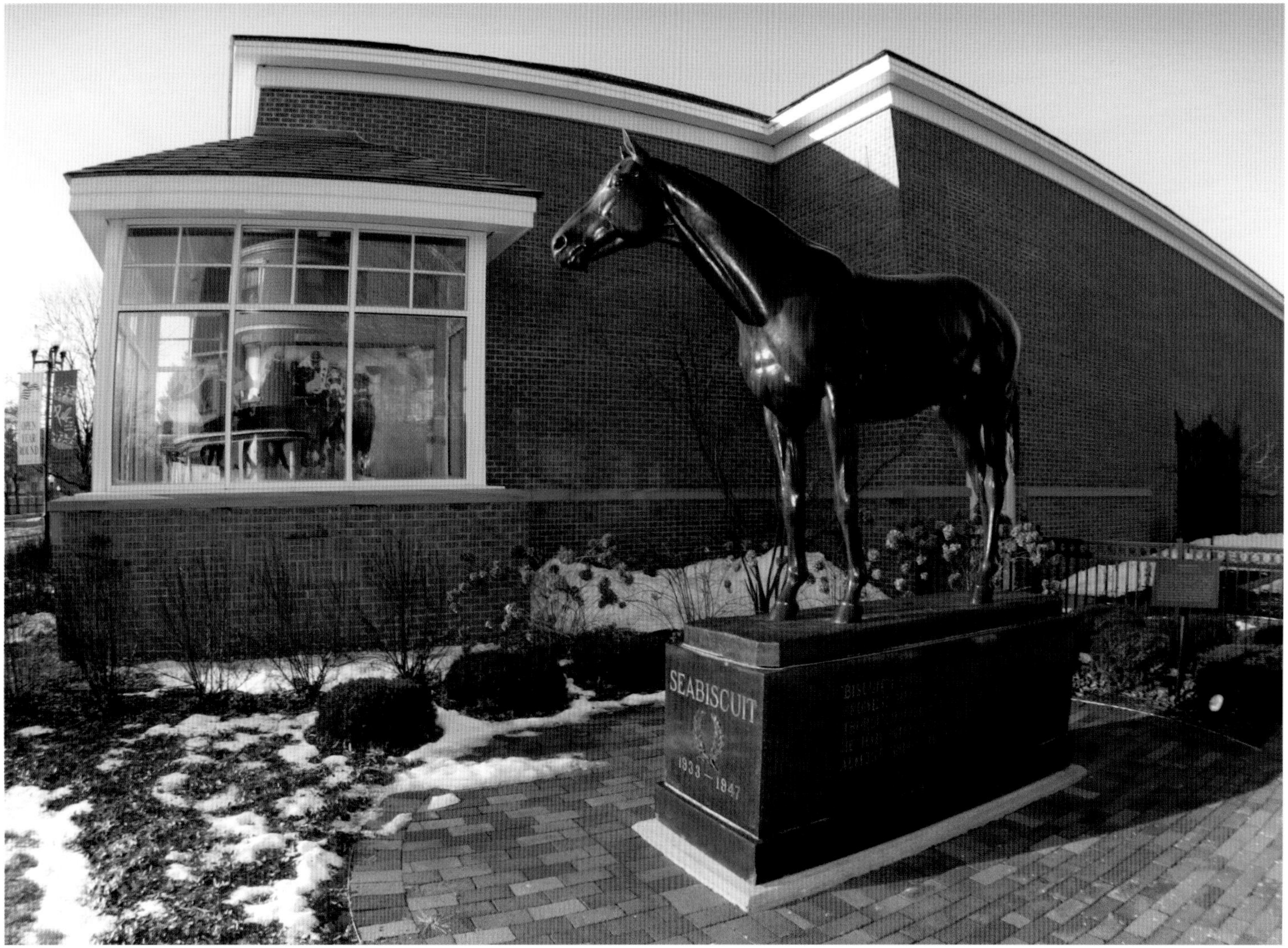

THE NATIONAL MUSEUM OF RACING AND HALL OF FAME, on Union Avenue across from the racetrack, features a wide variety of exhibits and programs.

The remains of Heaton Park (left) gallop eternally in the Anatomy Room and Seabiscuit (above) views Union Avenue.

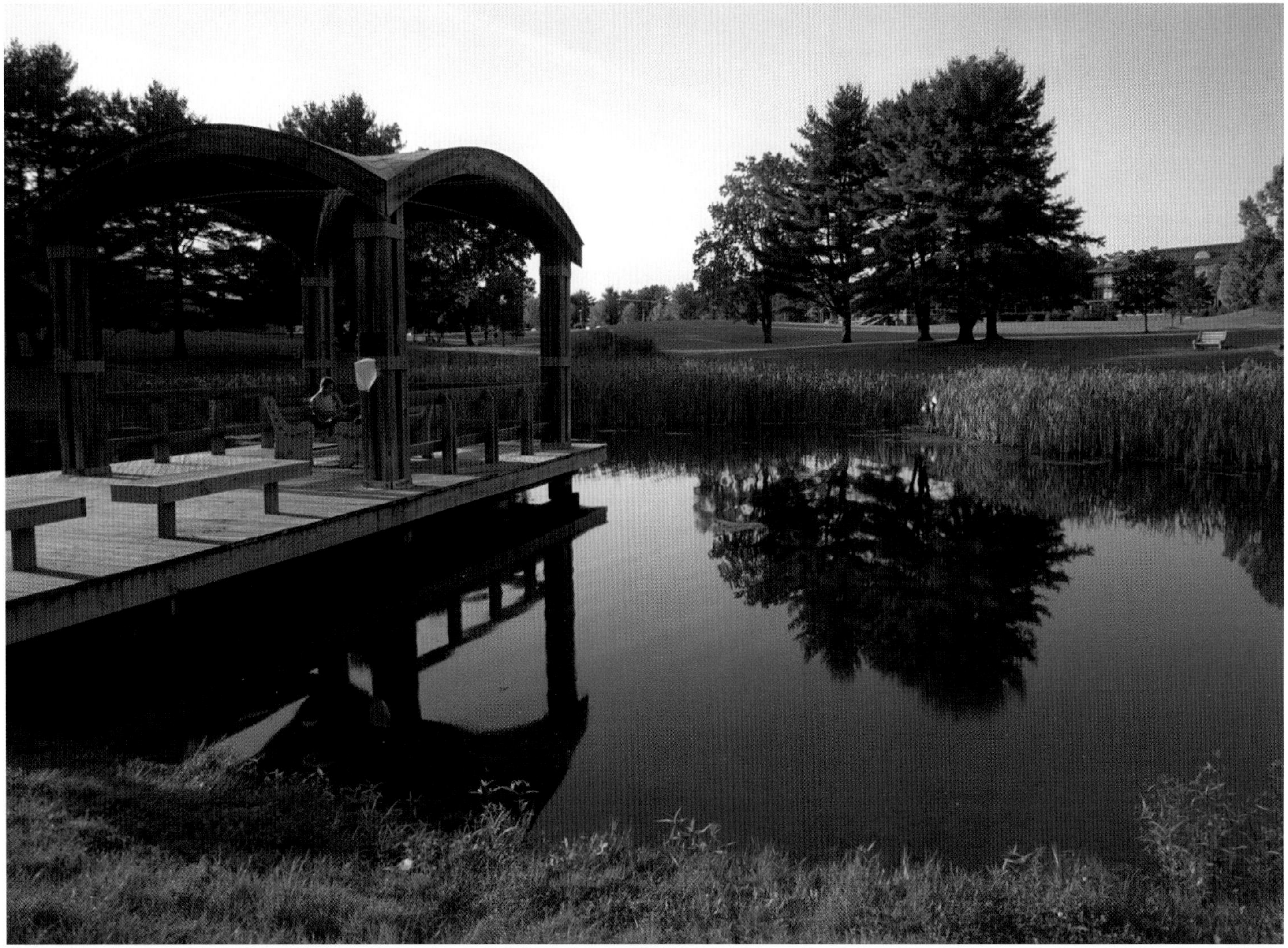

SKIDMORE COLLEGE, founded in 1903, is located off of North Broadway. The beautiful, expansive campus features the popular Tang Teaching Museum and Art Gallery (right).

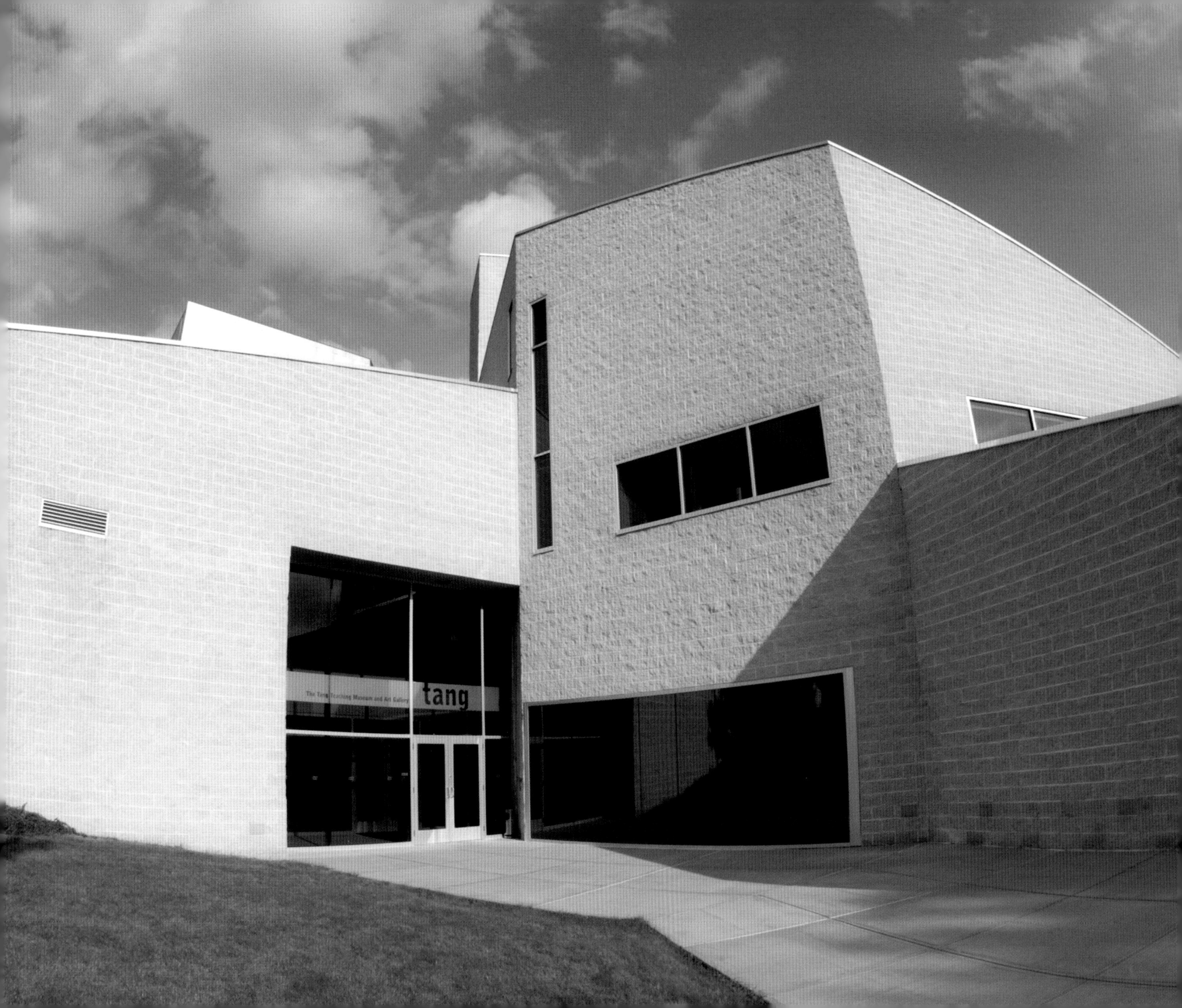
tang

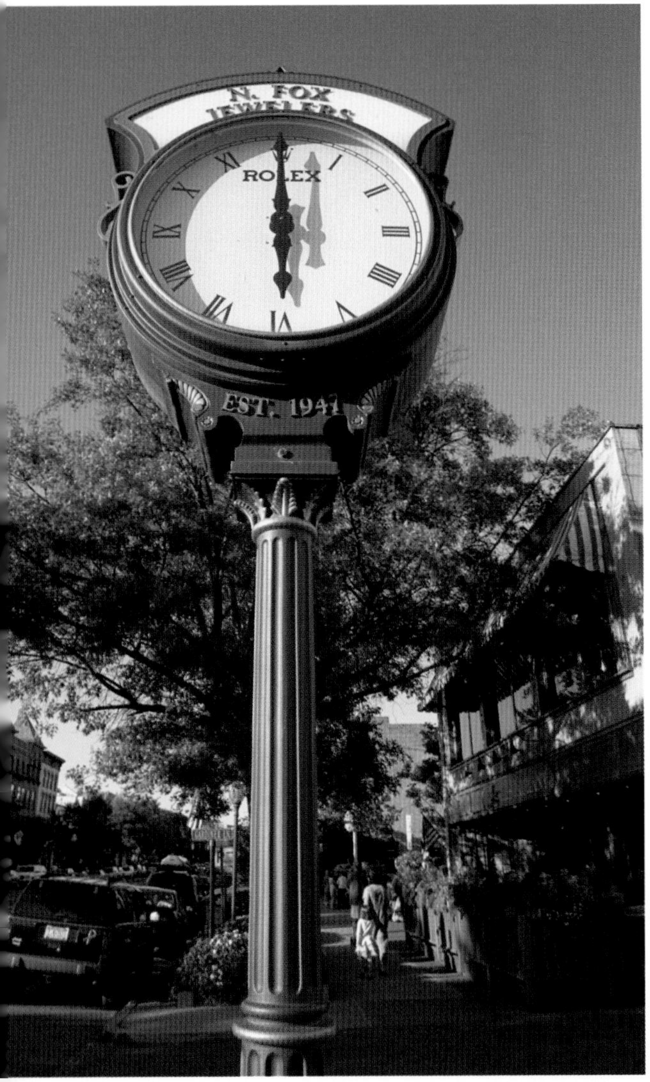
N. FOX
JEWELERS
ROLEX

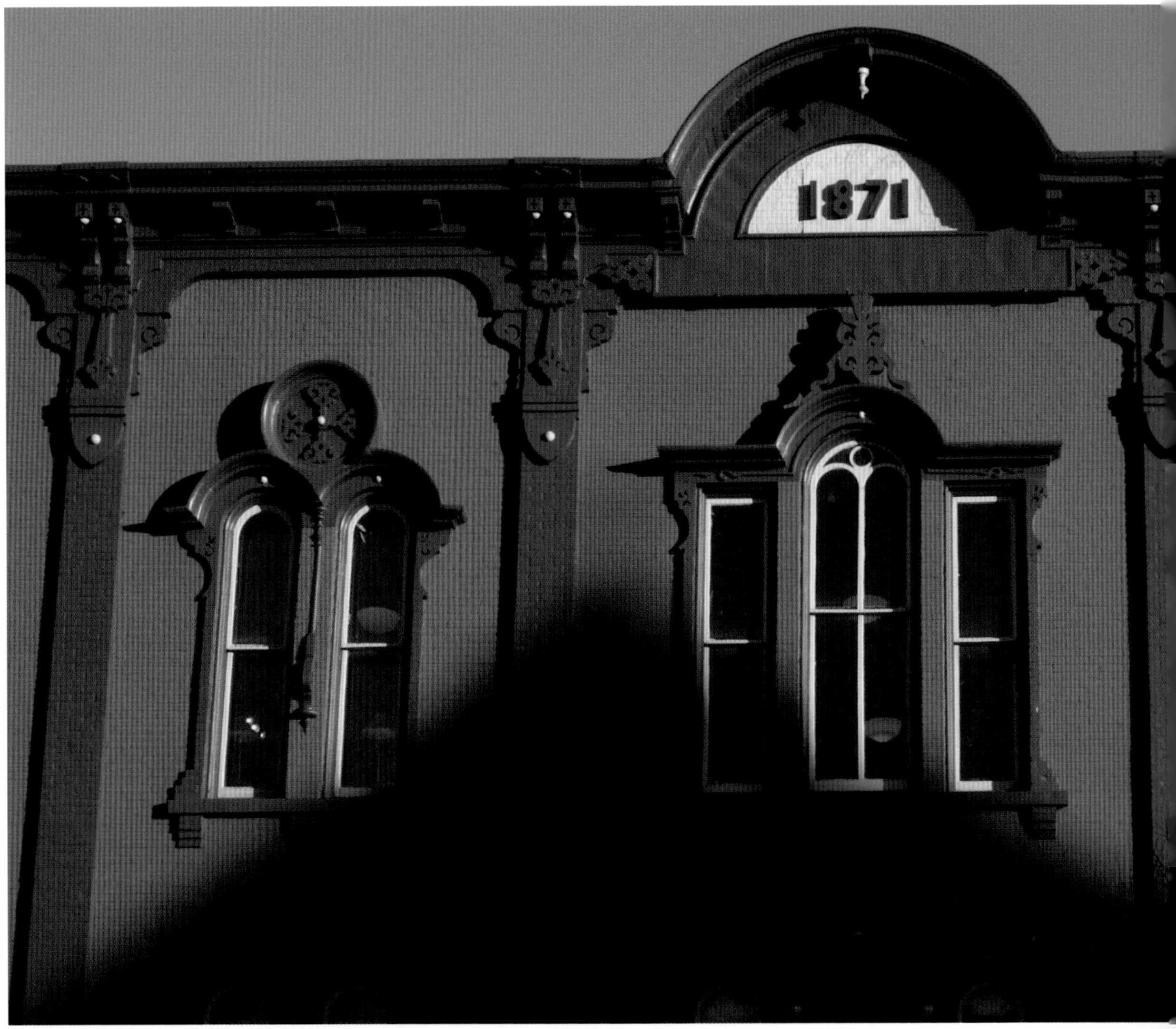
1871

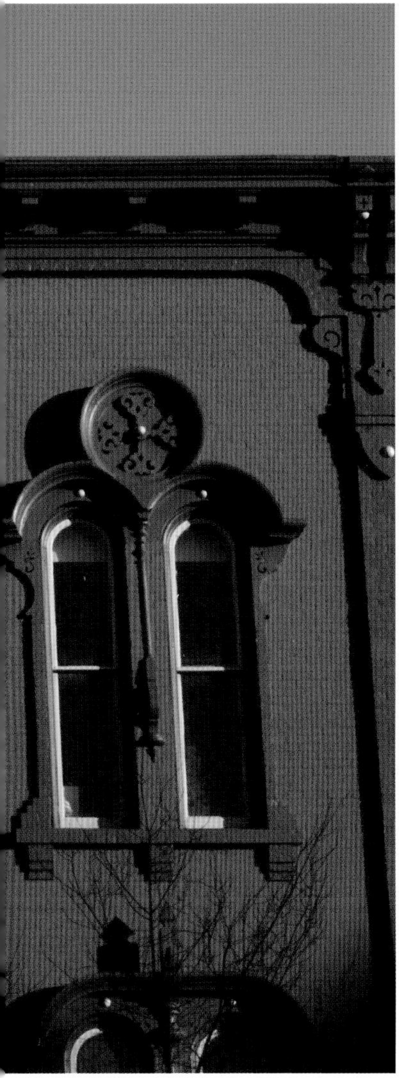

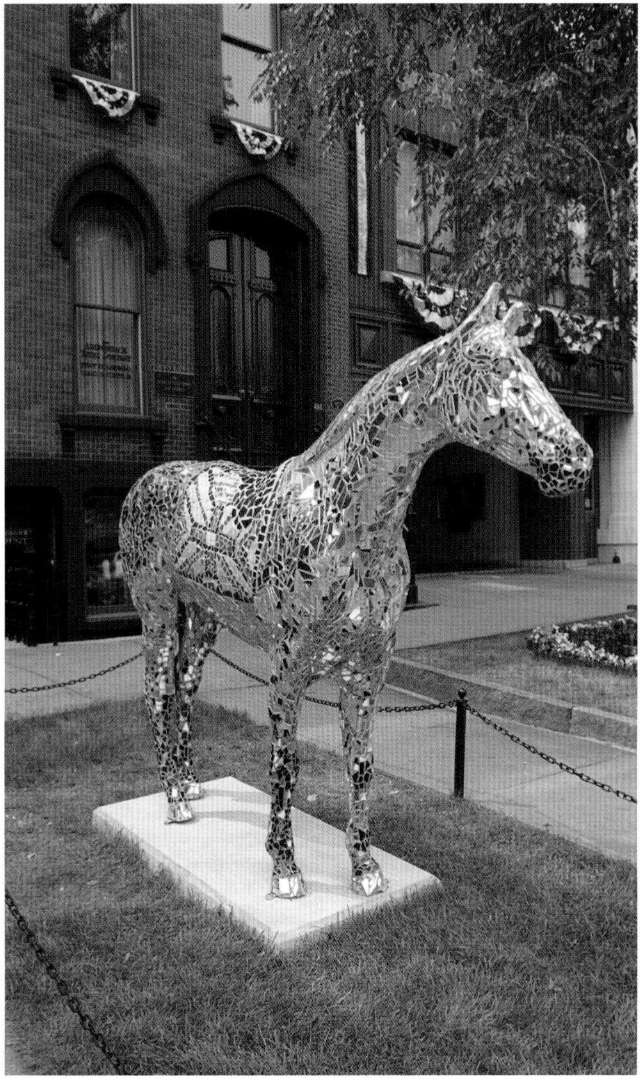

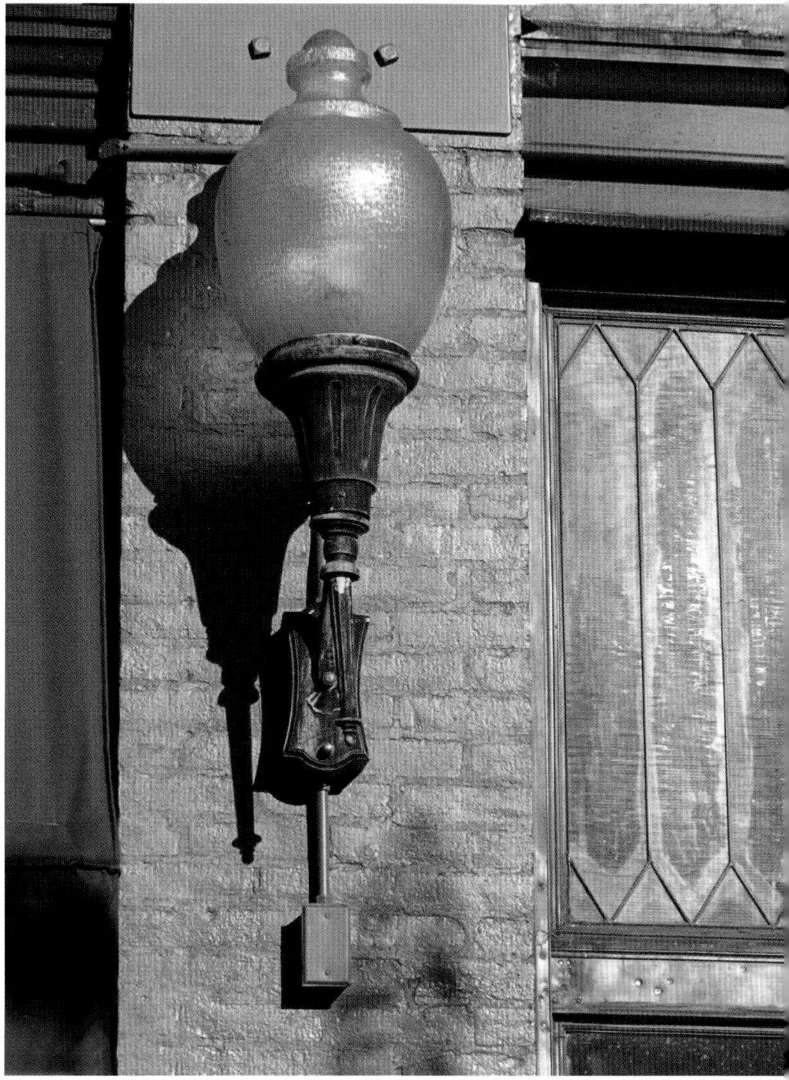

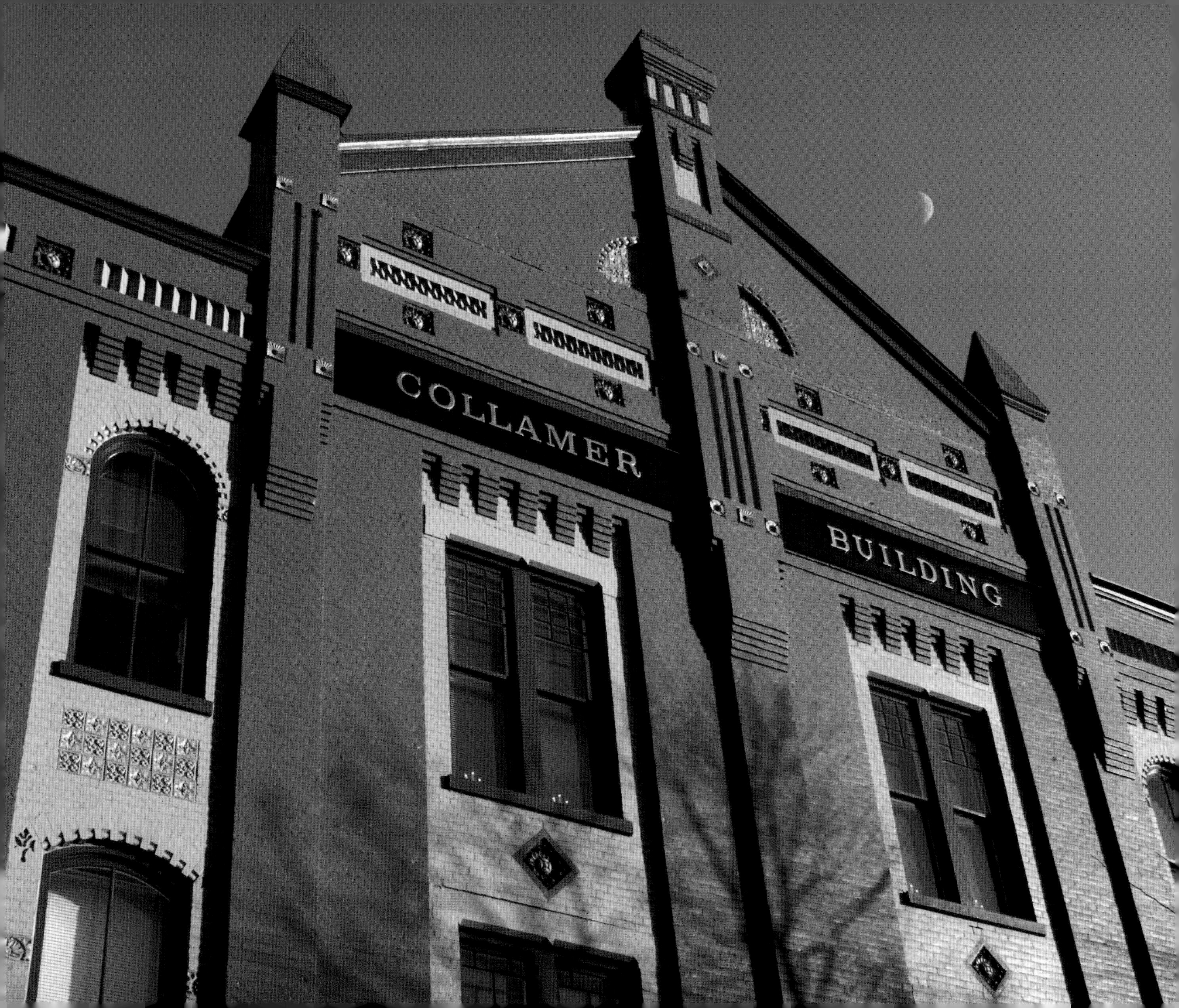
COLLAMER
BUILDING

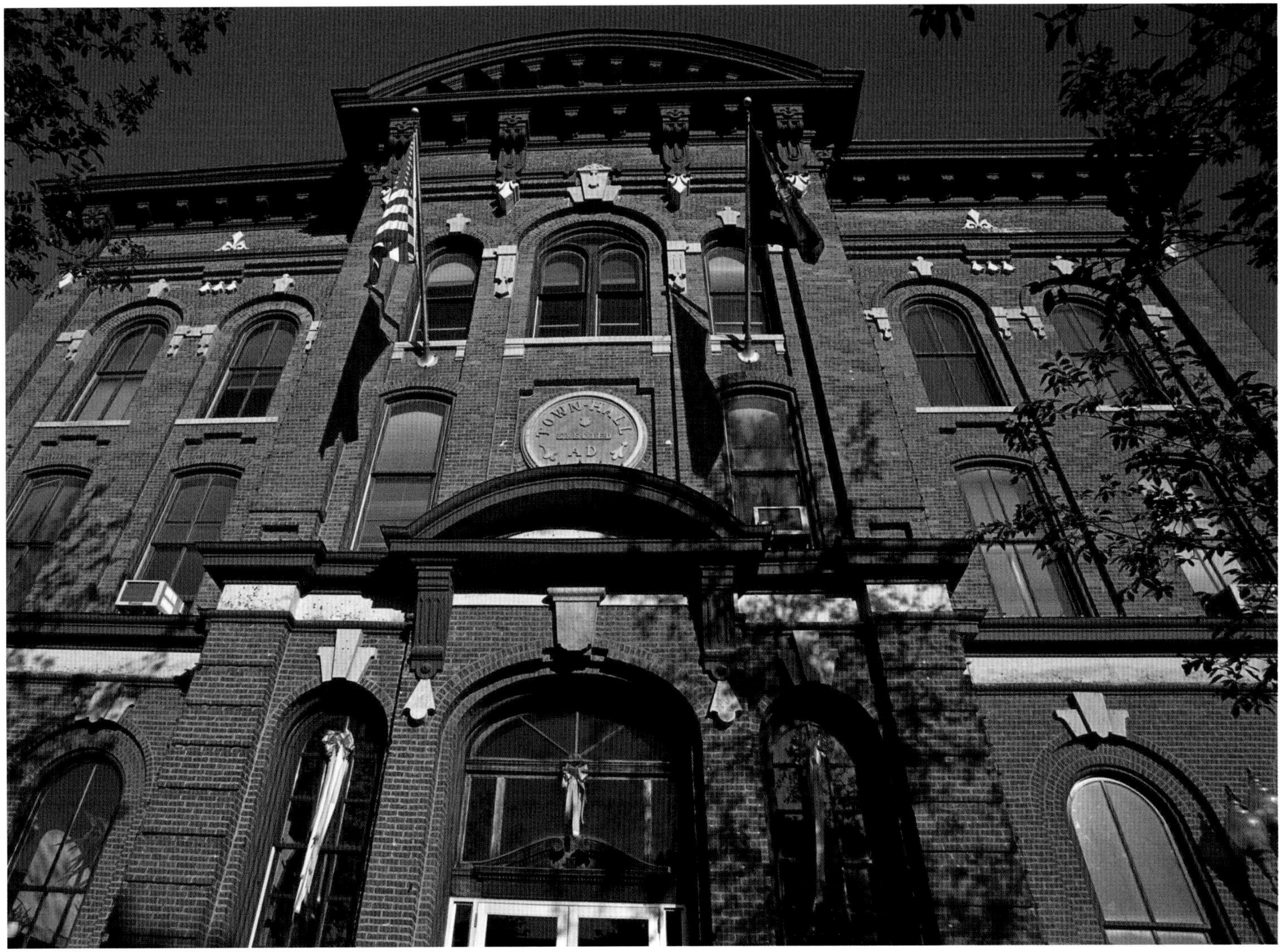

THE COLLAMER BUILDING AND TOWN HALL are a few of the classic old buildings featured on Broadway.

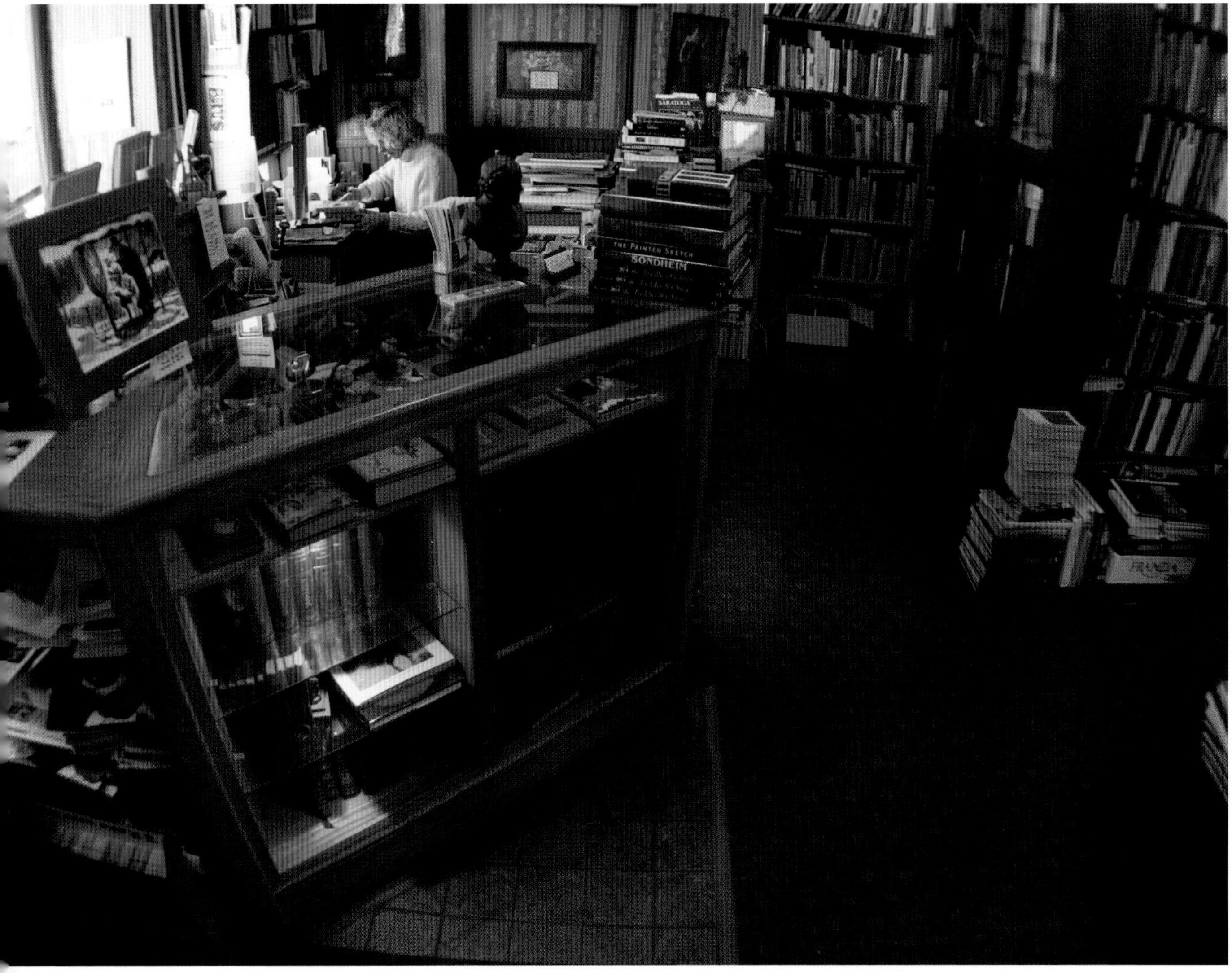

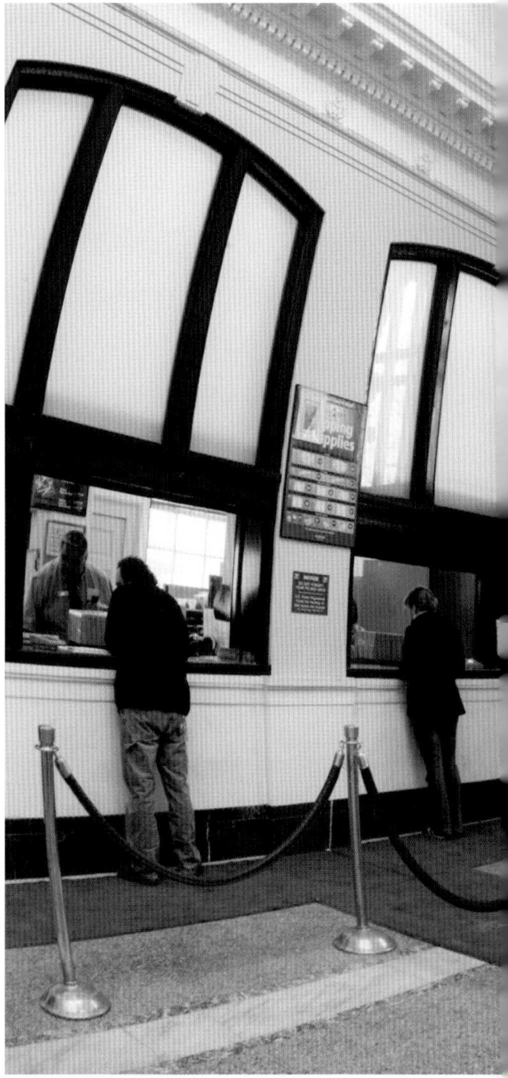

LYRICAL BALLAD BOOKSTORE (ABOVE) is one of many cherished Saratoga mainstays.

THE BROADWAY POST OFFICE (CENTER, RIGHT) features American realist Guy Pène du Bois' remarkable 1930s murals, depicting the glamorous world of the track and city.

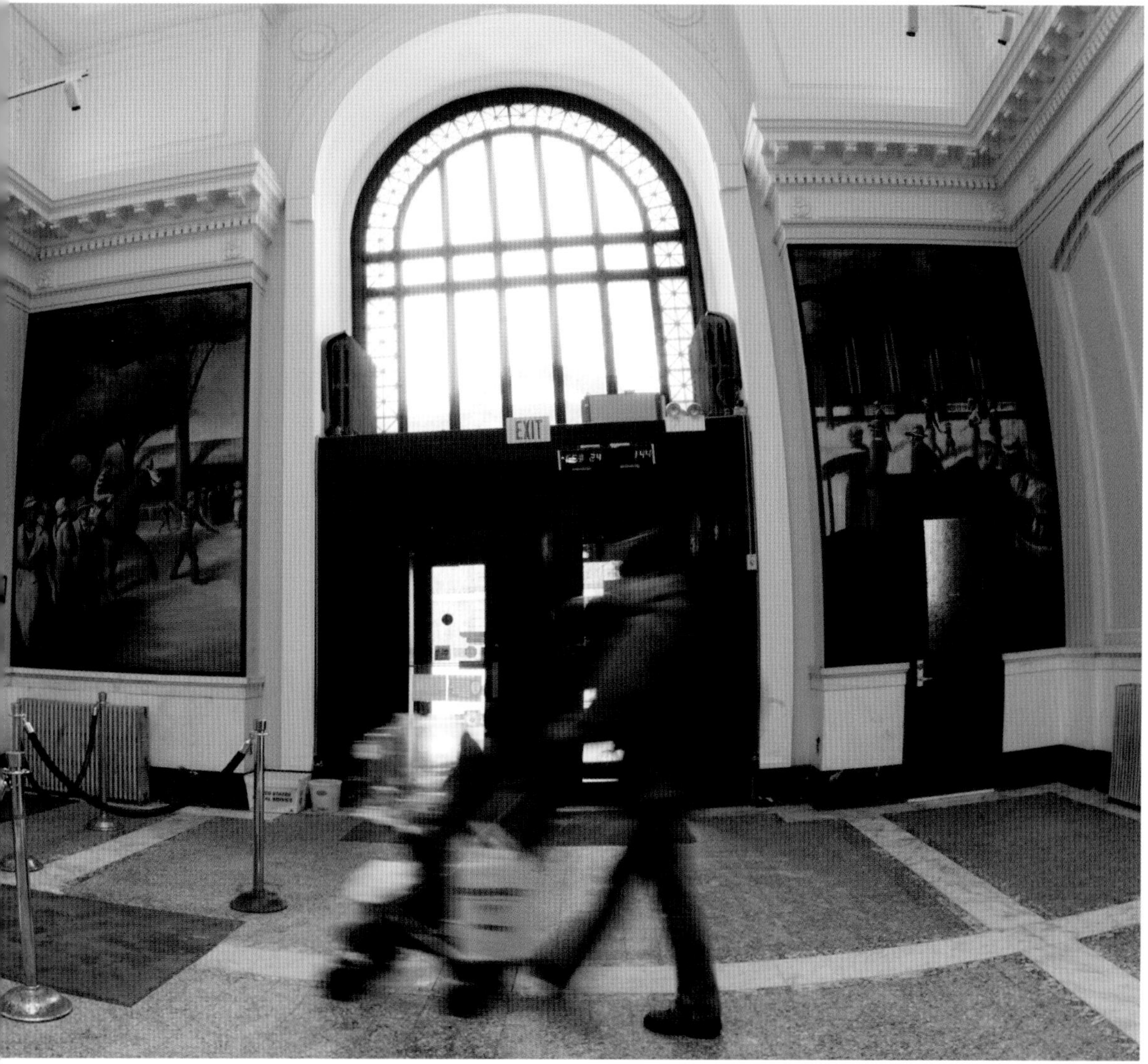
EXIT

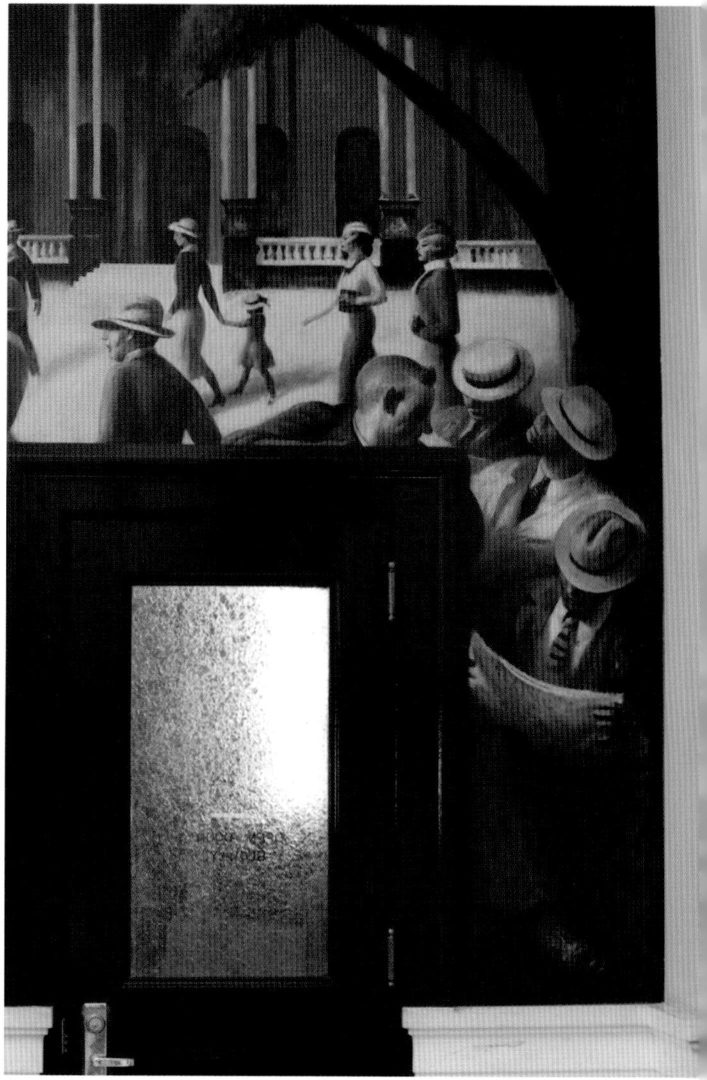

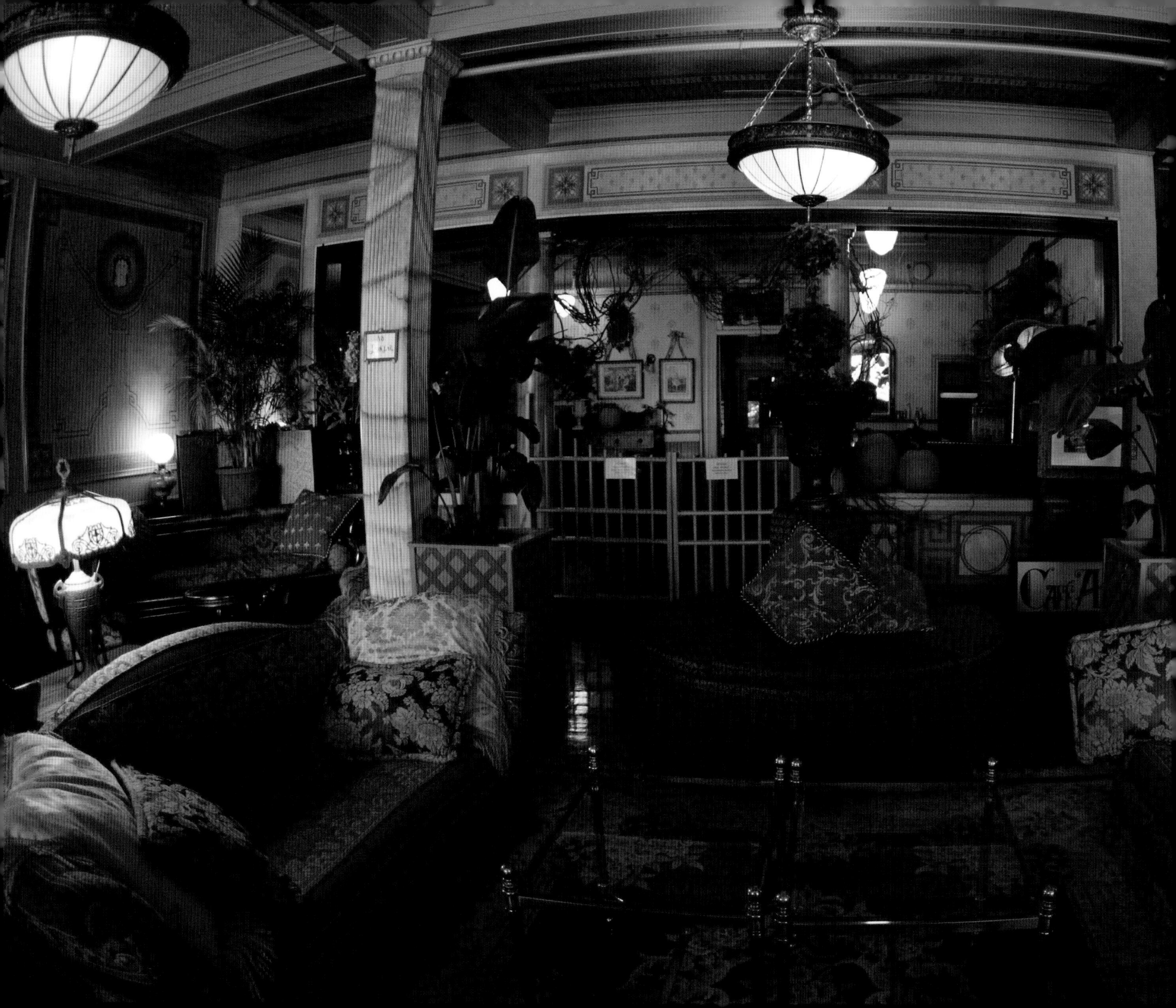

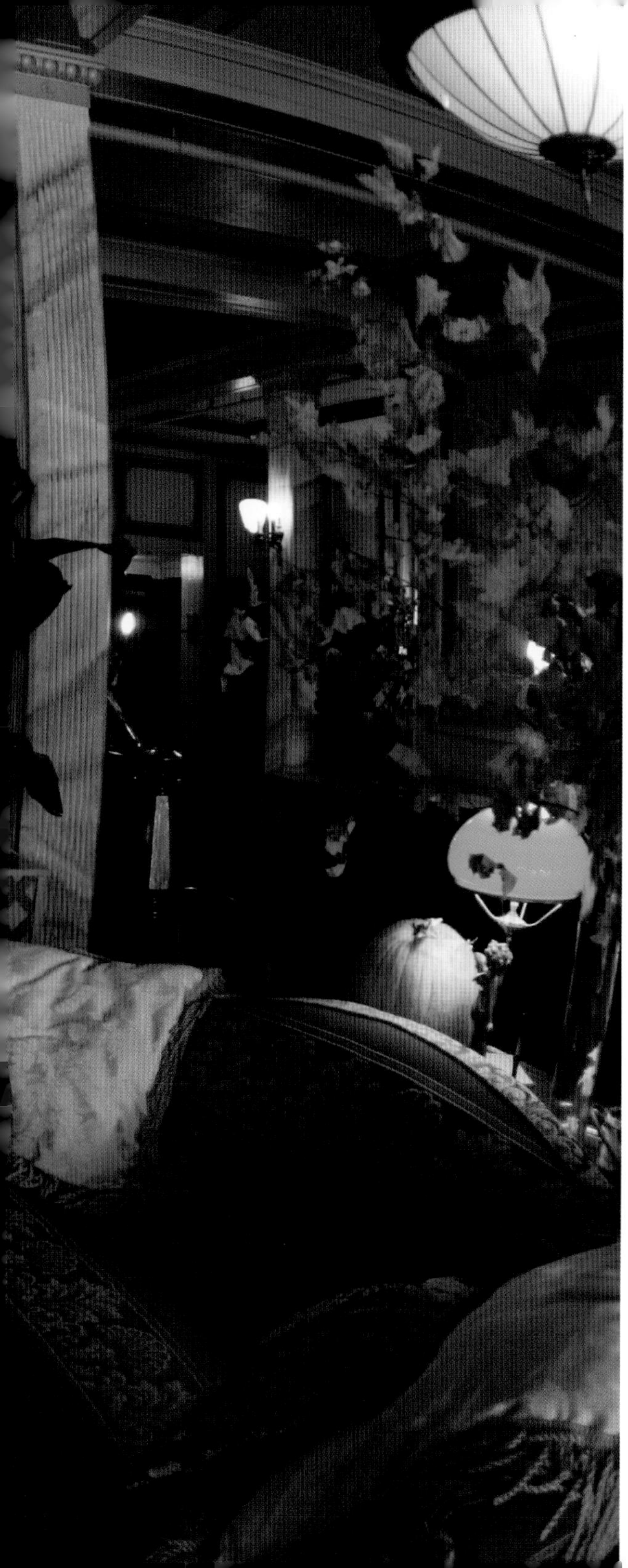

THE ADELPHI HOTEL, constructed in 1877, is a grand example of Saratoga's Victorian era, featuring unique architecture, ornate trappings, and an extravagantly appointed lobby.

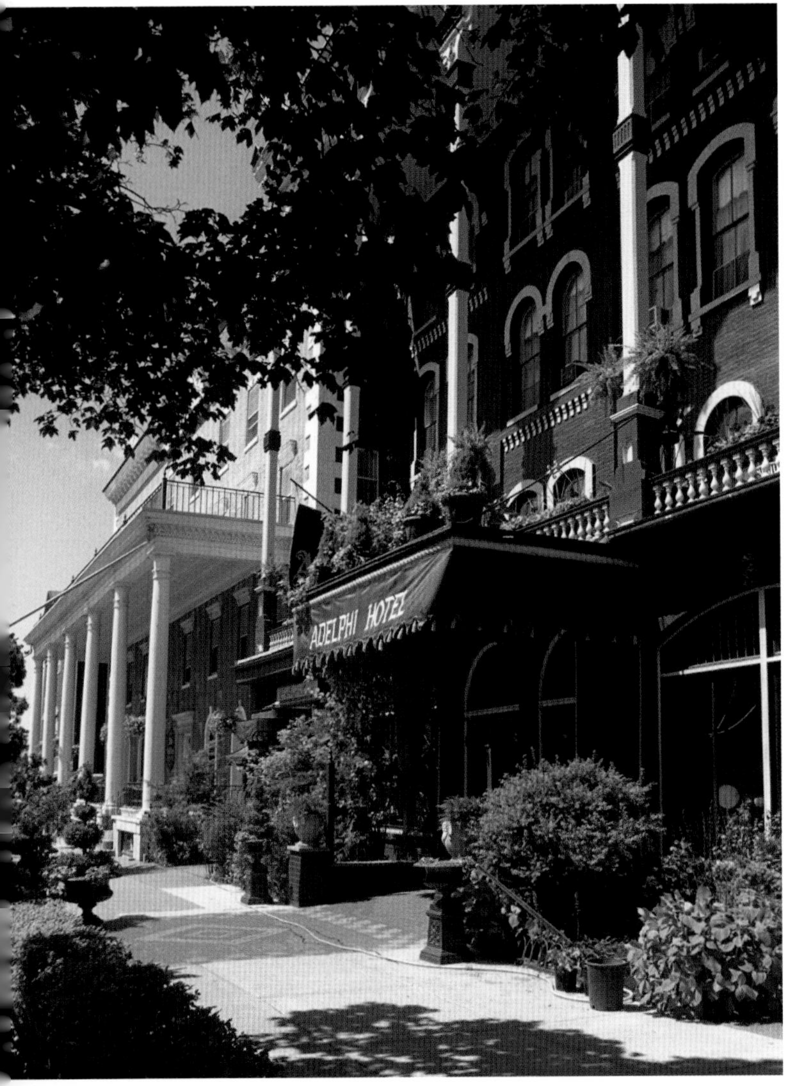

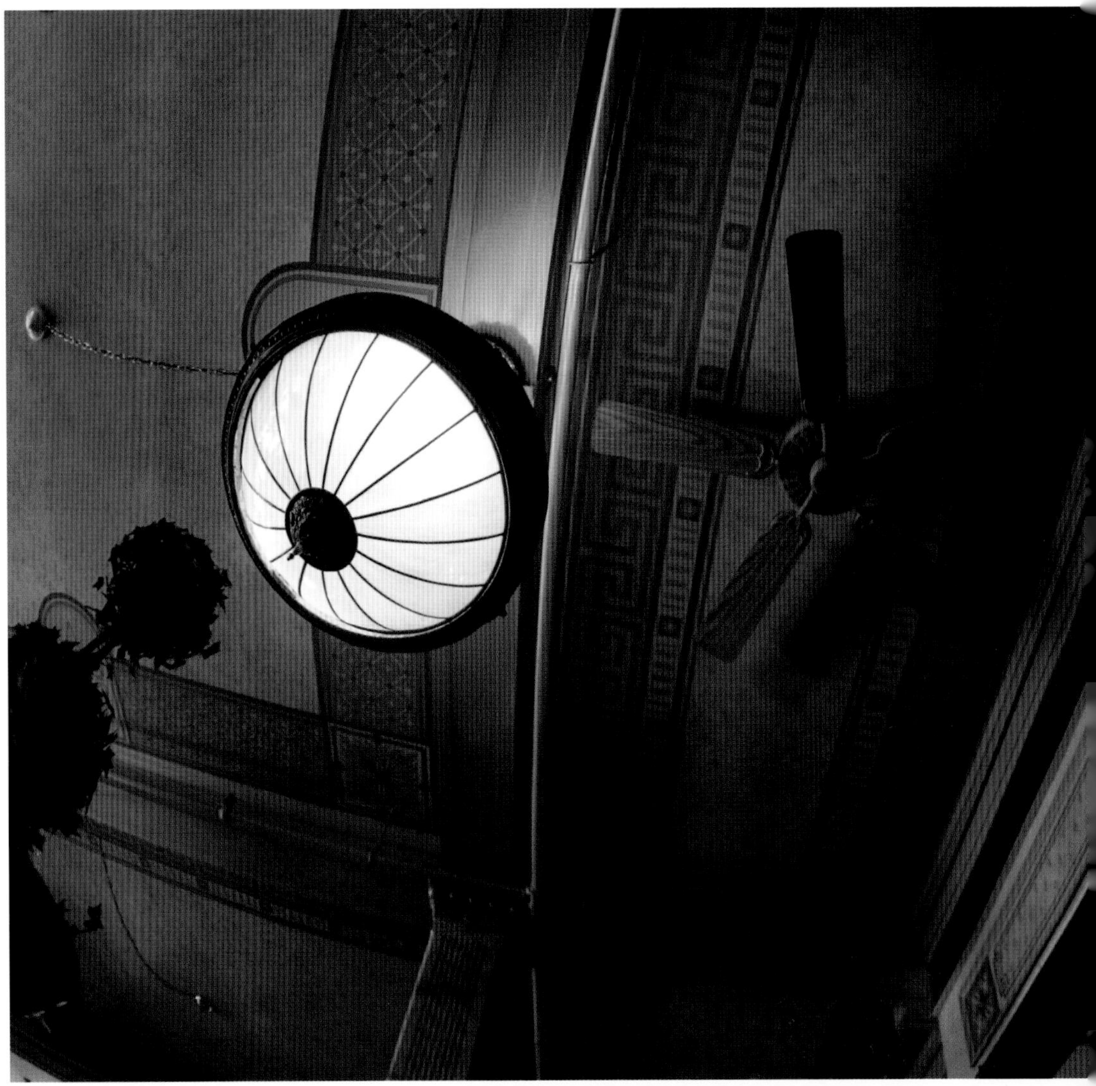

ADELPHI HOTEL DETAILS — The hotel is famous, in part, for its beautiful upstairs piazza (second from right), where guests relax and overlook the Broadway scene.

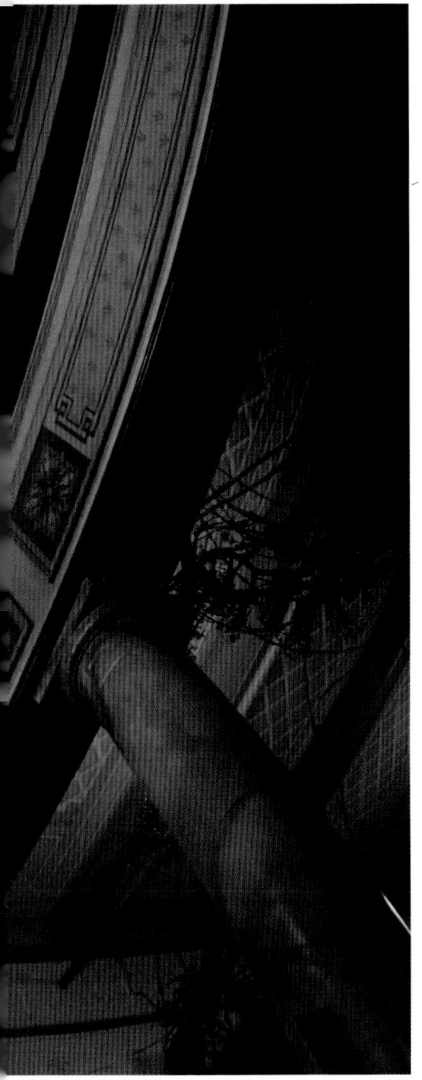
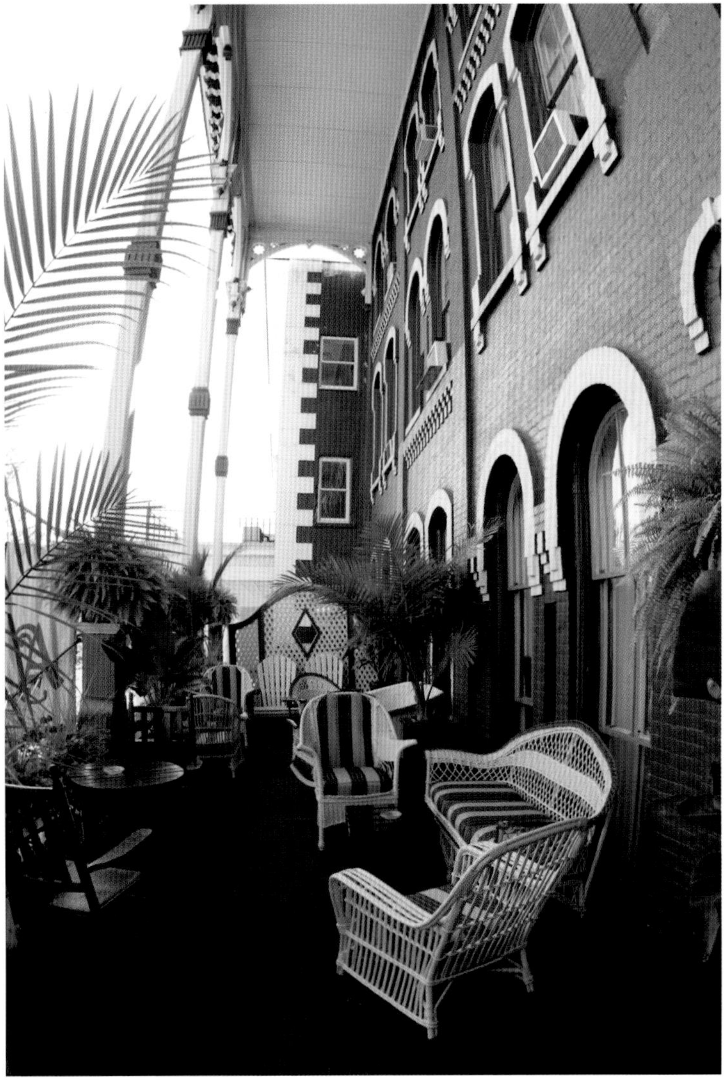
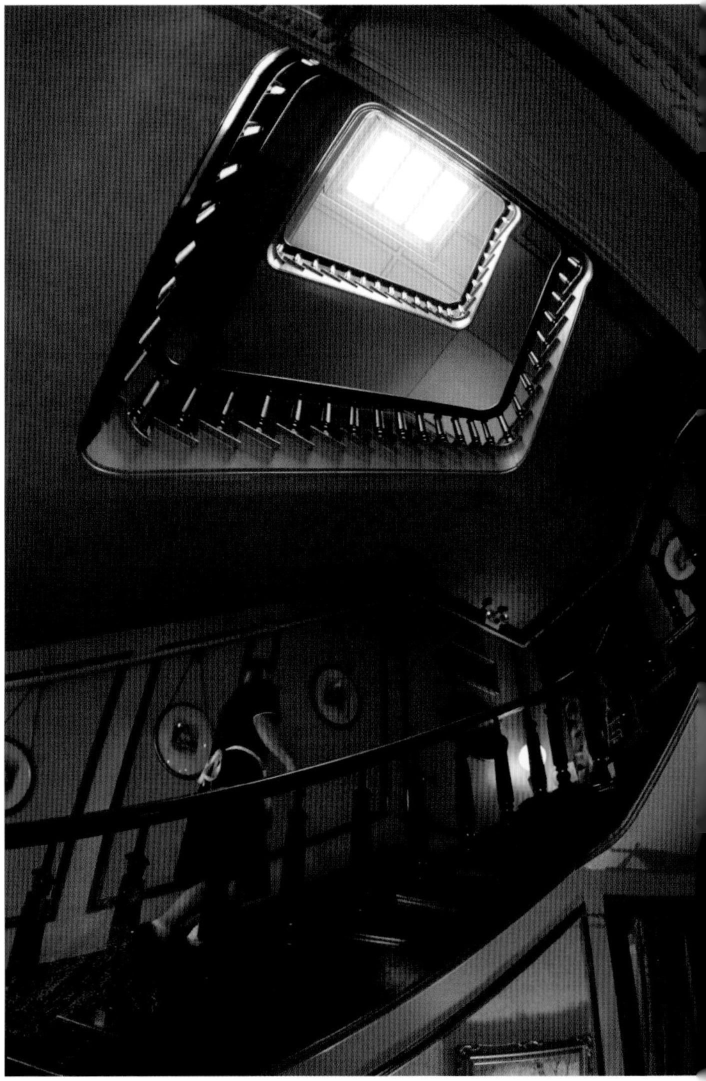

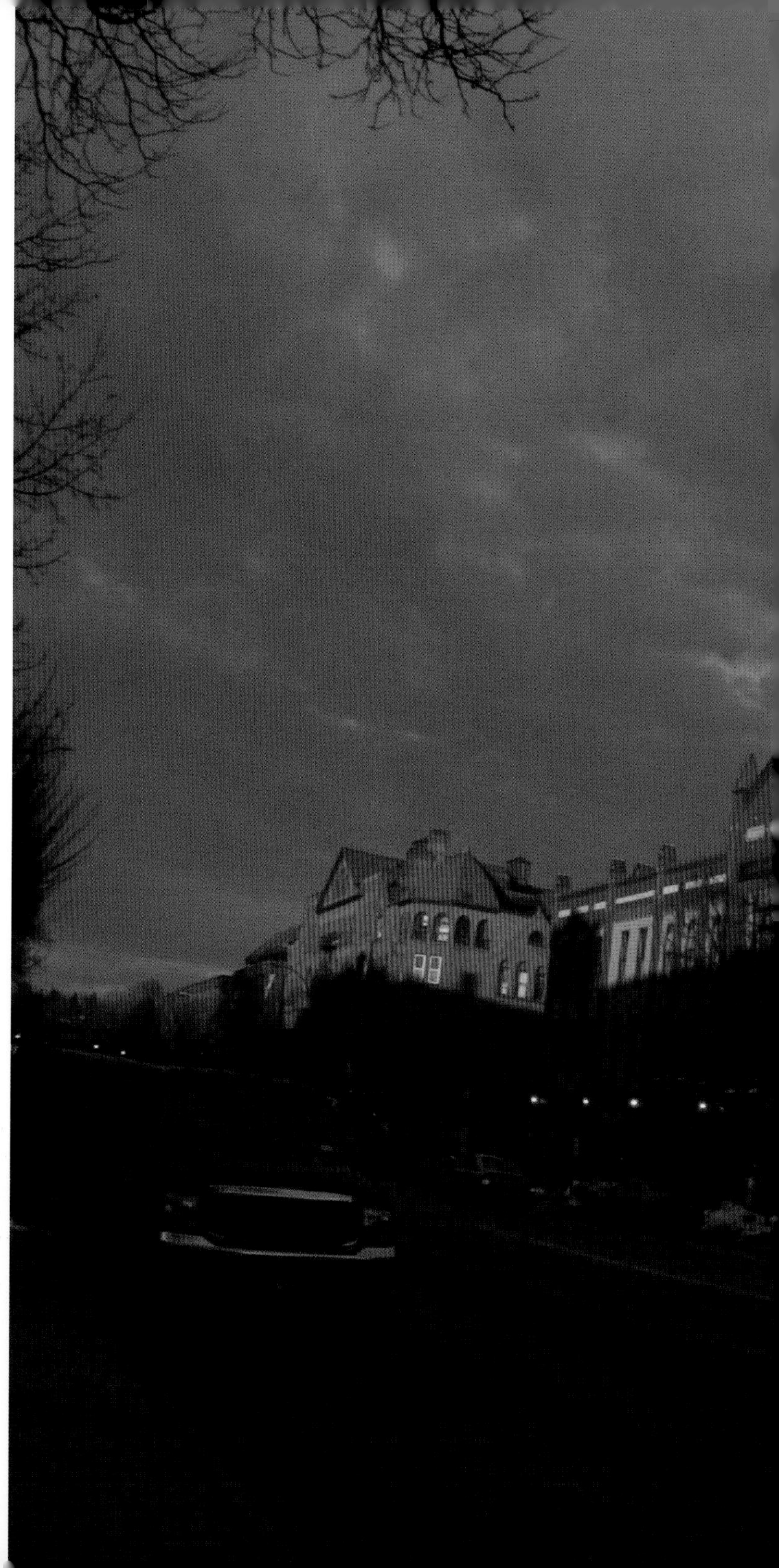

 BROADWAY, late afternoon light. The town hall is at right.

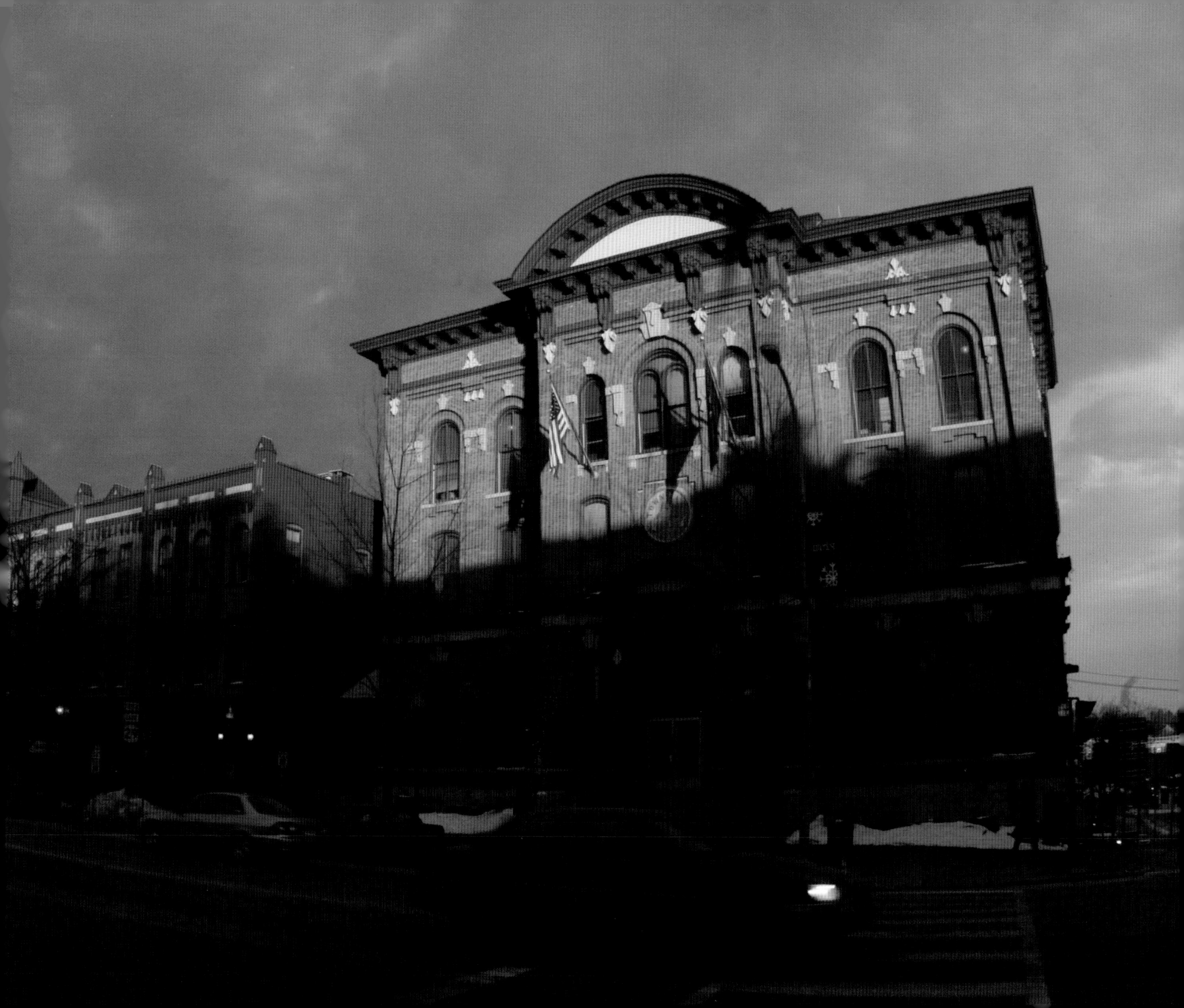

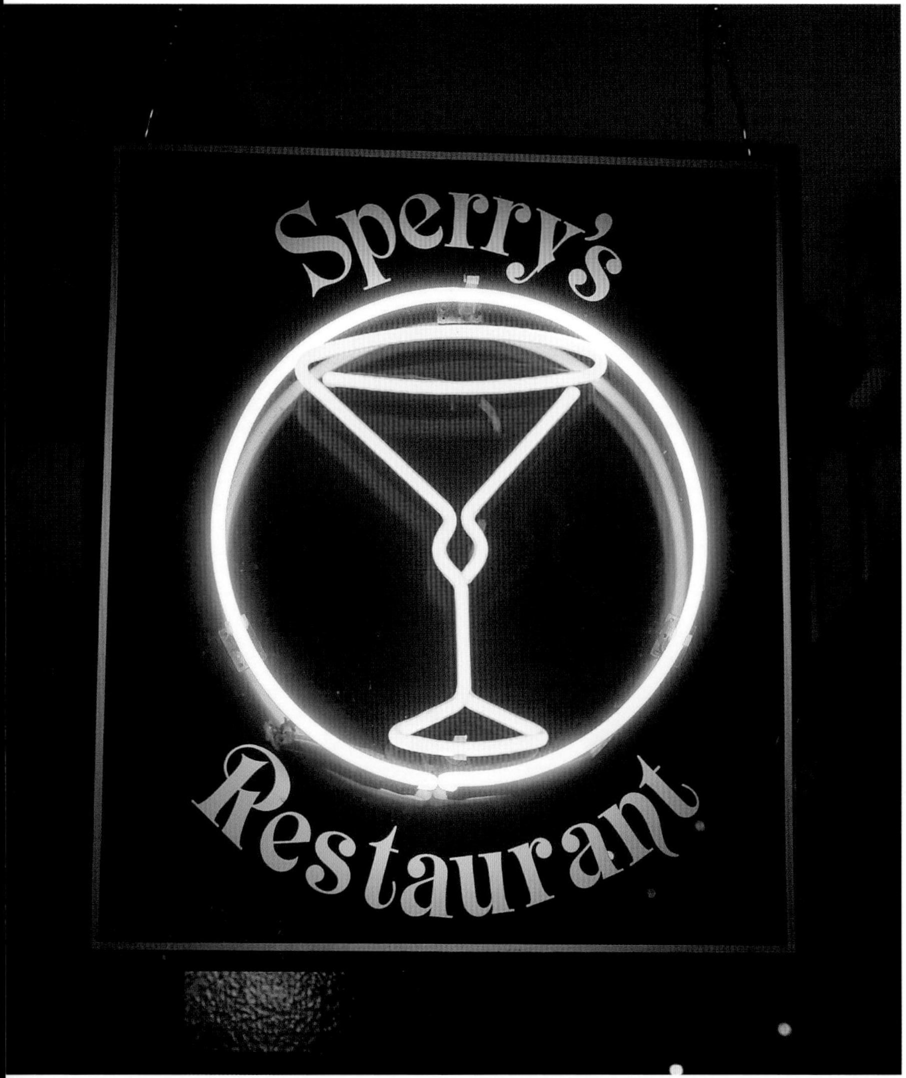

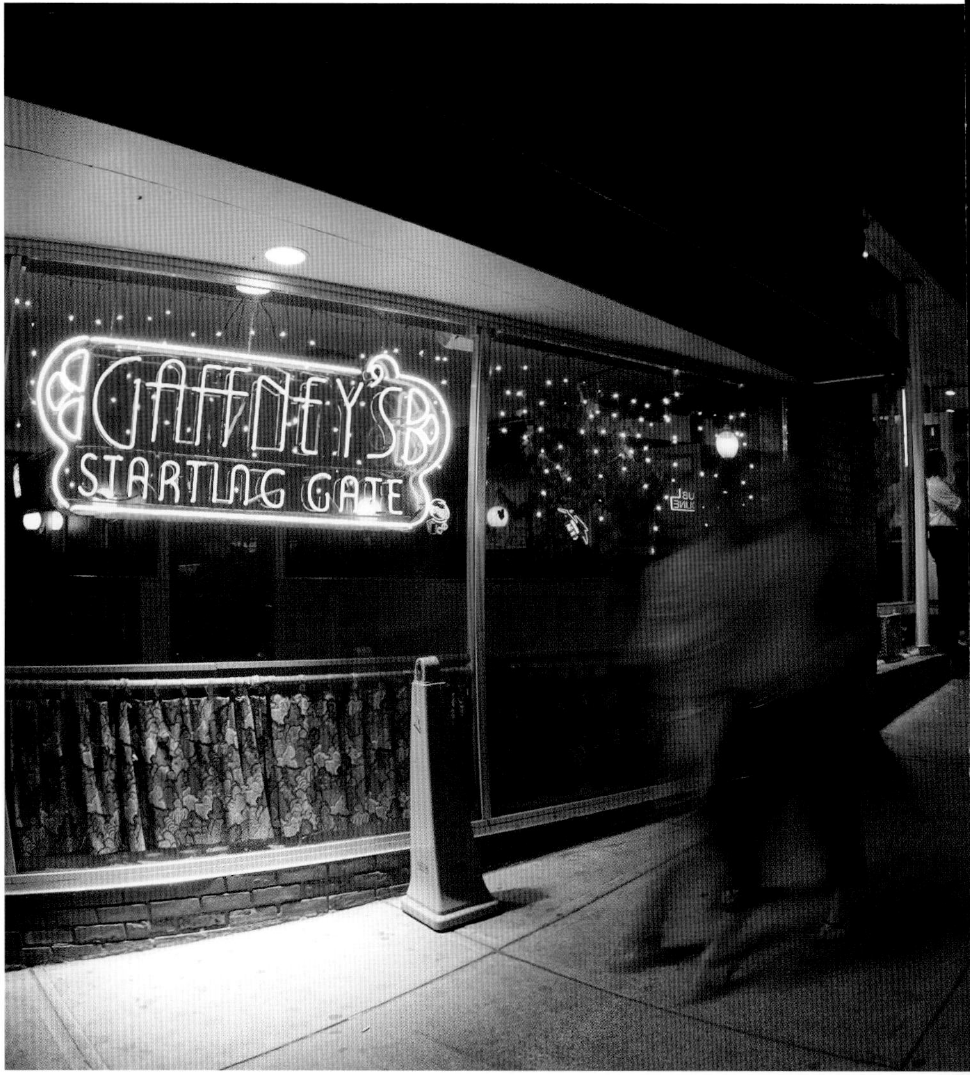

 SARATOGA NIGHTLIFE is both varied and vibrant.

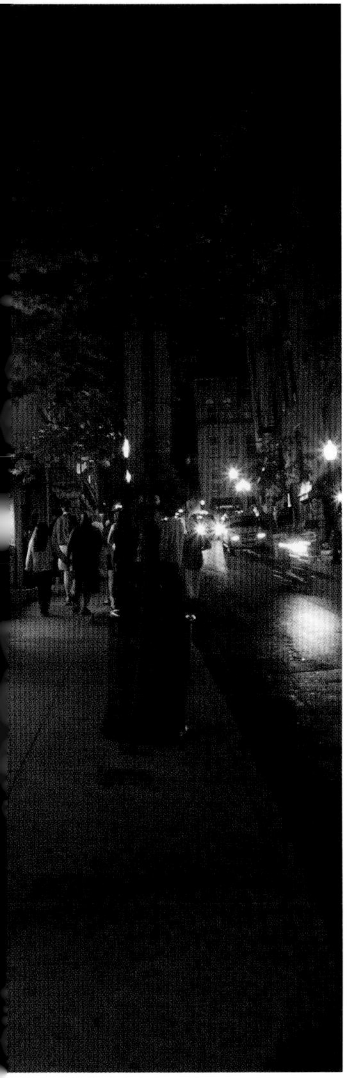

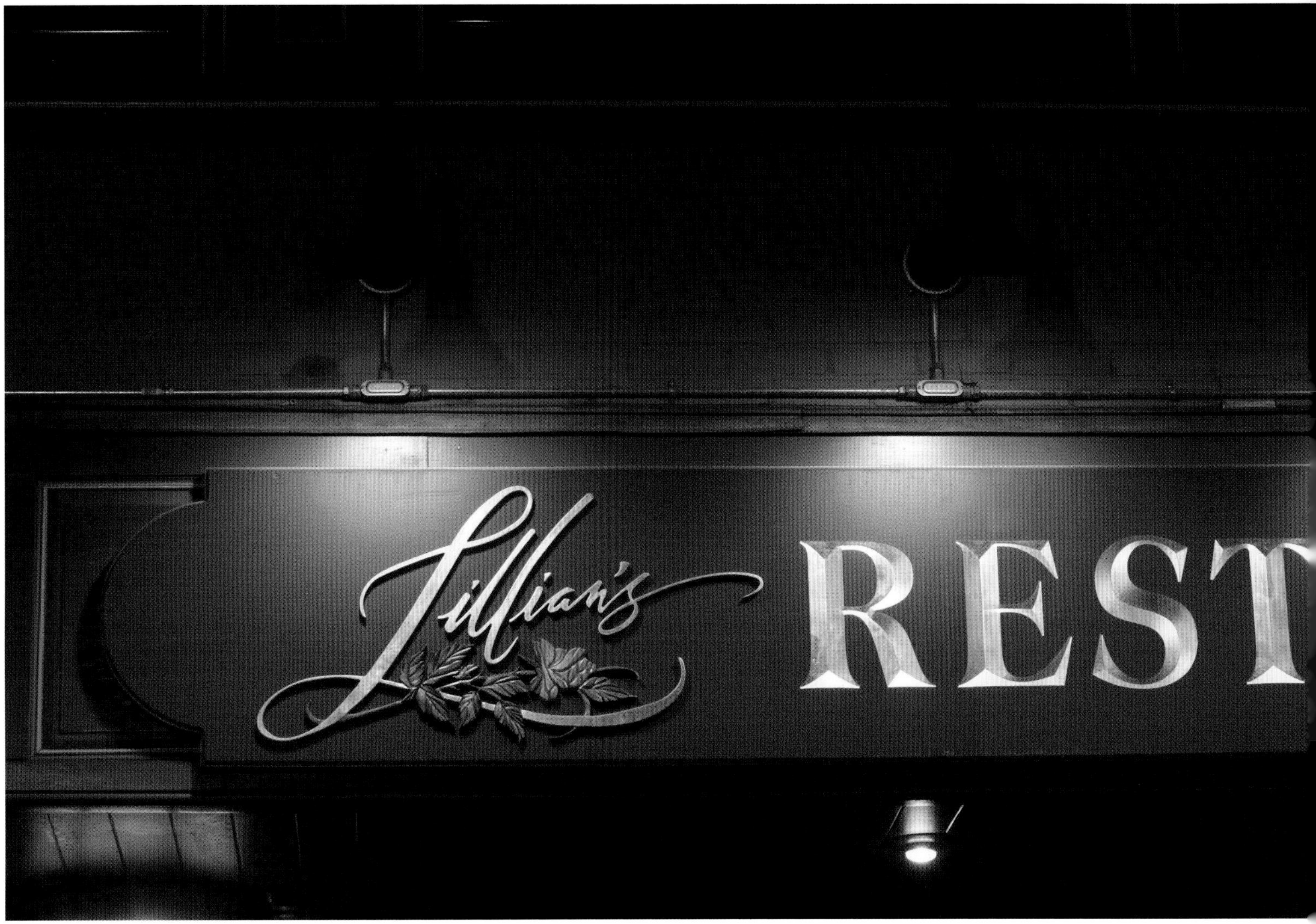
Lillian's
REST

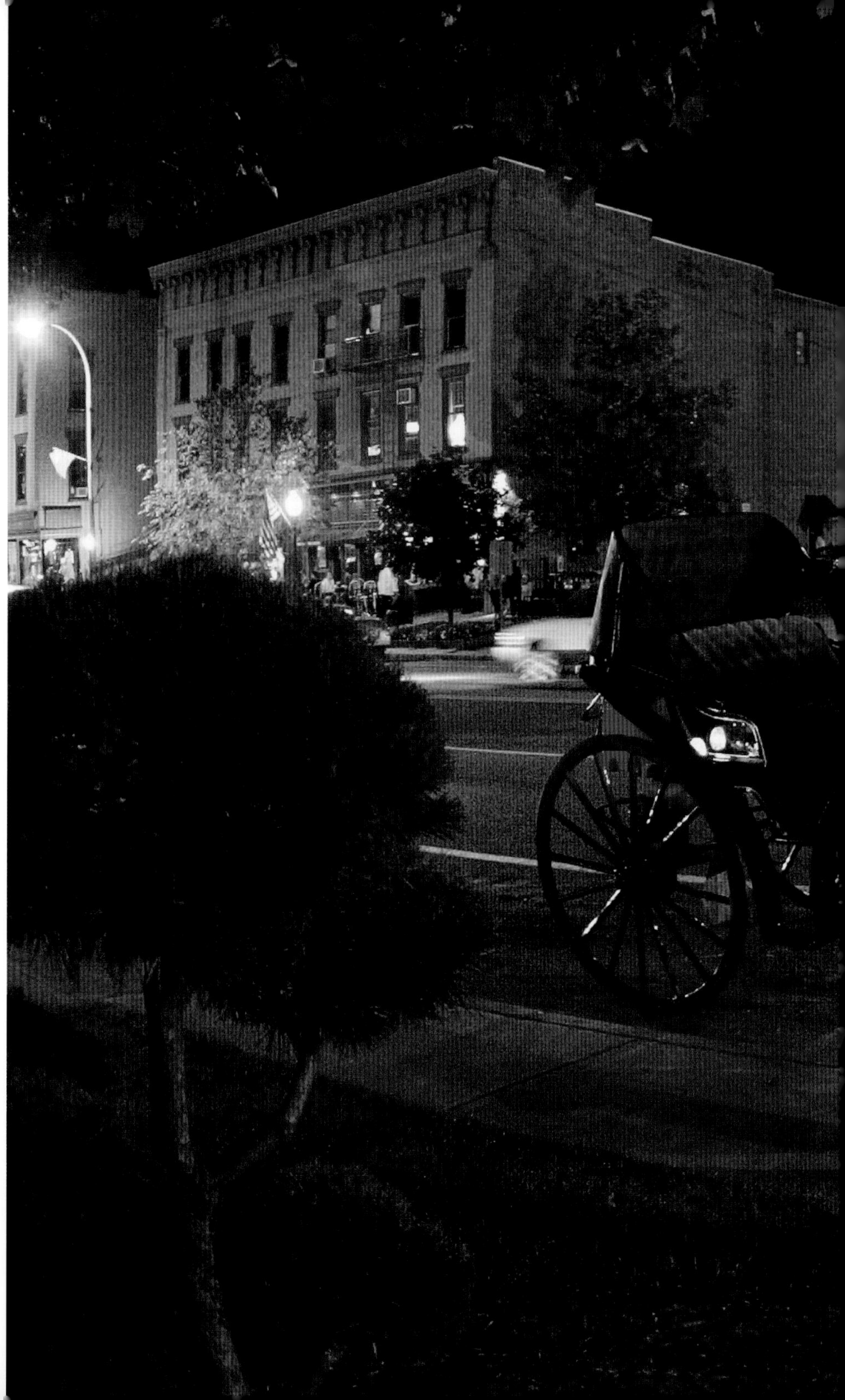

 AUGUST EVENING ON BROADWAY as a carriage horse and its driver await tourists wanting a nighttime tour.

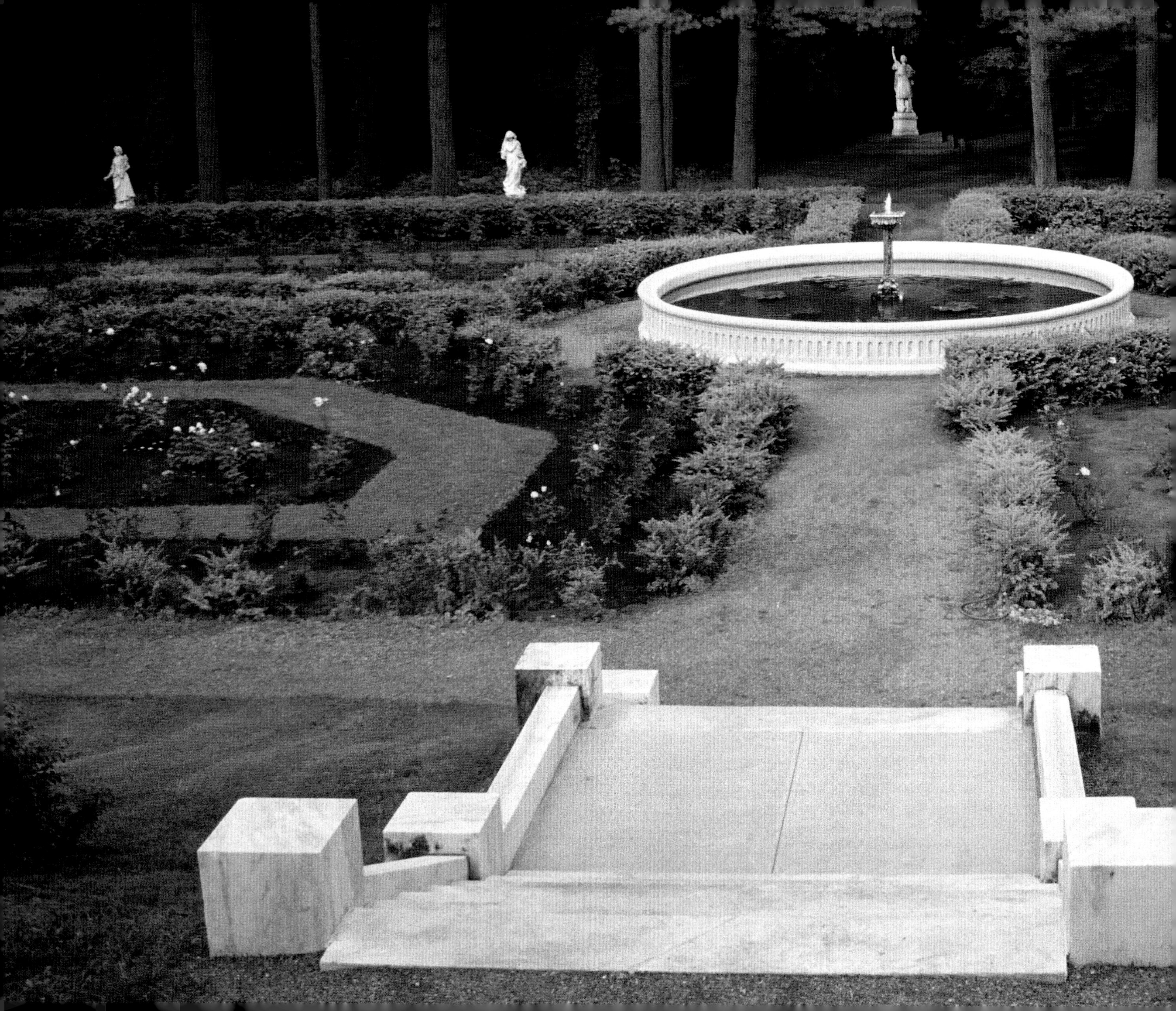

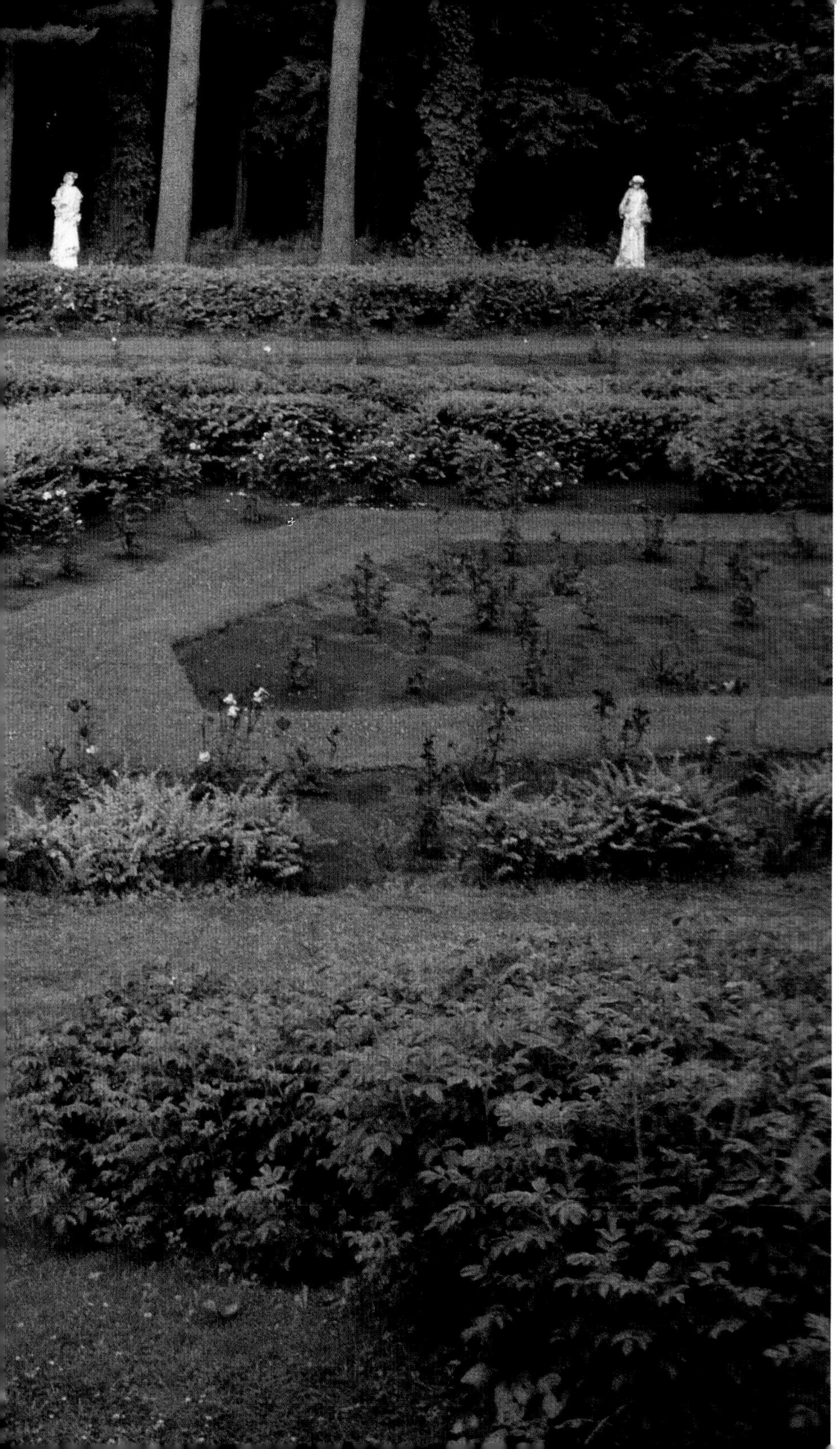

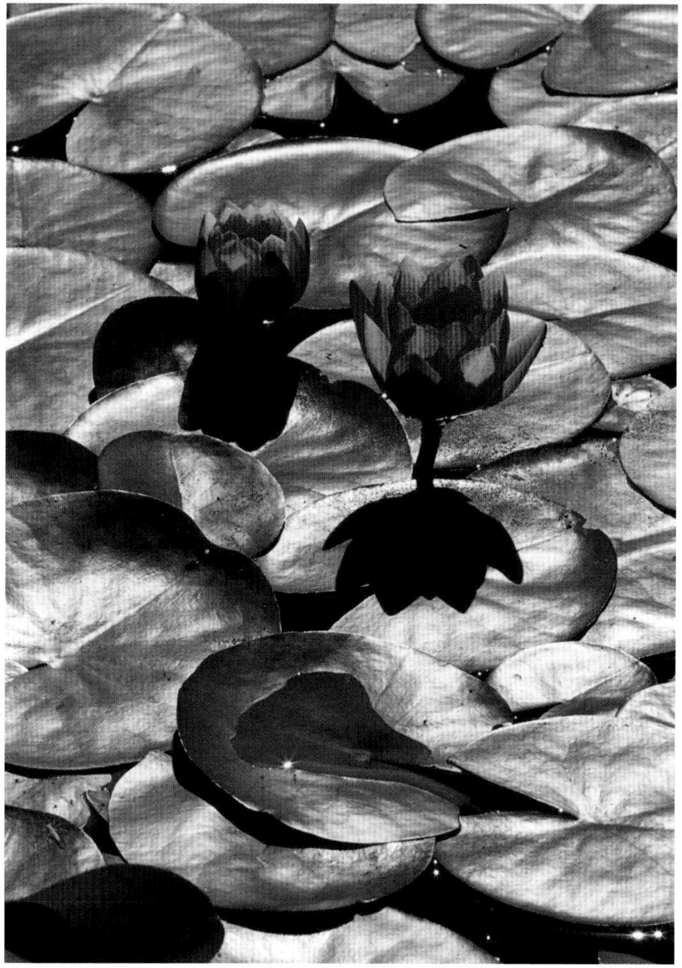

Yaddo

Yaddo, the famed artists' retreat, is an idyllic, wondrous property adjacent to Saratoga Race Course. It has fueled the dreams of Saul Bellow, Aaron Copland, and Leonard Bernstein, just to name a few. Truman Capote fell in love at Yaddo; Sylvia Plath spent happy days there.

And it was all due to one woman's vision more than a century ago.

Katrina Trask was a gifted playwright and poet; her husband Spencer, a successful financier. They were philanthropists on a grand scale, and Yaddo is their most remarkable legacy.

The property has always seemed destined for creative energies. Before the Trasks' time, the expansive property contained a popular tavern. It is said that Edgar Allan Poe wrote part of "The Raven" while wandering near a pond there.

The Trasks purchased the land in 1881 as a home for their growing family. By 1889, however, all four of their children had died in childhood. In 1891 their beloved mansion burned to the ground. They built a new one two years later.

Beset by tragedies, the couple carried on, and in 1899 while walking in the woods, Katrina experienced an epiphany. She finally understood their destiny: Yaddo was to become an artists' retreat. Spencer wholeheartedly embraced Katrina's vision, and the couple devoted the rest of their lives to that end.

Four years after Katrina's death in 1922, the first artists arrived to live Katrina's dream. And so it has been for some eighty years for nearly 5,500 artists.

While the main mansion is for residents and guests only, the gardens are open to the public. Some explore the woods or sit by ponds thought inspirational to Poe. Towering trees form a wondrous canopy, beneath which every color in nature resides.

The gardens reflect a magical, bygone time, with roses of seemingly every color, size, and type. Water bursts from fountains and trickles through worn rock gardens as aging statues watch the day. Large, multi-colored fish drift lazily in pools, and lily pads with happy blooms greet summer days.

More than a century after Katrina had her prophetic vision, she and Spencer live on here. Many believe Katrina still wanders the grounds. More than one visitor has seen her diaphanous figure, sitting in the rose gardens or descending the mansion staircase.

I hope the Trasks' legacy has brought her peace. Their beloved Yaddo has brought peace and inspiration to countless others.

THE ROSE GARDEN (PREVIOUS), a gift from Spencer Trask to his wife, was designed by the couple. Four statues represent the seasons; in the woods, the Christalan statue stands proud.

YADDO ROCK GARDEN

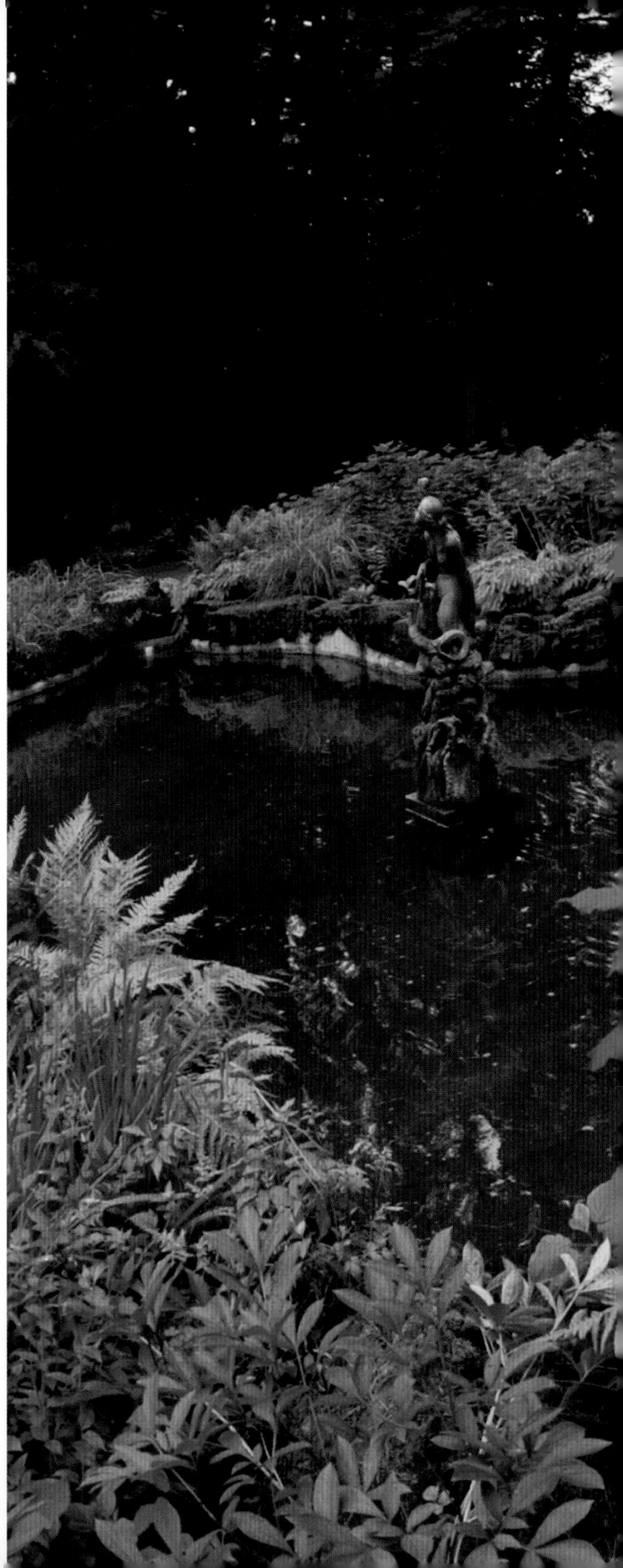

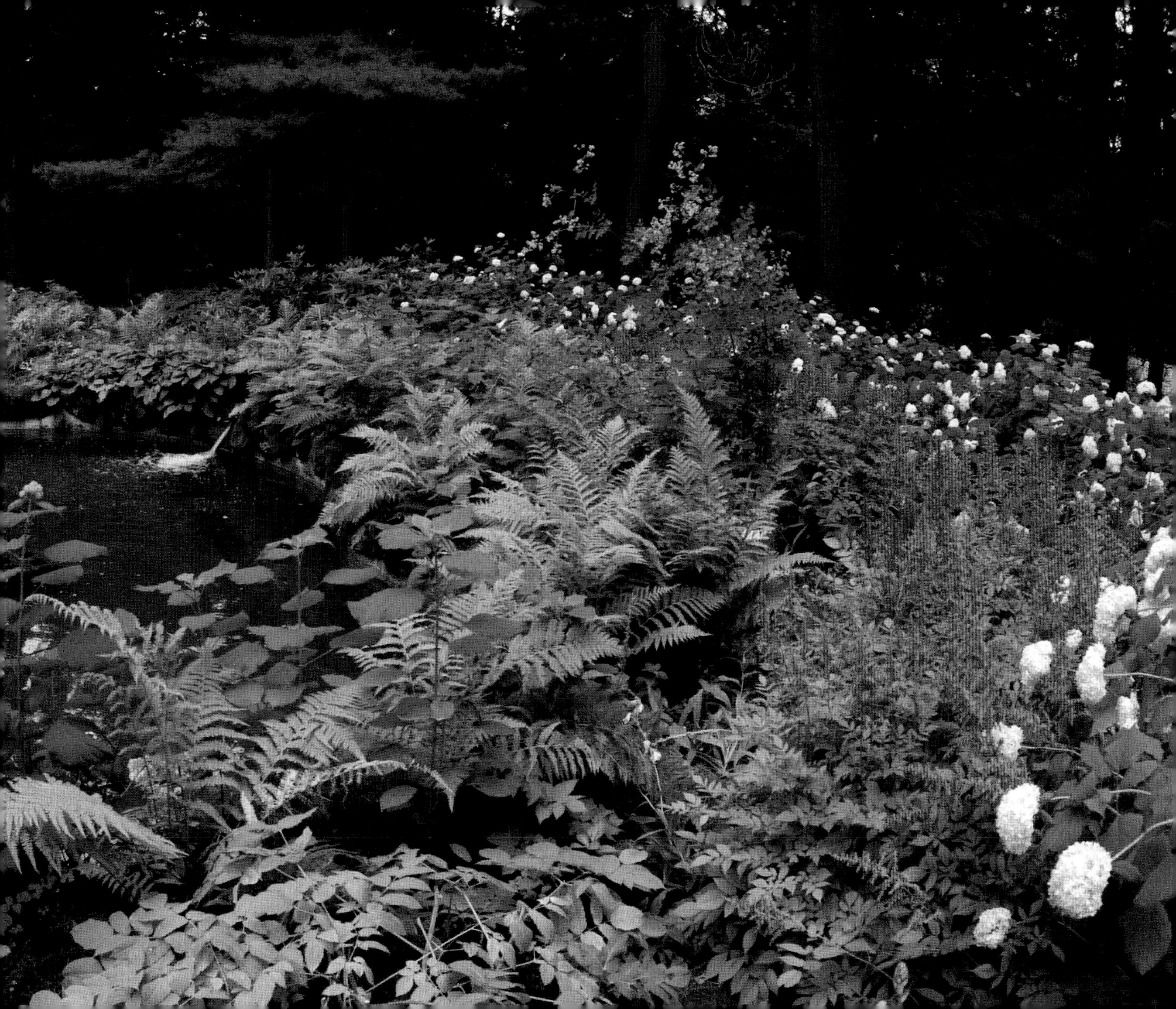

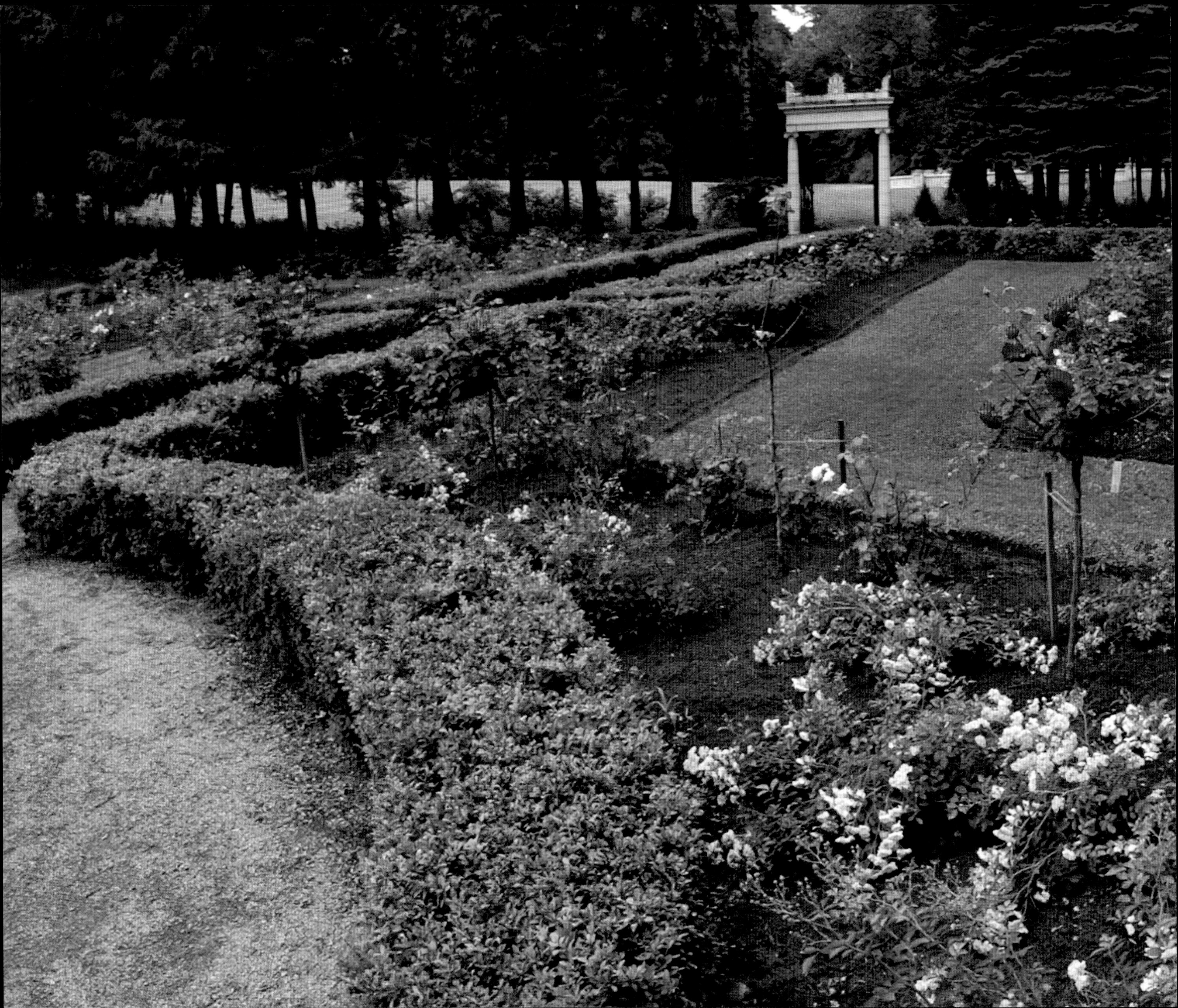

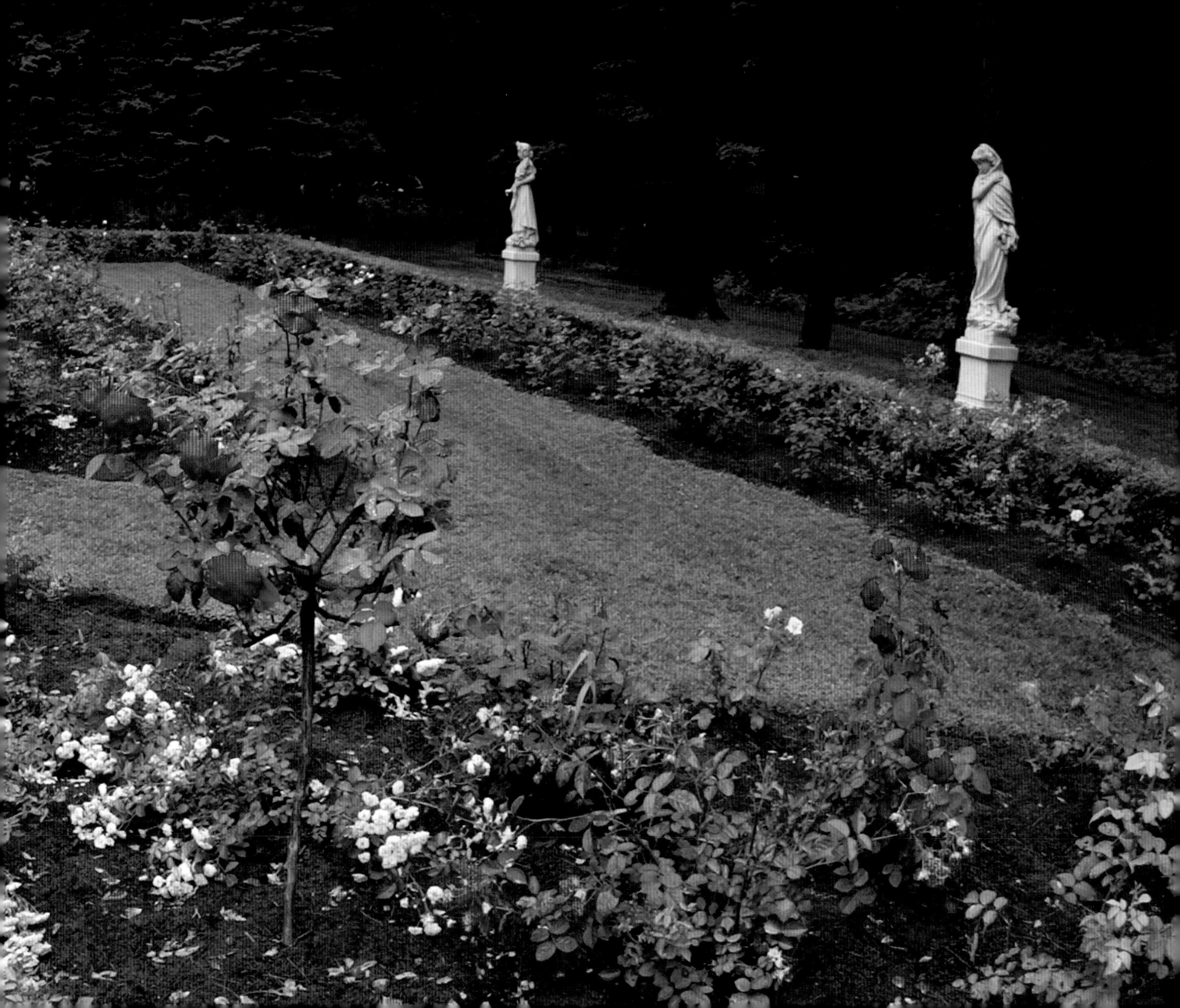

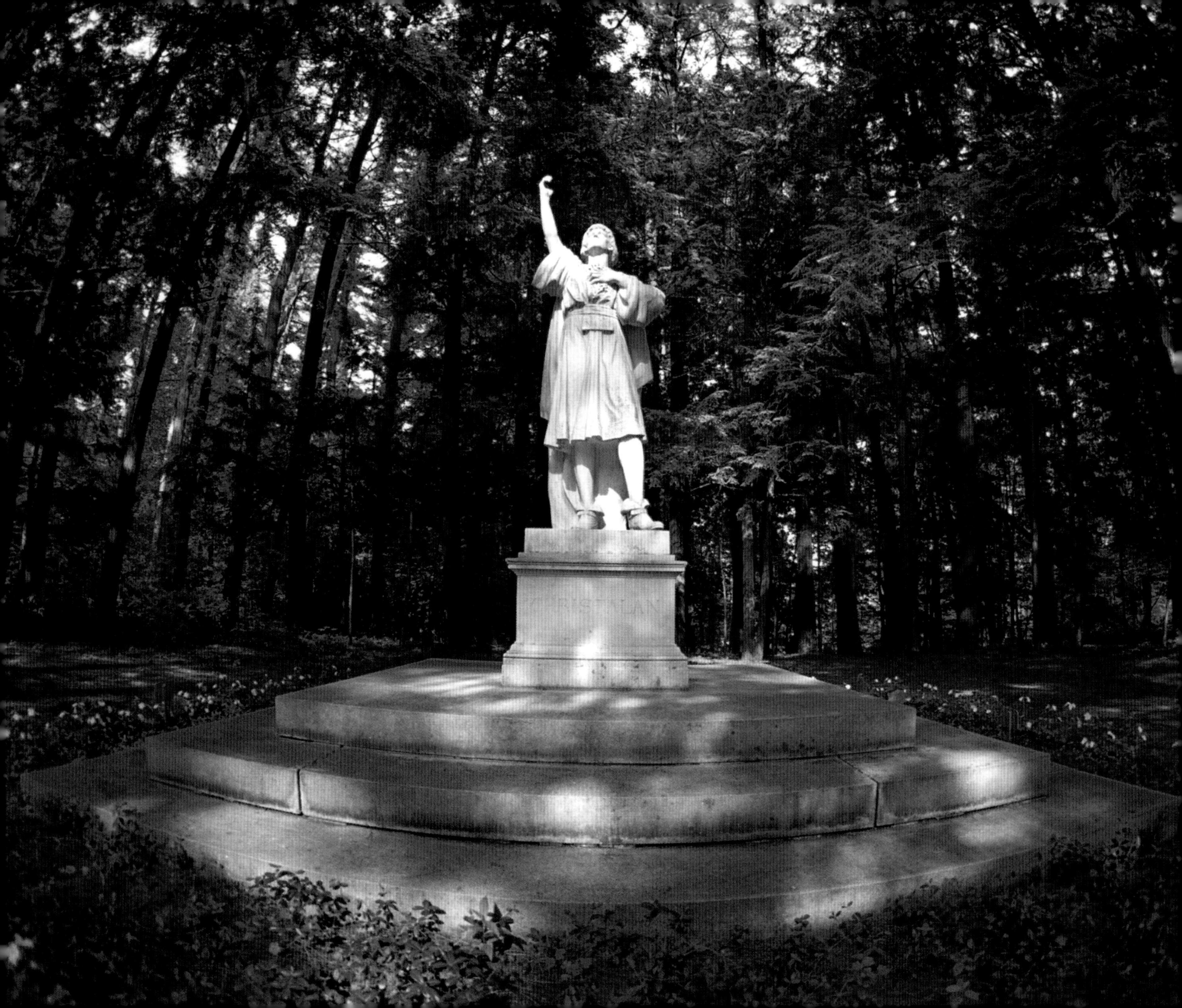

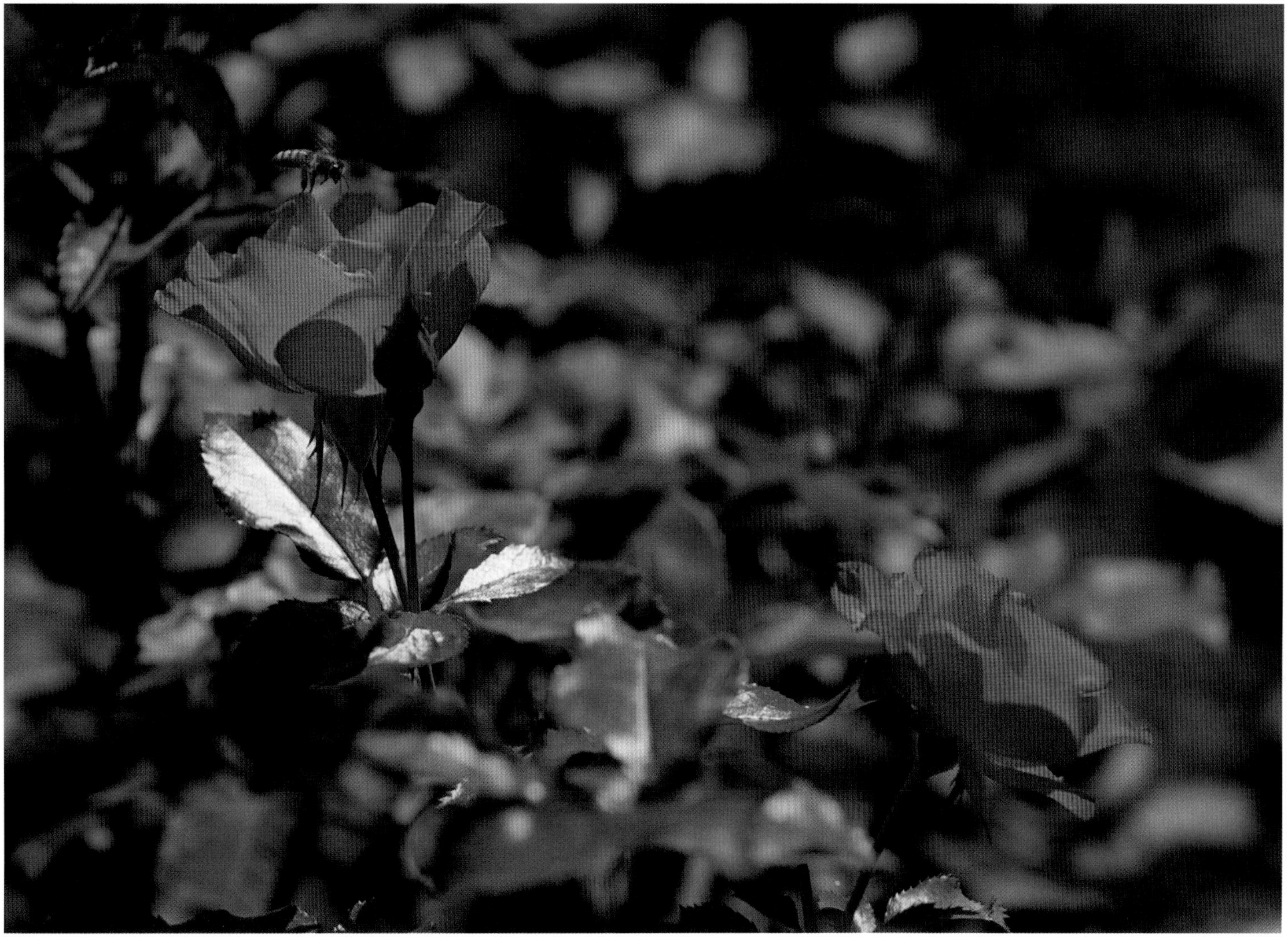

THE YADDO ROSE GARDEN (PREVIOUS, ABOVE) in late summer.

THE CHRISTALAN STATUE (LEFT), crafted by William Ordway Partridge as a memorial to the Trasks' four children (all of whom died in childhood), represents youth, chivalry, and victory over mortality.

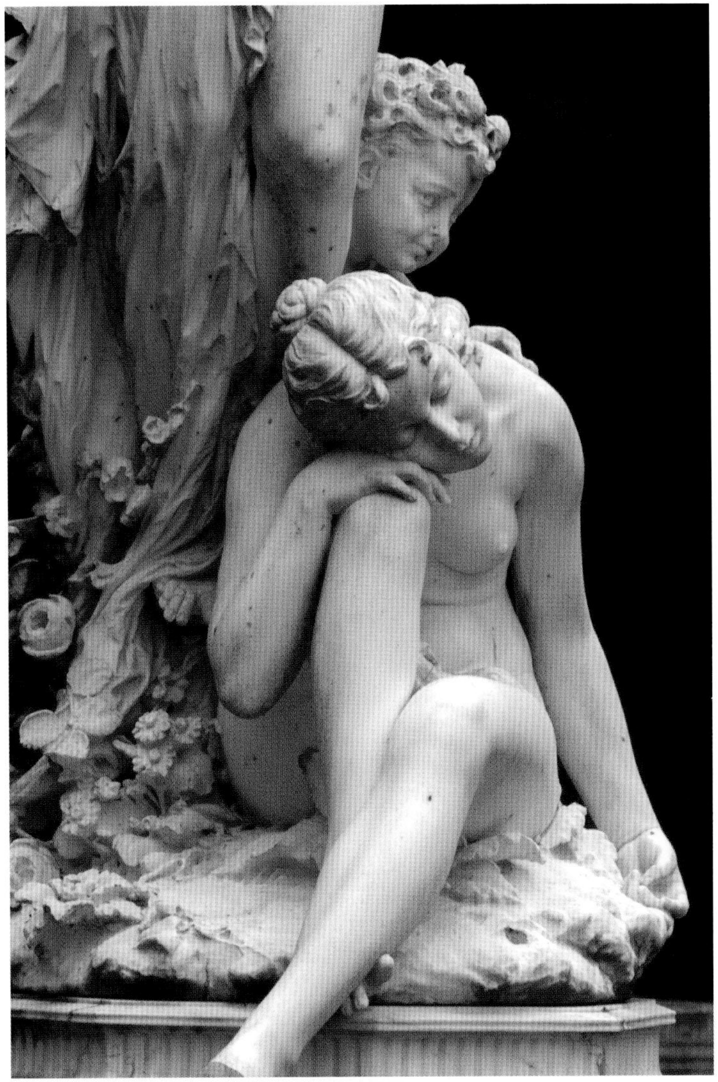

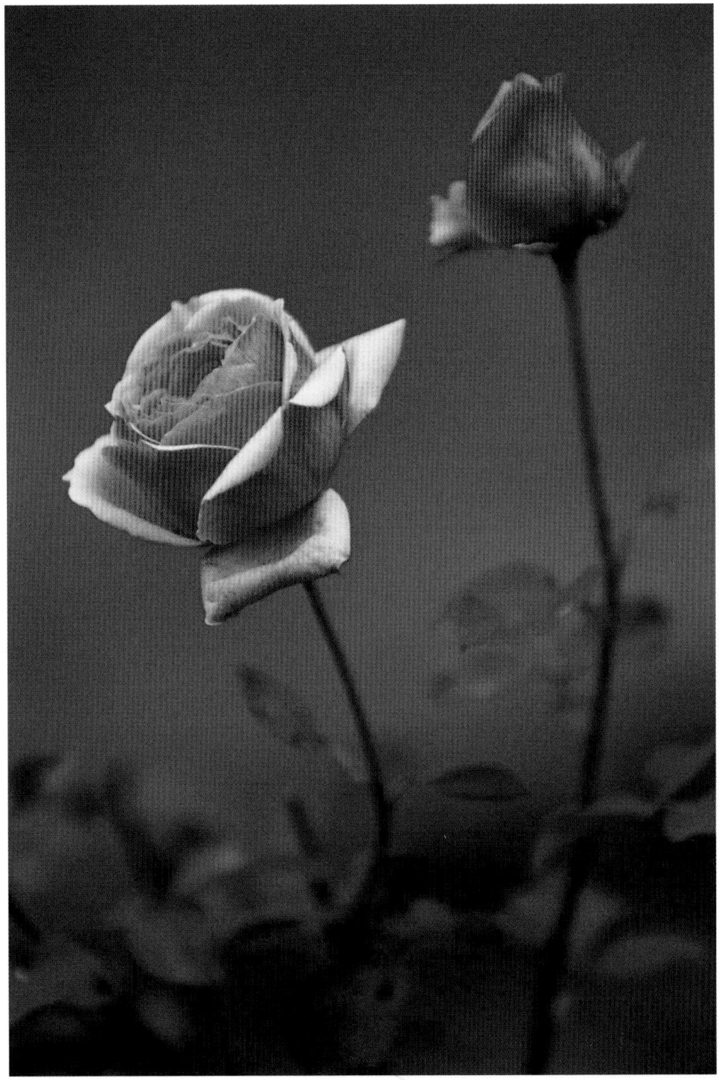

YADDO was so named by the Trasks' four-year-old daughter, Christina, in 1881. Christina told her mother, "Call it 'Yaddo,' Mamma, for it makes poetry! Yaddo, shadow — shadow, Yaddo!"

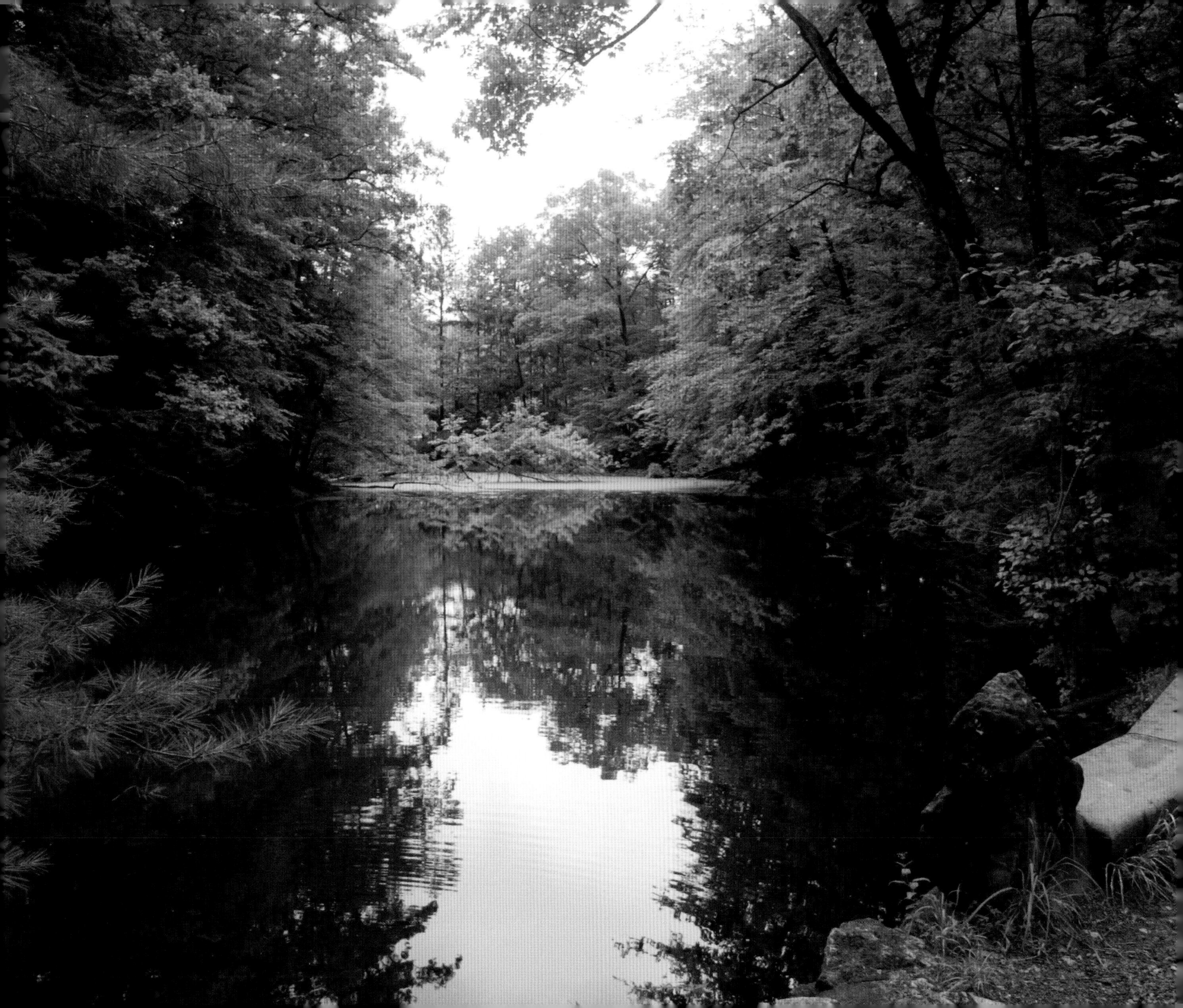

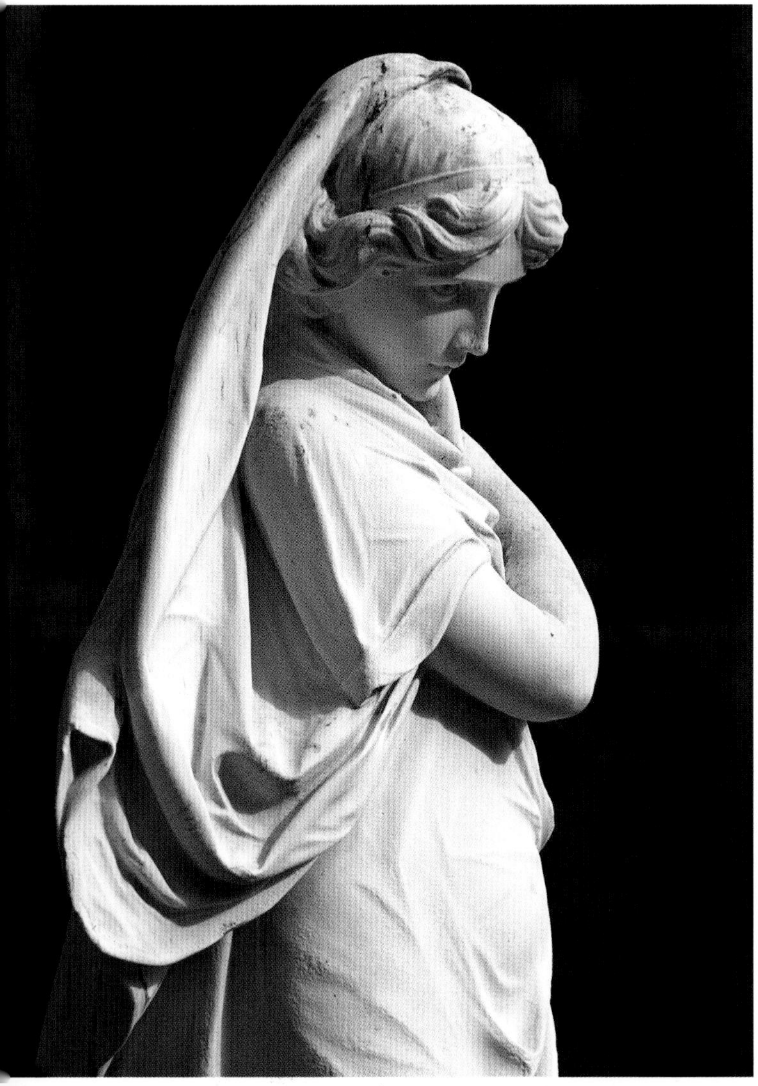

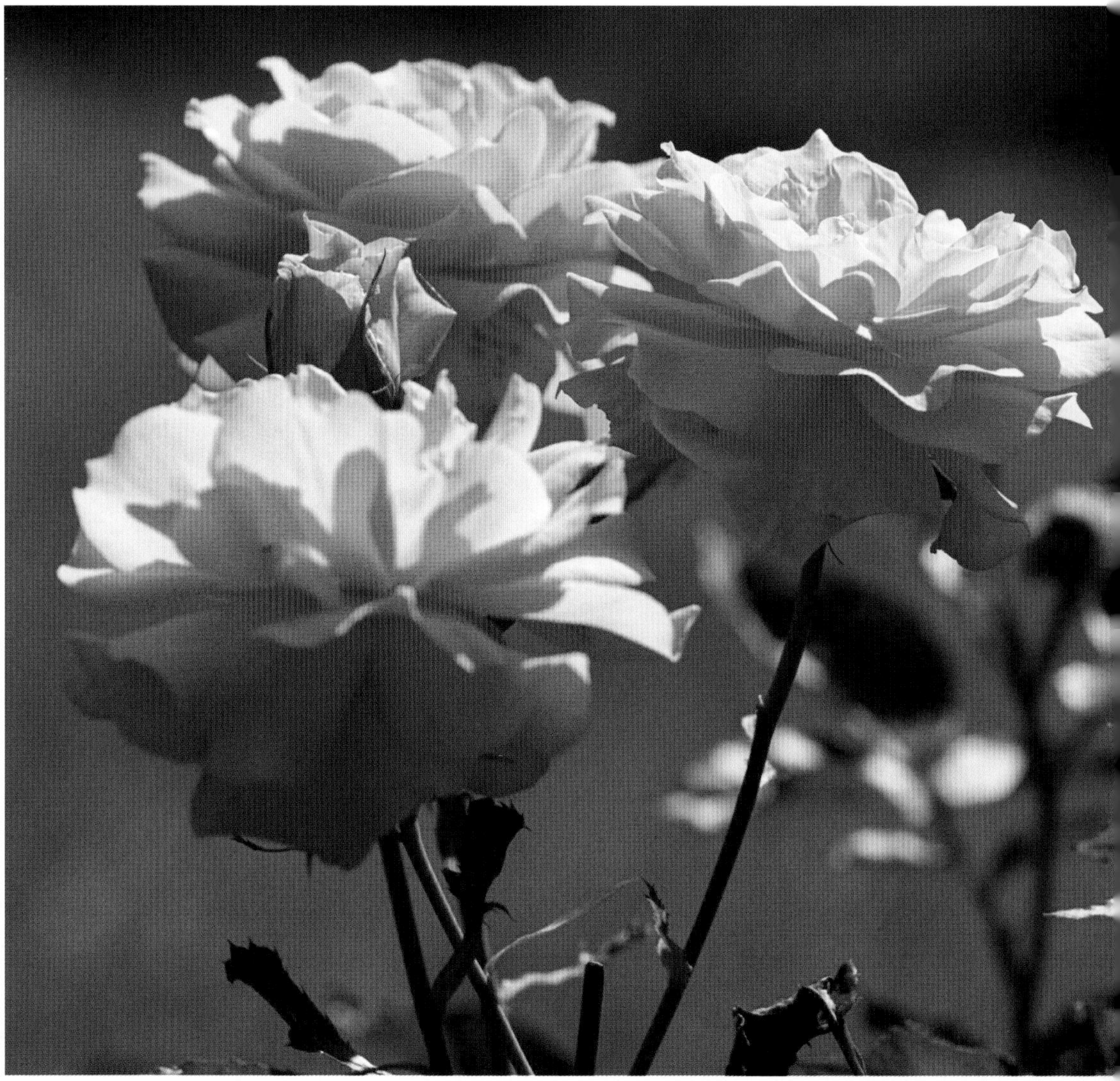

YADDO BEAUTIES — The Yaddo sundial (right) features a poem written for Katrina by longtime friend Henry van Dyke.

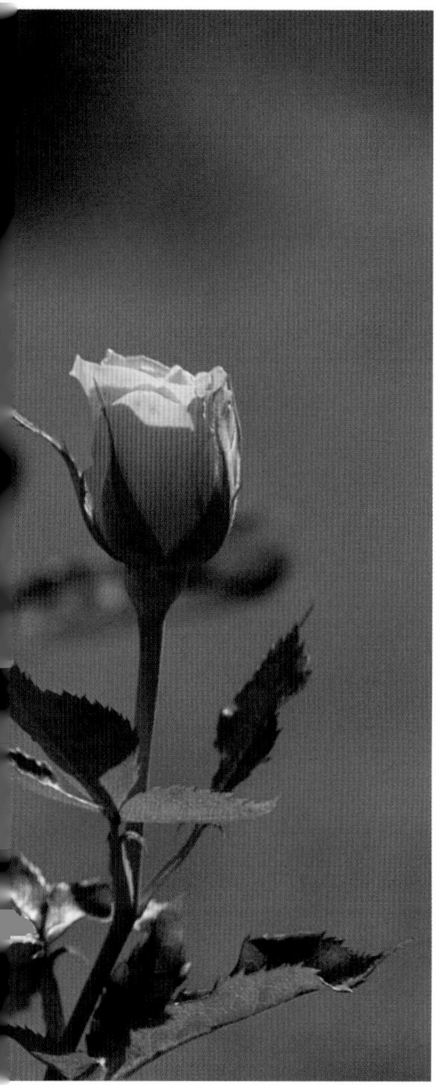

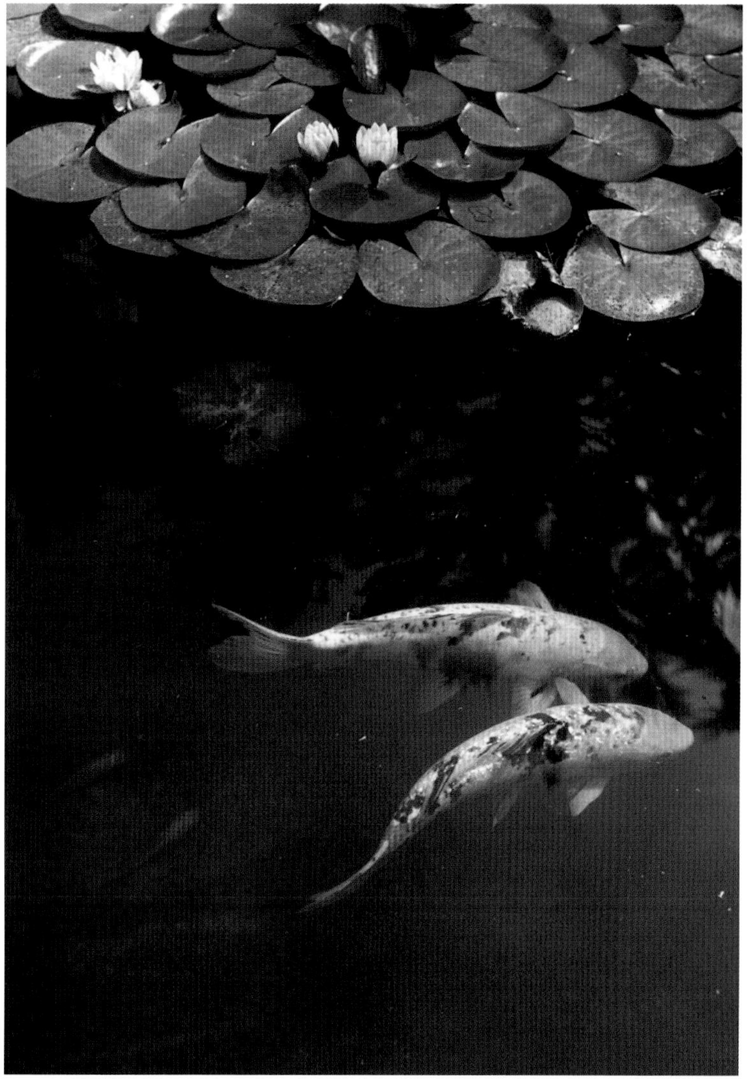

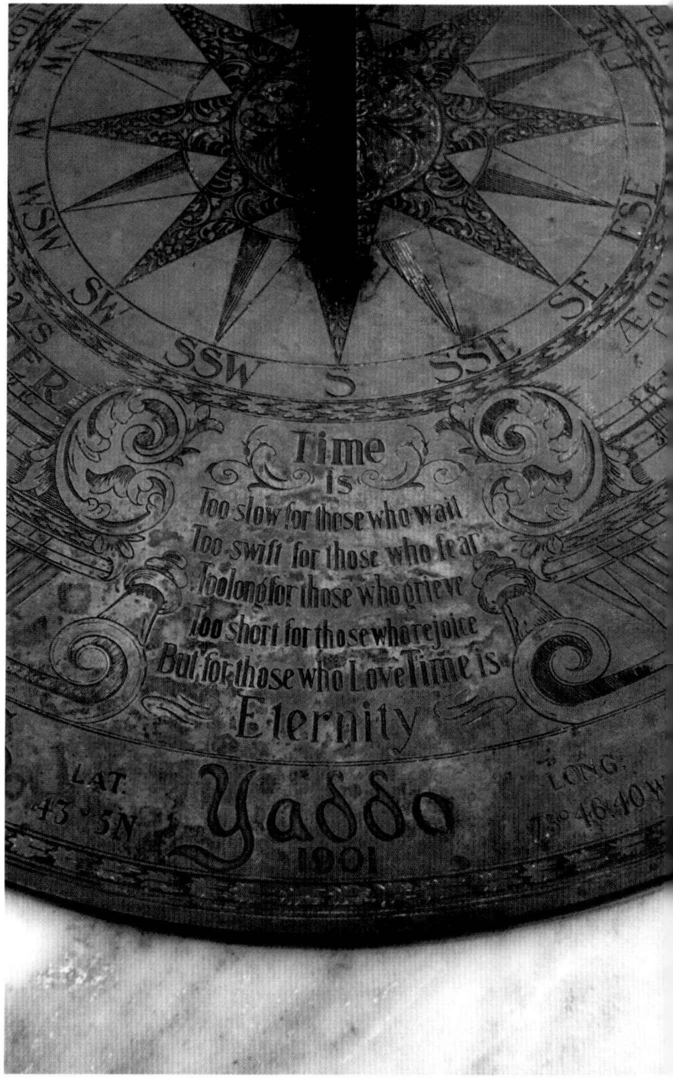
WSW
SW
SSW
S
SSE
SE
ESE
Time
is
Too slow for those who wait
Too swift for those who fear
Too long for those who grieve
Too short for those who rejoice
But for those who Love Time is
Eternity
LAT.
LONG.
Yaddo
1901

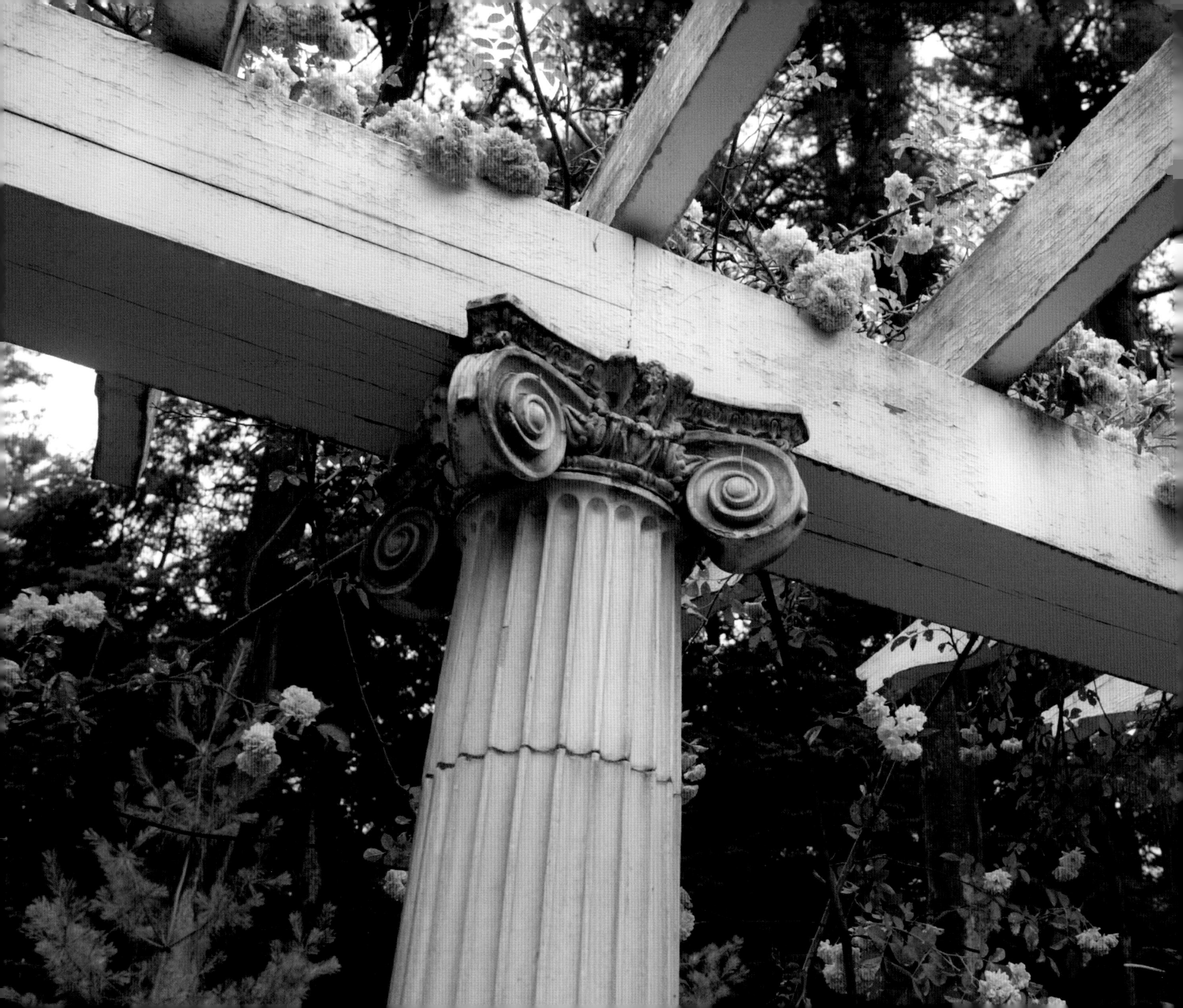

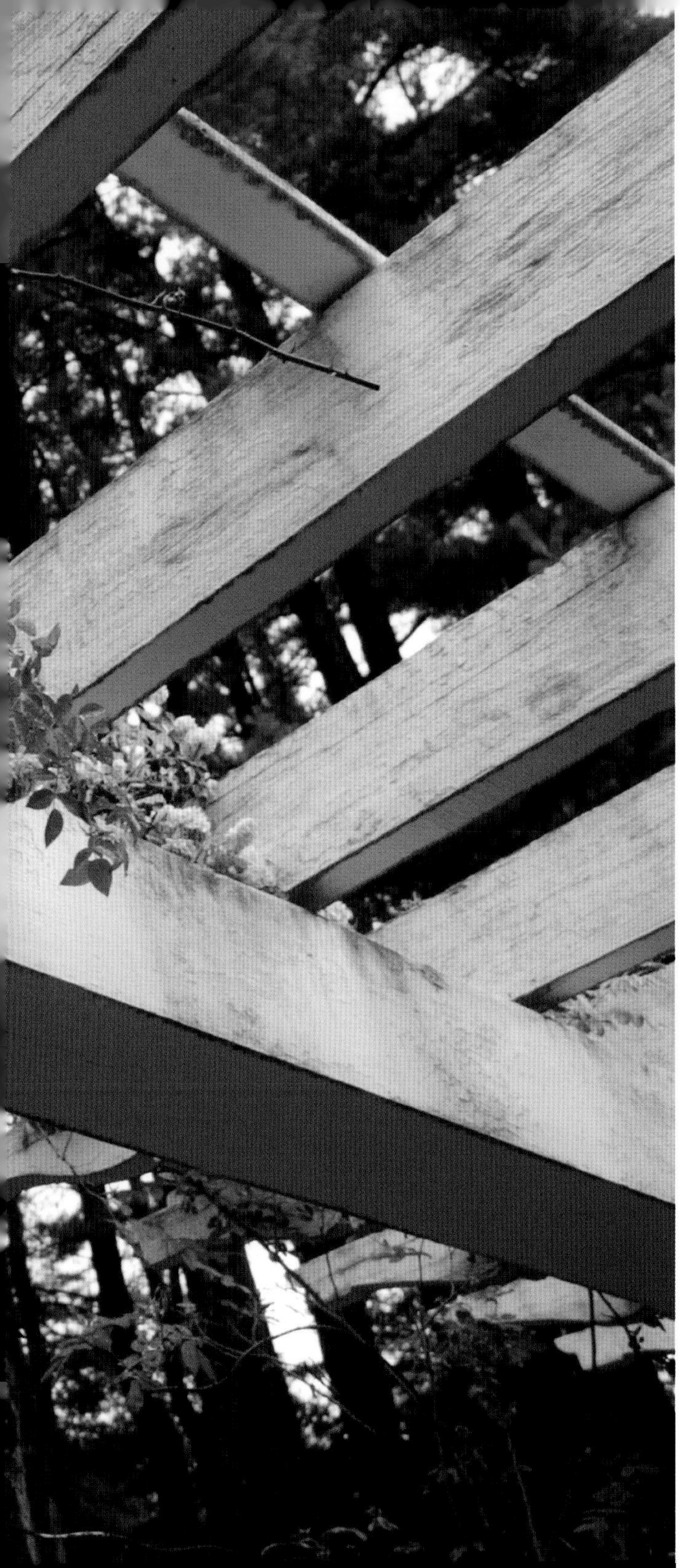

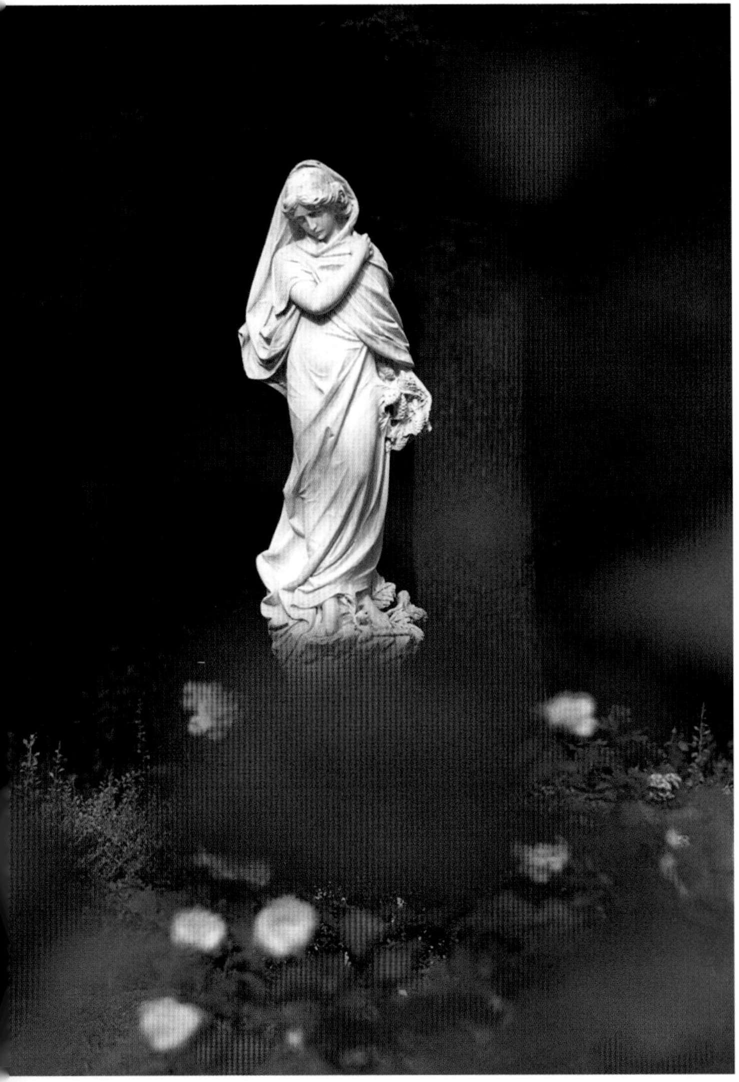

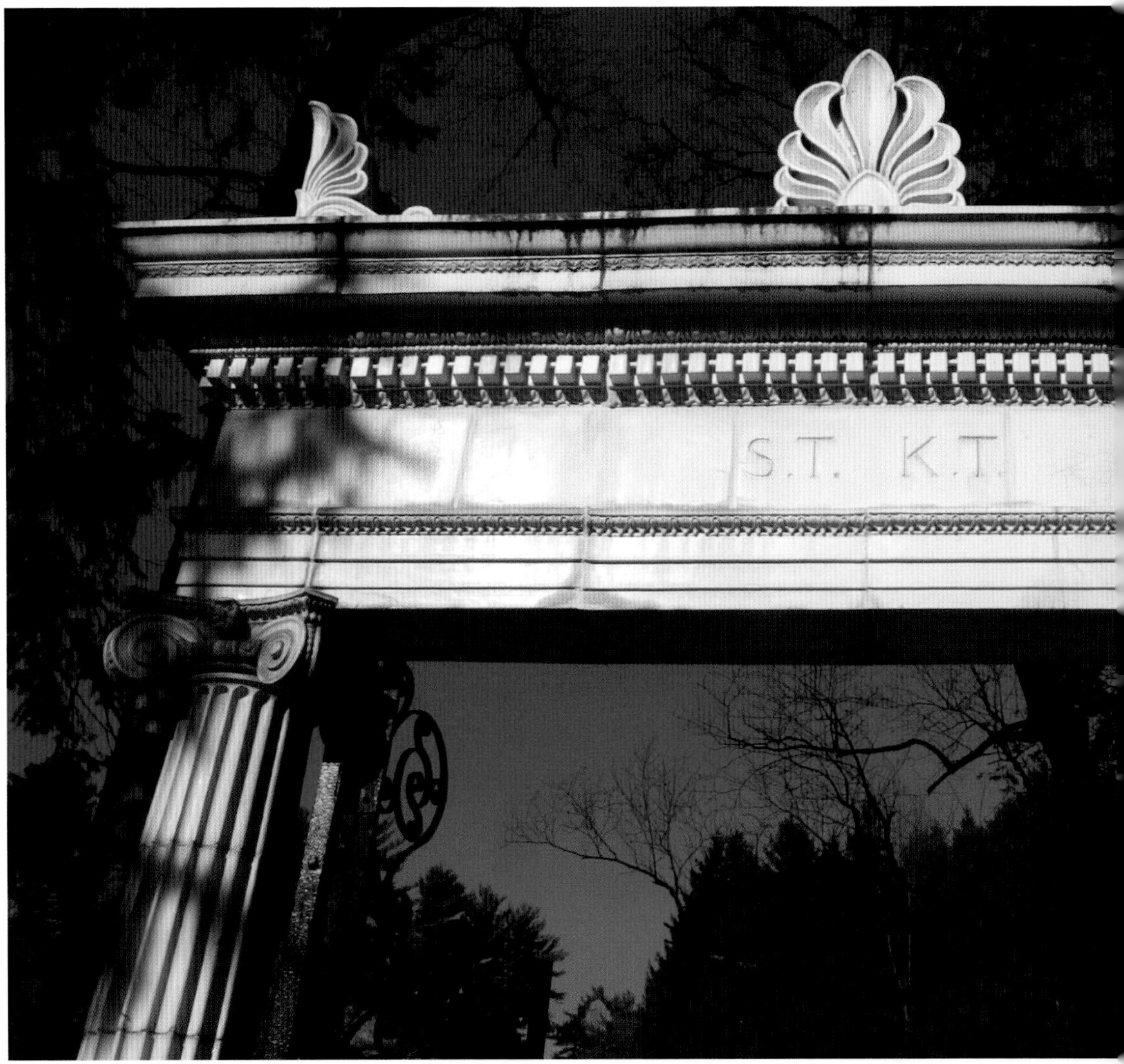

SPENCER AND KATRINA TRASKS' INITIALS (CENTER) grace the beautiful rose garden entryway.

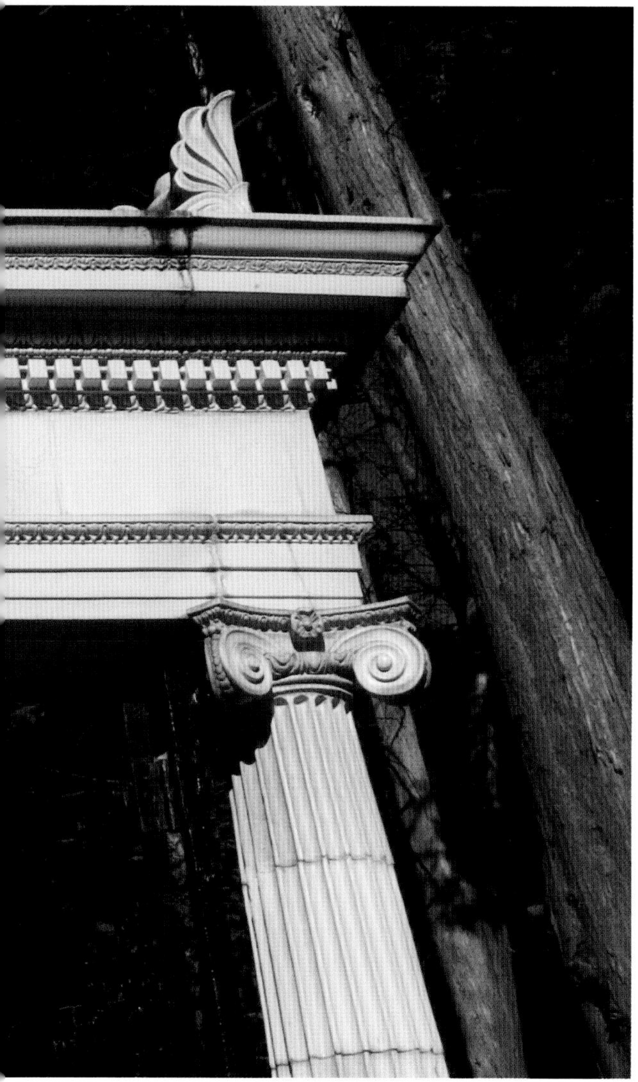

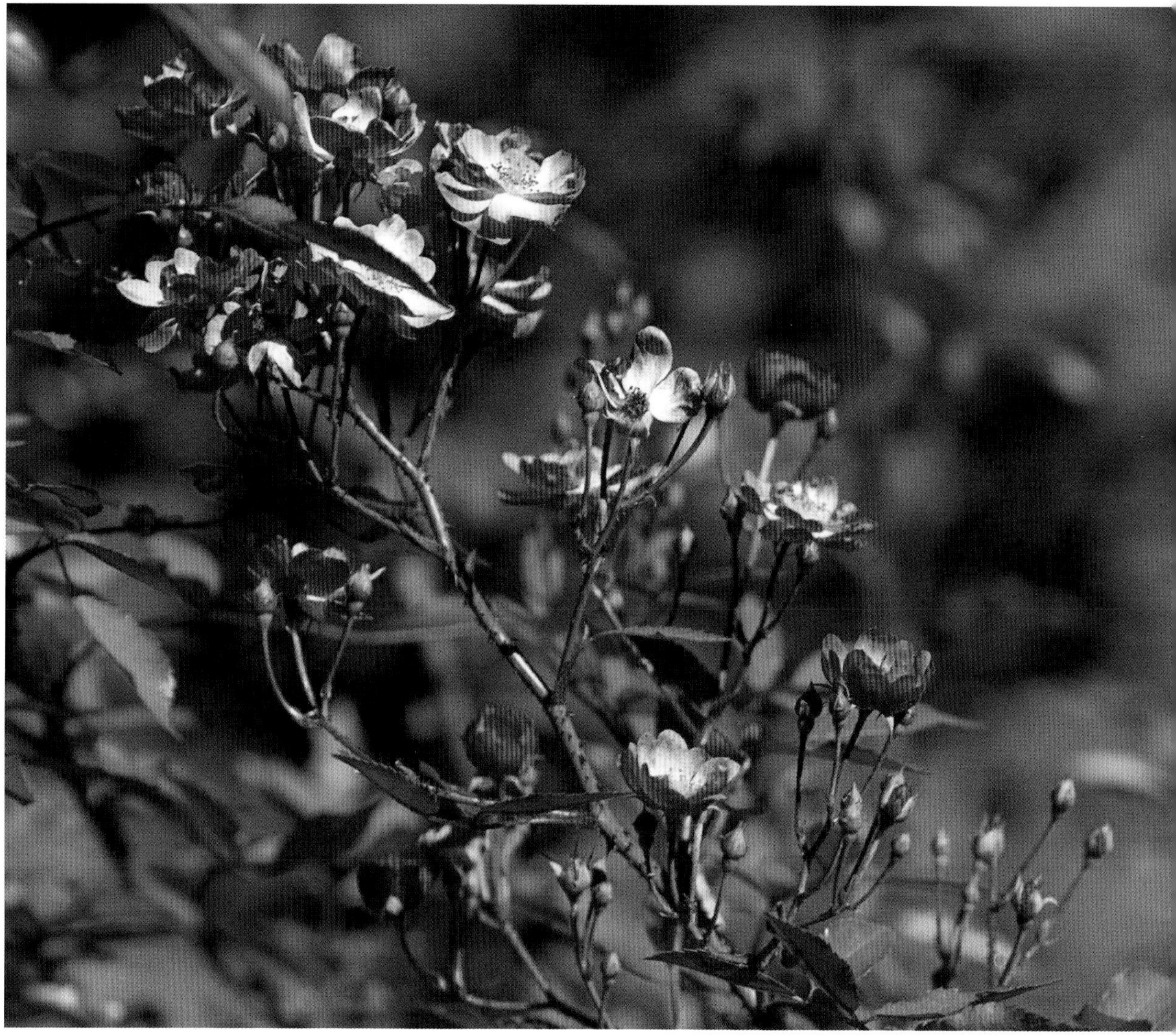

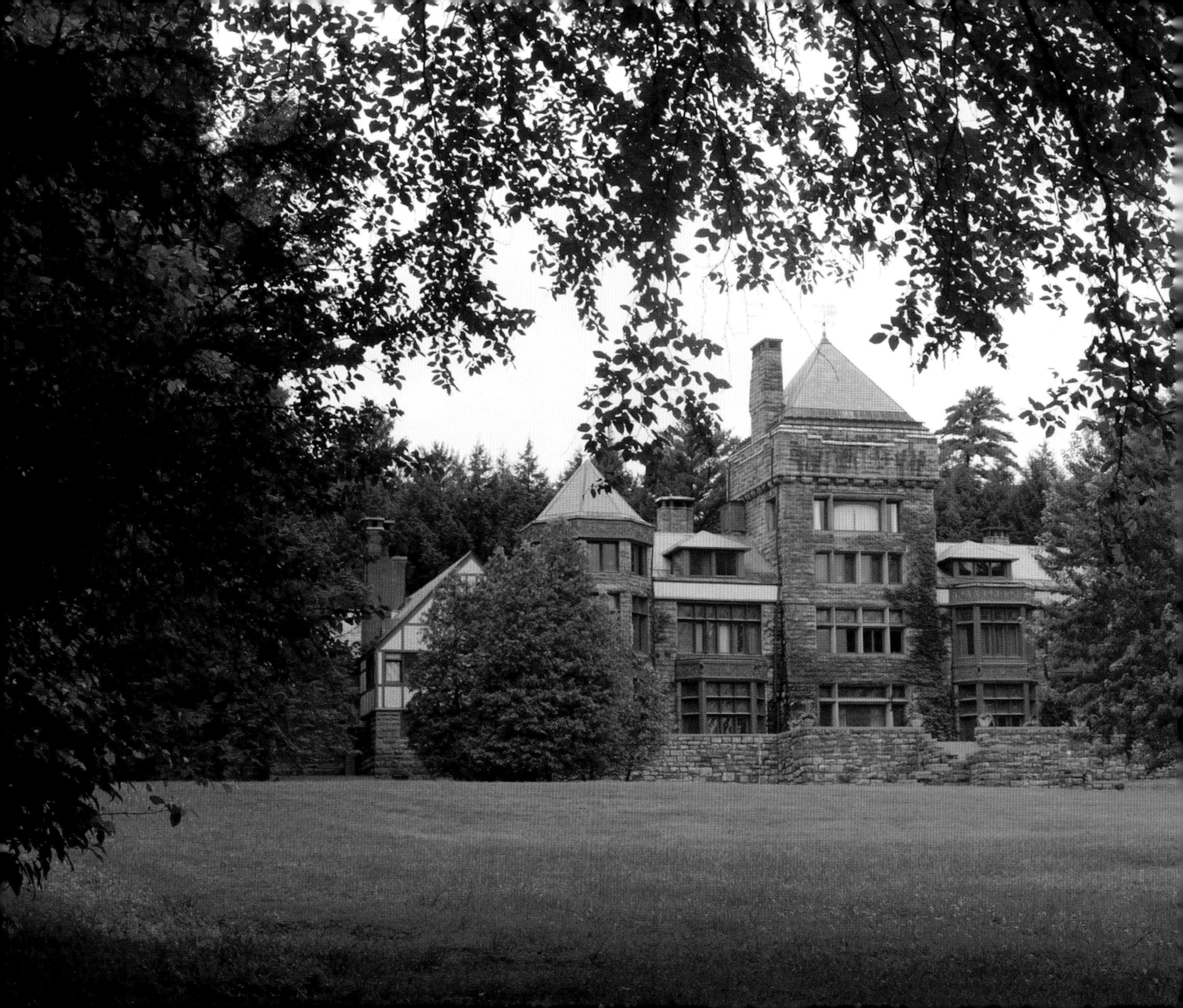

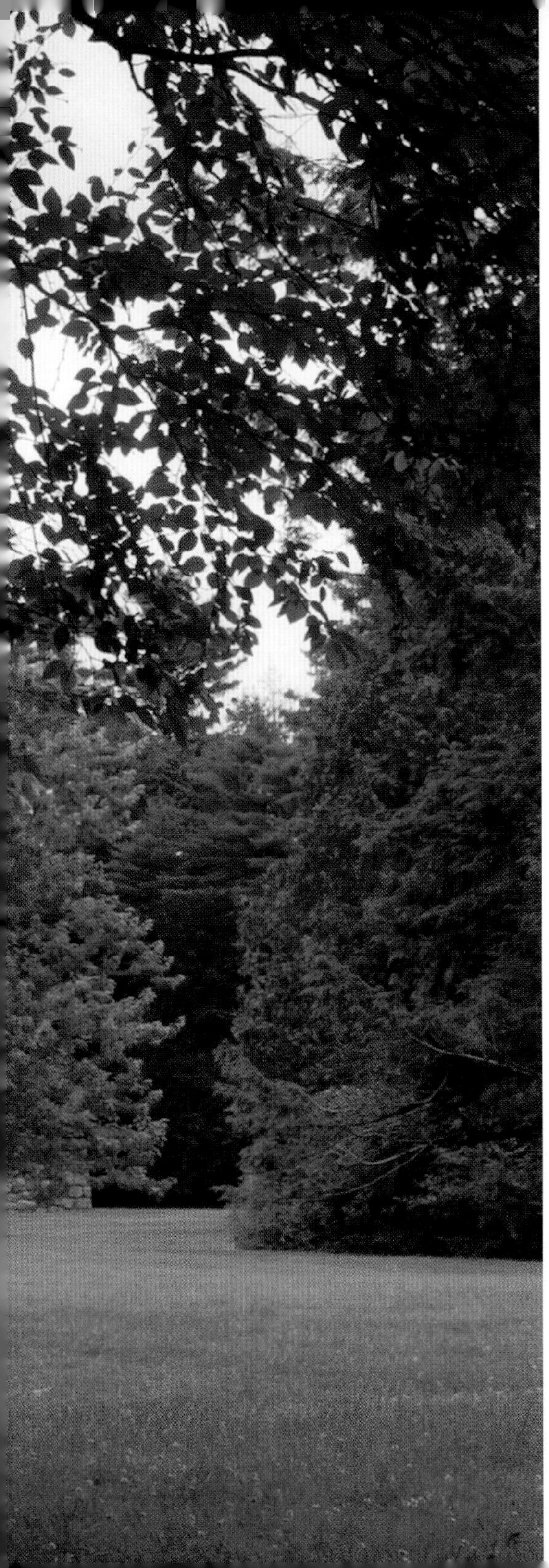

THE YADDO MANSION
Yaddo has hosted nearly 5,500 artists, including such immortal names as Truman Capote, John Cheever, Leonard Bernstein, Aaron Copland, Langston Hughes, Sylvia Plath, Mario Puzo, Katherine Anne Porter, and Henri Cartier-Bresson.

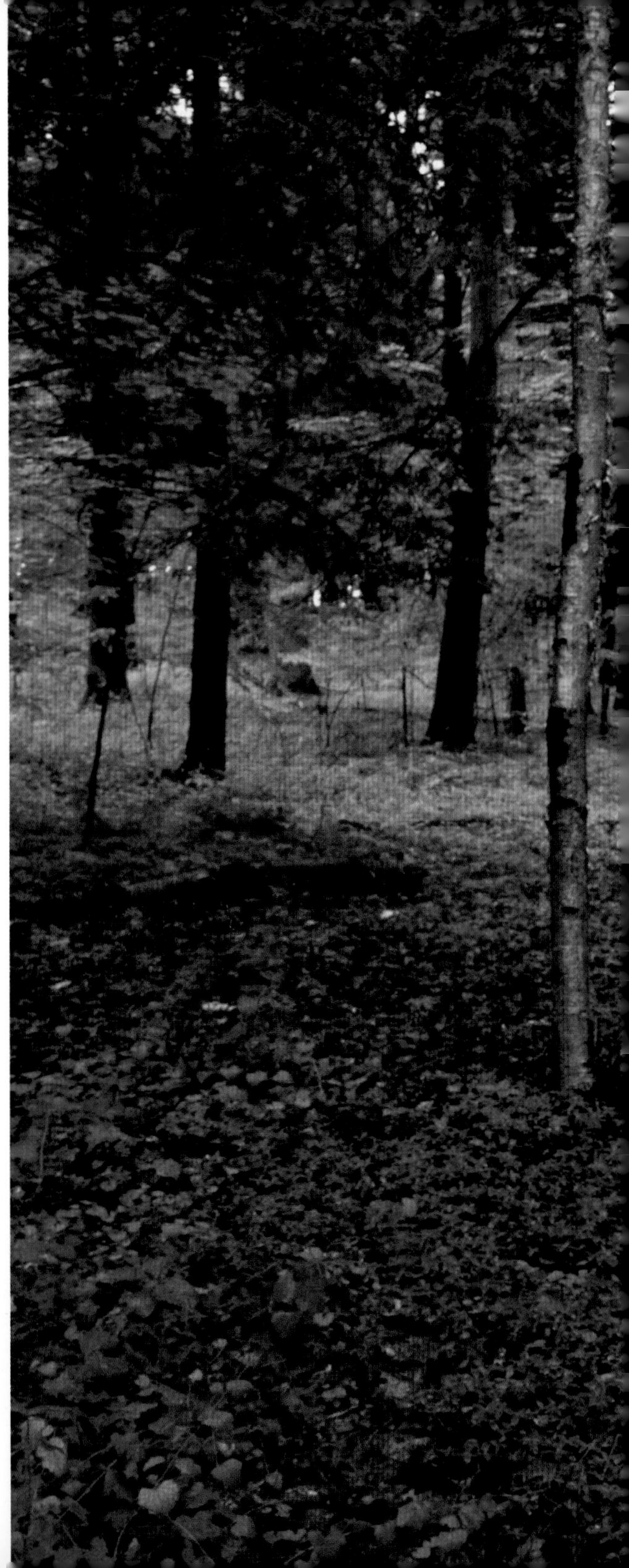

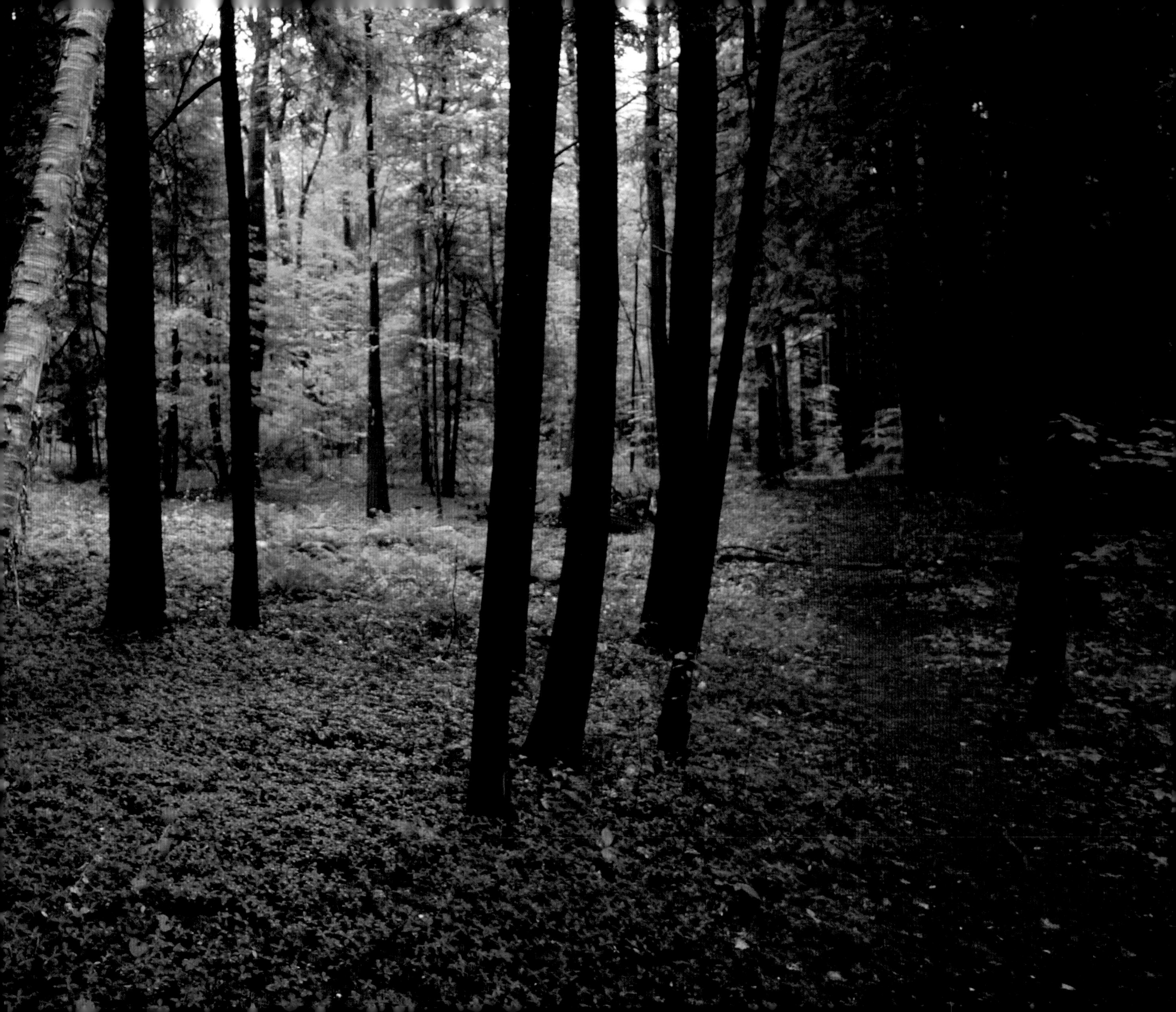

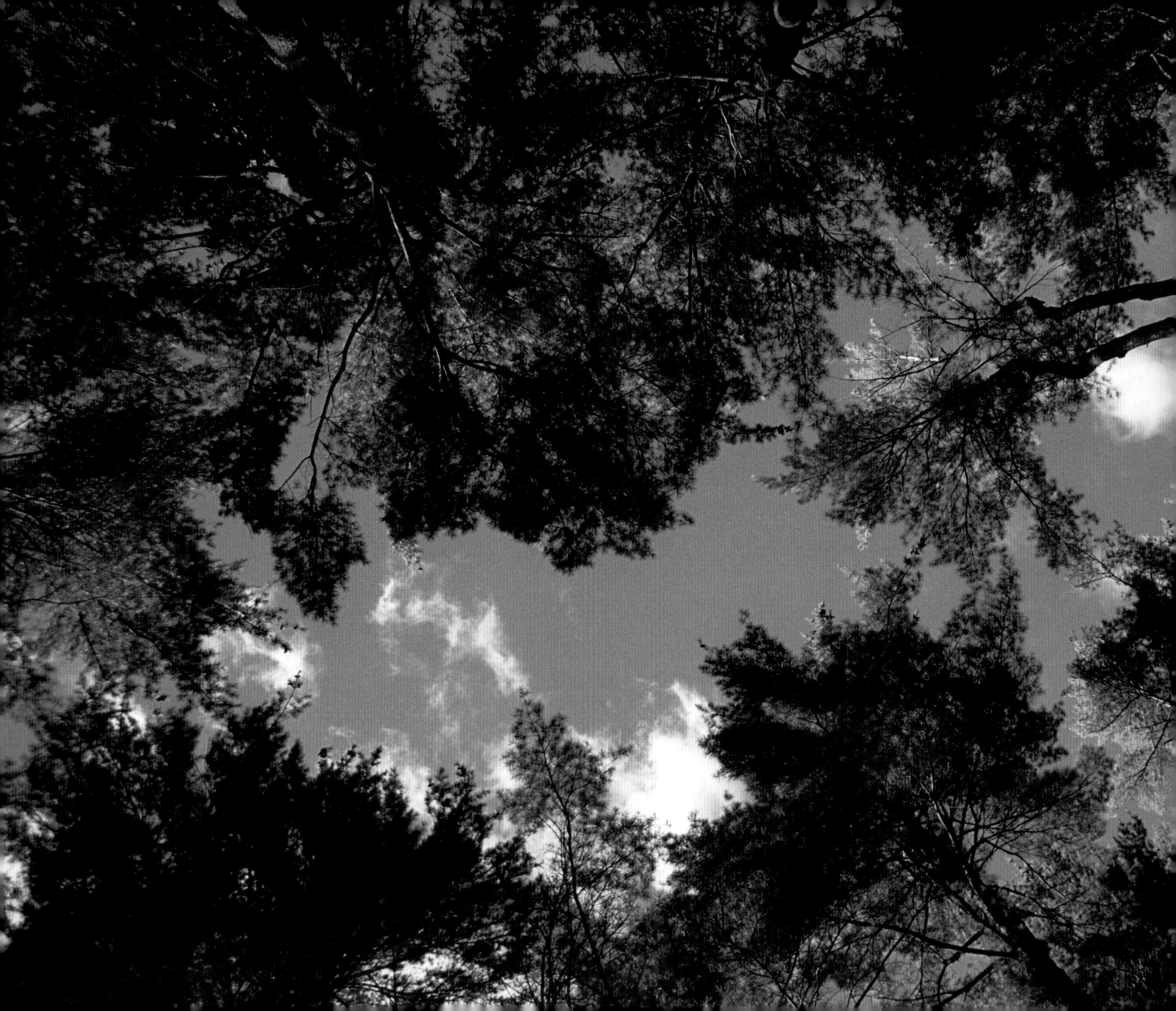

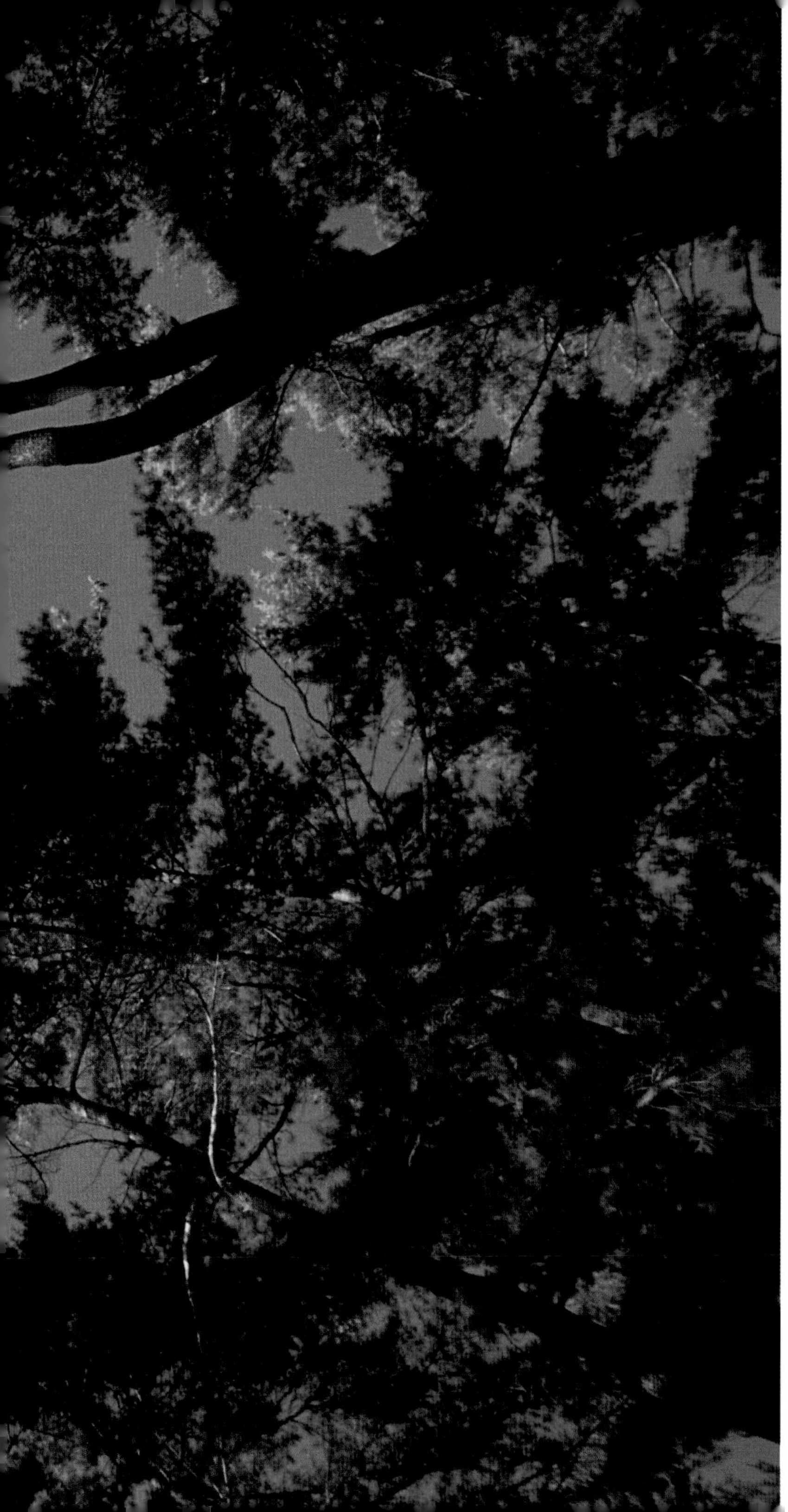

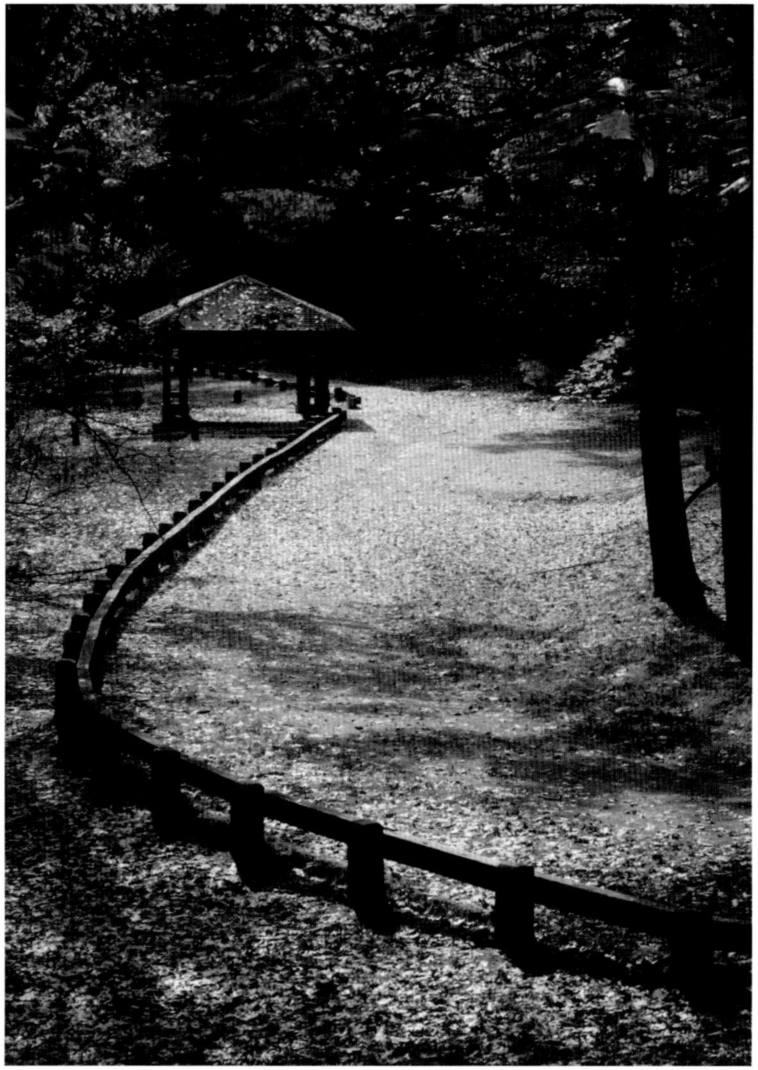

Saratoga Outings

The National Trust for Historic Preservation named Saratoga Springs one of America's Dozen Distinctive Destinations, and the city has received the prestigious Great American Main Street Award. But Saratoga's charms extend well beyond city limits.

In an area rich with treasures, visitors are drawn by the Saratoga Spa State Park and National Historical Park, Petrified Sea Gardens, and Saratoga Lake. Beautiful rural roads offer relaxing day trips, and the racino offers nighttime excitement.

The State Park, a national landmark with numerous buildings on the National Historic Register, charms visitors on sun-washed days. People spread out on blankets, toss softballs, and cook burgers on the grills. Many play golf, swim, promenade down the Avenue of the Pines, or partake of spring waters.

The nearby Saratoga battlefield sparks the imagination and haunts the senses. The battles here are considered among the most decisive in world history — and the turning point of the Revolutionary War.

It is easy to imagine 1777 when the Americans, fighting for independence, were disheartened by a series of agonizing defeats by the British. Yet here, on these now quiet, rolling lands, the Americans first forced a British surrender.

On early mornings and late afternoons, when the tour road is closed, the ghosts of some fifteen hundred lost soldiers seem to come to life. Mists and sunlight play tricks on the imagination as owls hoot, bullfrogs sing, and deer slip through the shadows.

The Petrified Sea Gardens lies just west of Saratoga. Winding nature trails are rich with myrtle, flowers, mushrooms, and trees. A 300-year-old Iroquois pine towers overhead. Two rare trees, the ginkgo leaf and Dawn redwood, were once thought extinct and are considered "living fossils." Yet it is other fossils — nearly an acre of exposed stromatolites, some 500,000 years old — that have drawn curious tourists since the 1930s.

A time-honored Saratoga tradition takes place on evenings when Standardbreds command center stage at the harness track.

The first-recorded horse race in the city was a harness race won by Lady Suffolk in 1847. The aging, near-white trotter was so beloved in her day she became inspiration for a still-popular folk song, "The Old Gray Mare."

Nowadays, as trotters and pacers clip-clop through the dark of night, the harness track also offers a popular gaming facility — a racino.

From morning till night, whether one prefers quiet history or glitzy action, the Saratoga area always entertains.

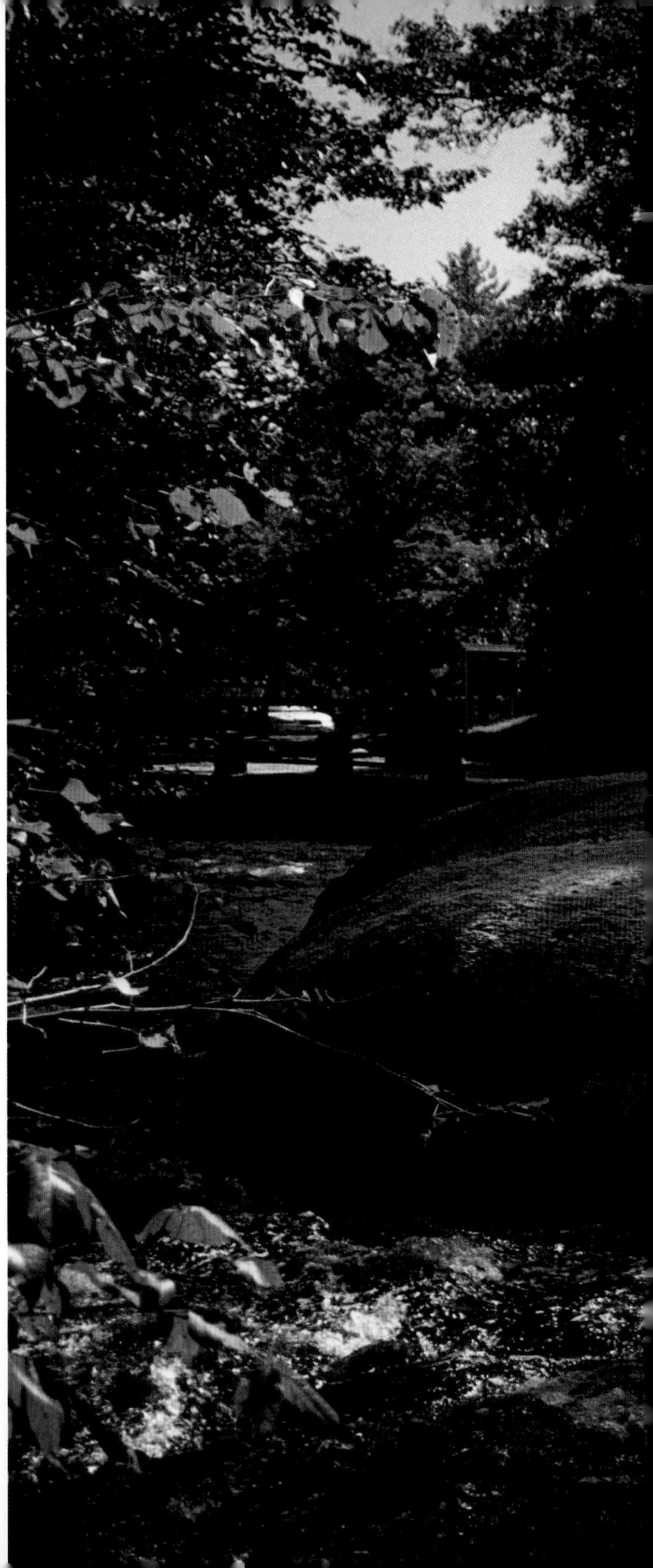

AVENUE OF THE PINES (PREVIOUS, LEFT), Saratoga Spa State Park.

"THE GEYSER," as locals call the popular island spouter in the state park.

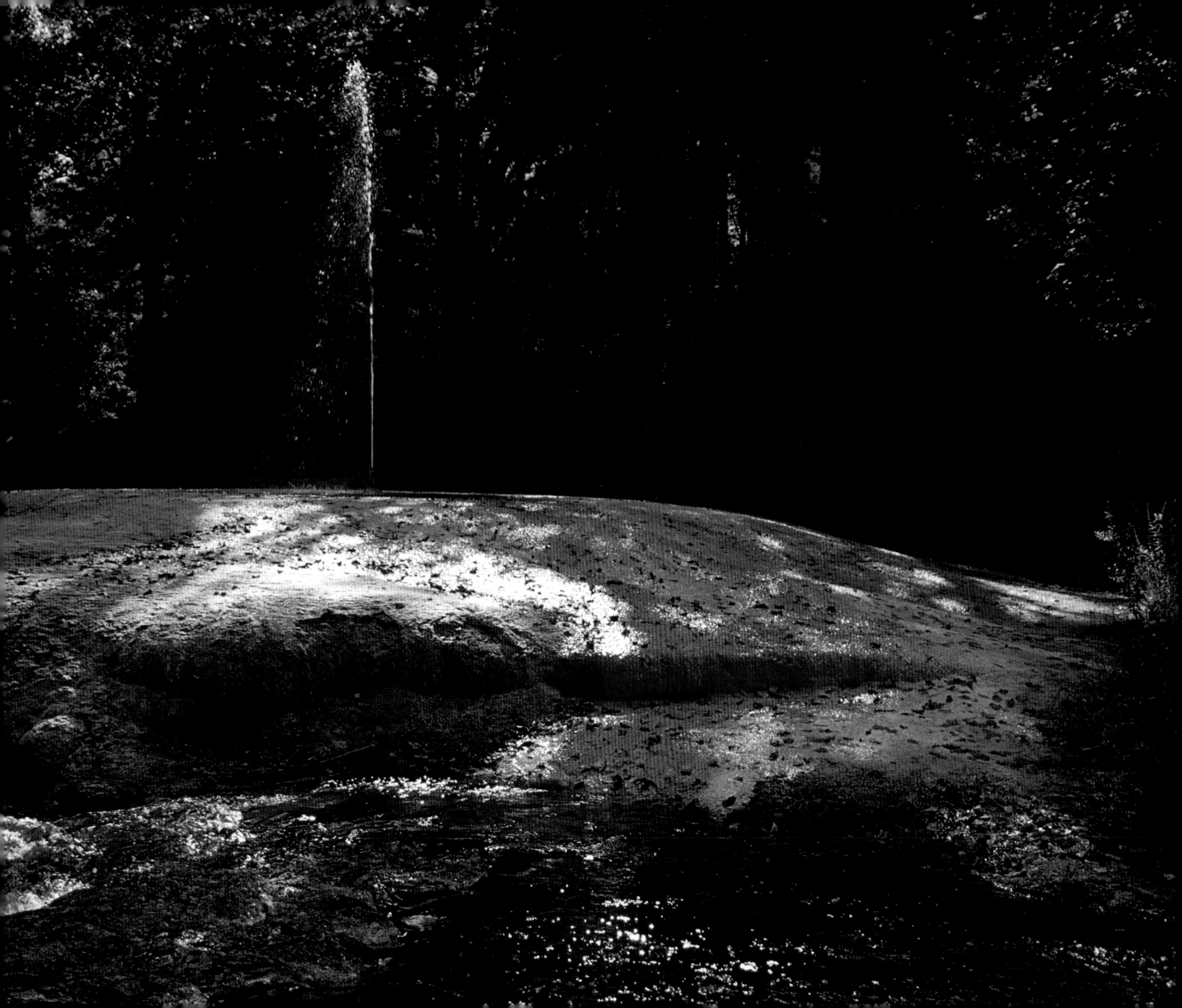

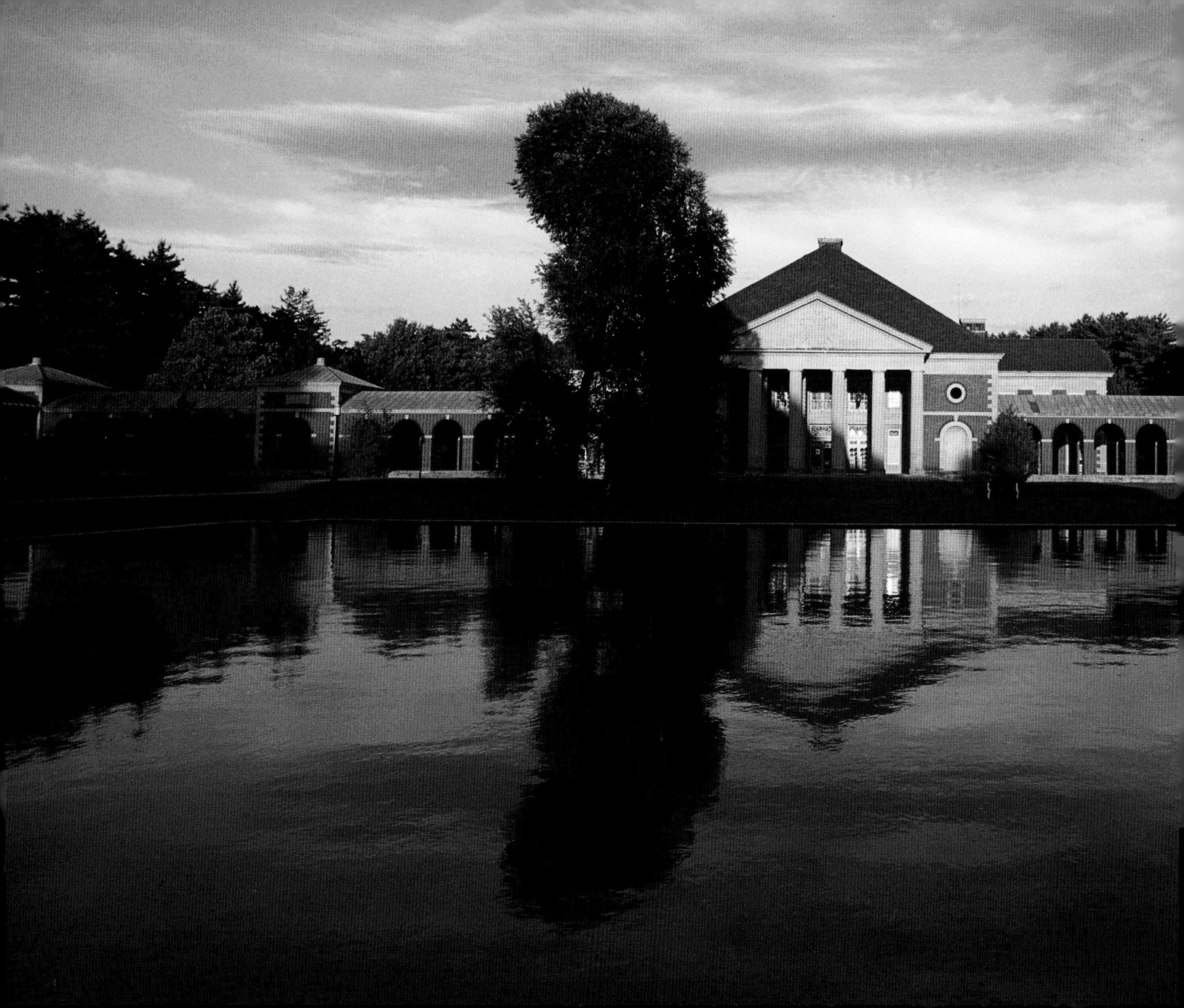

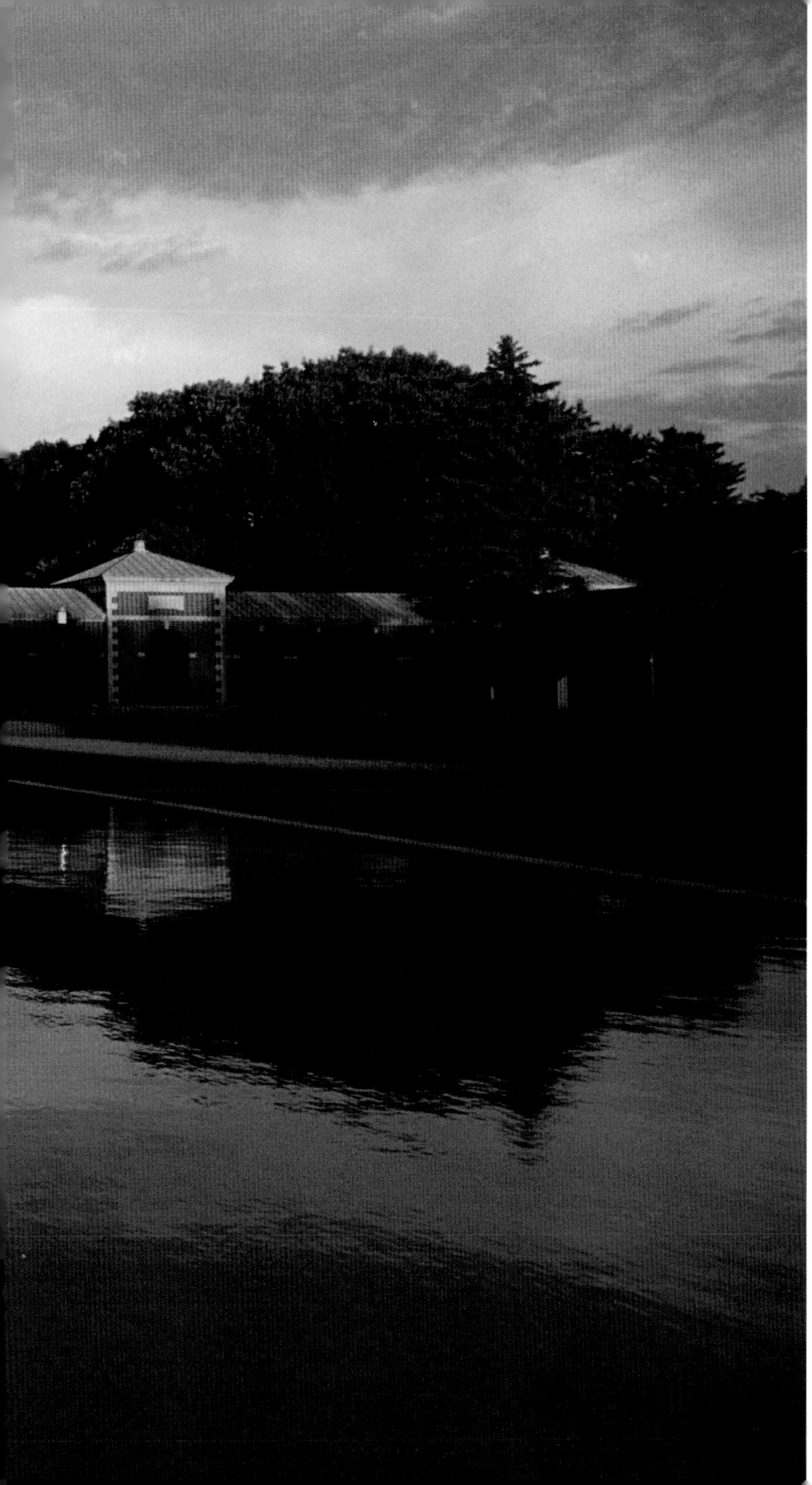

THE SARATOGA SPA STATE PARK ADMINISTRATION BUILDING in late-afternoon light.

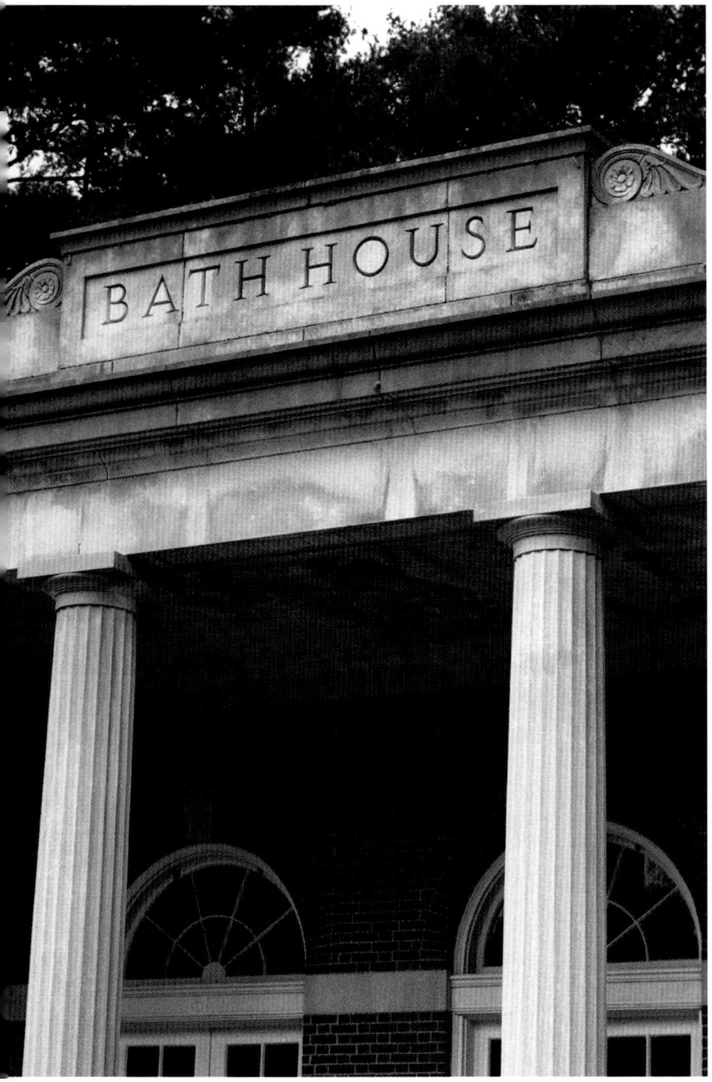

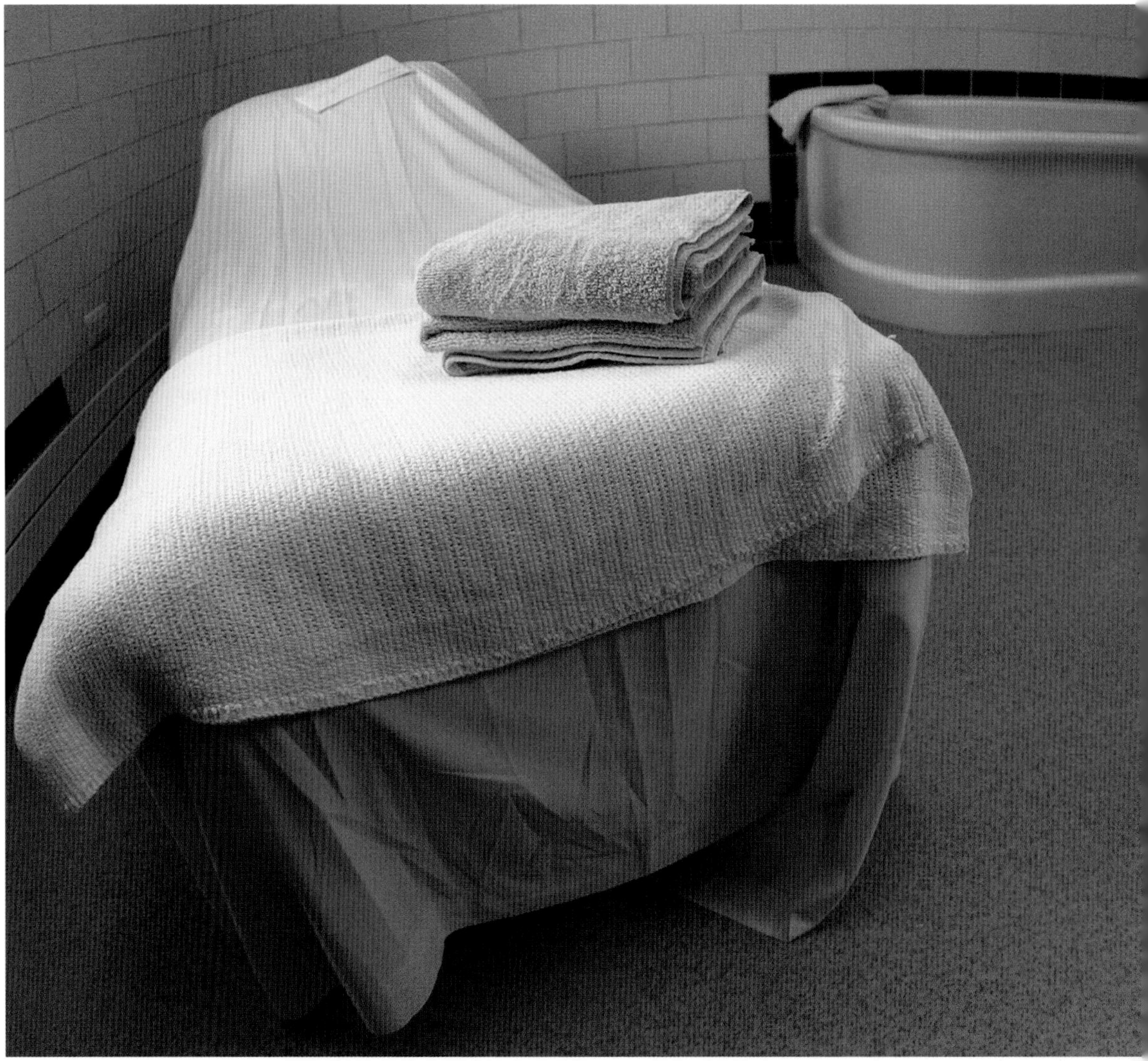

138 **QUEEN OF THE SPAS** — Saratoga has several area facilities, including Roosevelt Baths (center) at the state park, that offer relaxing baths and other pampering services.

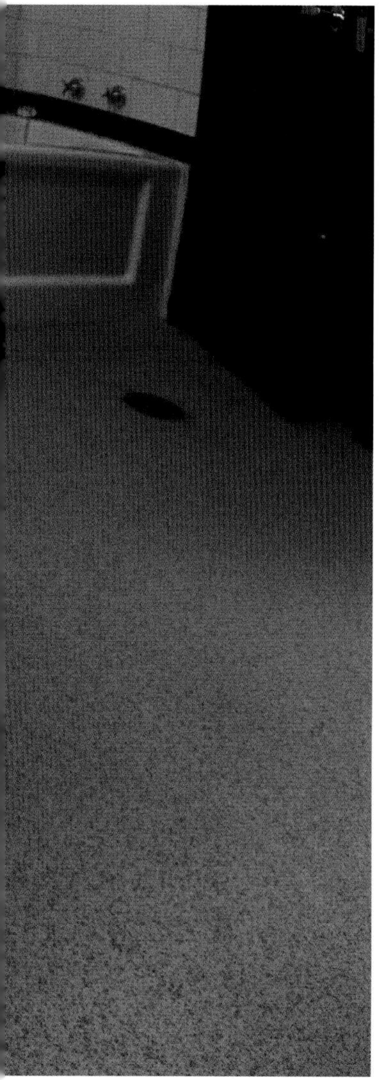

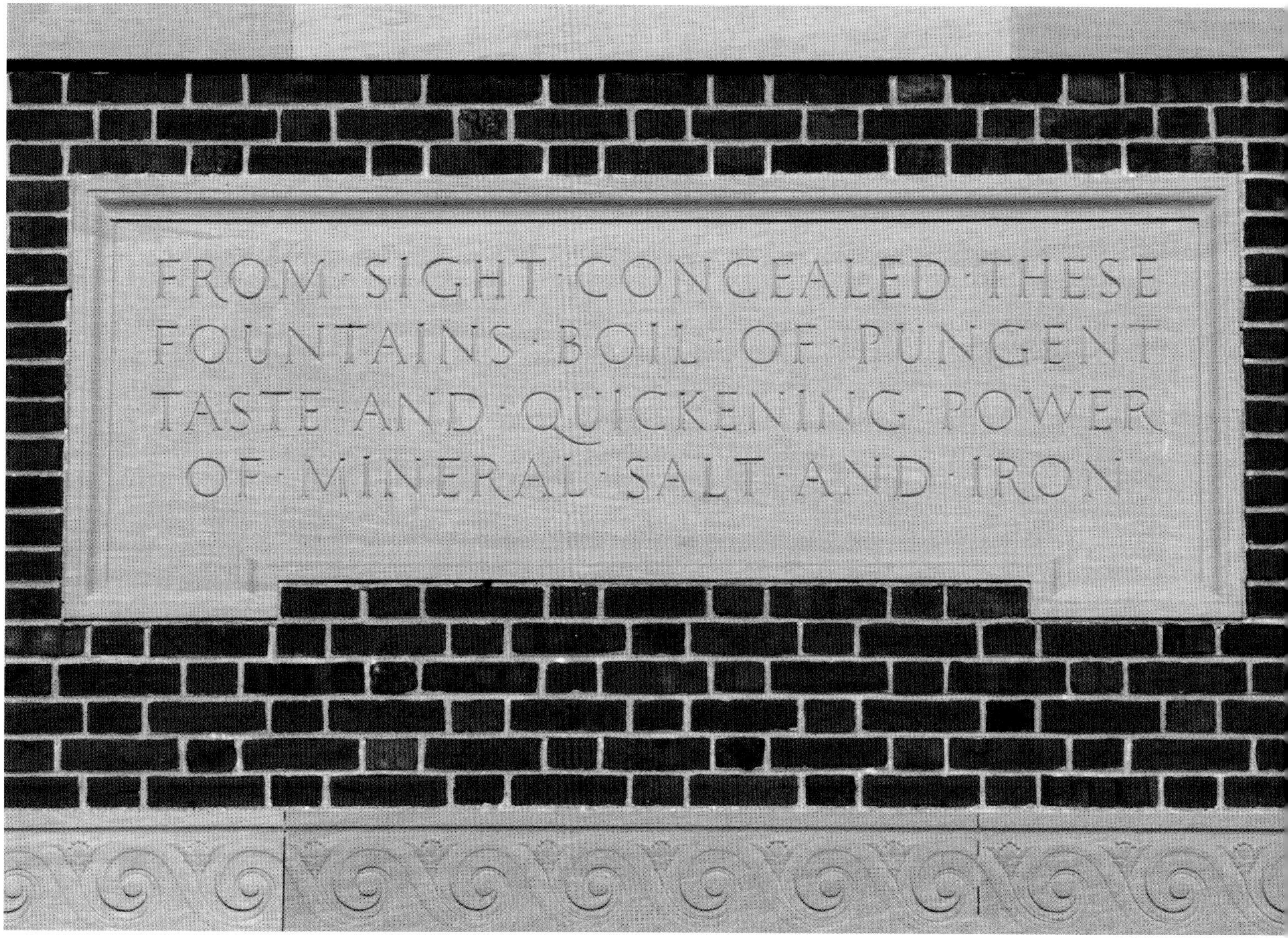
FROM·SIGHT·CONCEALED·THESE
FOUNTAINS·BOIL·OF·PUNGENT
TASTE·AND·QUICKENING·POWER
OF·MINERAL·SALT·AND·IRON

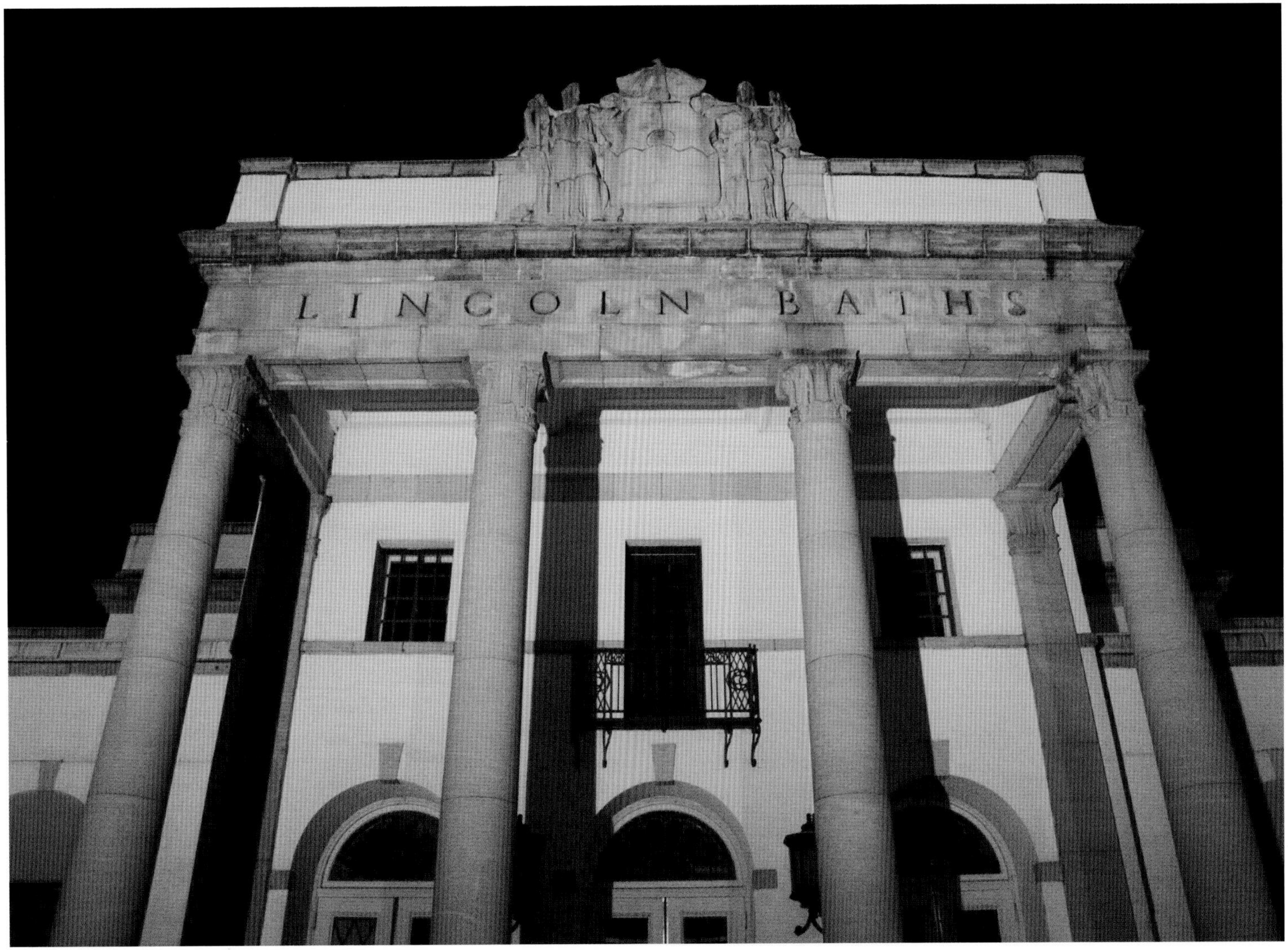

LINCOLN BATH HOUSE, a grand Saratoga landmark, at the state park.

NATIONAL MUSEUM OF DANCE AND HALL OF FAME is housed in the former Washington Bath House, adjacent to the Lincoln Bath House.

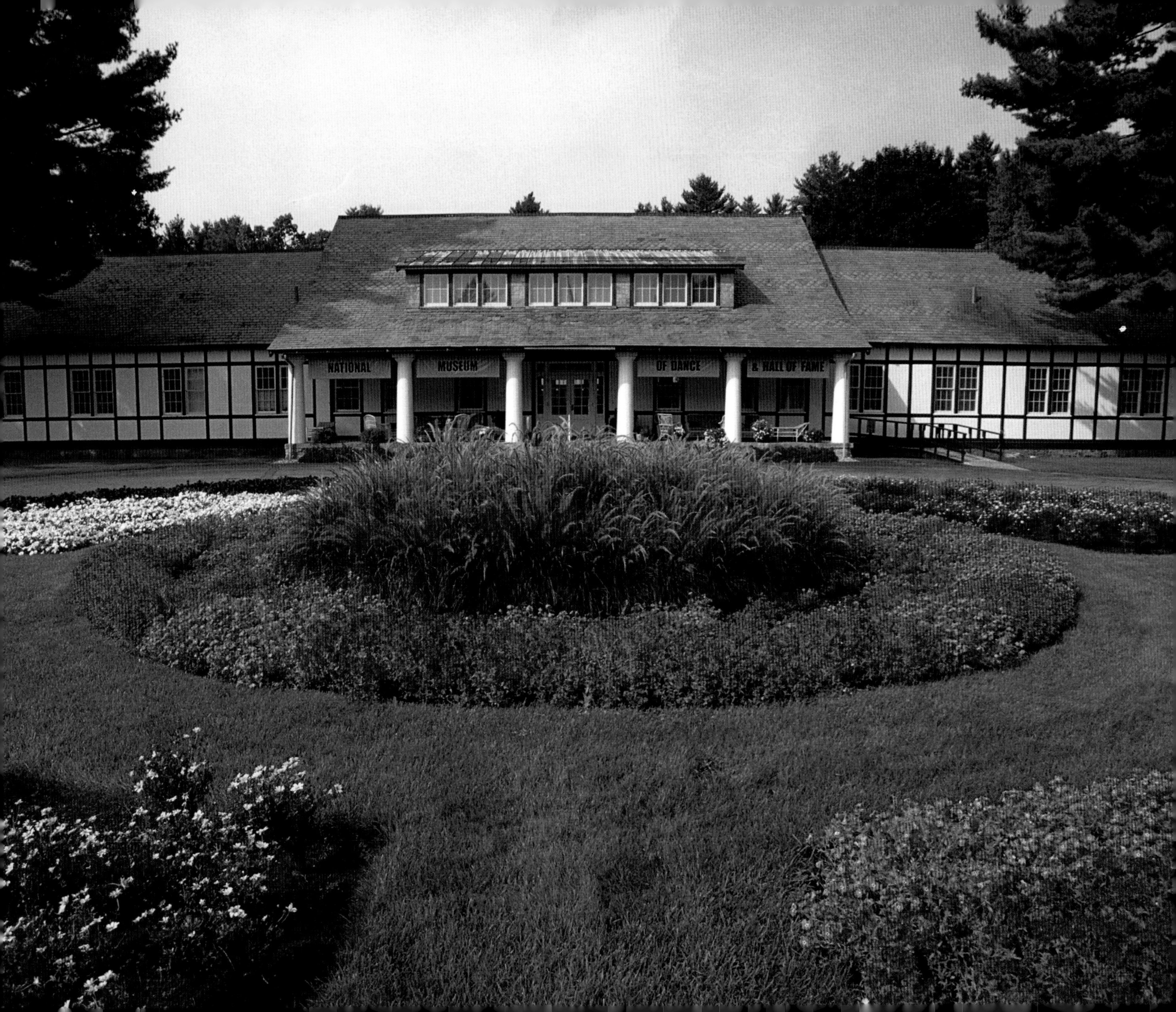
NATIONAL
MUSEUM
OF DANCE
& HALL OF FAME

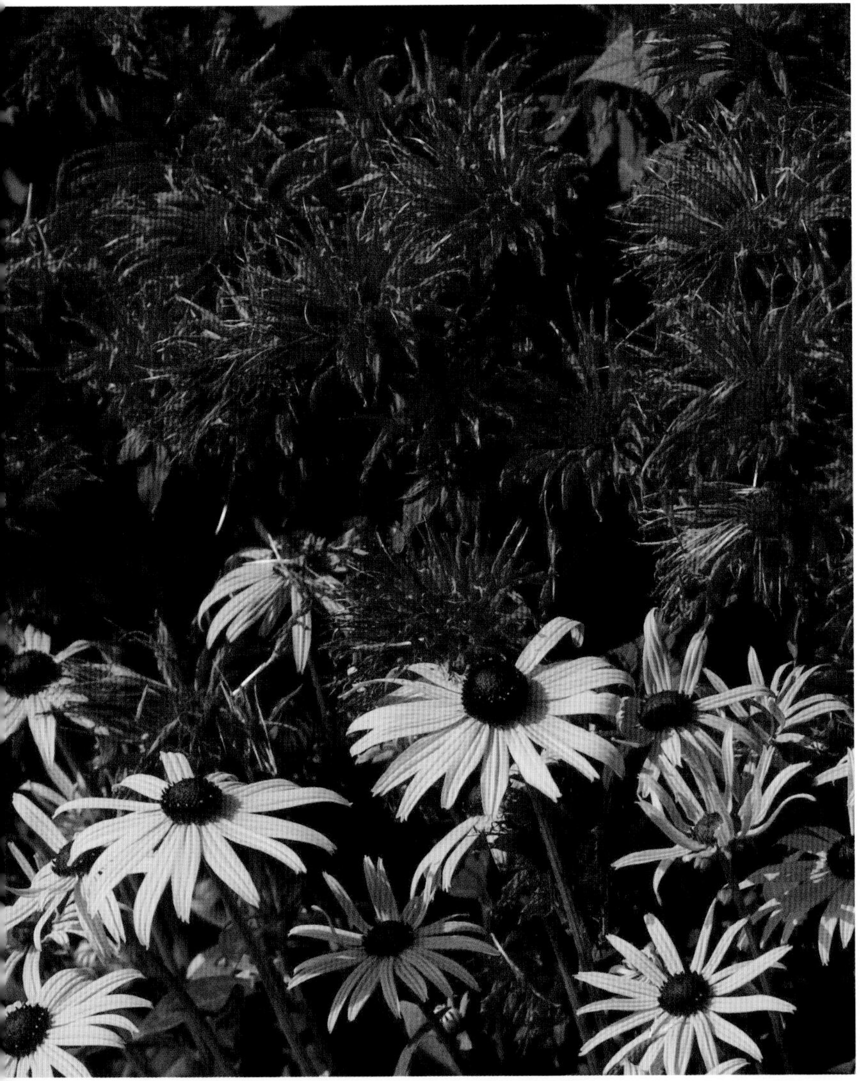

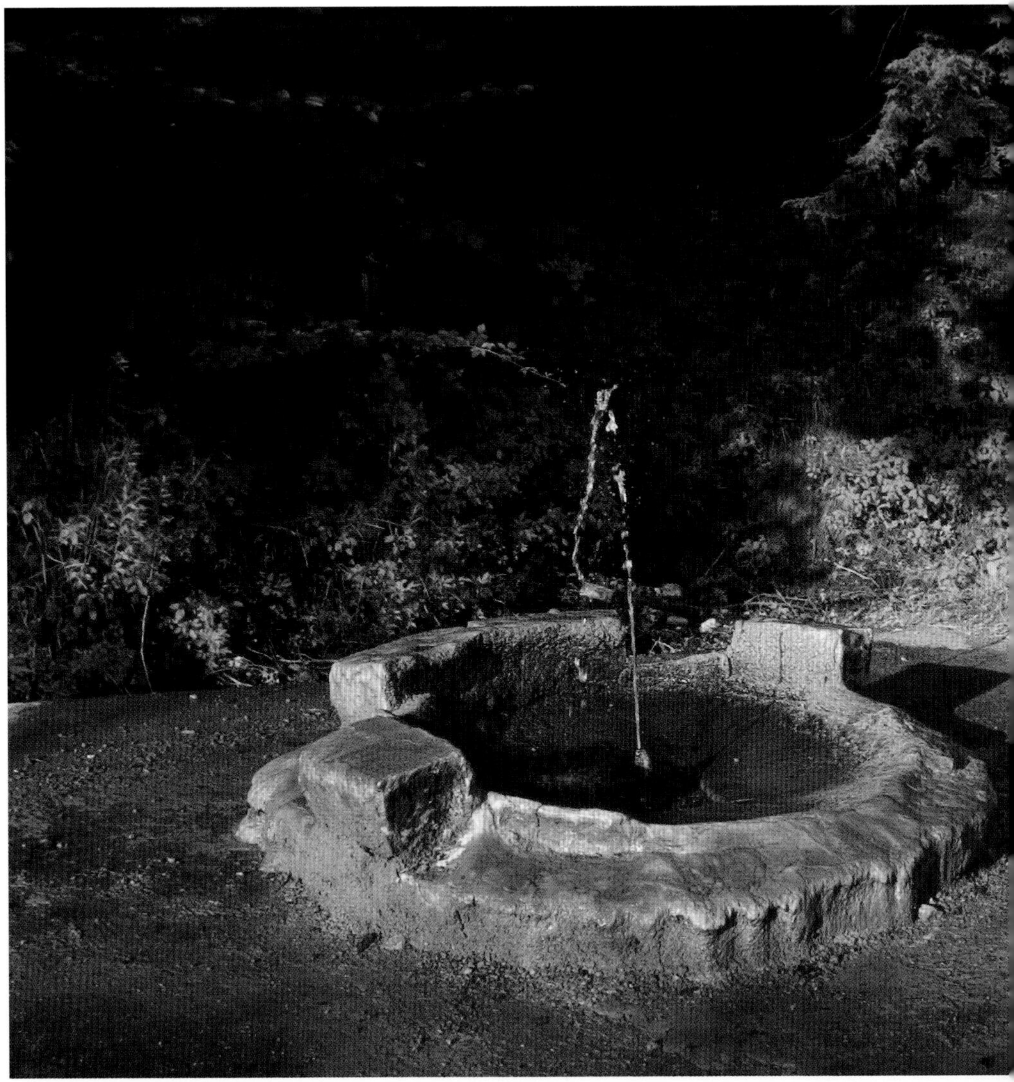

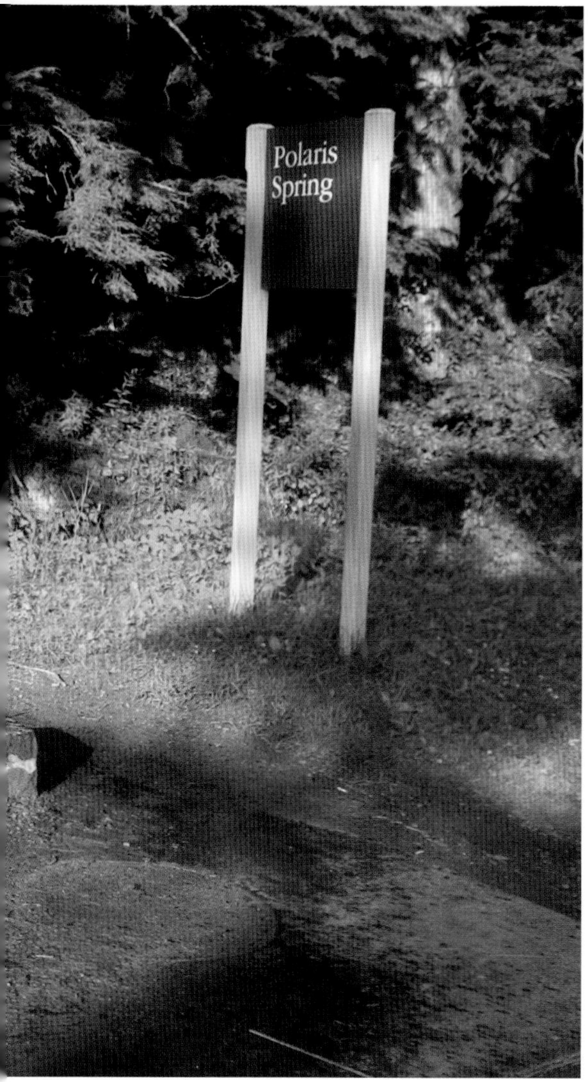
Polaris
Spring

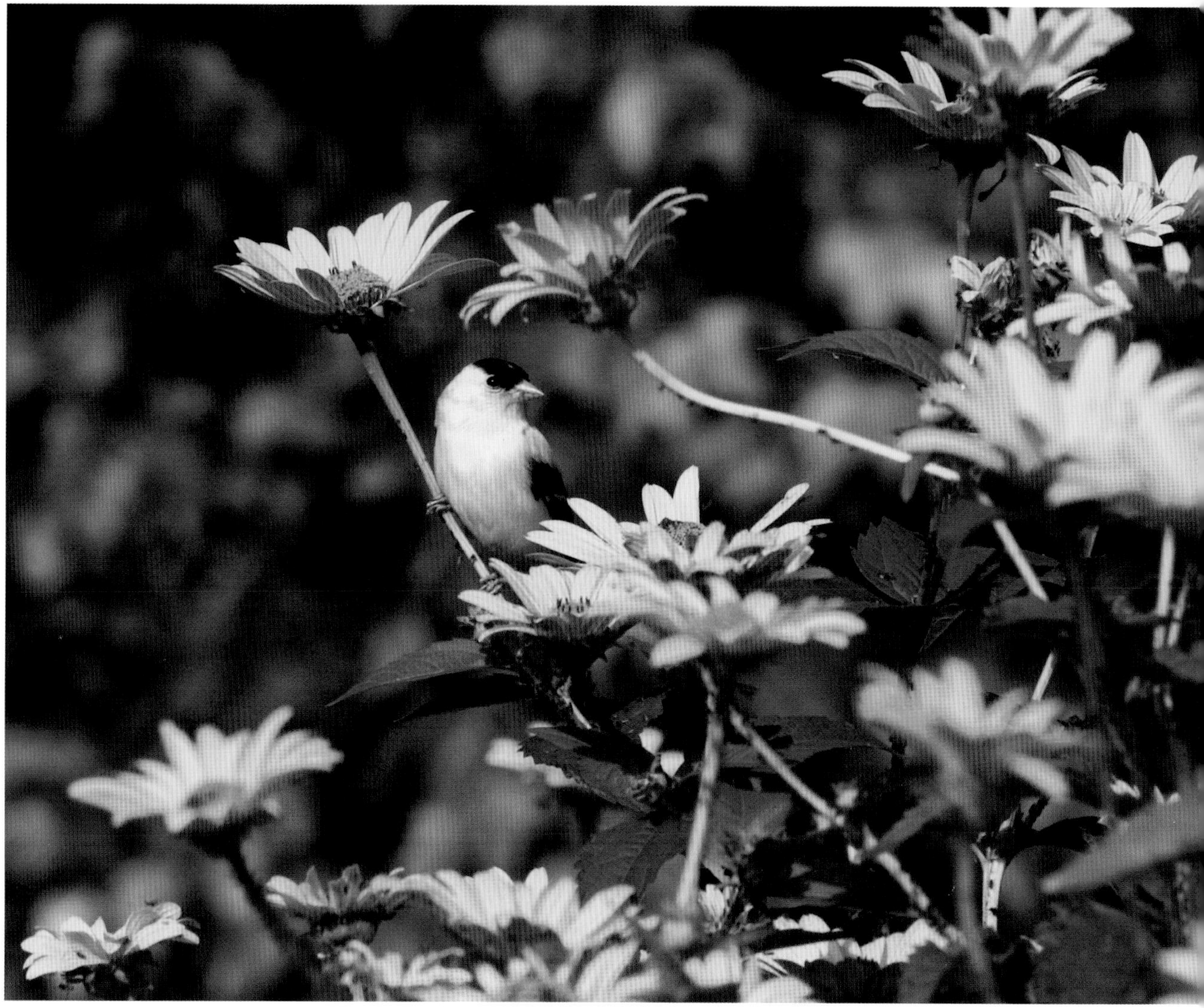

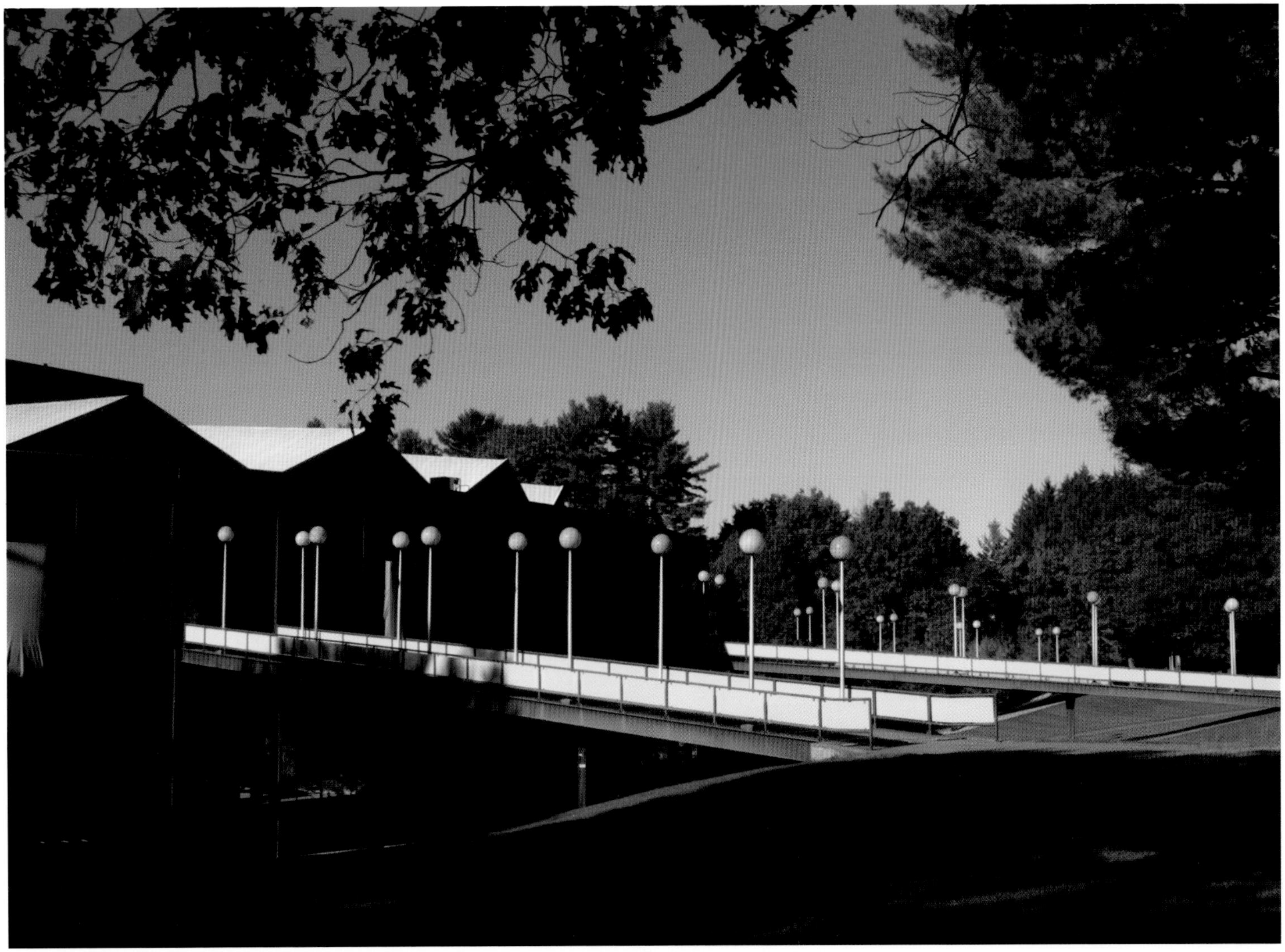

SARATOGA PERFORMING ARTS CENTER, the summer home to such institutions as the Philadelphia Orchestra and the New York City Ballet.

THE ORENDA SPRING runoff, a beautiful scene visible from a SPAC walkway.

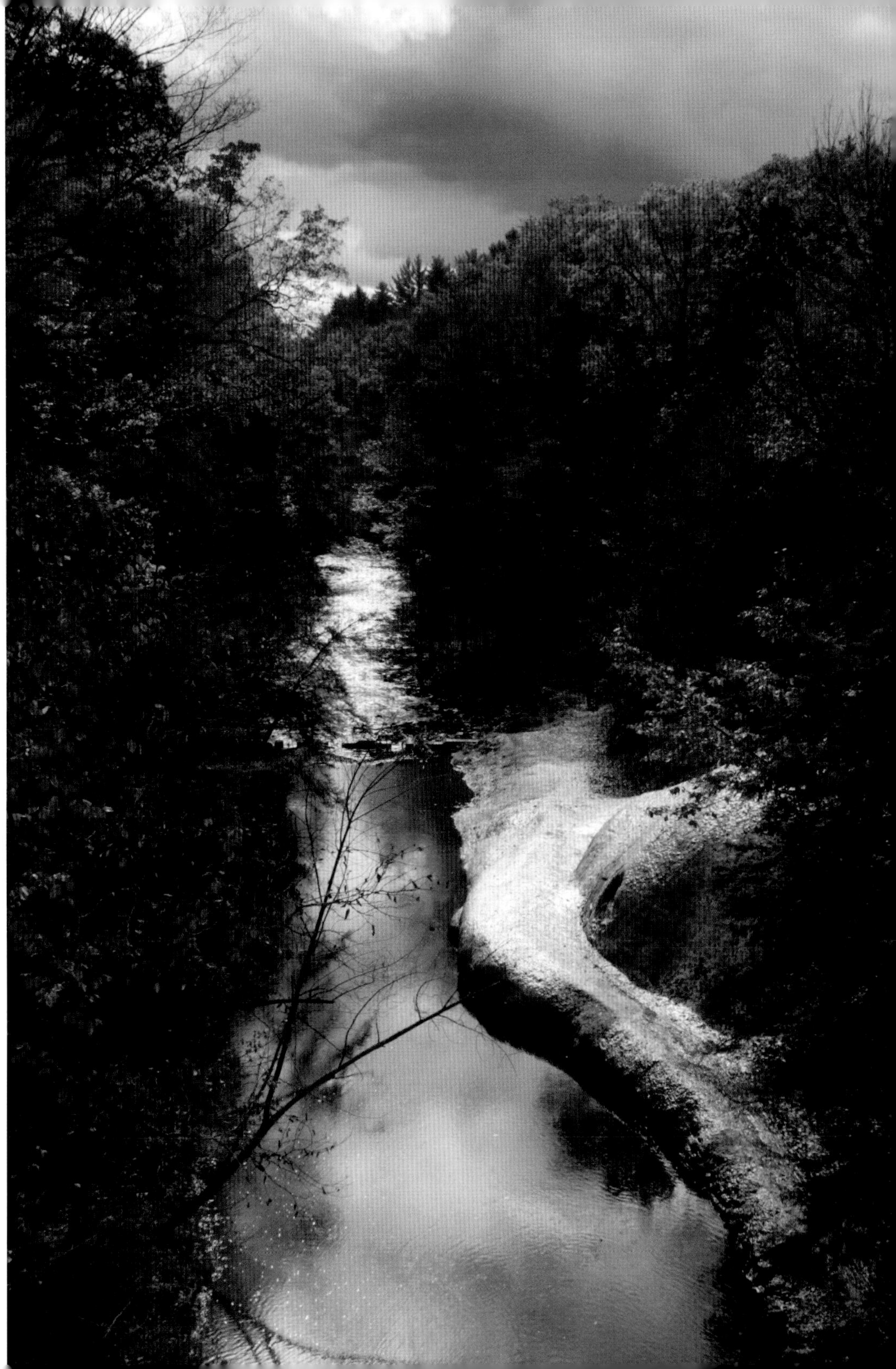

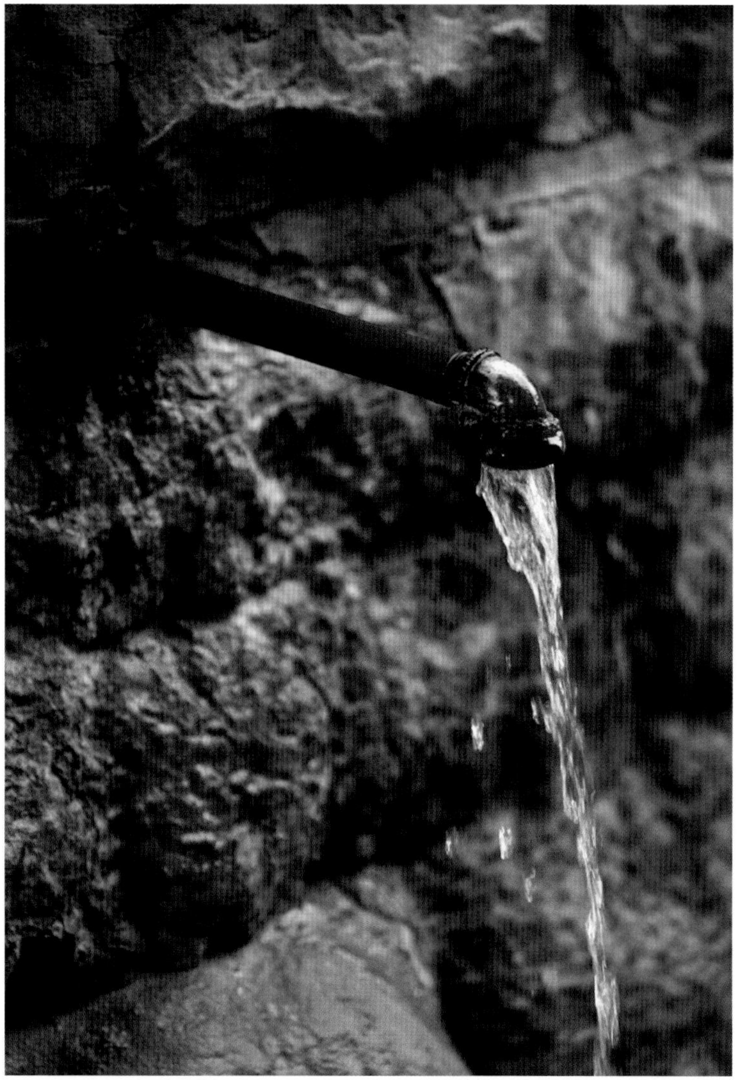

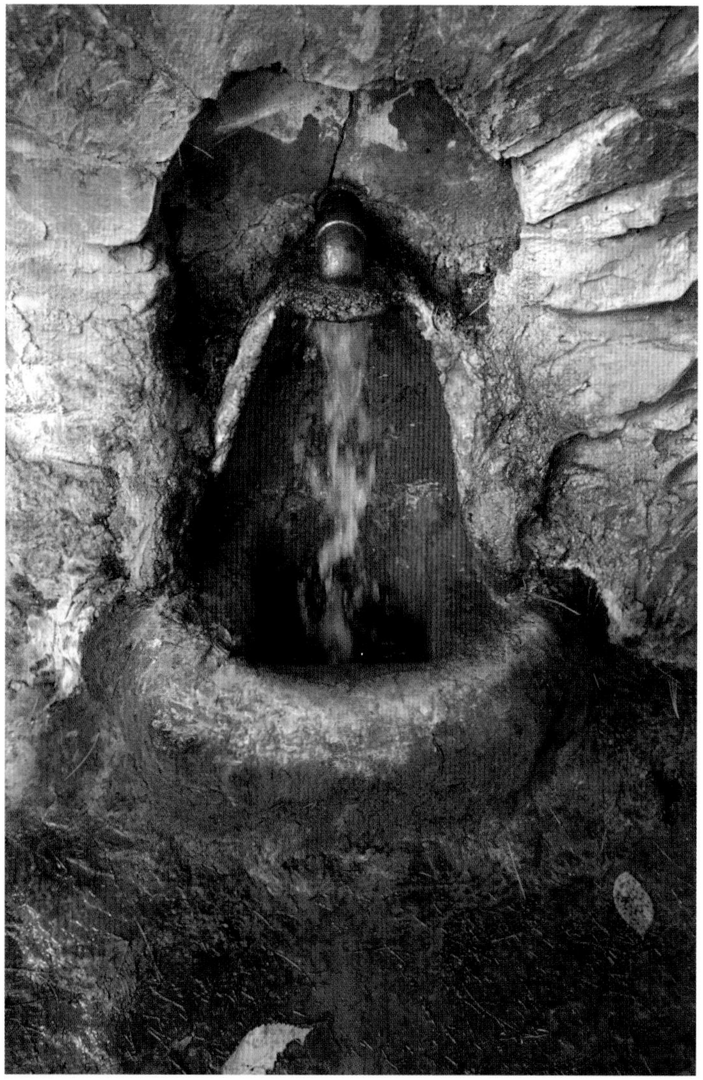

STATE PARK SPRINGS
Mineral deposits from the Orenda Spring (center)
forever capture — and eventually "fossilize" — fallen leaves.

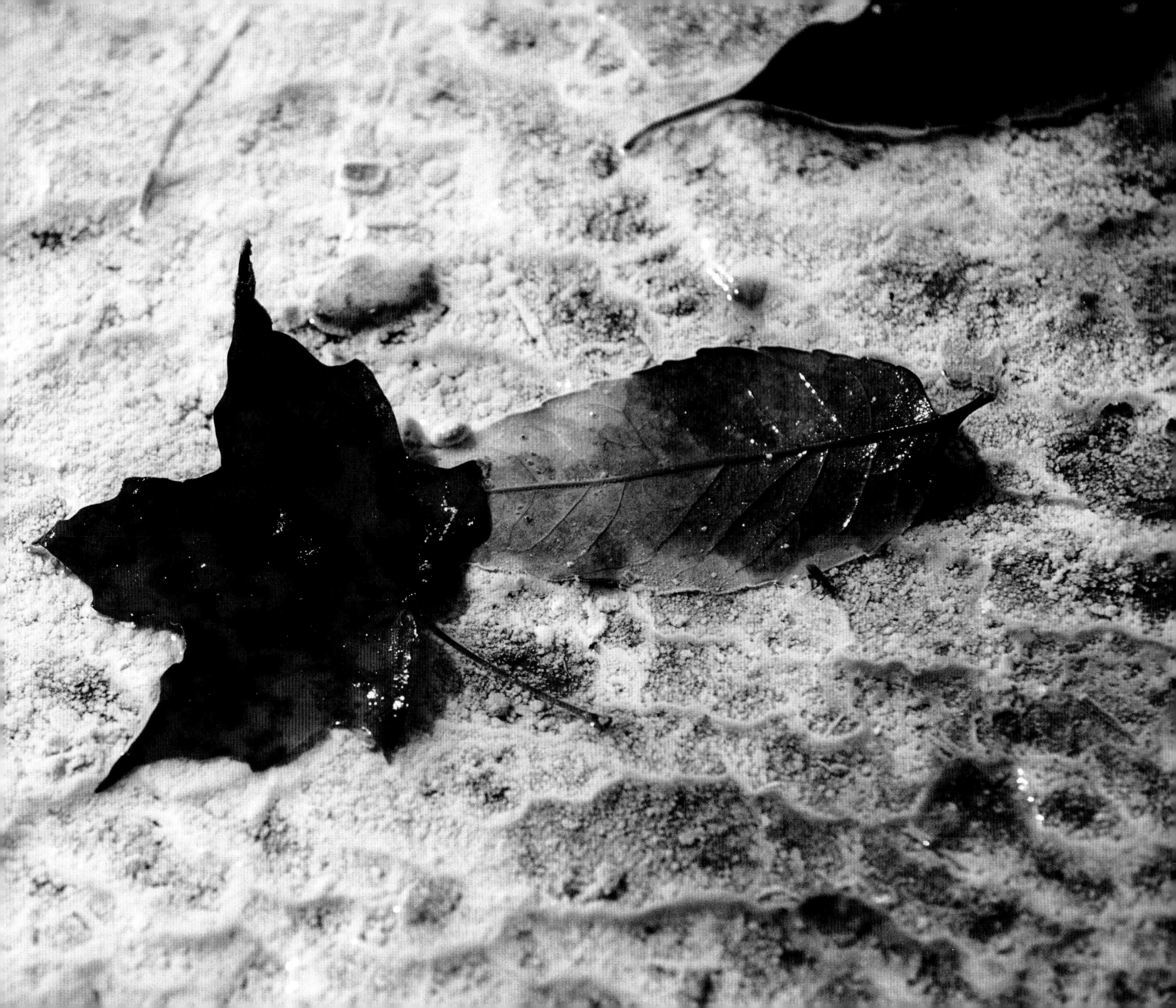

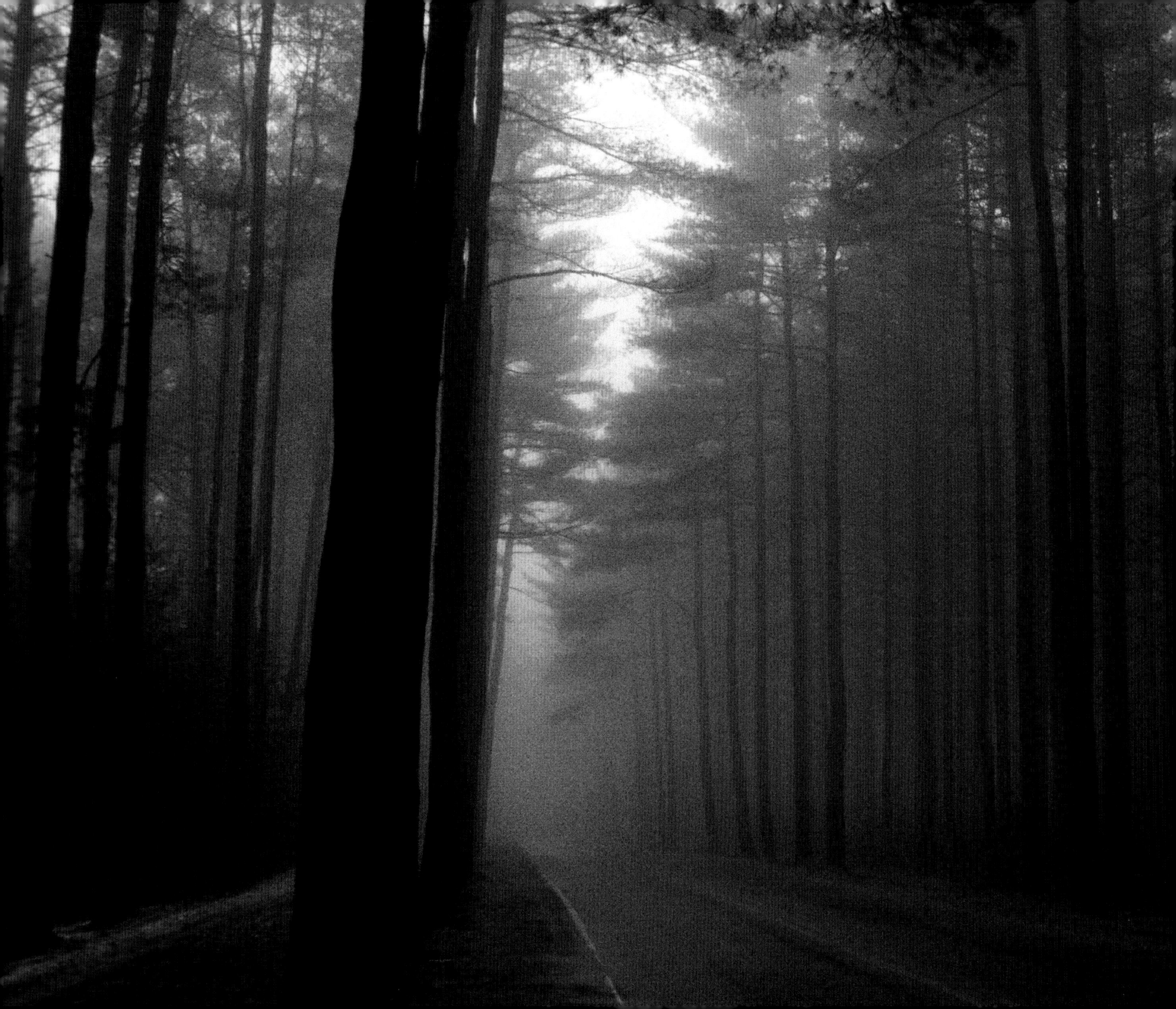

THE AVENUE OF THE PINES is a popular scenic roadway through the state park.

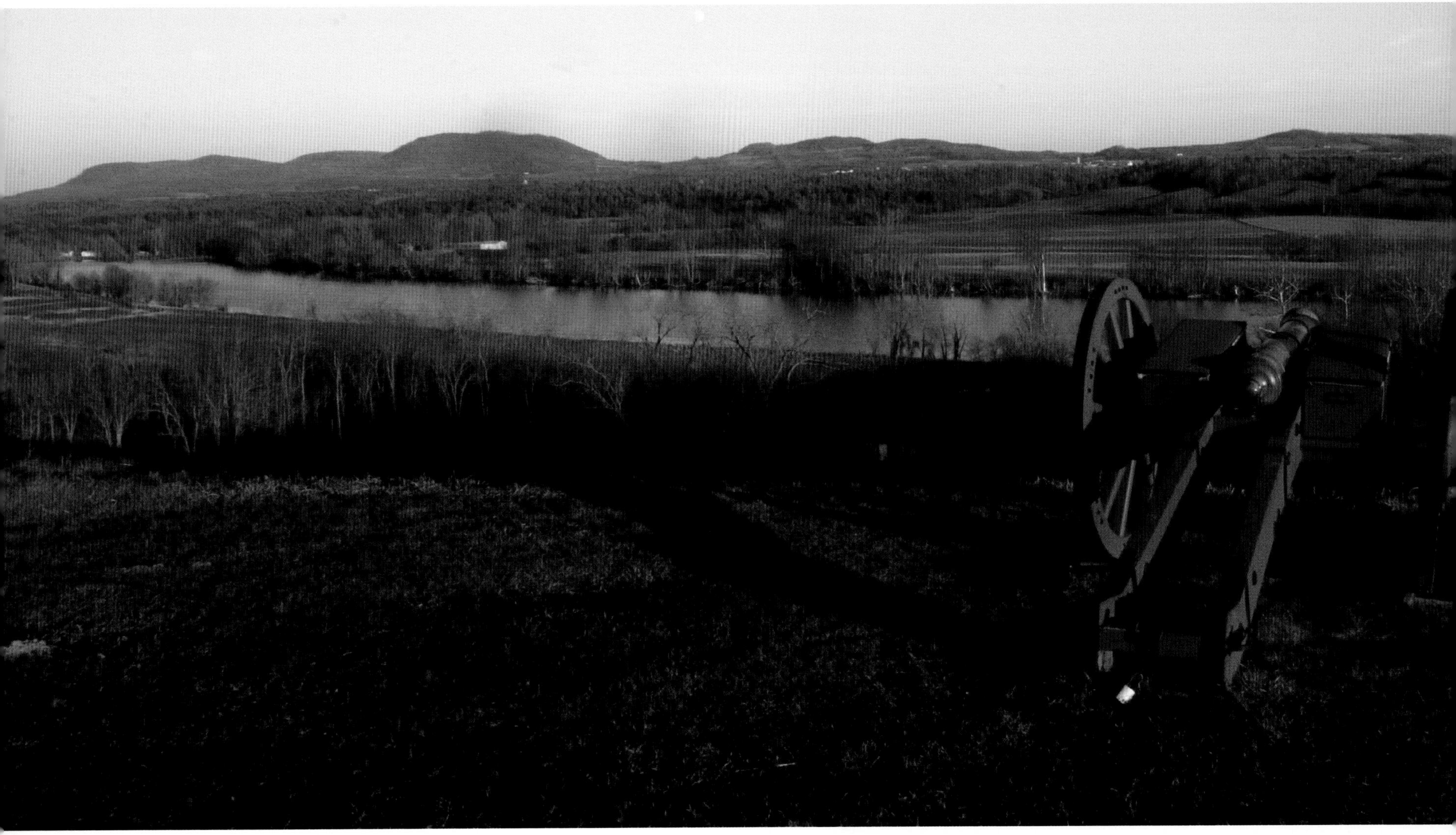

 THE SARATOGA BATTLEFIELD, Hudson River overview.

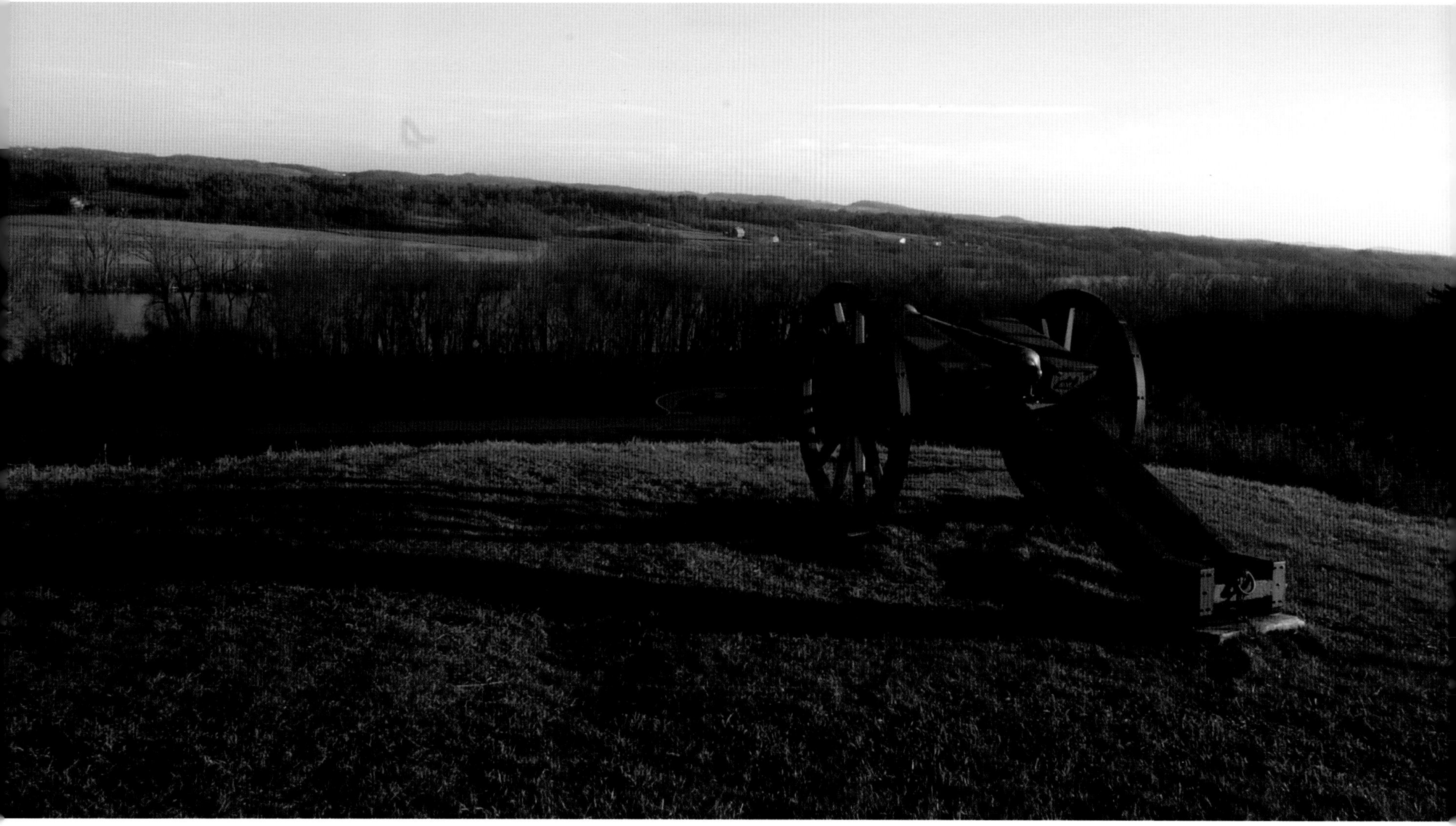

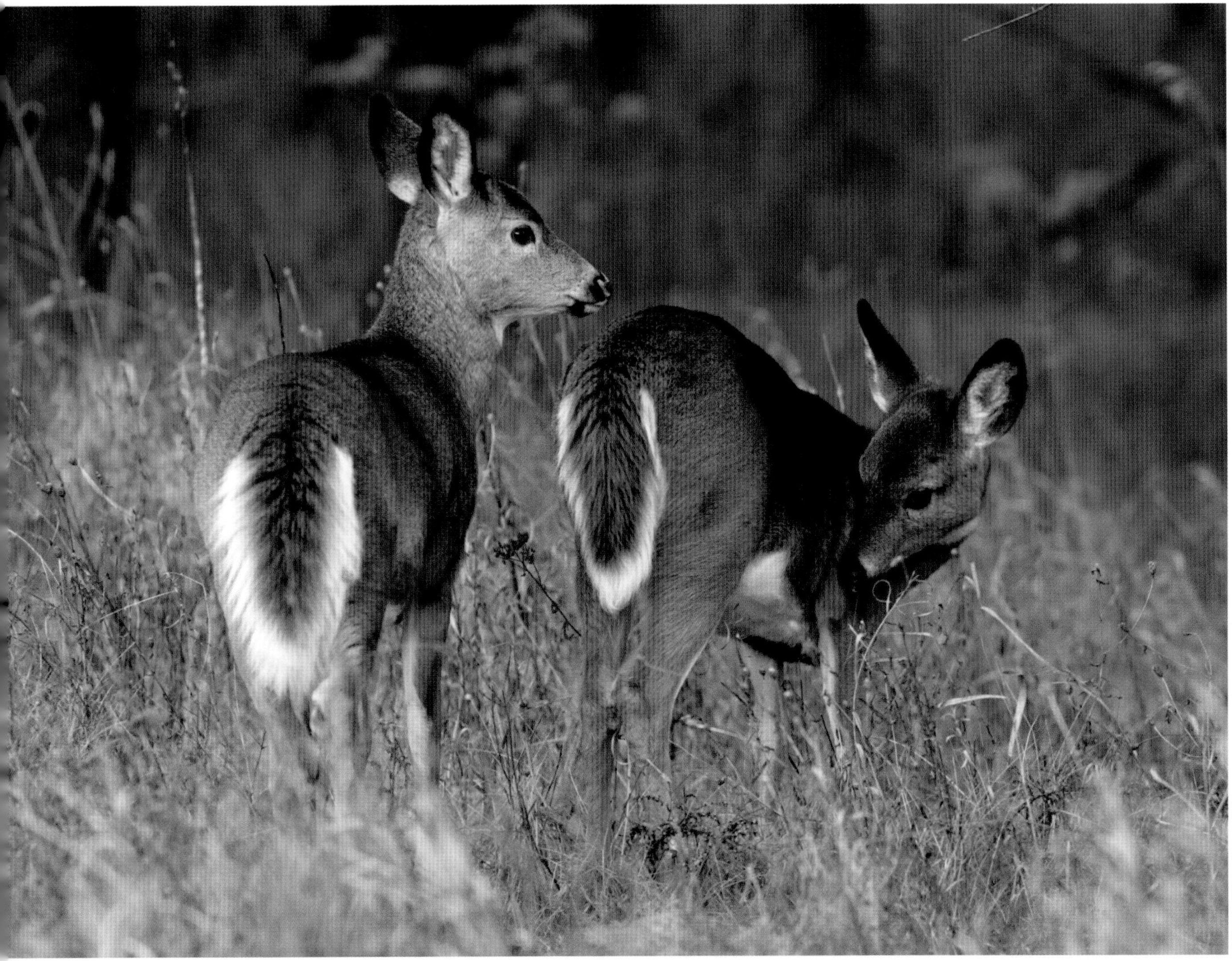

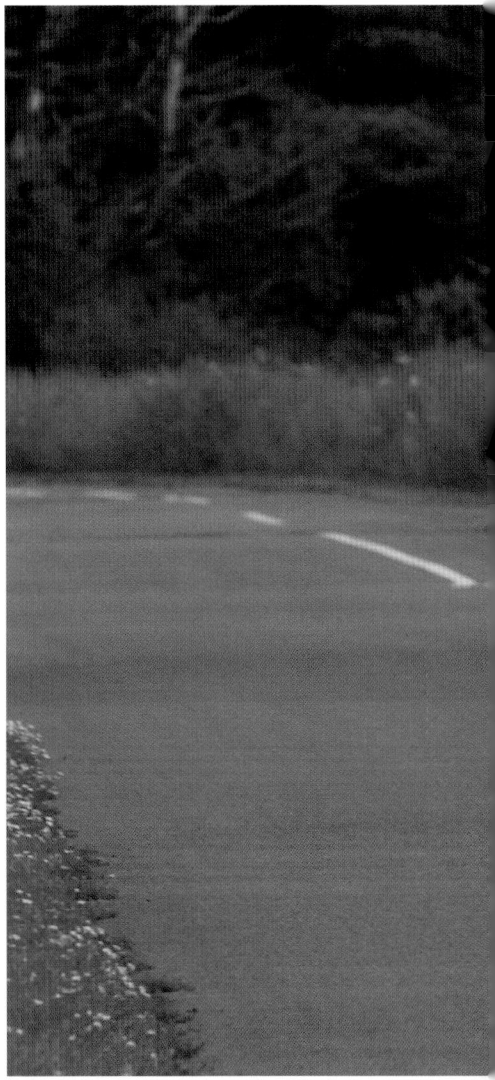

YOUNG WHITE-TAILED DEER wander the battlefield, as do bikers, hikers, historians, and tourists.

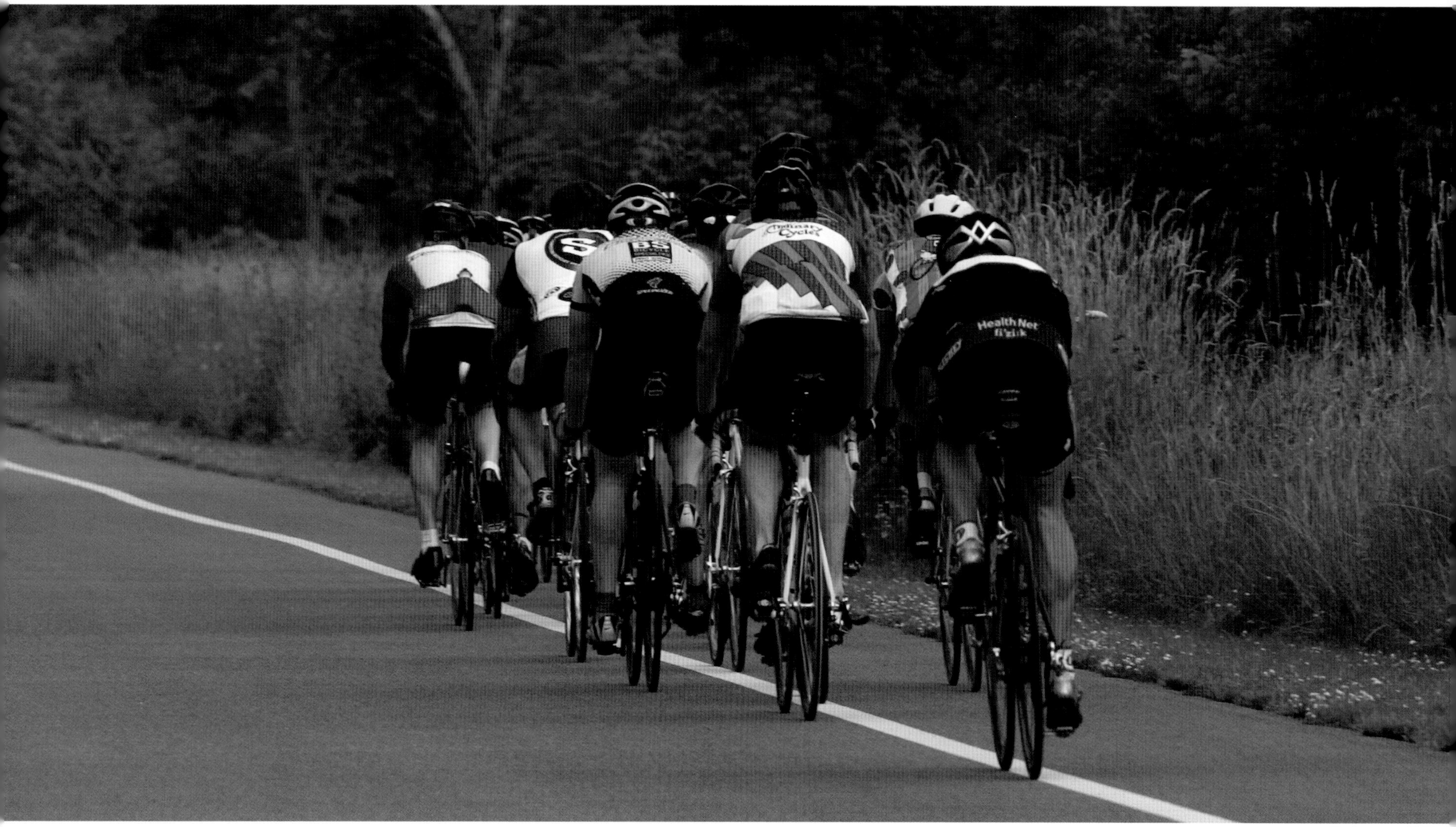
Health Net

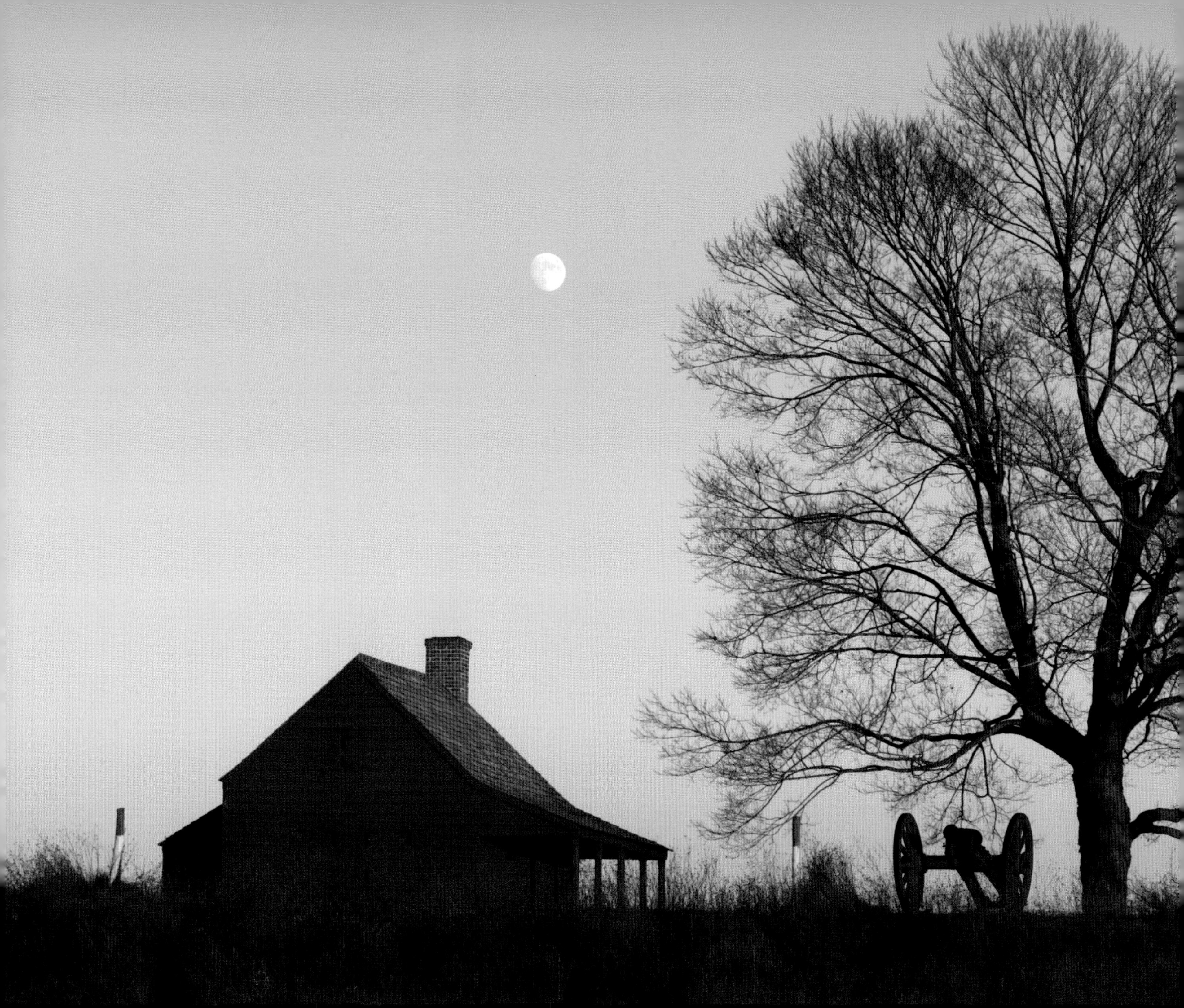

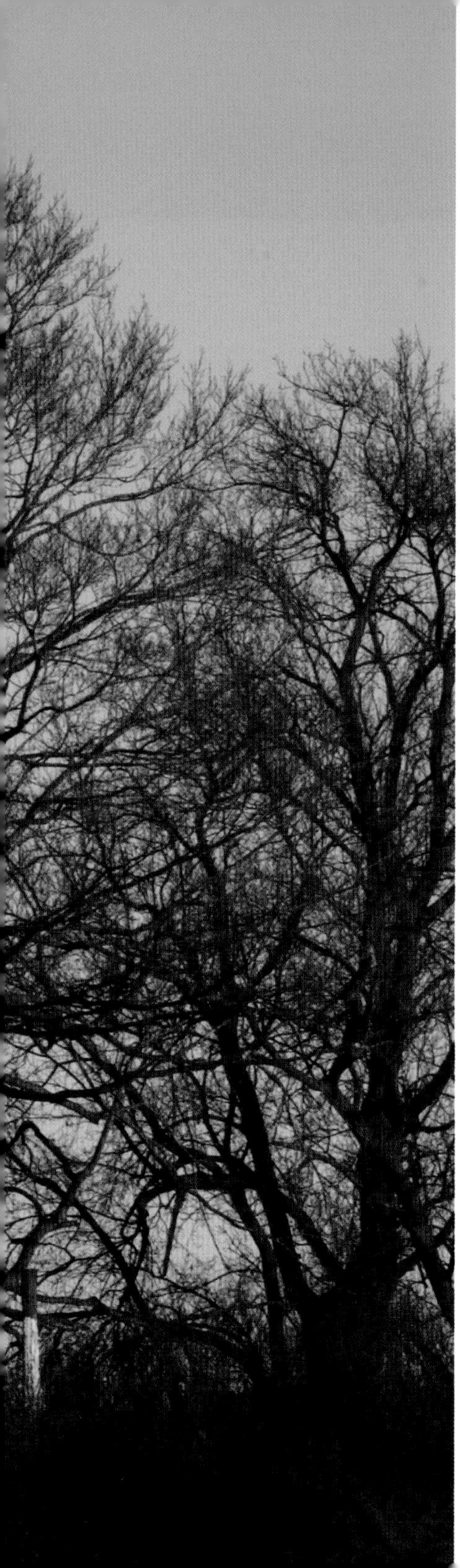

THE NEILSON HOUSE is the only battlefield structure still standing from the time of the Battles of Saratoga.

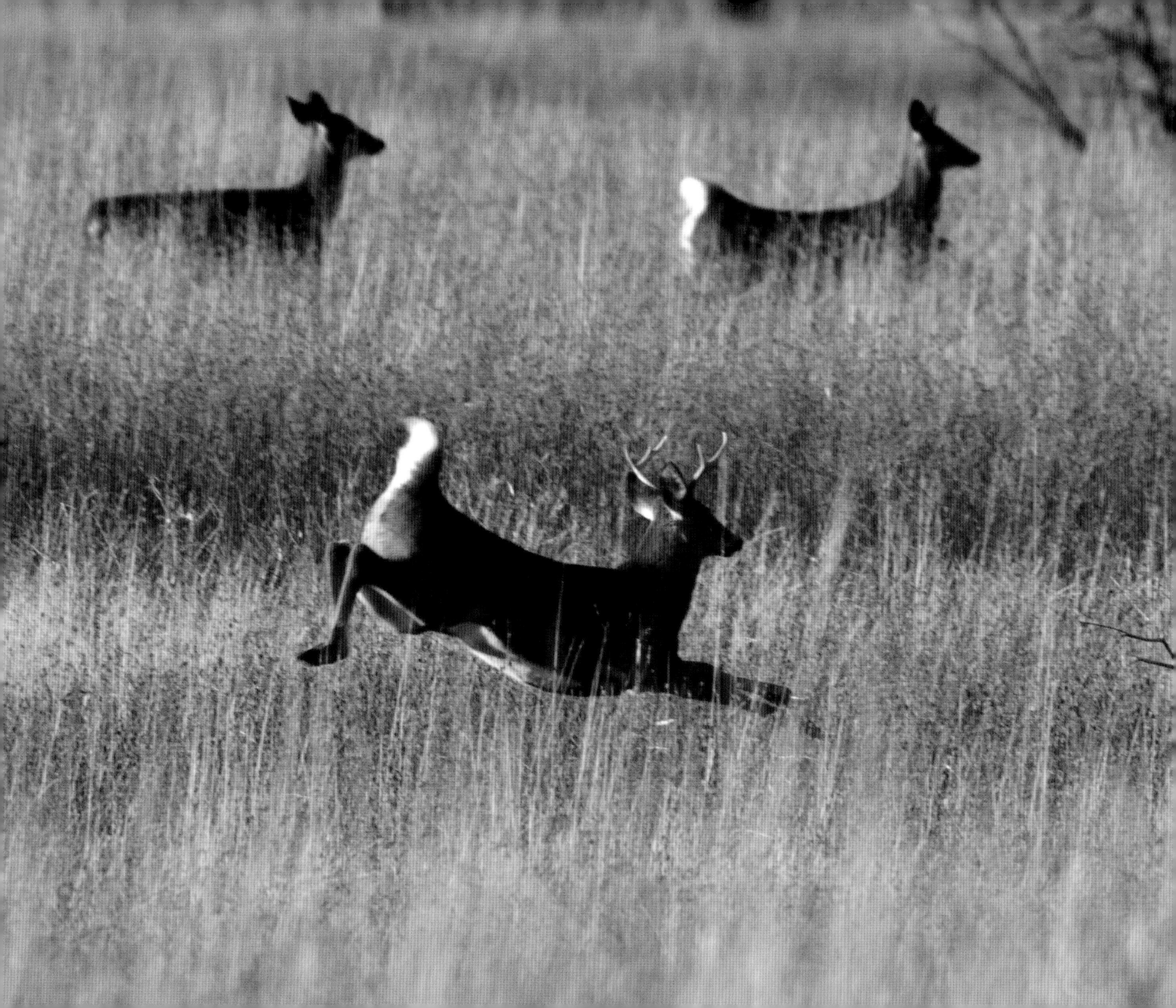

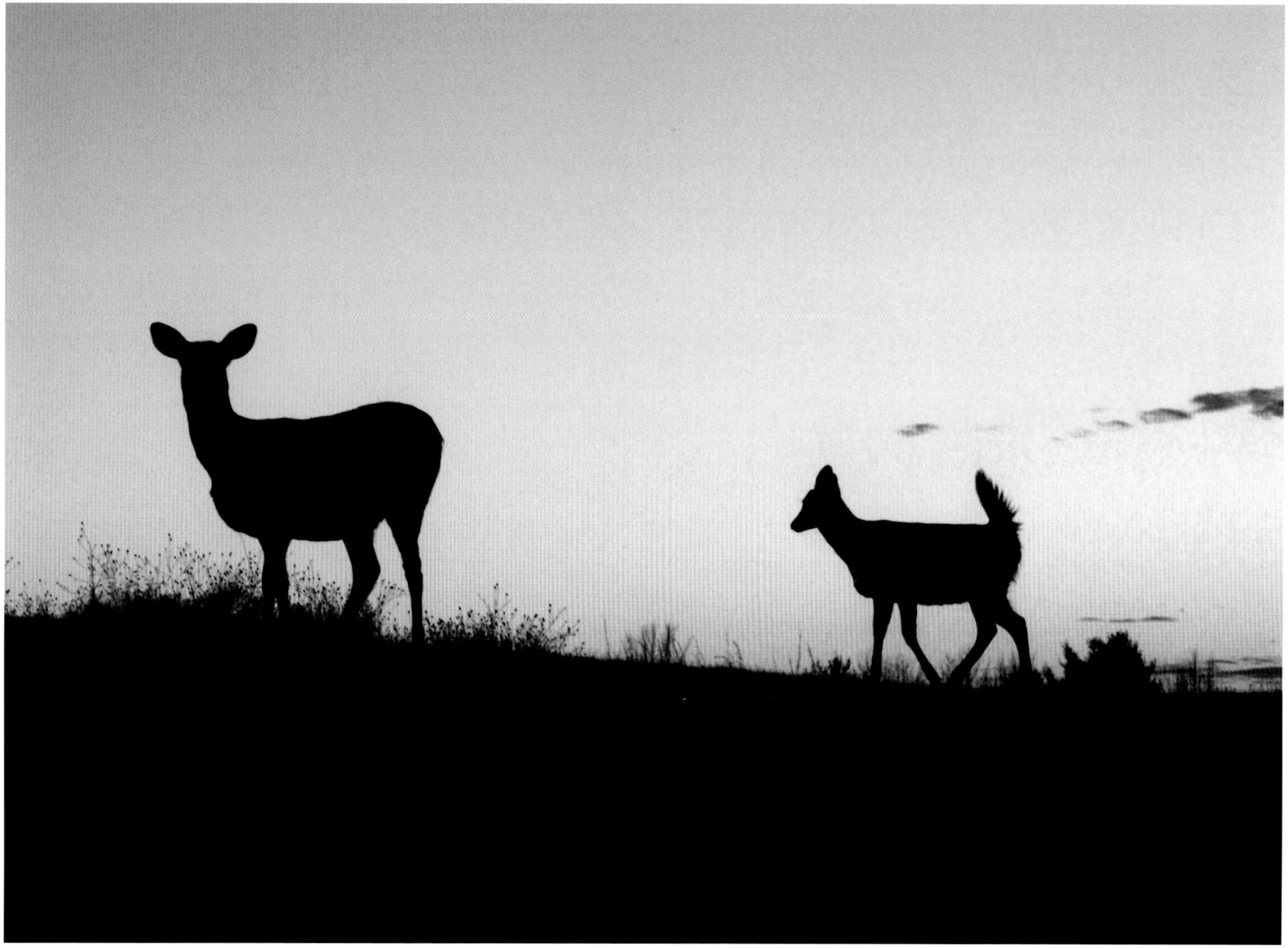

WHITE-TAILED DEER are plentiful throughout the protected lands of the battlefield.

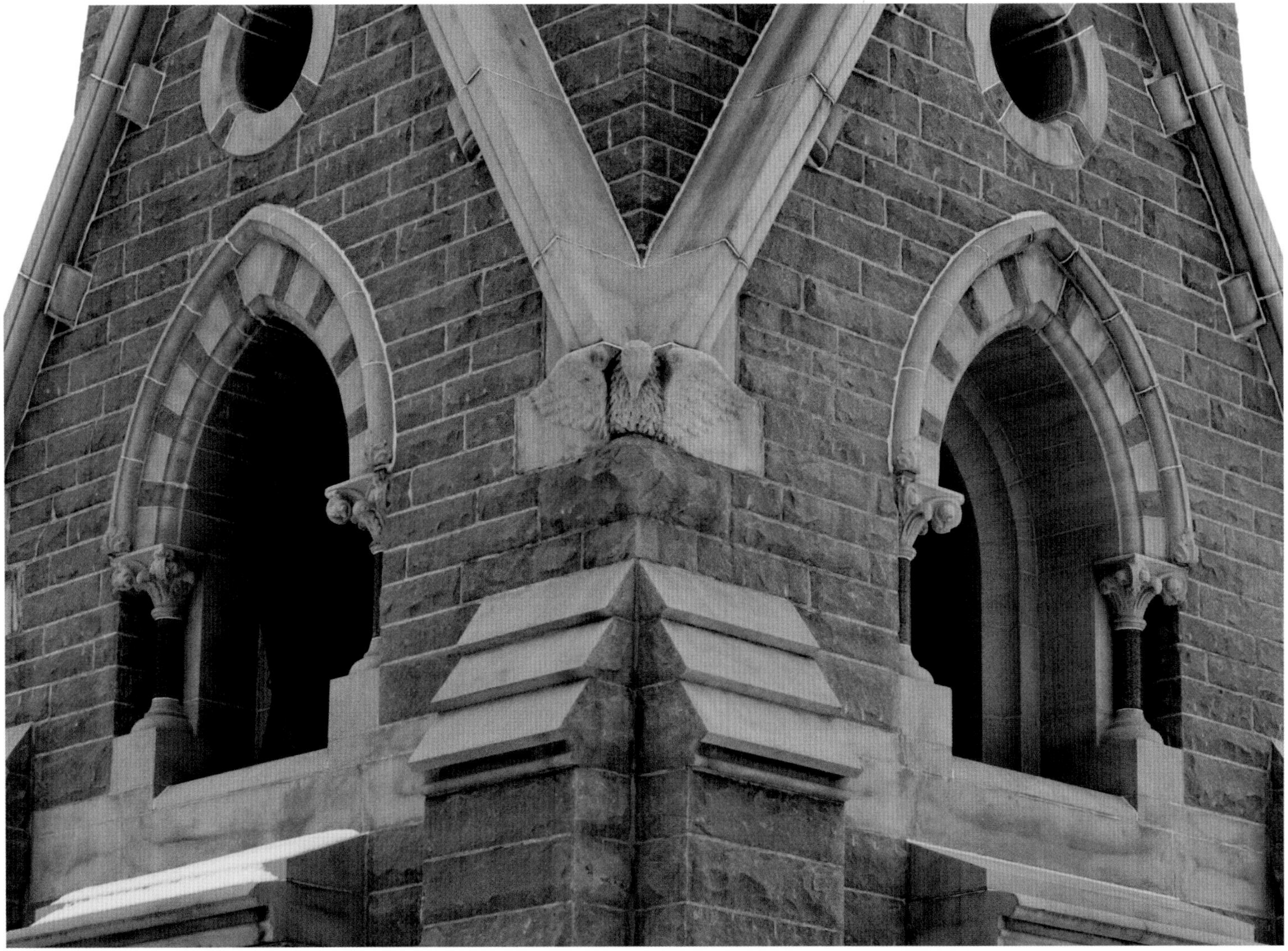

158 **THE SARATOGA MONUMENT,** located eight miles from the battlefield, commemorates the Battles of Saratoga. The figures on the 155-foot-high monument honor the major American contributors to the battles, with the exception of eventual traitor Benedict Arnold, whose niche is statueless.

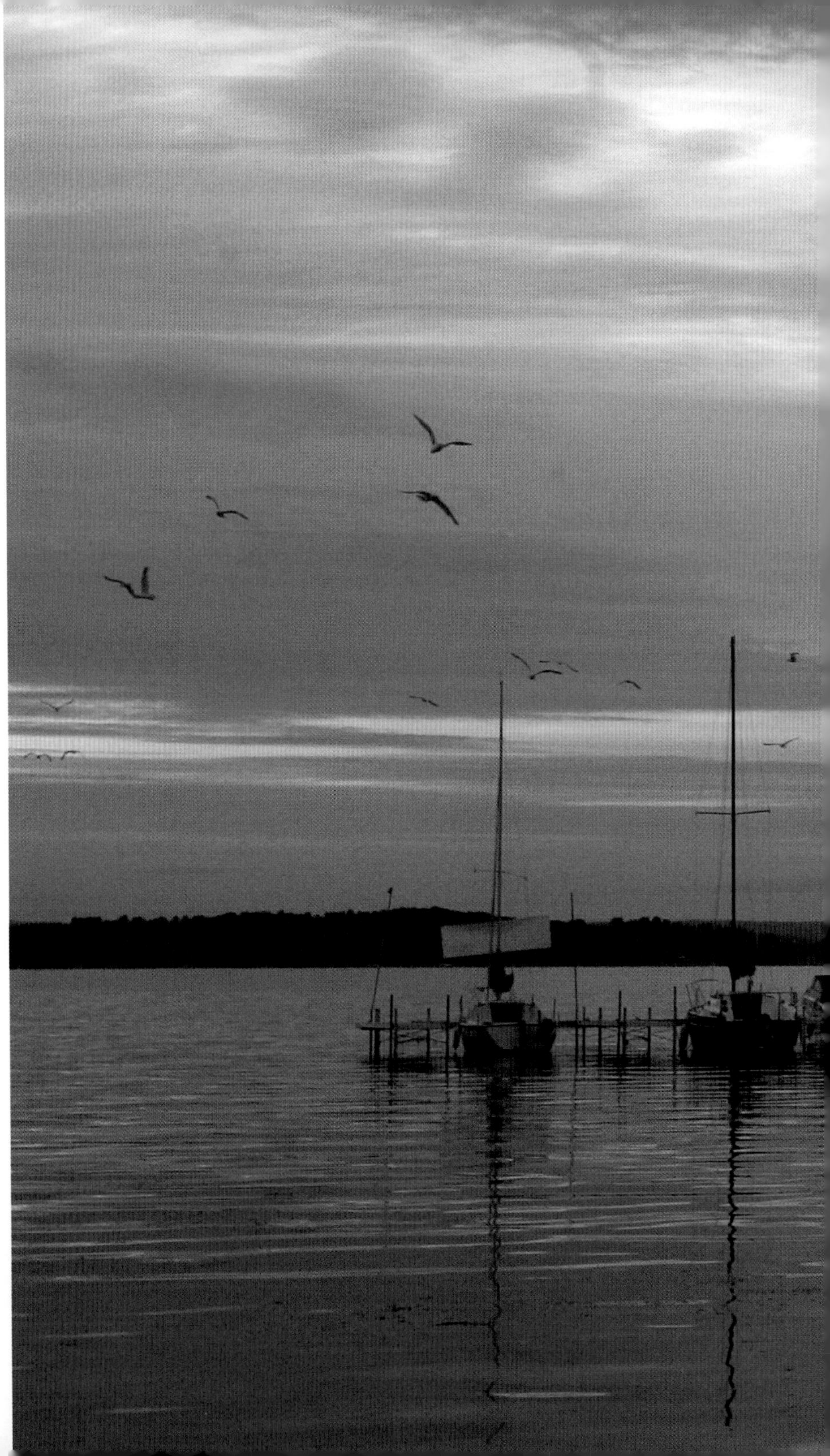

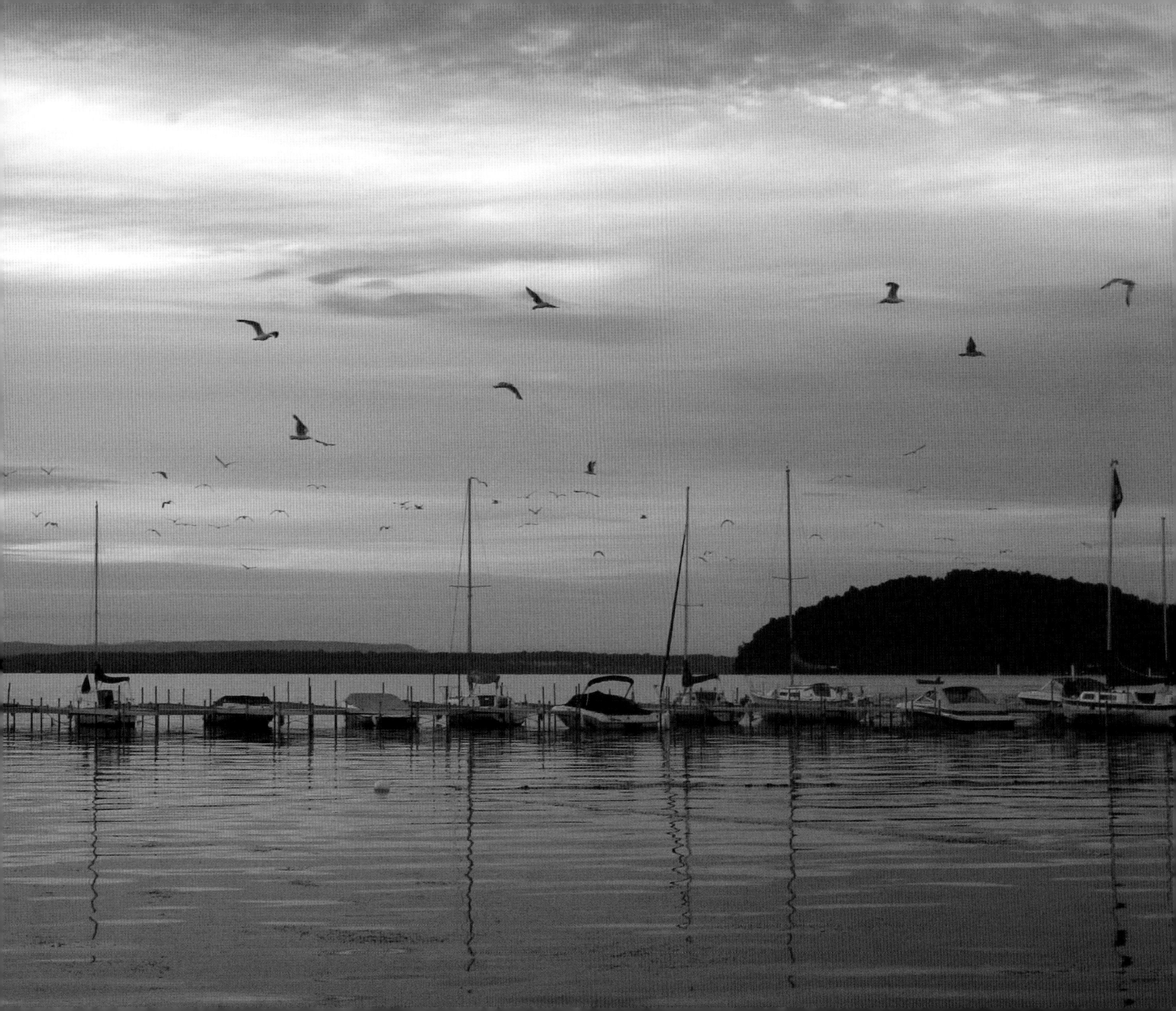

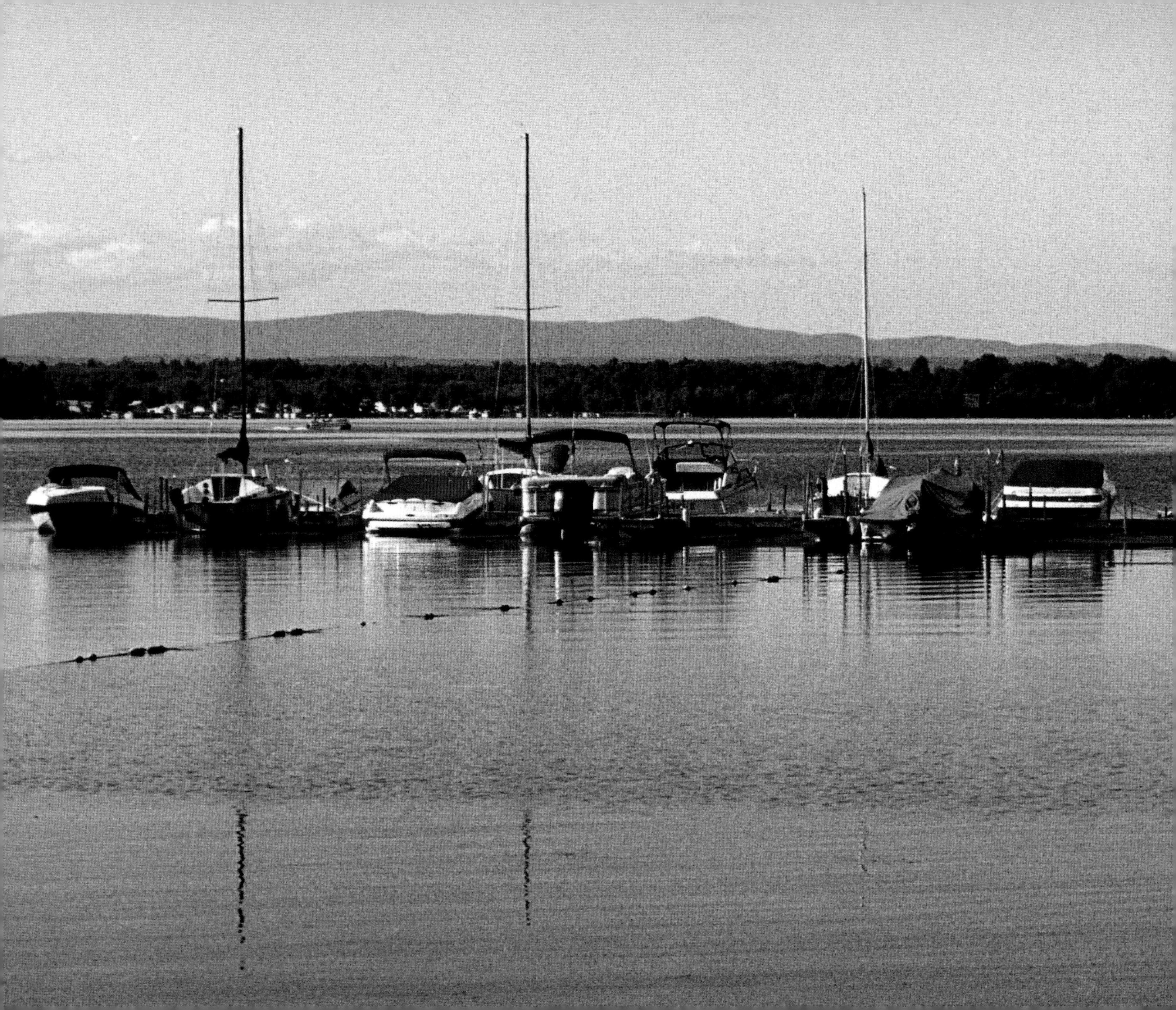

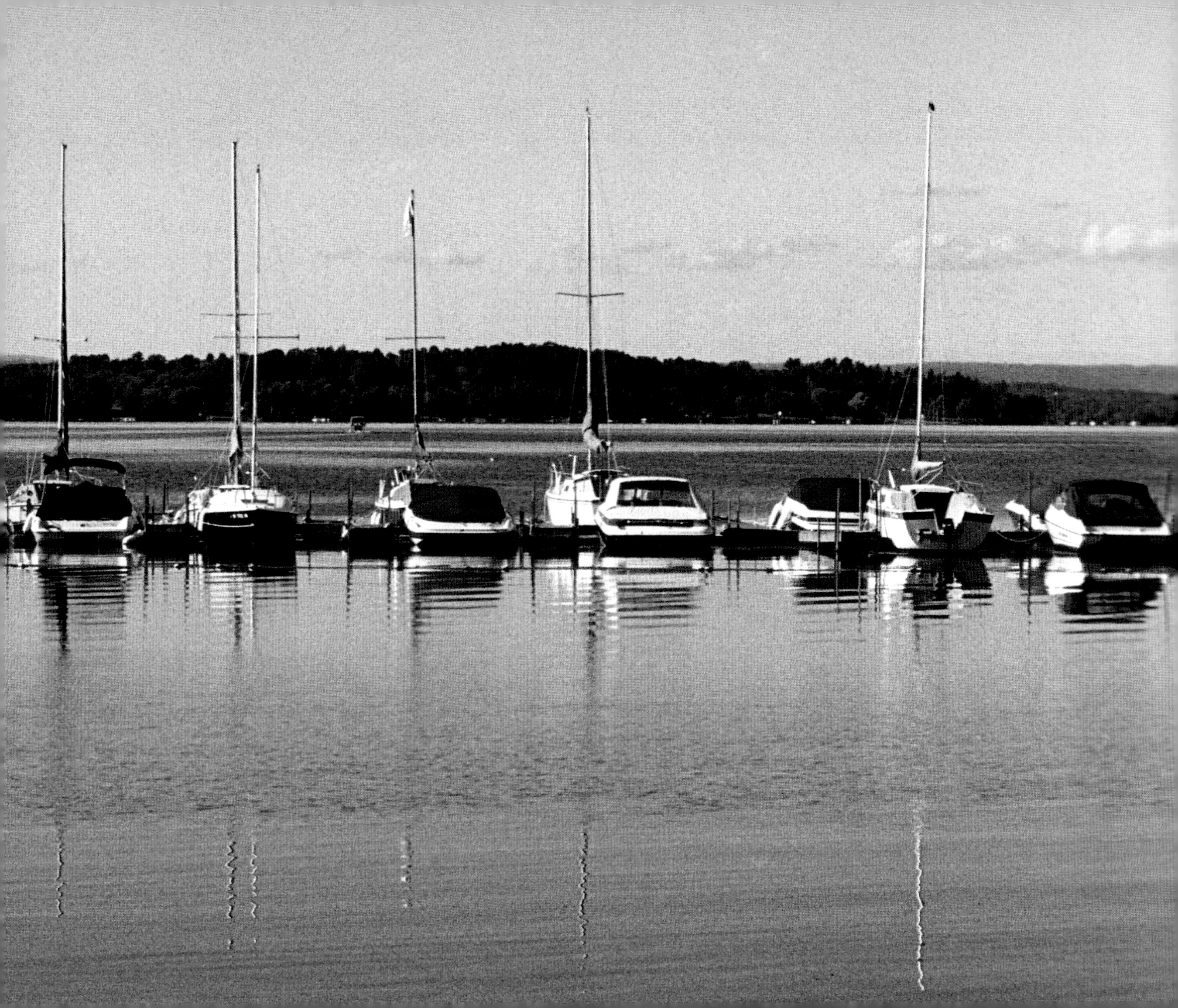

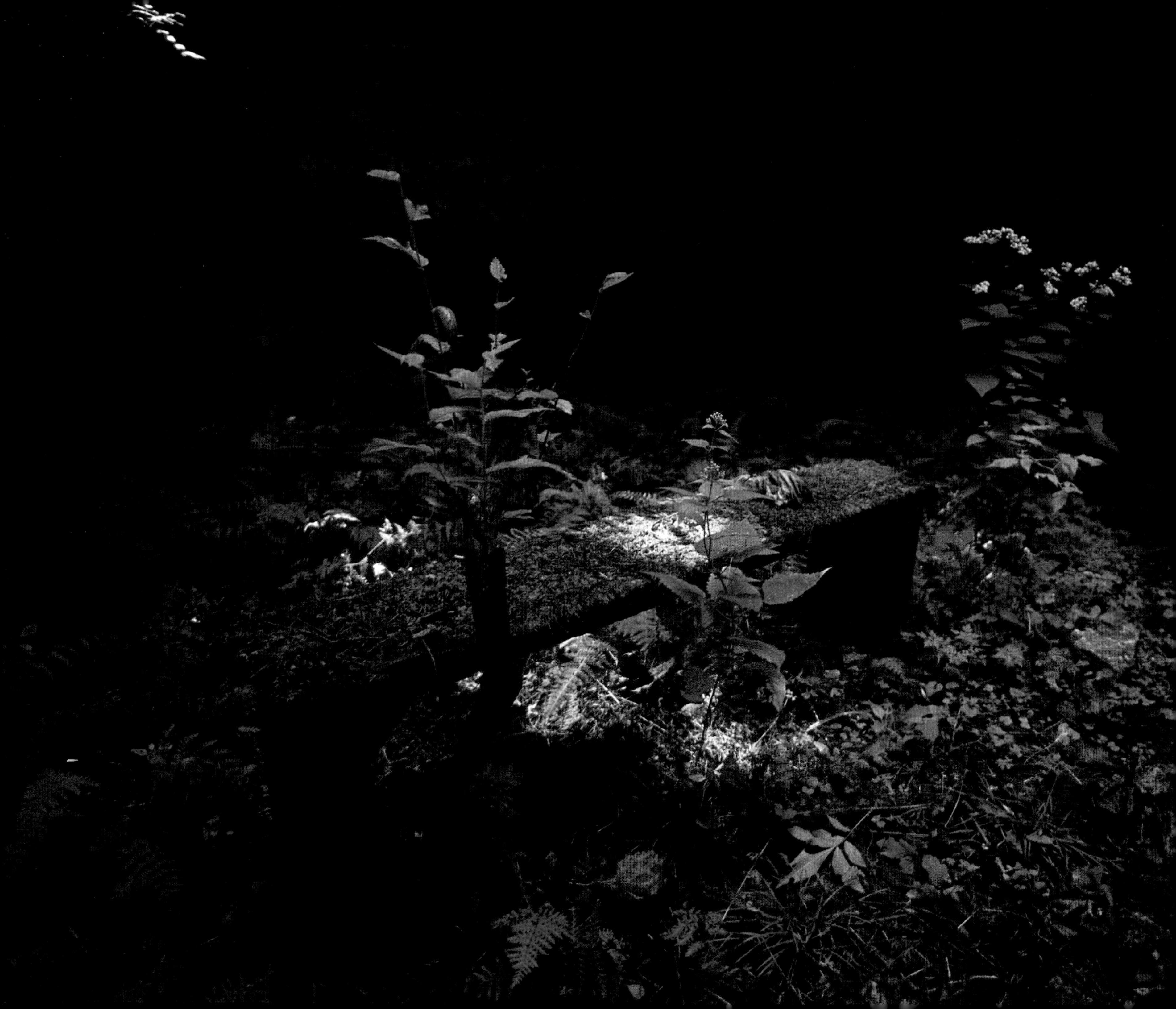

BENCH IN THE PETRIFIED SEA GARDENS, a national landmark that features natural wonders and relaxing nature trails.

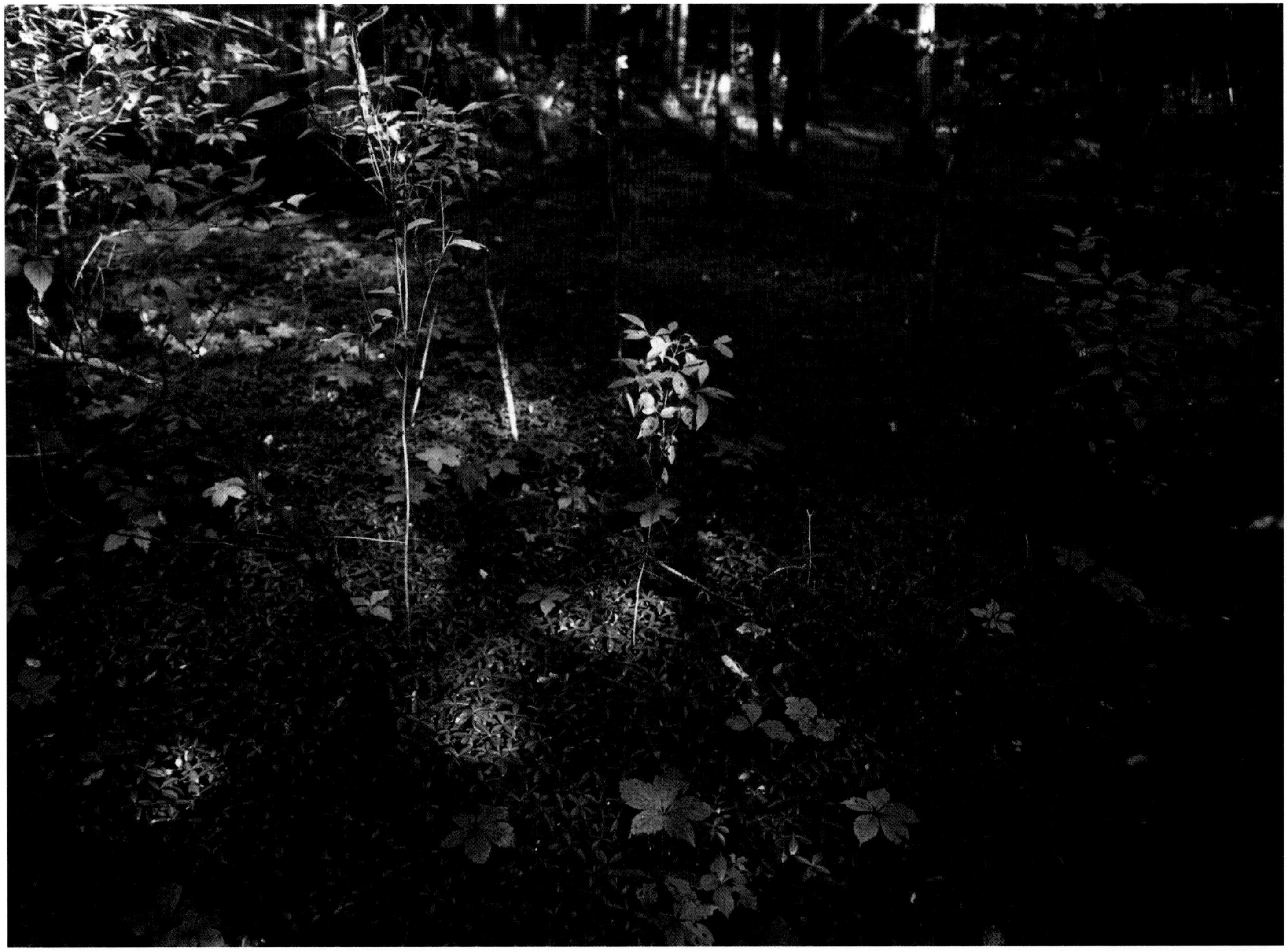

THE SPLIT STONE GROUP (RIGHT), in the Petrified Sea Gardens, aligns with the solstice and appears to include an altar used by Native Americans.

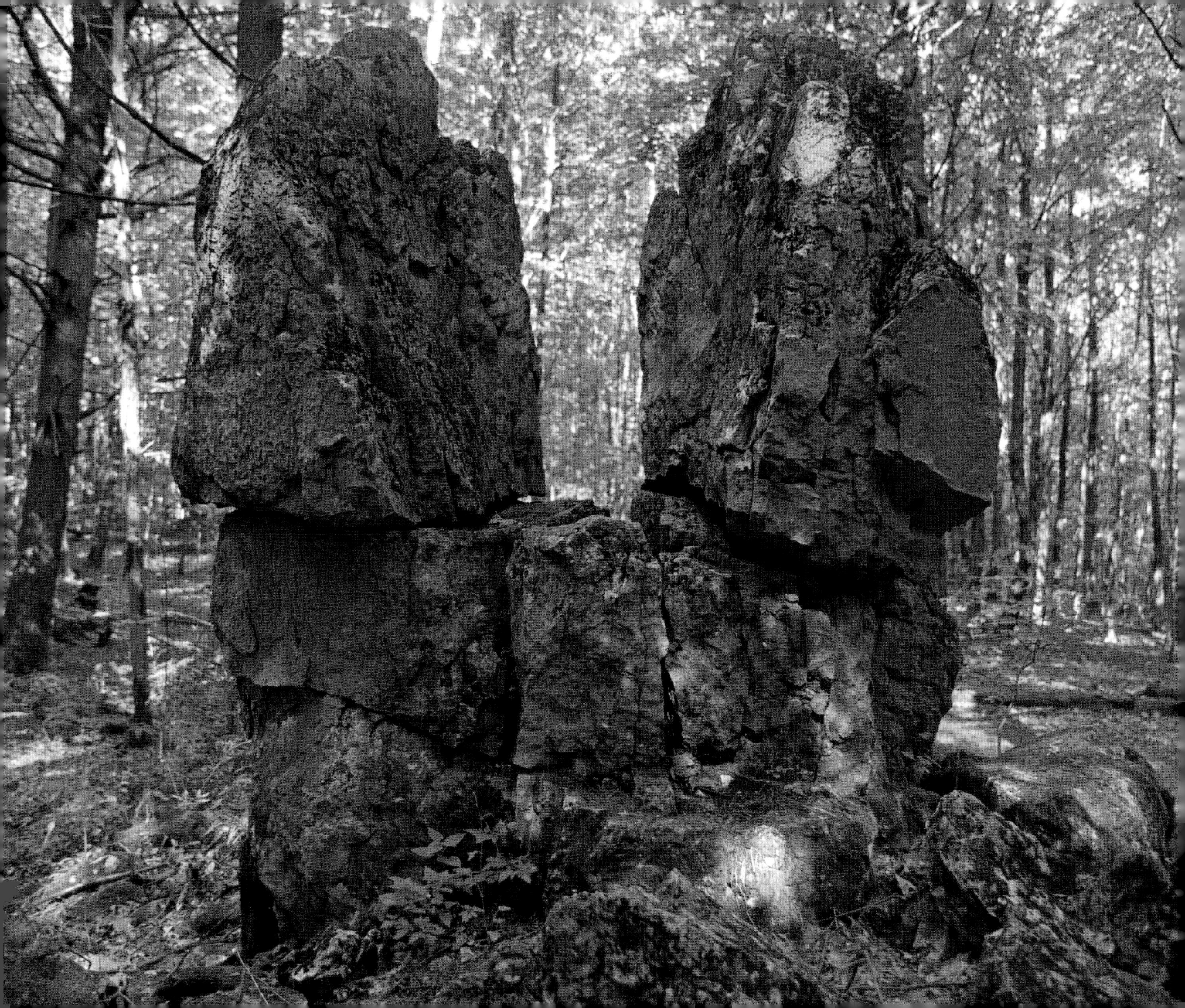

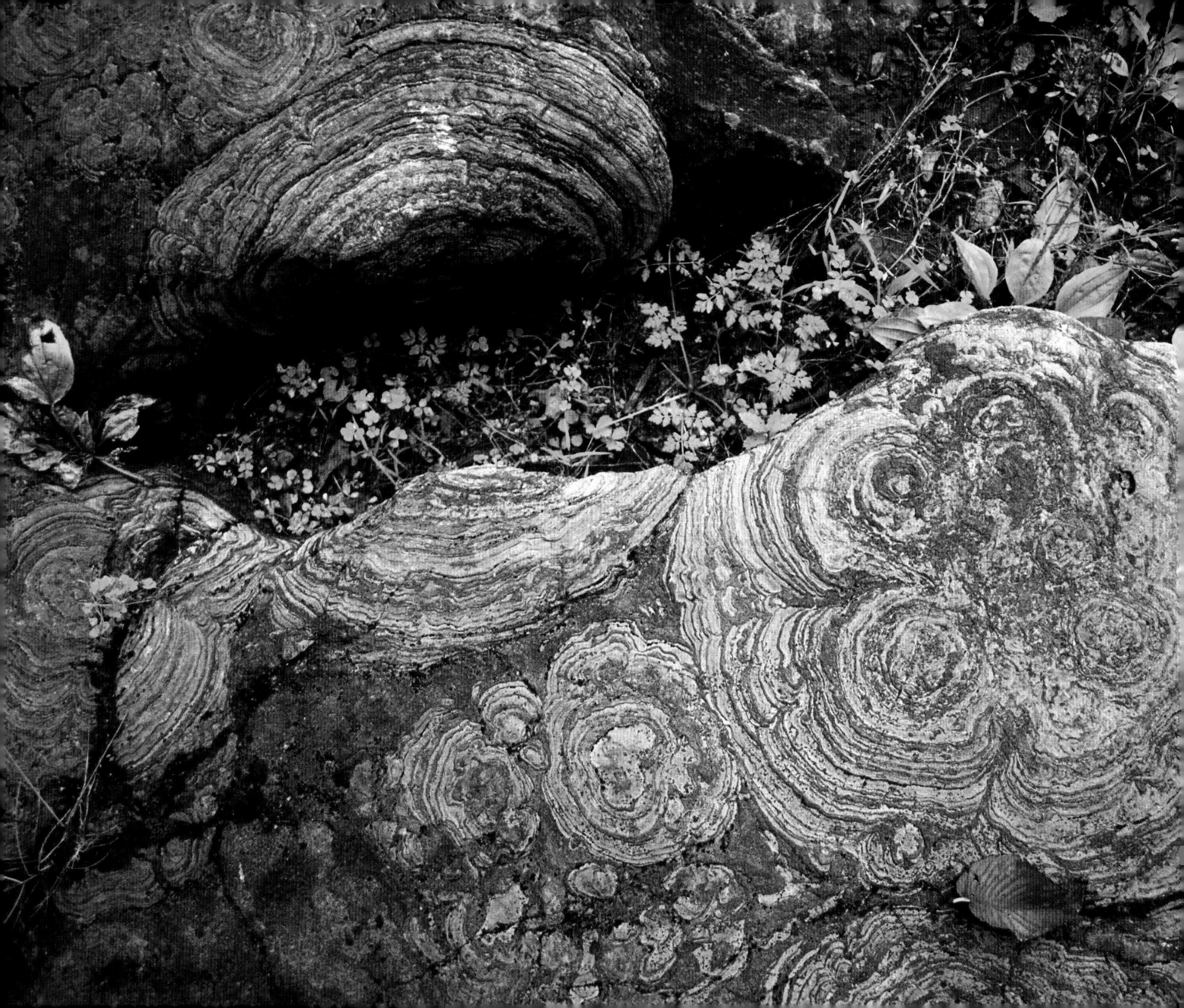

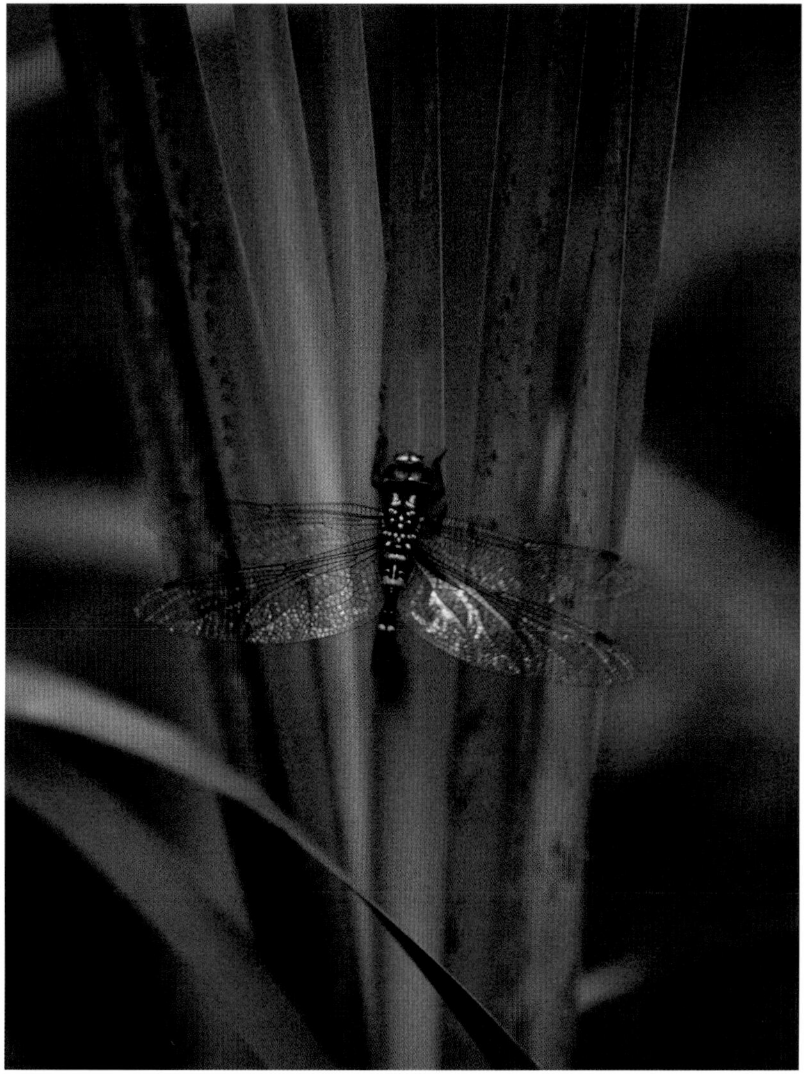

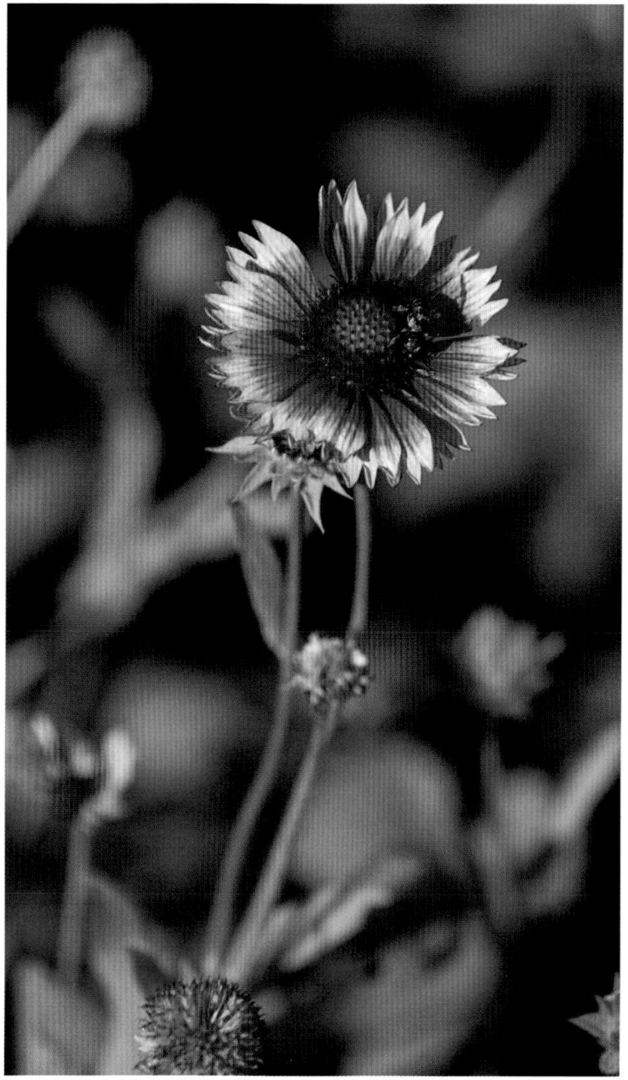

THE PETRIFIED SEA GARDENS features 500-million-year-old fossils called stromatolites, remnants of a tropical ocean shoreline.

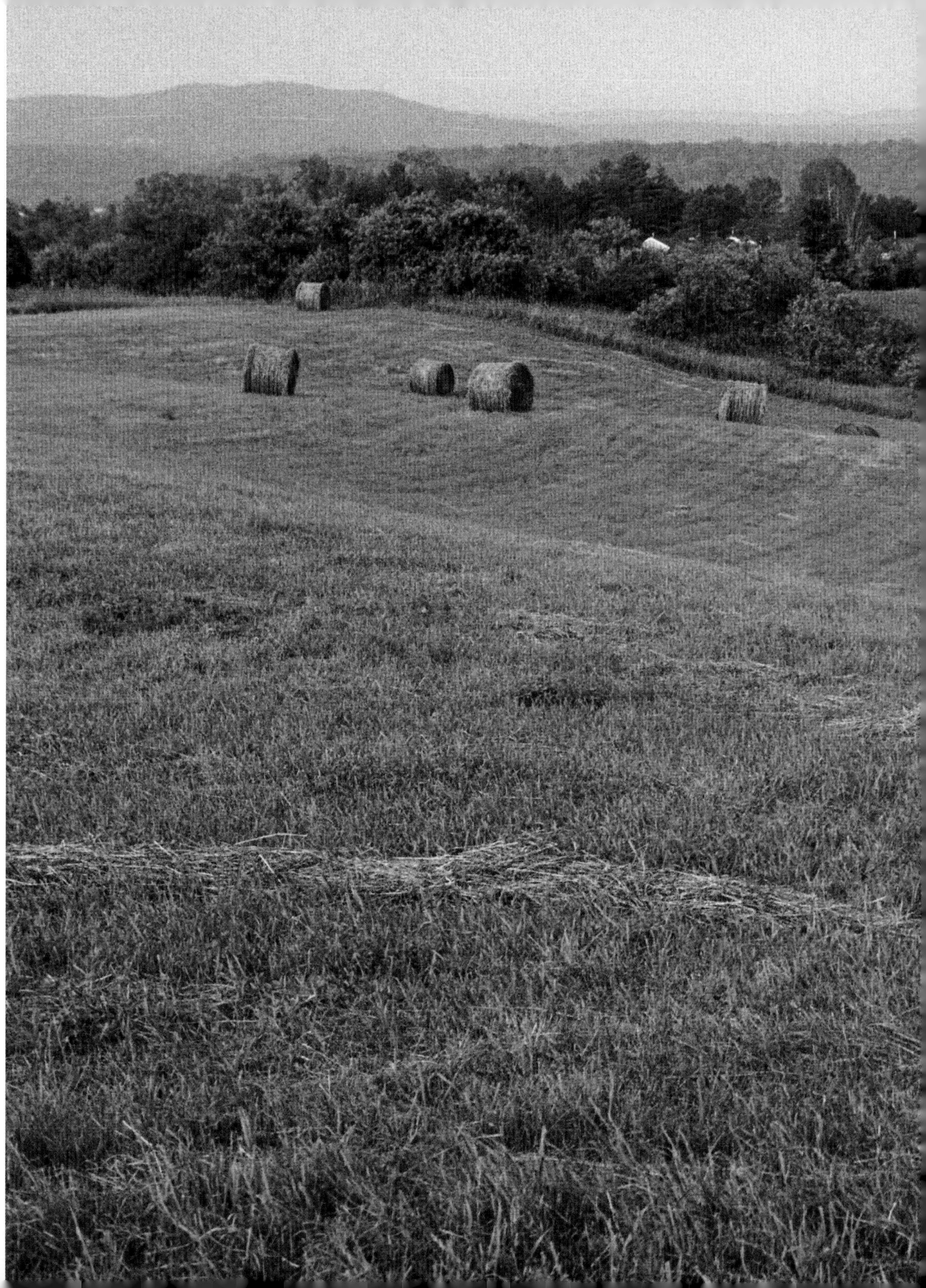

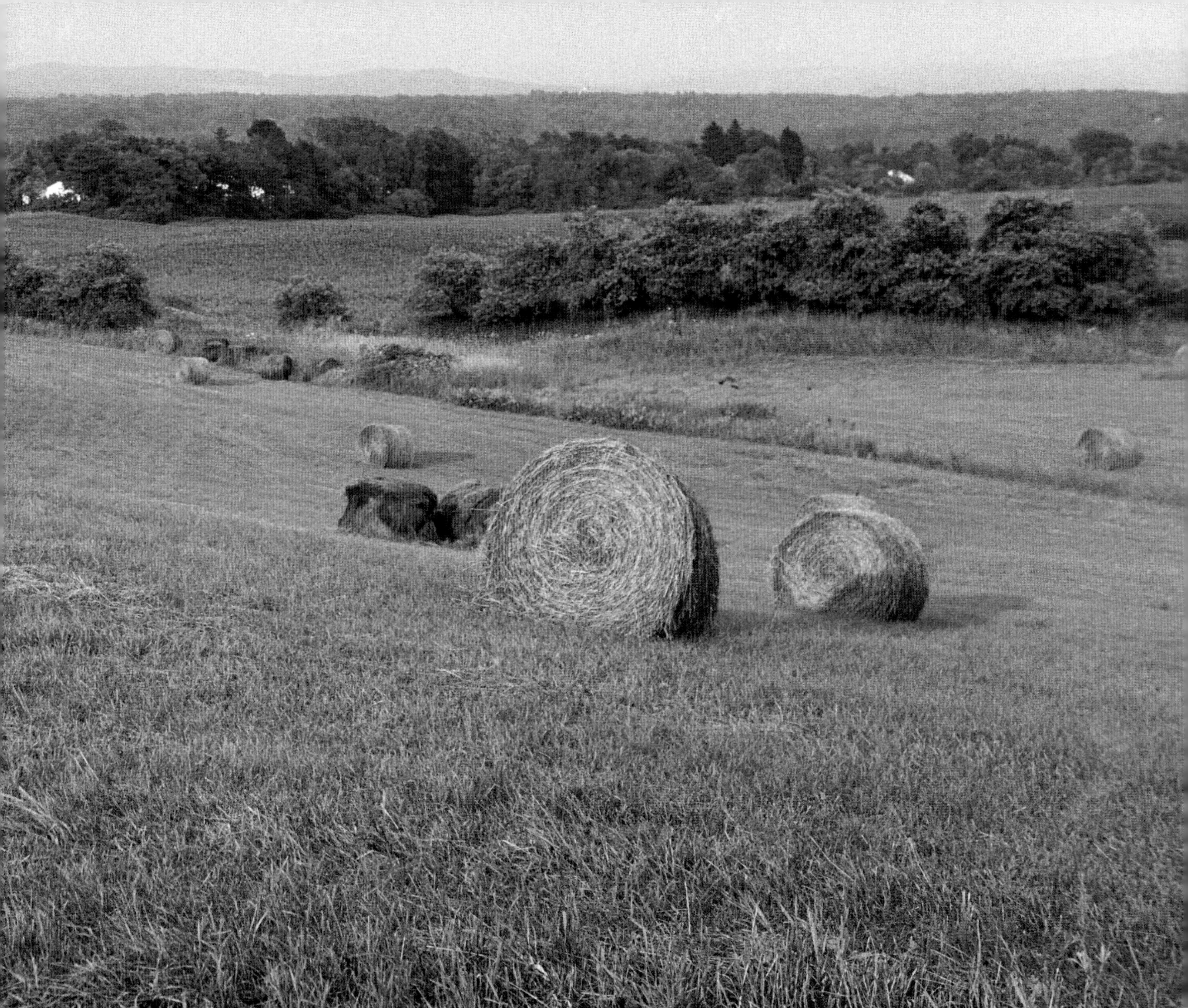

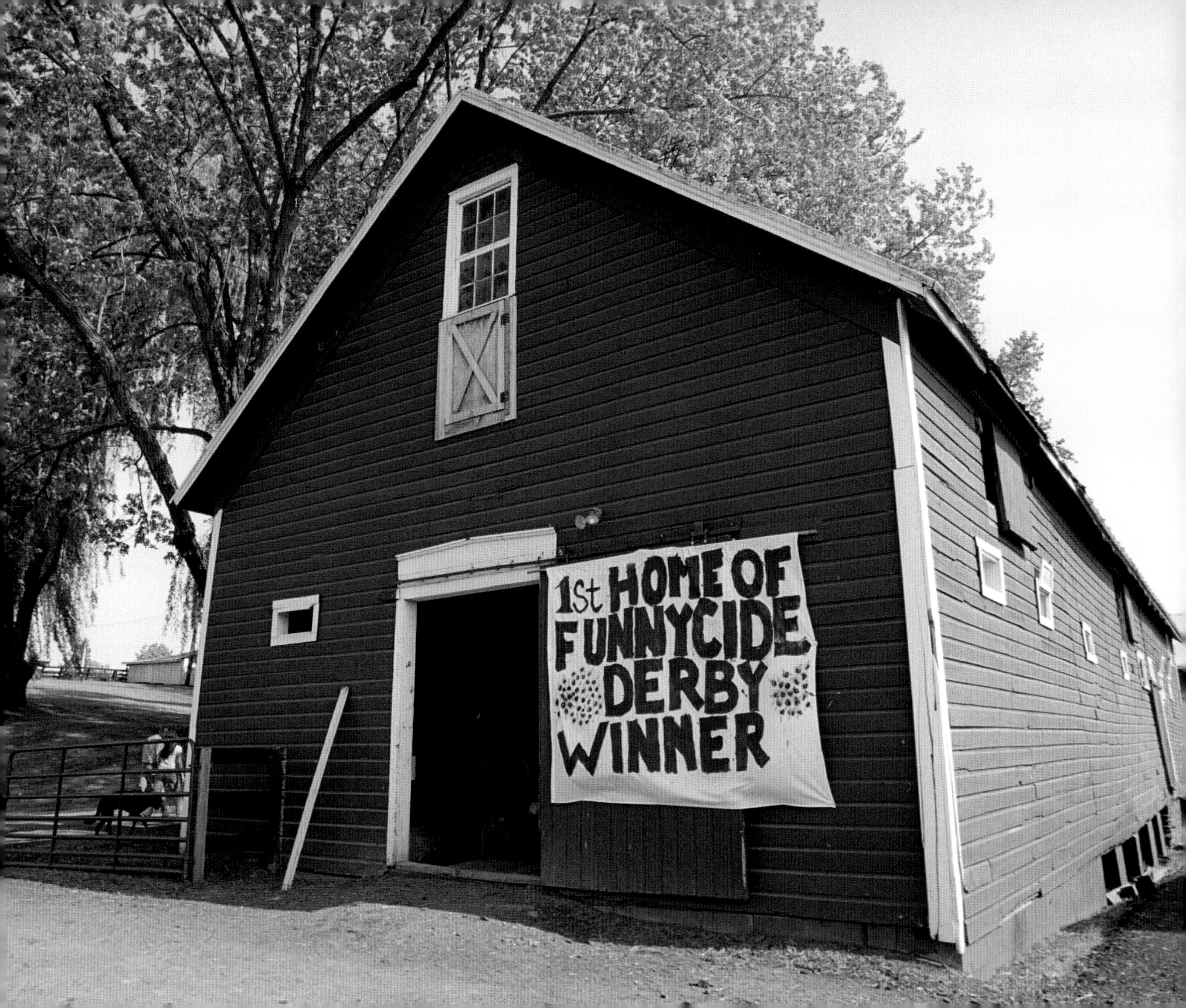
1st HOME OF
FUNNYCIDE
DERBY
WINNER

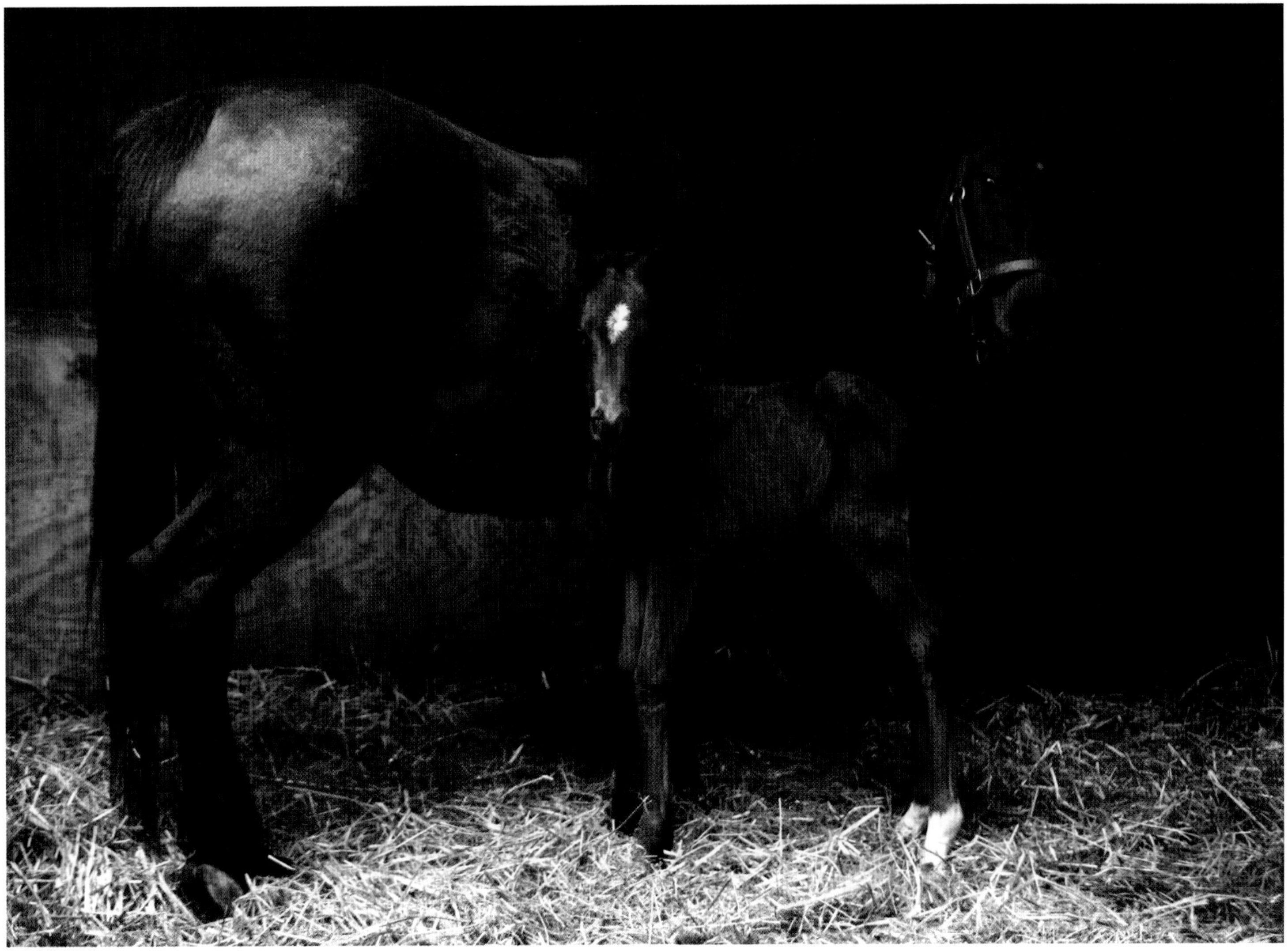

MCMAHON OF SARATOGA THOROUGHBREDS (LEFT) shows its pride in 2003 Kentucky Derby winner Funny Cide.

NEW ARRIVAL — A day-old foal and her dam at Mill Creek Farm.

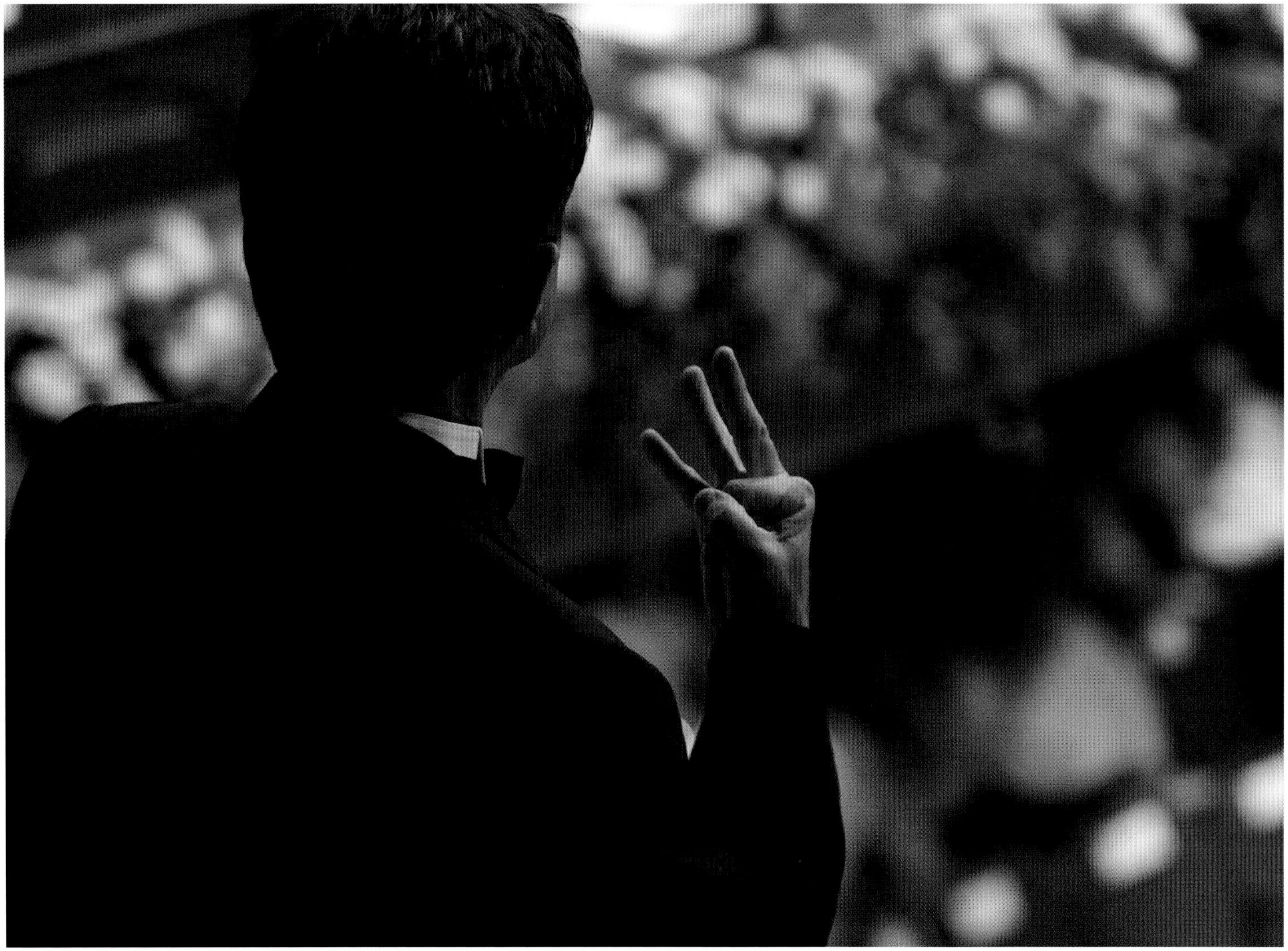

 SALES NIGHTS — At the Fasig-Tipton yearling sales, horsemen buy horses for prices sometimes reaching into the millions. Fans and tourists also enjoy the glittery scene, perhaps more for the exorbitant prices and buyers' Rolls-Royces than for the horseflesh.

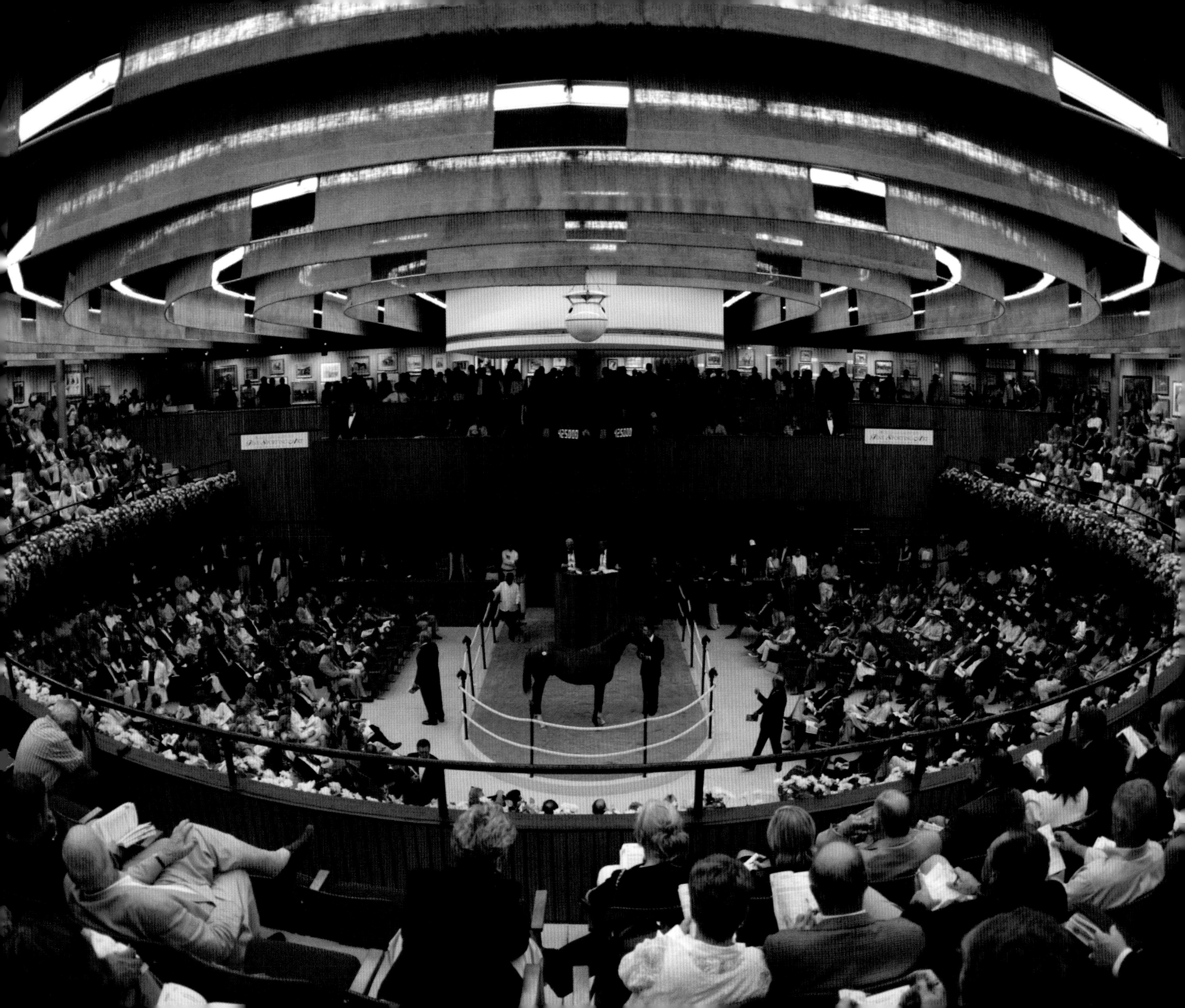
425000
425000

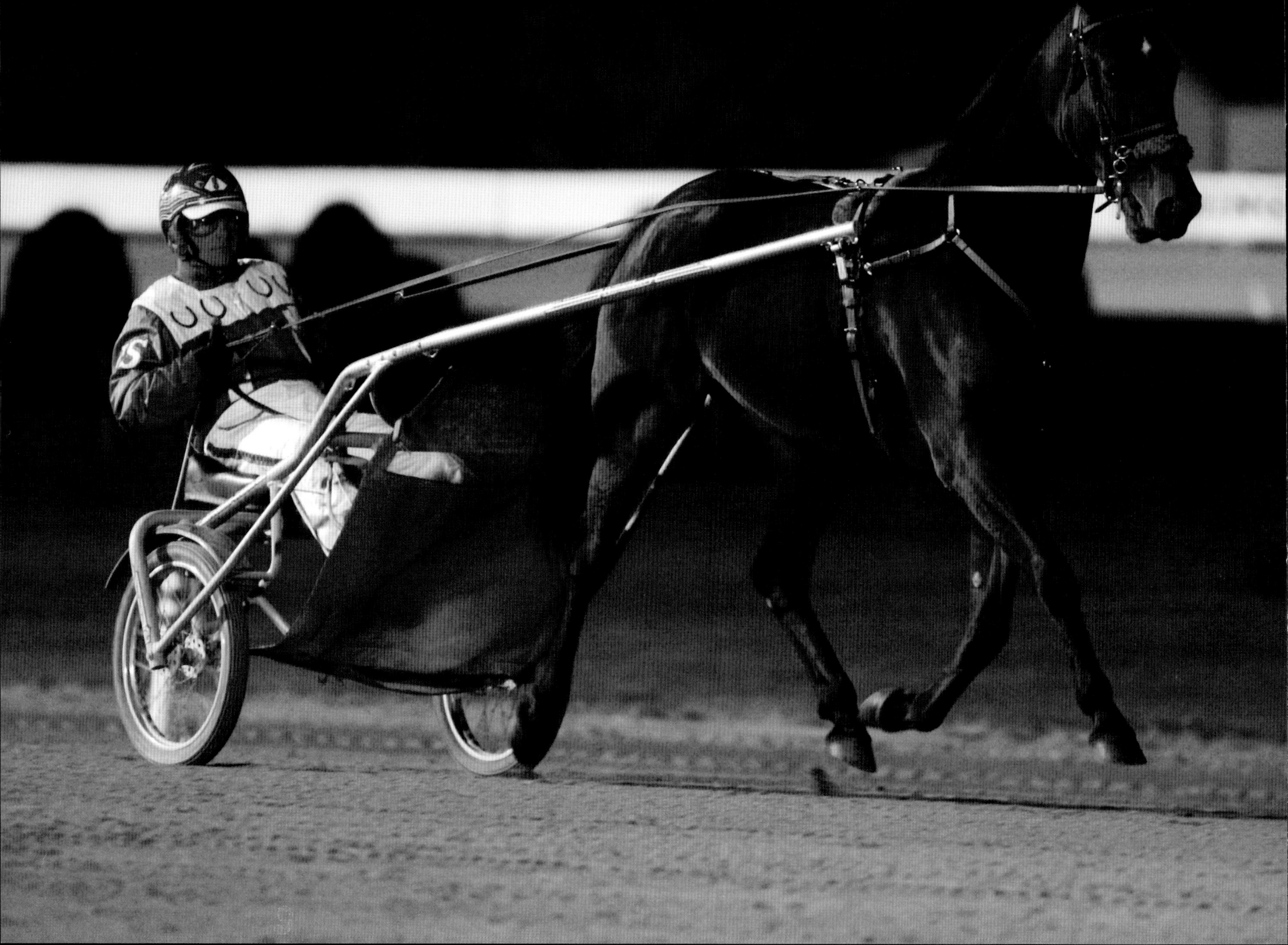

BUNNY LAKE, the 2001 Harness Horse of the Year, at her retirement ceremony in 2004 at Saratoga Gaming and Raceway.

THE "RACINO," which opened in 2004 at Saratoga Gaming and Raceway.

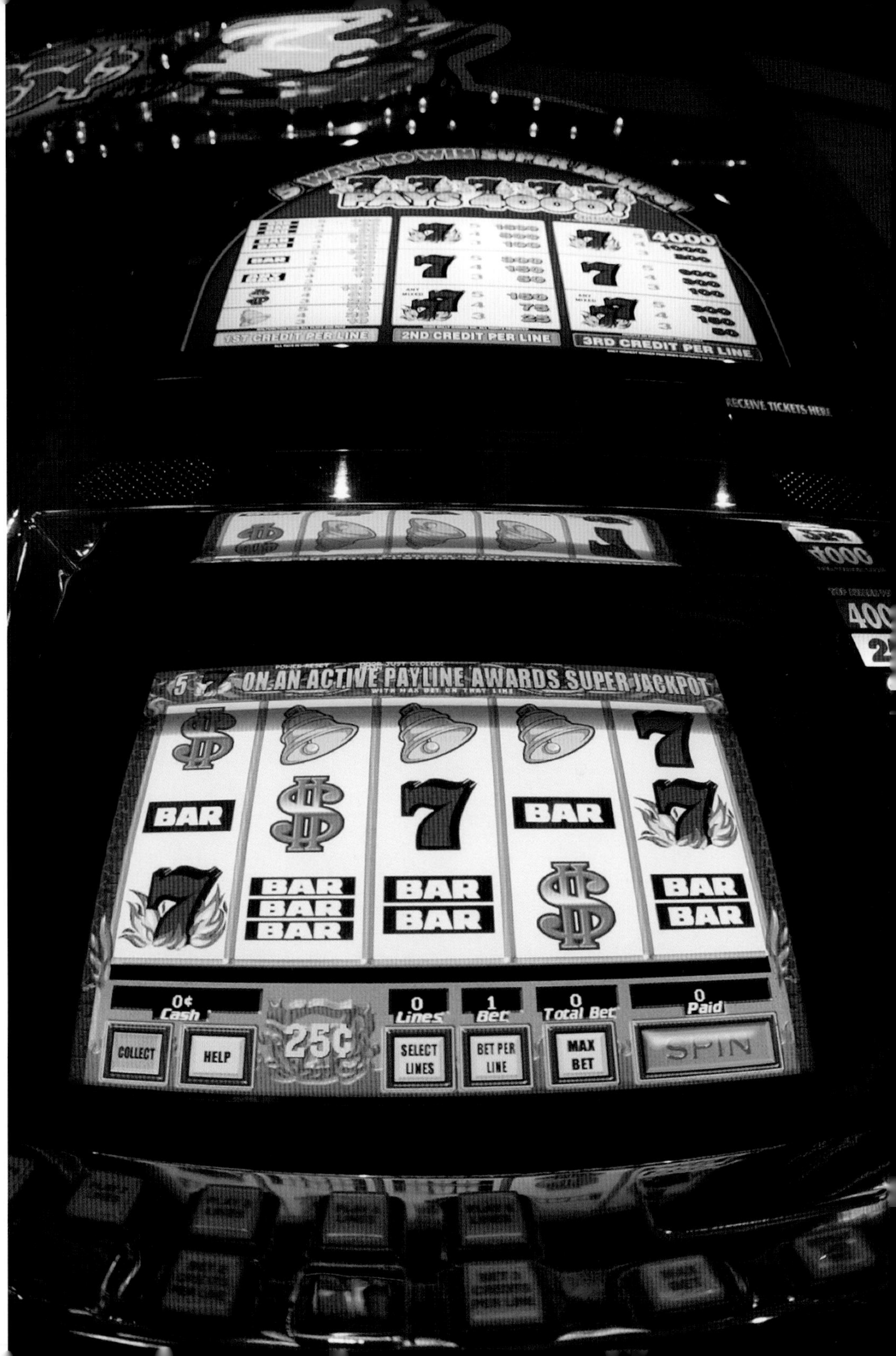

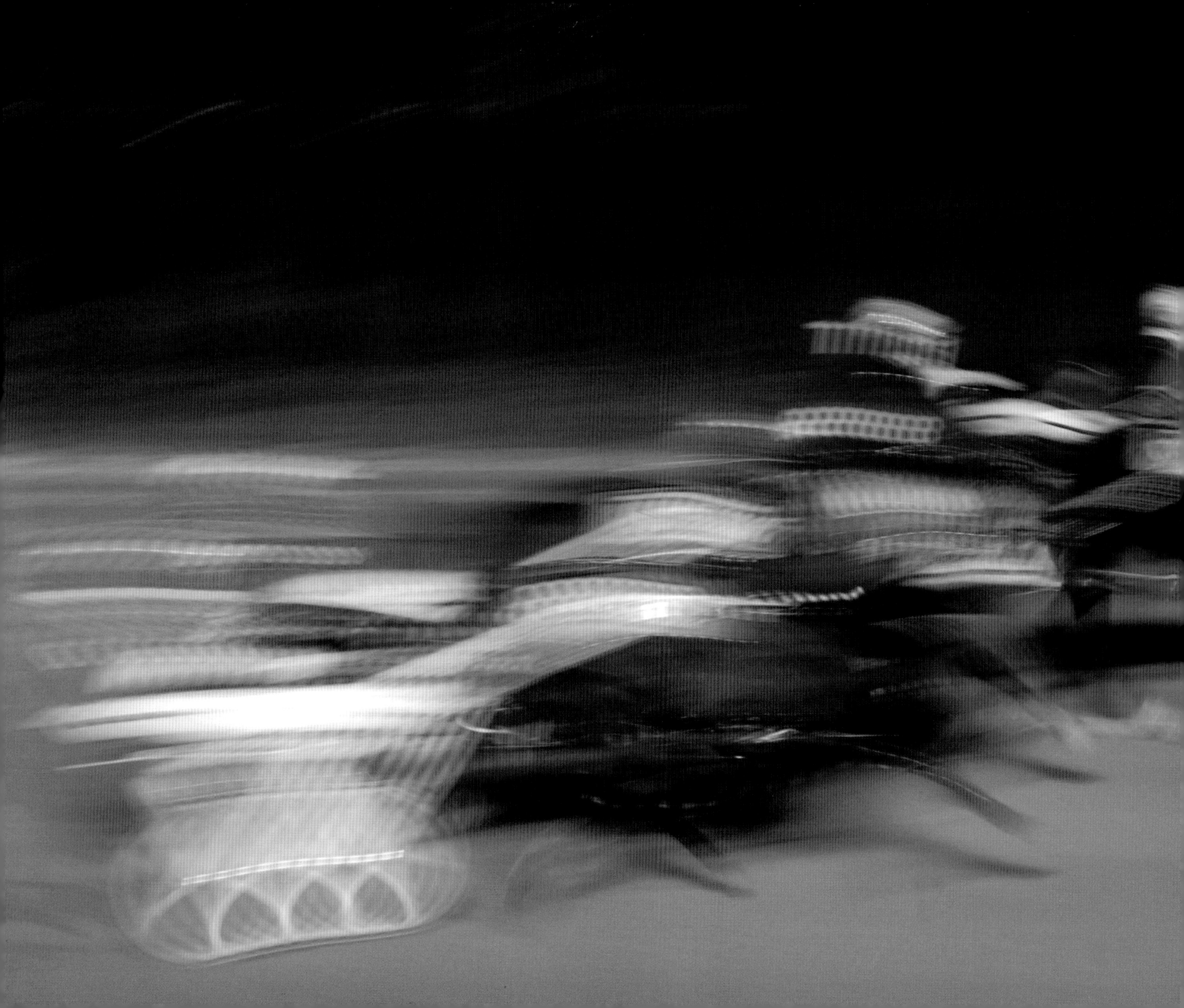

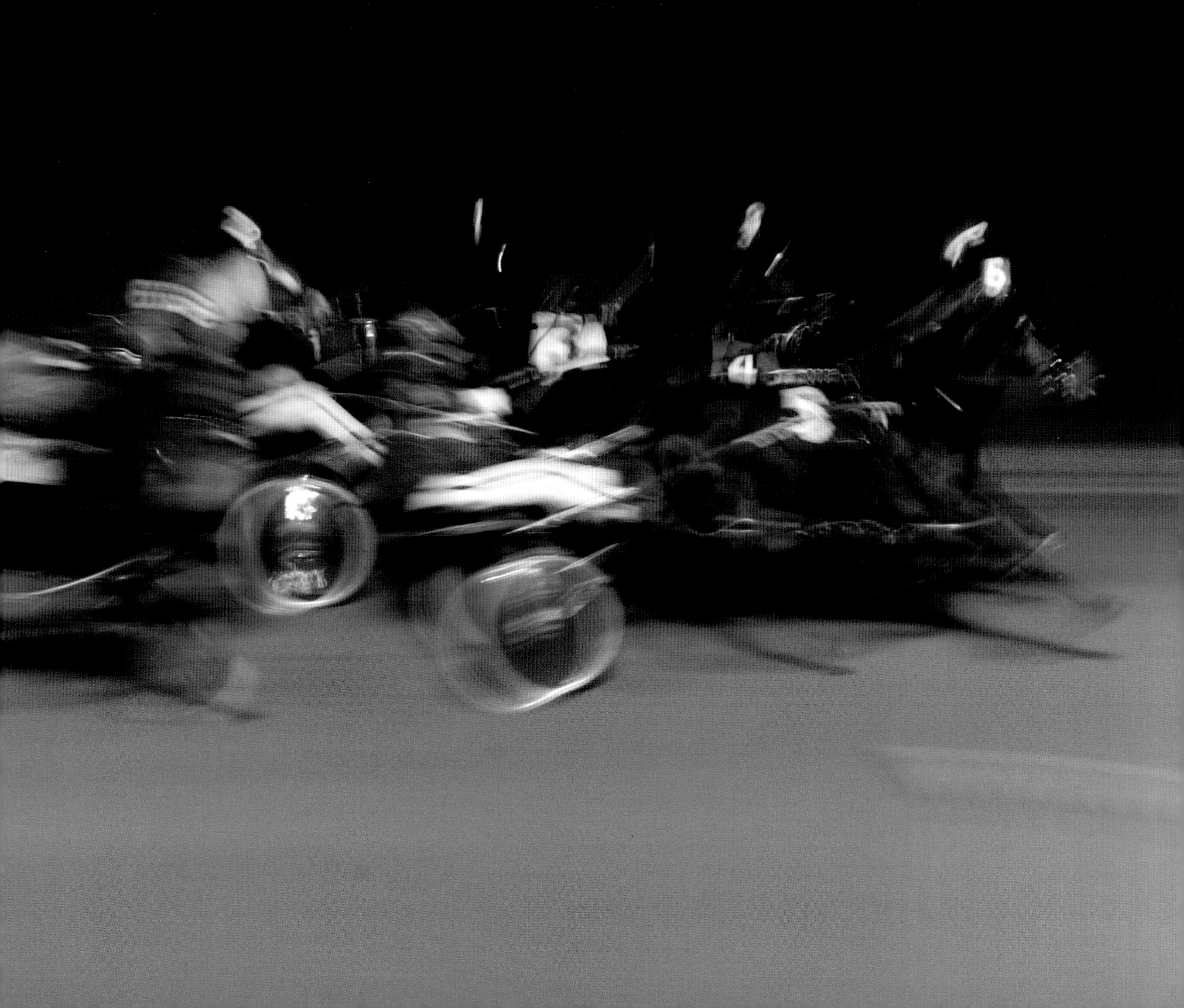

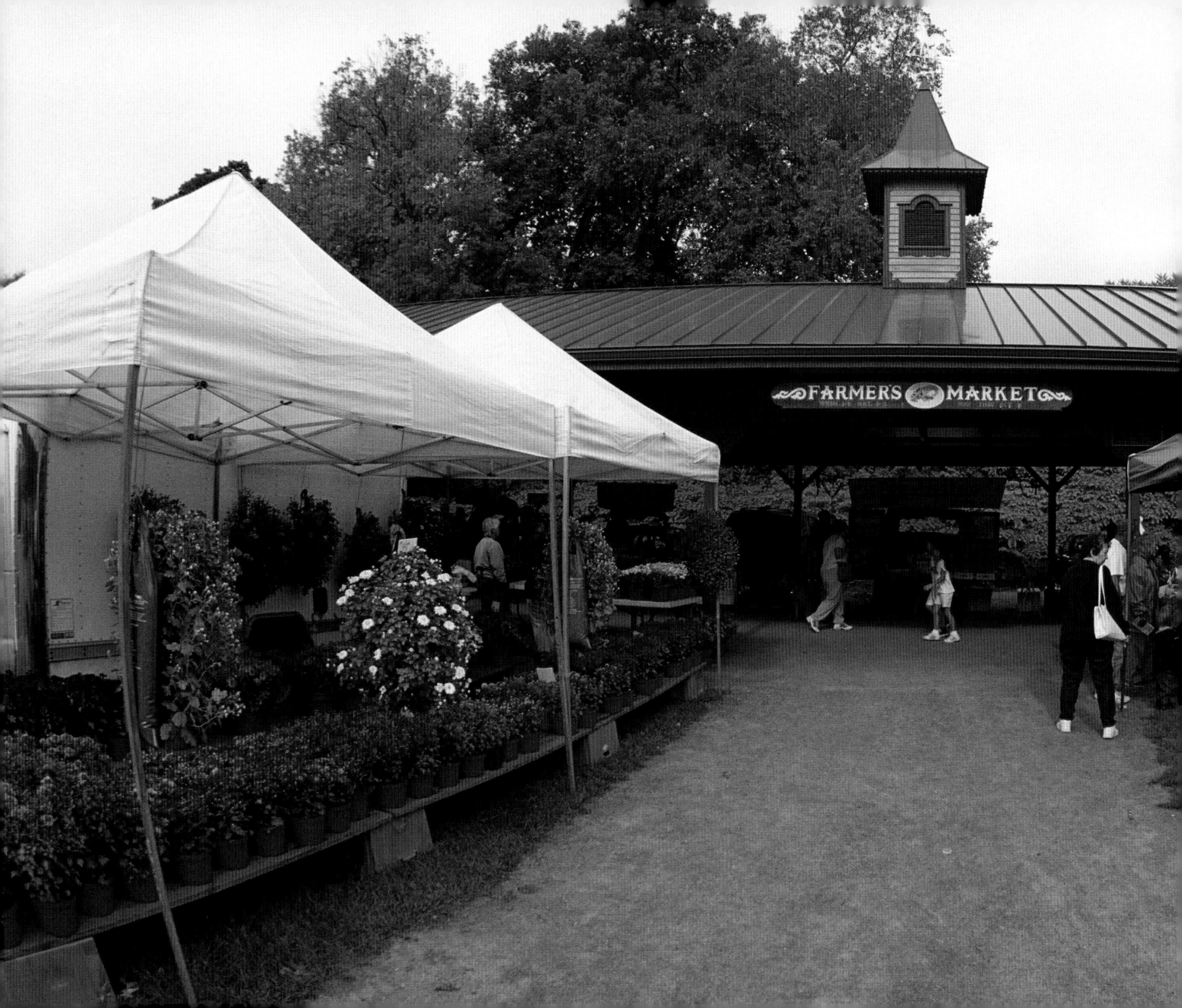
FARMER'S MARKET

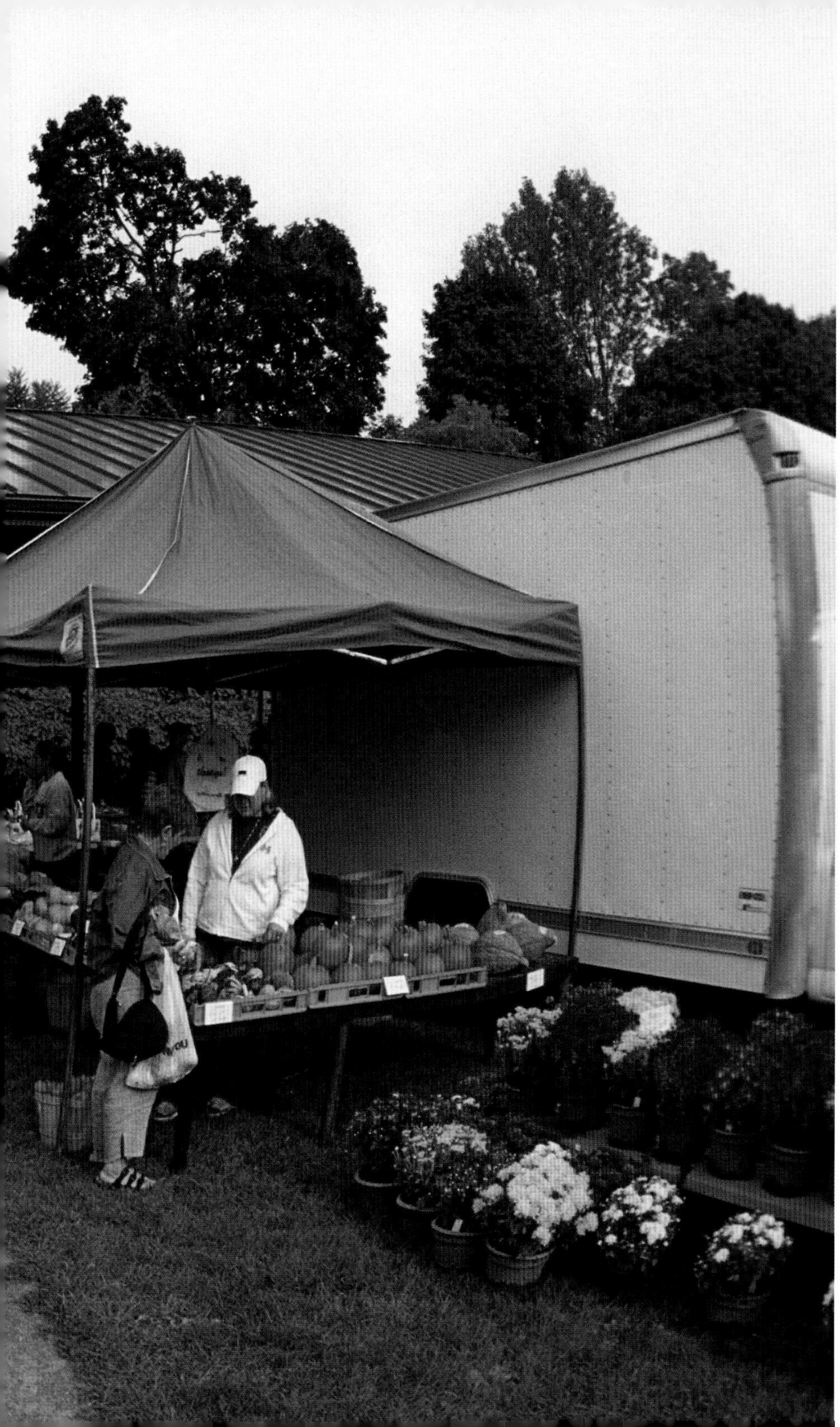

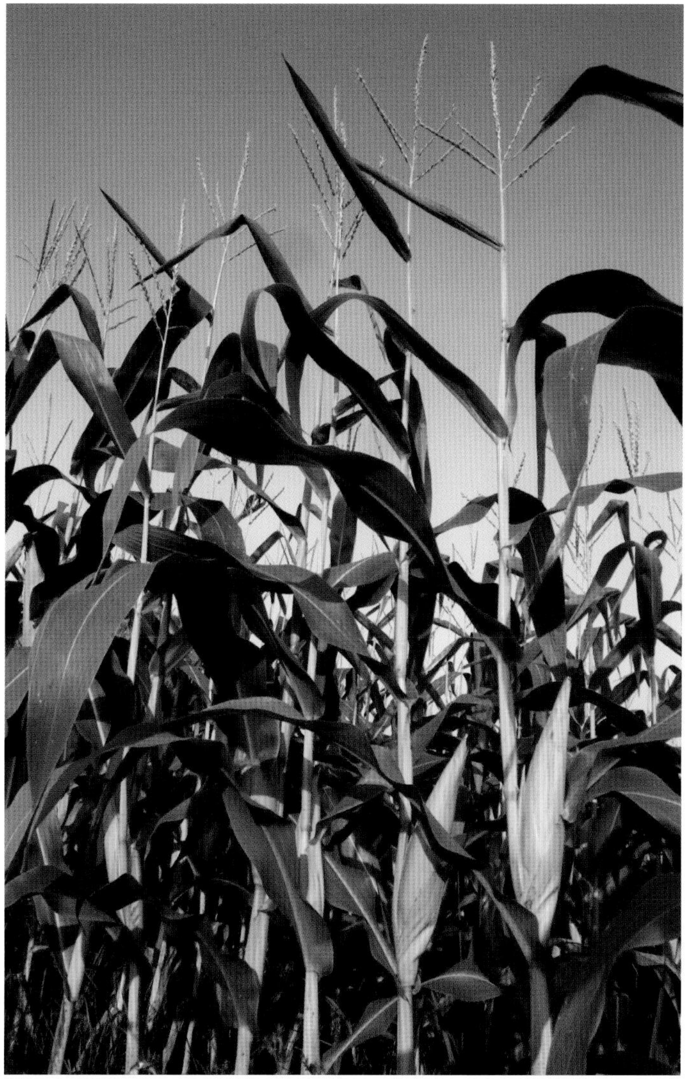

Saratoga Seasons

The four seasons paint beautifully diverse scenes with a palette most resplendent.

For many year-round residents spring is Saratoga's most anticipated season. After the prolonged chill of winter, tentative light green shoots peek through melting snows. The sun creeps closer. Daylight hours lengthen.

Trees bud, birds sing on high, and flowers — snowdrops, crocus, then daffodils — bloom everywhere. At local farms foals take wobbly first steps, kindling hopes of the next Funny Cide. Farmers prepare their fields as apple trees burst with fragrant blossoms.

Families stroll through Congress Park, delighting in the world's reawakening. Ducks guard nests and hope for generous, bread-toting tourists. Children eagerly wait their turn on the carousel.

As the greenery awakens and spreads, it melds into the rich, dark greens of summer.

Saratoga's population nearly doubles in summer. Many visitors enjoy the Performing Arts Center, parks, and bathhouses, and more than 66,000 crammed the racetrack in 2003 for a Travers Stakes Day record crowd.

Broadway is abuzz as tourists flit through seemingly countless restaurants, bars, and shops. Street musicians and horse carriages flavor the busy scene. In Congress Park, "Shakespeare in the Park" takes center stage.

When summer wanes, leaves burst like flames into brilliant gold, red, and orange. Last ears of corn jut skyward from browning stalks. Farmers hay their fields one last time, and fruit hangs heavily from apple trees. Every countryside road is rich with Grandma Moses scenes.

Many tourists linger, captivated by the stunning foliage and final warm days. Skidmore College is in full swing, the Farmer's Market remains busy, and Saratoga Spa State Park golfers appreciate the cooler temperatures.

And then winter comes, and brilliant leaves grudgingly turn brown and slip to earth. The snow flies.

While many question how residents tolerate winter's bitter chill, it's a remarkably beautiful season. On crisp, clear, snowy nights the deep blue world is quiet save the hushed sound of falling snow. The landscape is a pure one. The pace slows.

The Performing Arts Center and Adelphi Hotel shut their doors during winter months. Yet most local businesses remain open, and parking spots can be as elusive in January as in July. The city slows, but it does not hibernate. Locals brave the season in many ways, from ice fishing to cross-country skiing.

Finally, the crocuses and snowdrops return, and tourists begin making their summer plans. Saratoga Springs readies itself for another busy, bountiful year.

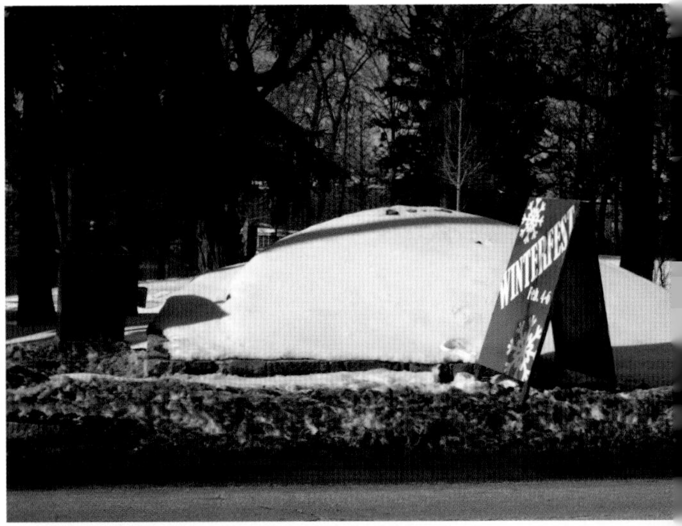

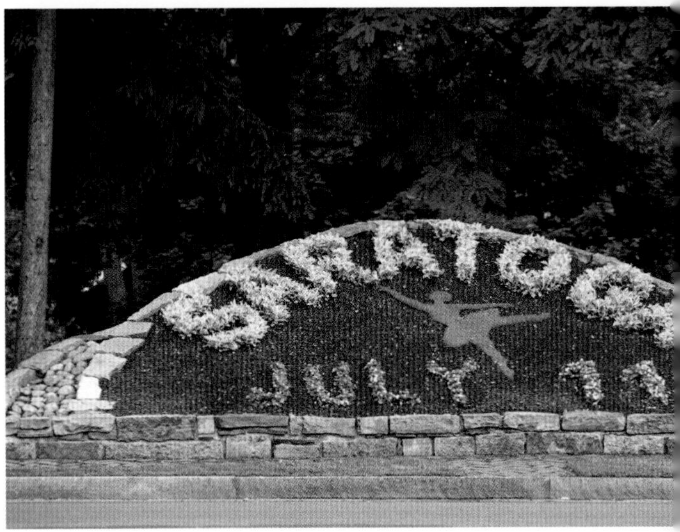

THIS WELL-KNOWN UNION AVENUE MESSAGE BOARD is changed daily during summer months.

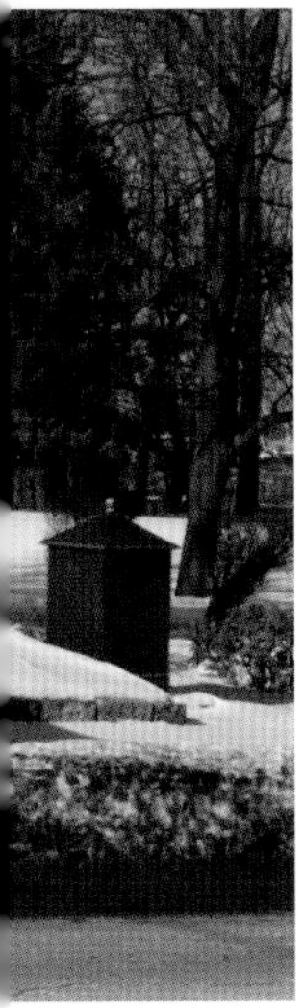

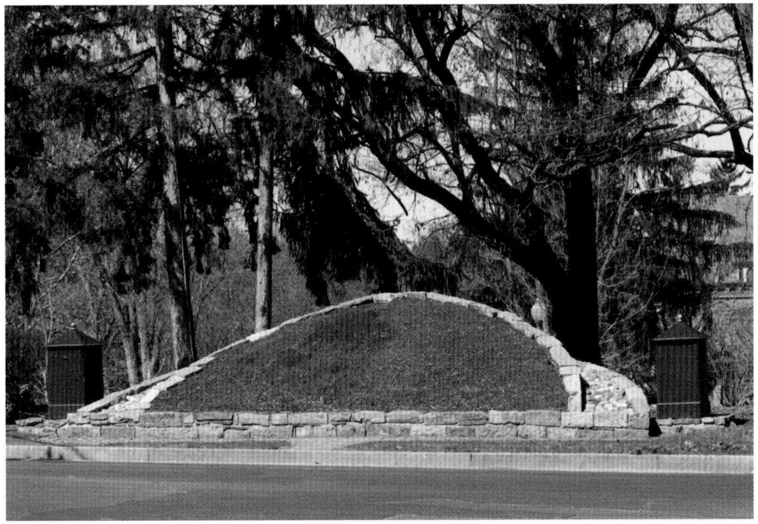

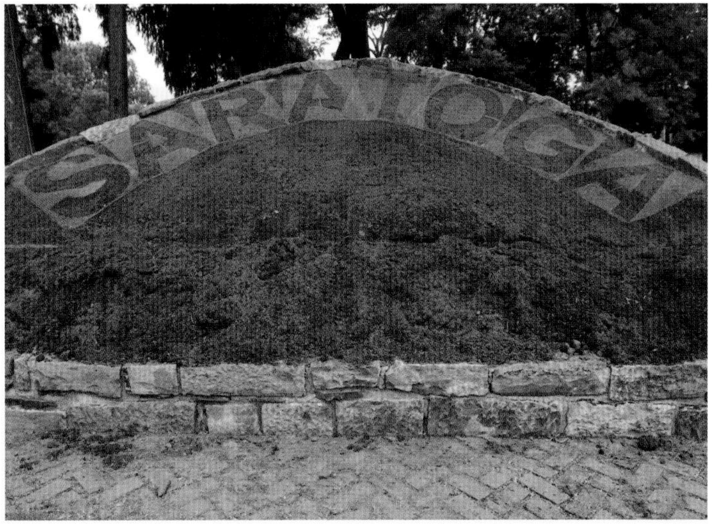
SARATOGA

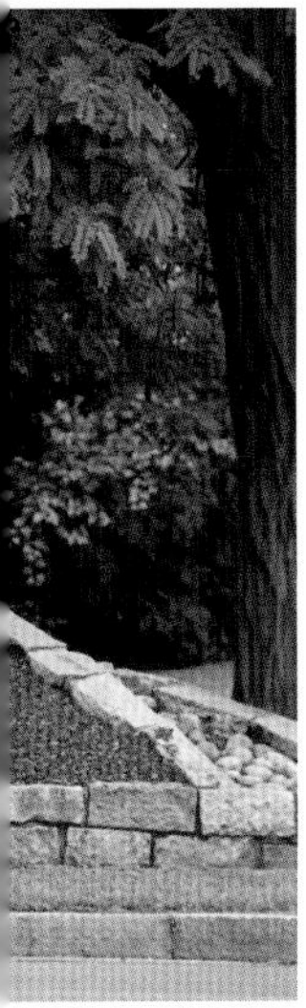

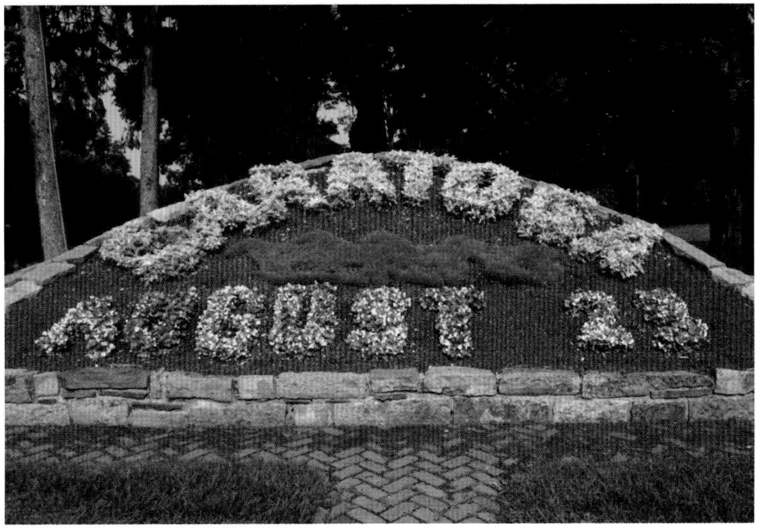

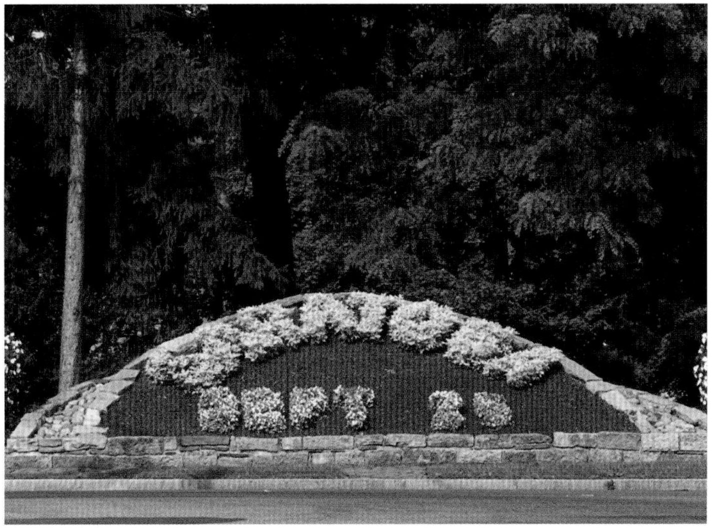

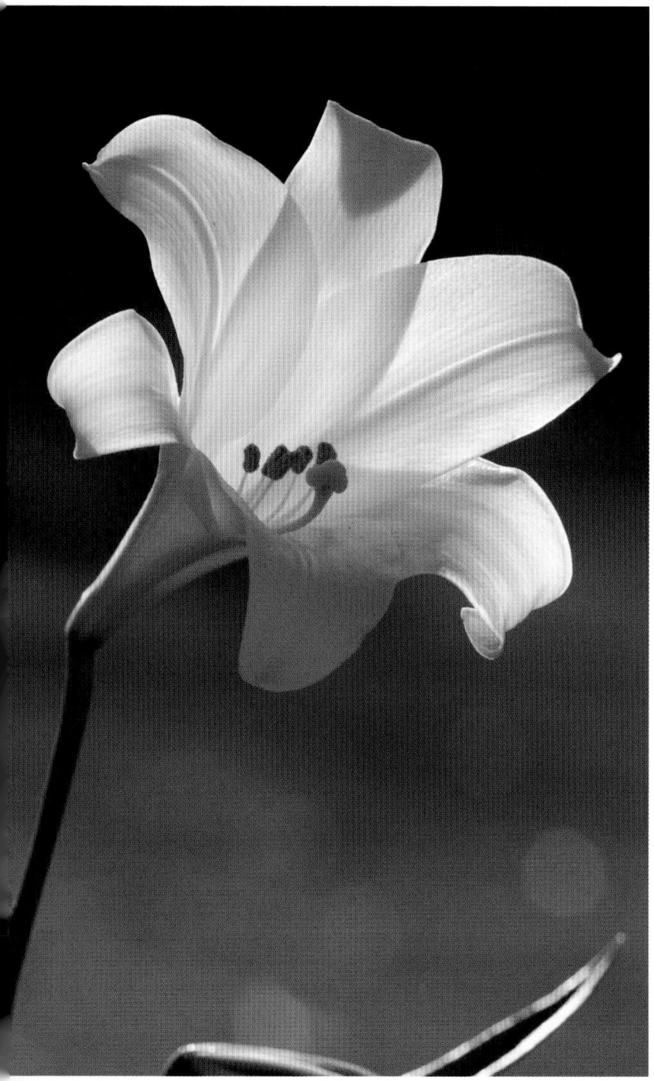

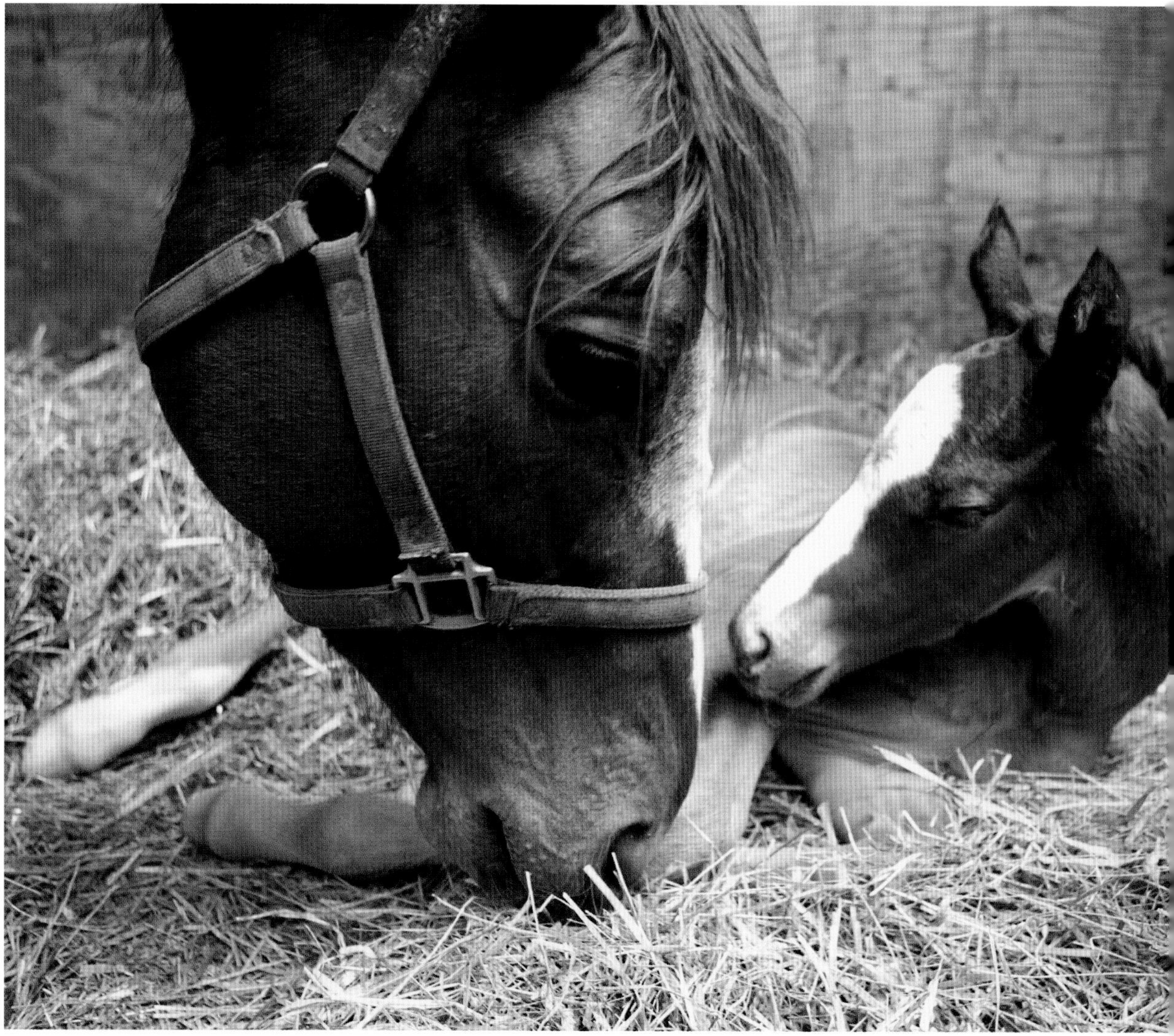

SPRING HAS SPRUNG — A Madonna lily, a mare and foal, and a Saratoga apple orchard in bloom.

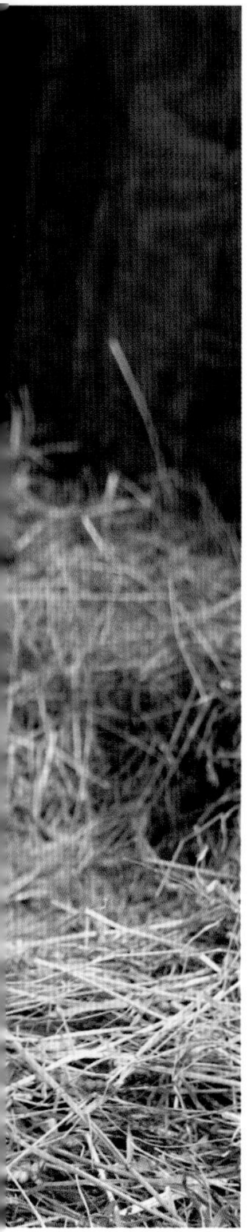

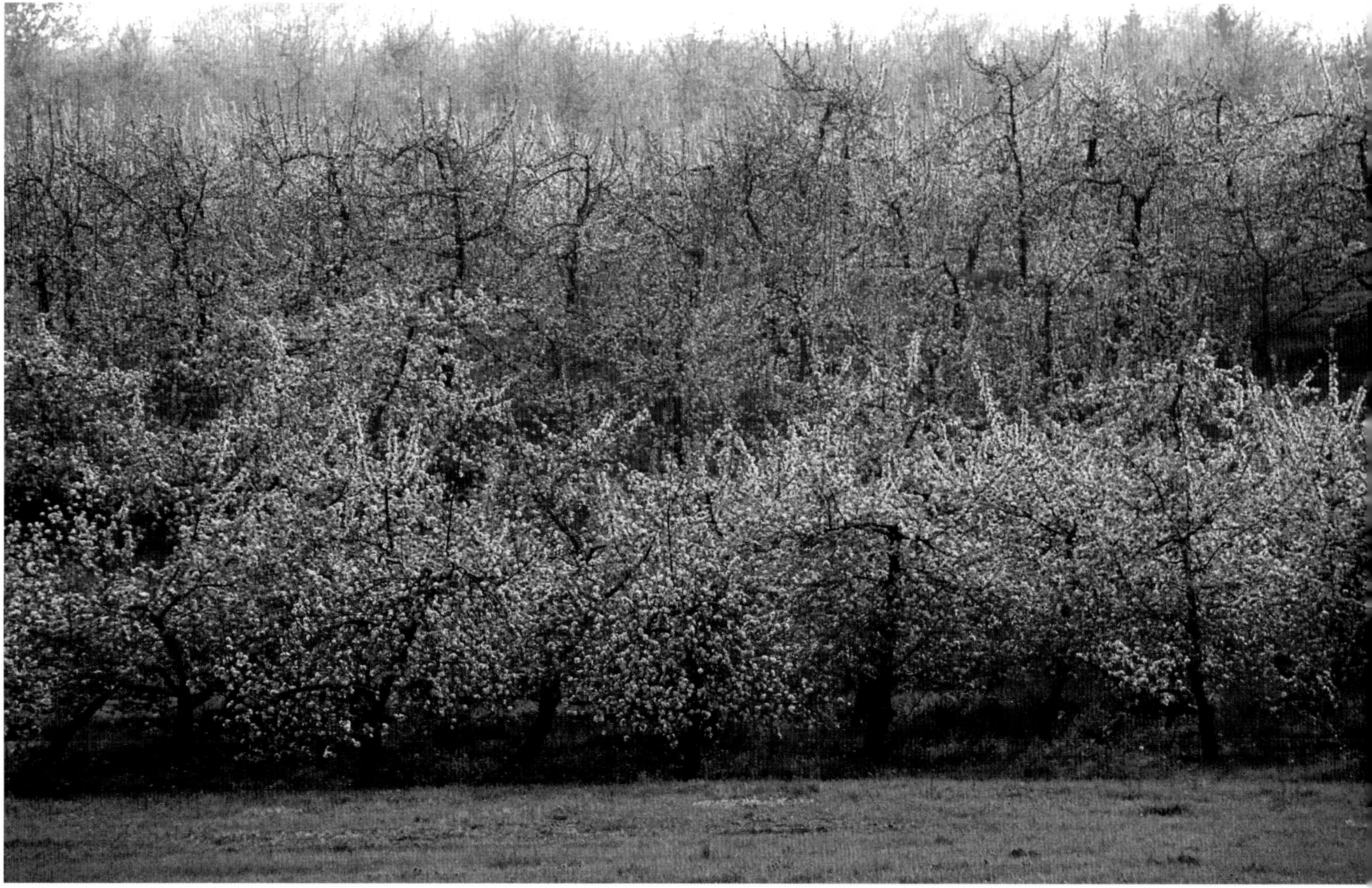

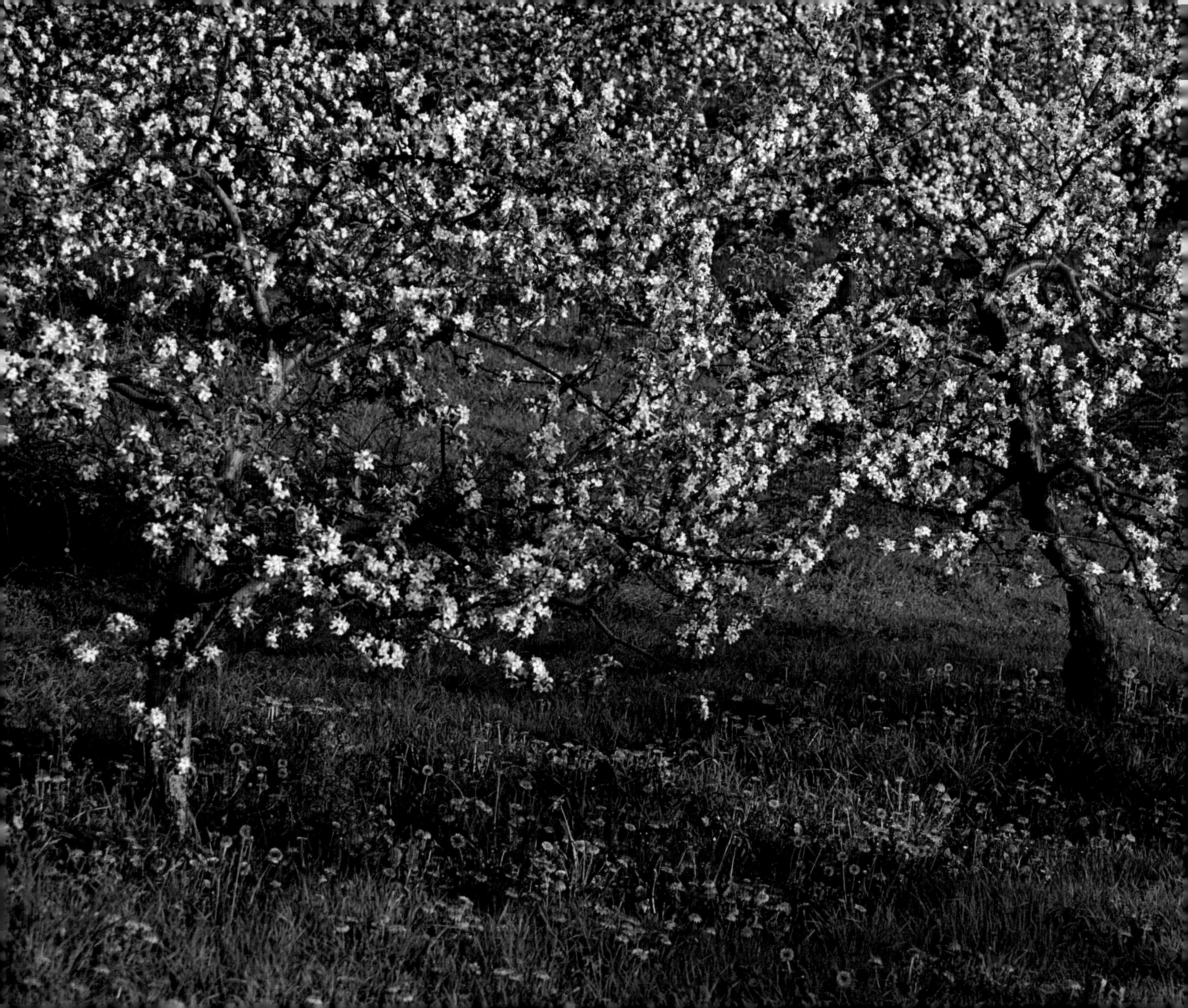

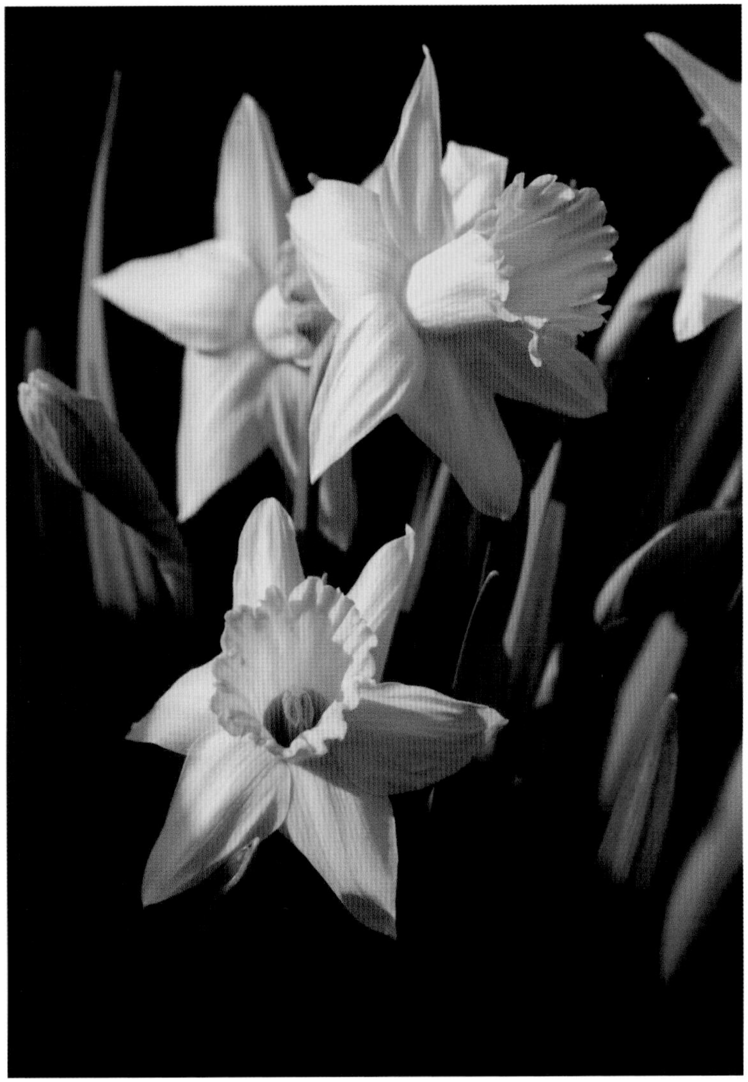

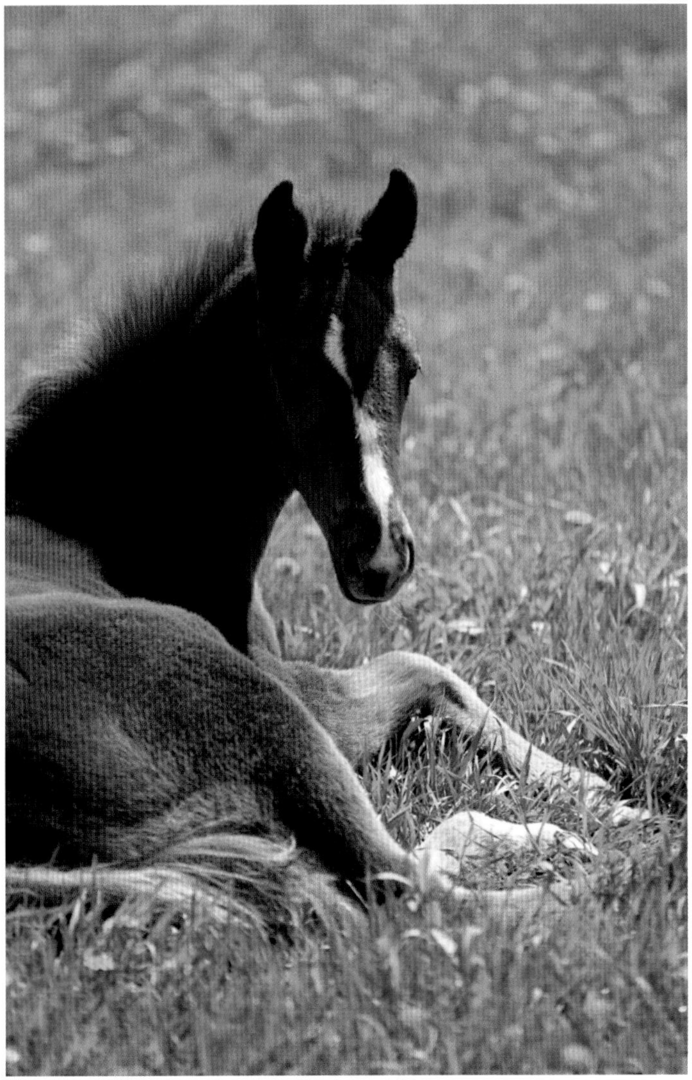

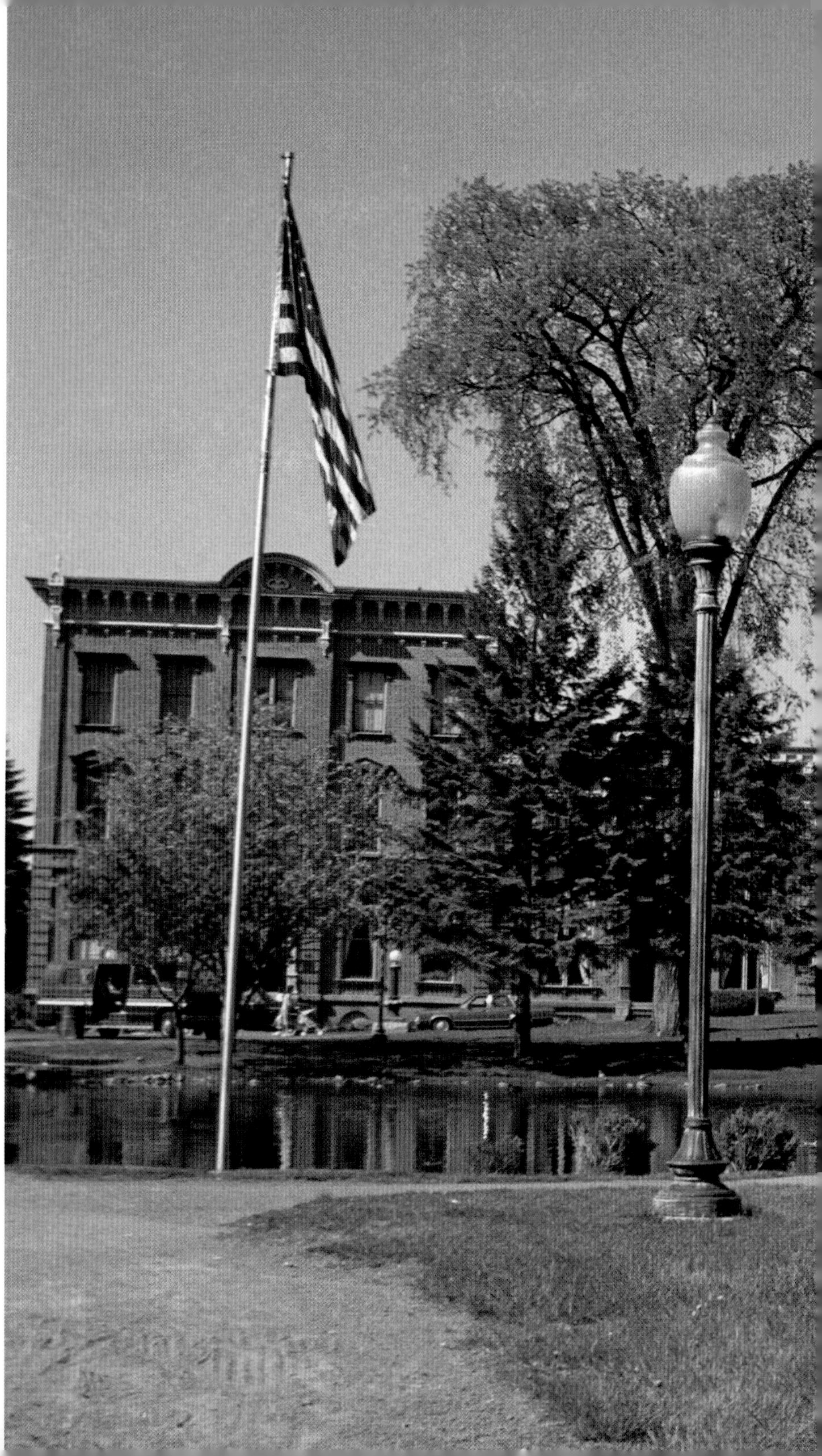

 CONGRESS PARK'S WAR MEMORIAL, with Canfield Casino in the background.

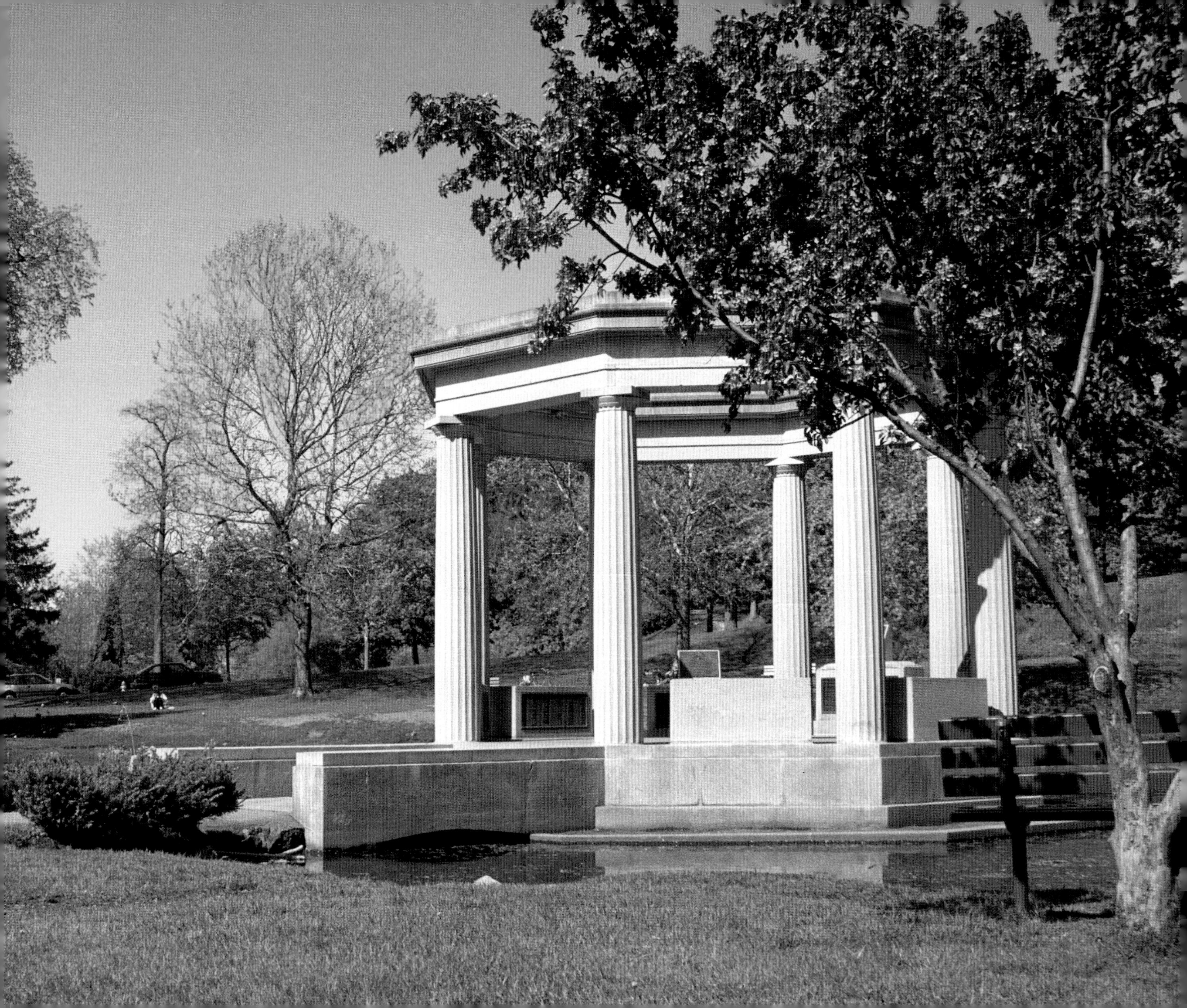

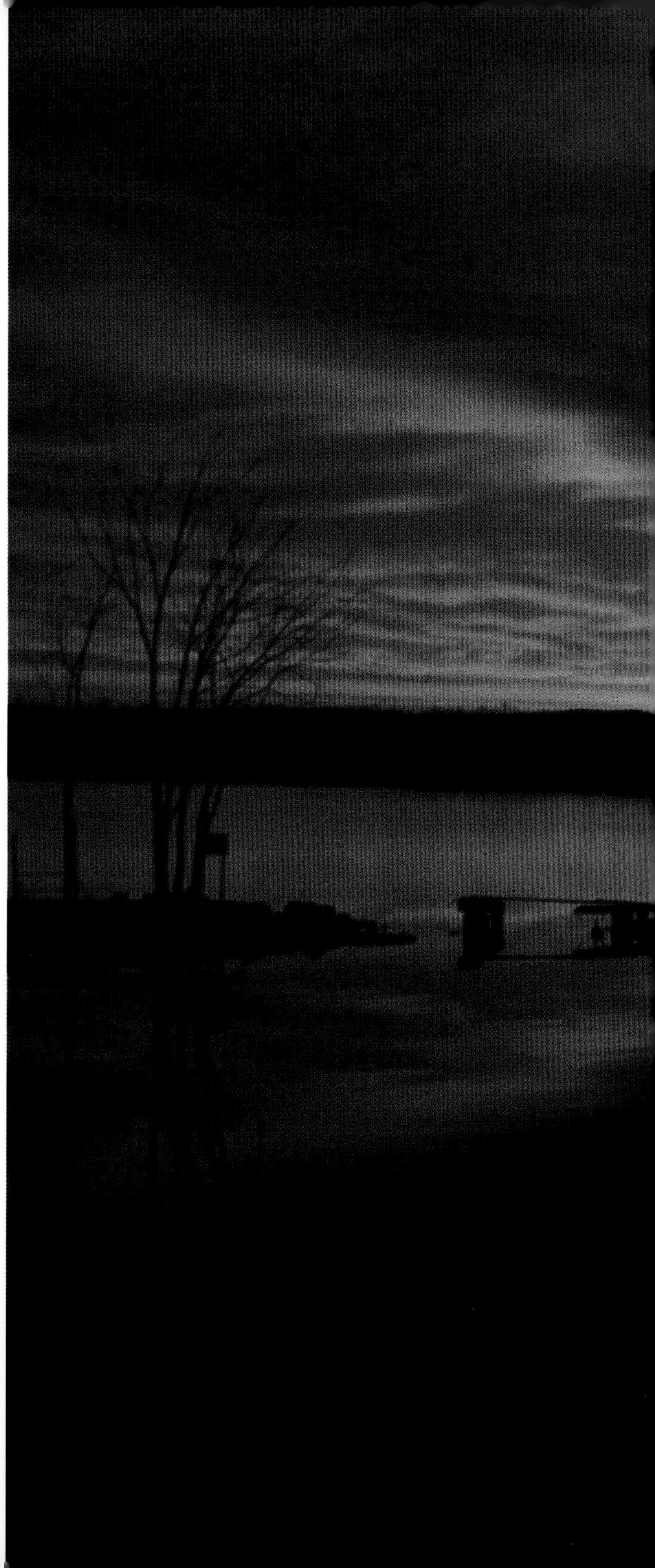

190 A SPRING SUNRISE ON SARATOGA LAKE

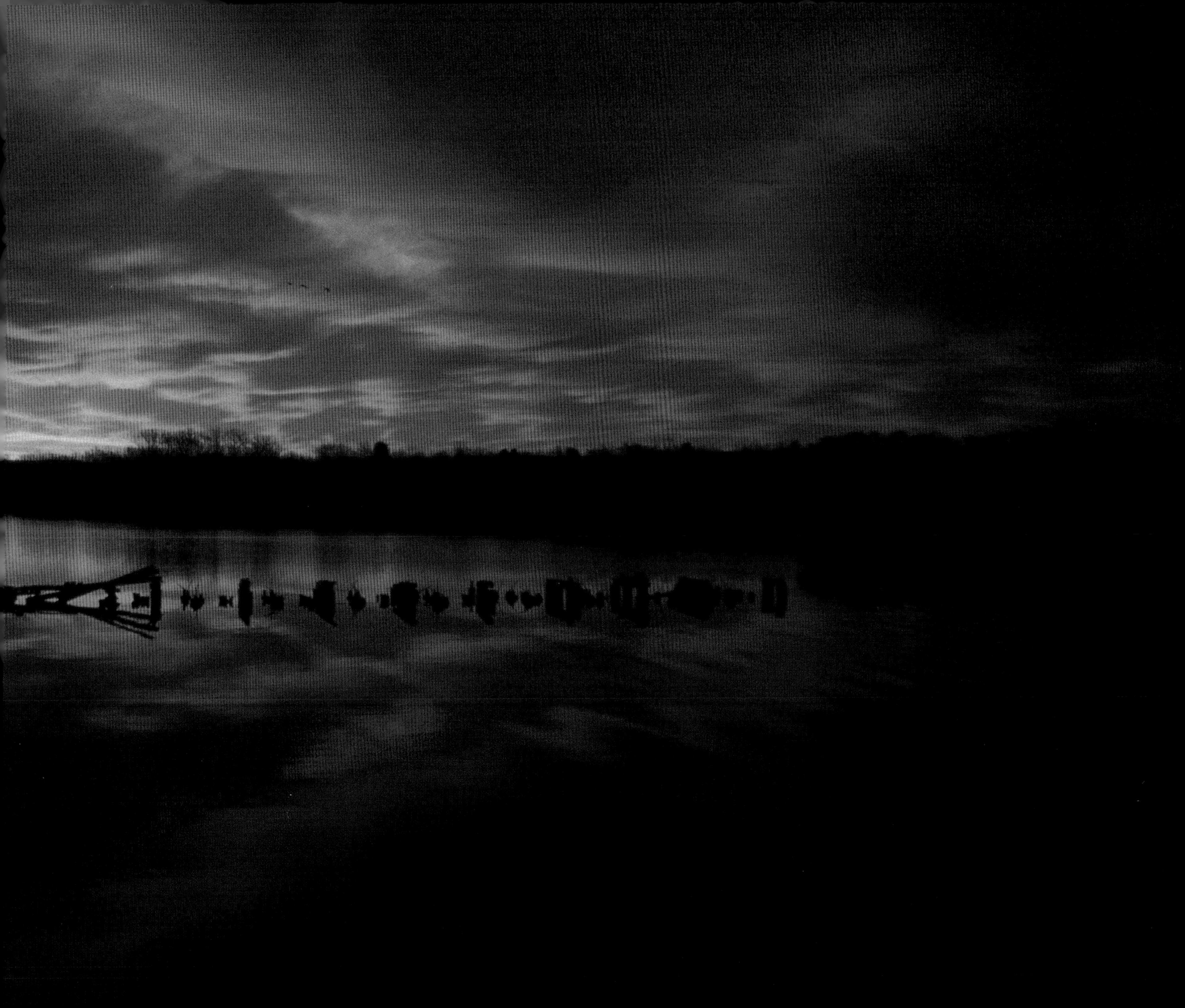

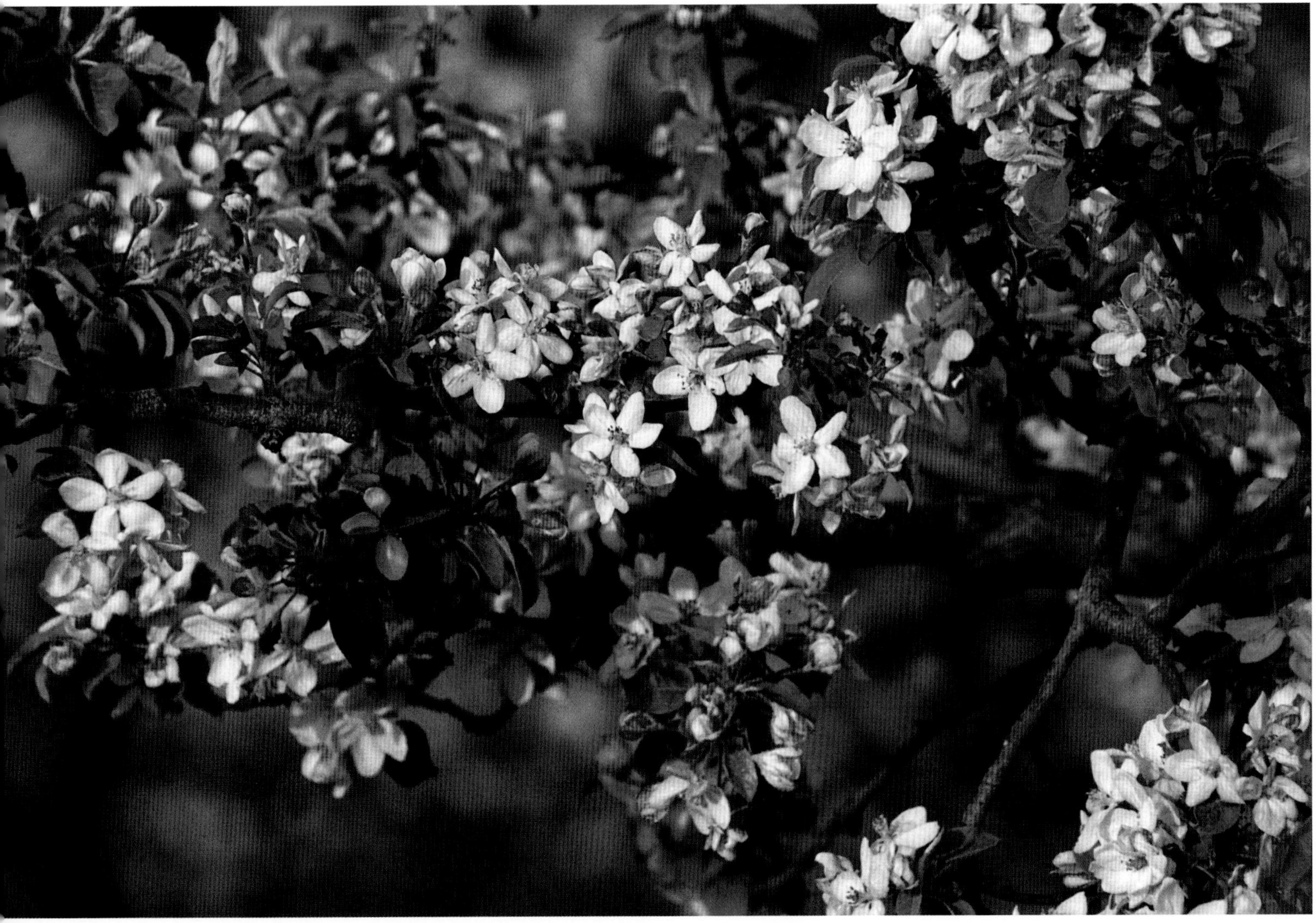

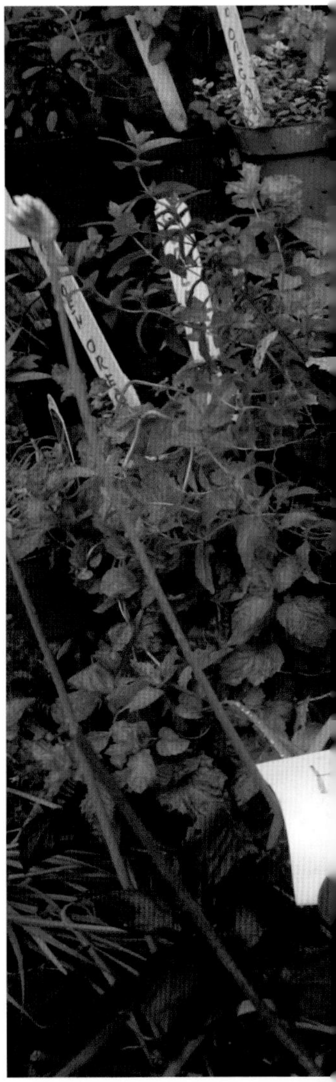

APPLE BLOSSOMS (ABOVE), and Farmer's Market summer scenes.

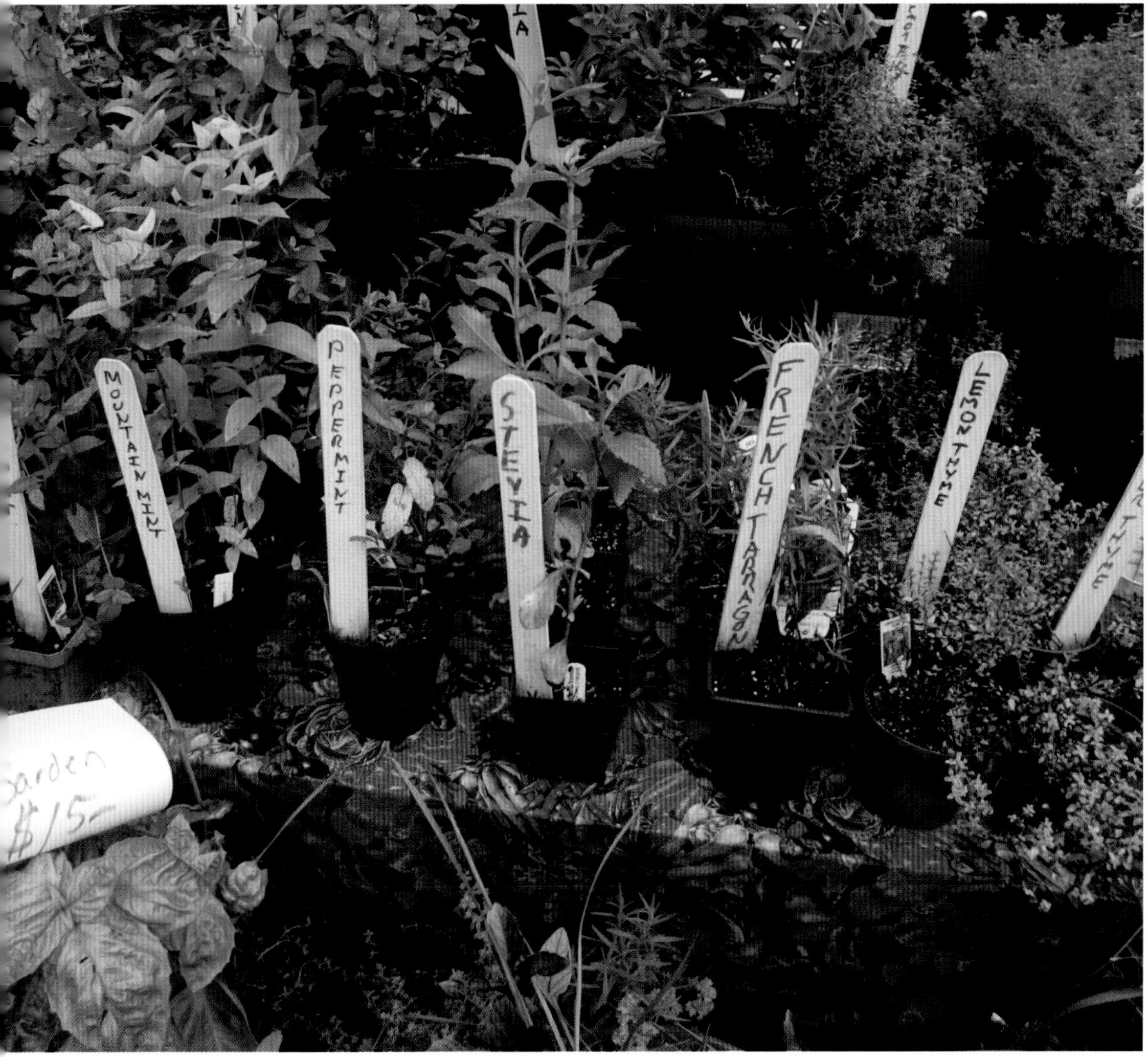
MOUNTAIN MINT
PEPPERMINT
STEVIA
FRENCH TARRAGON
LEMON THYME
$15

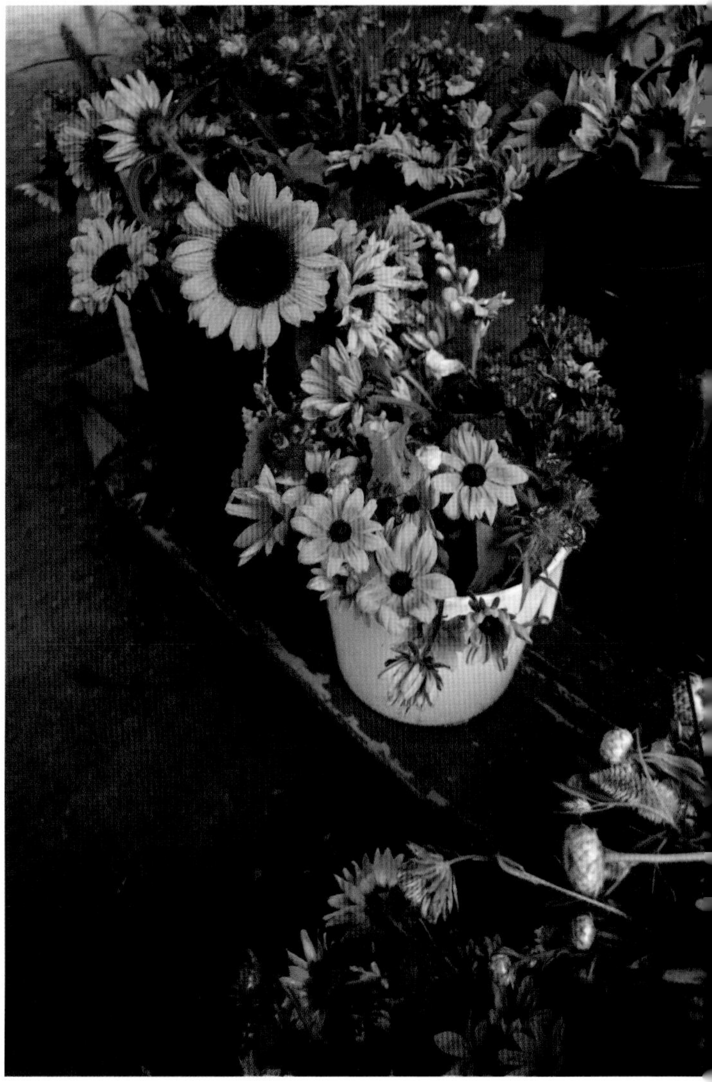

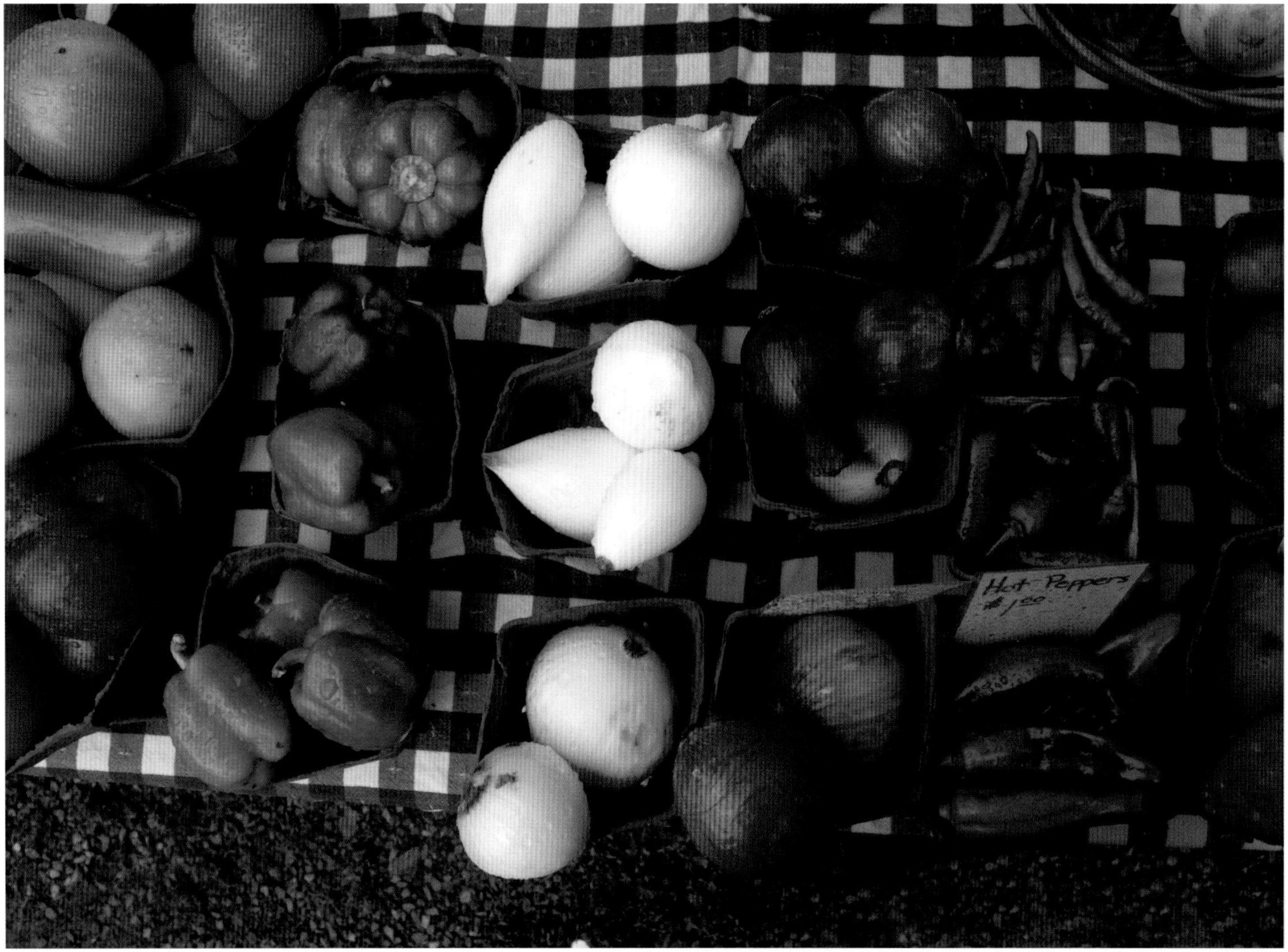
Hot Peppers
$1.00

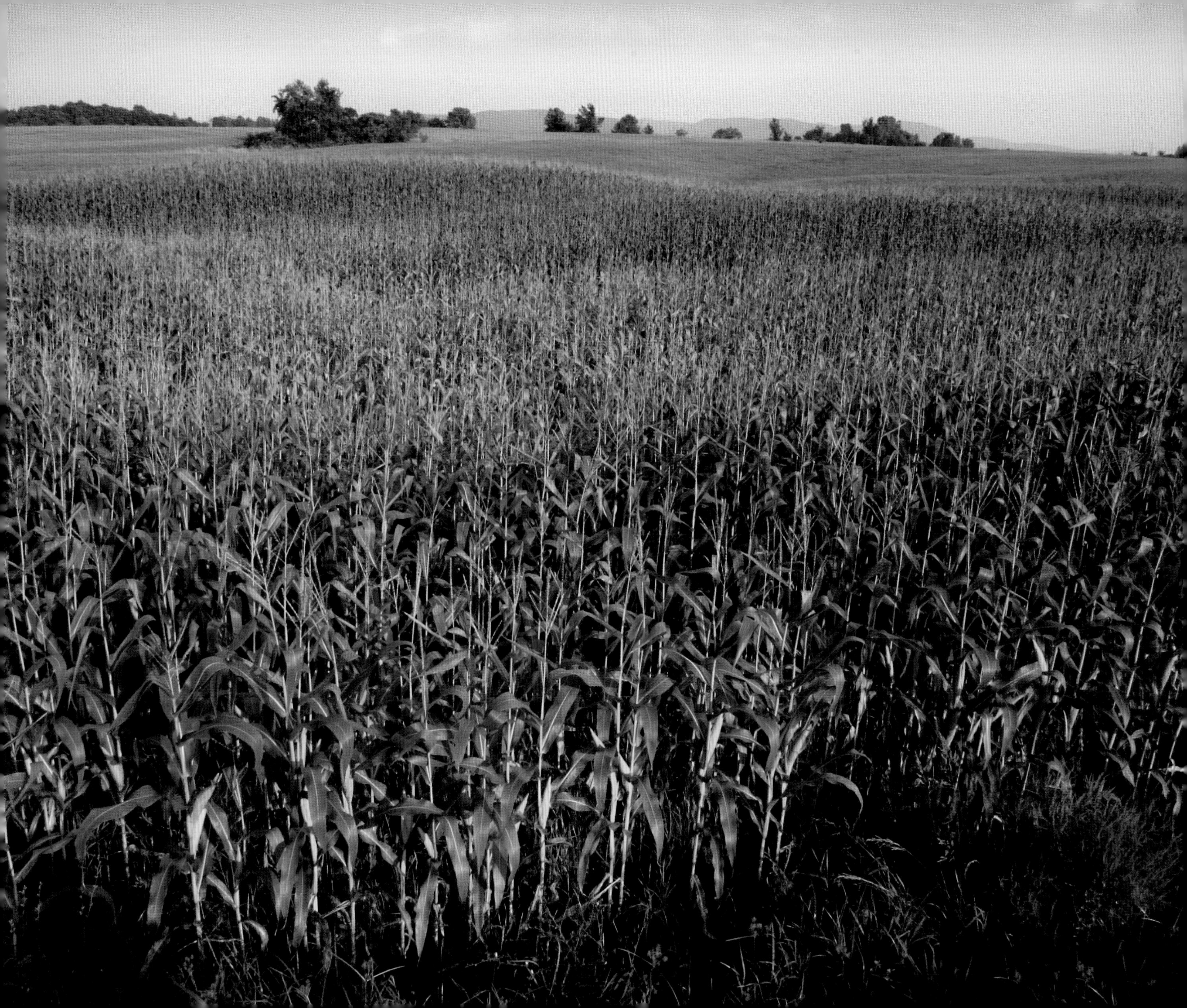

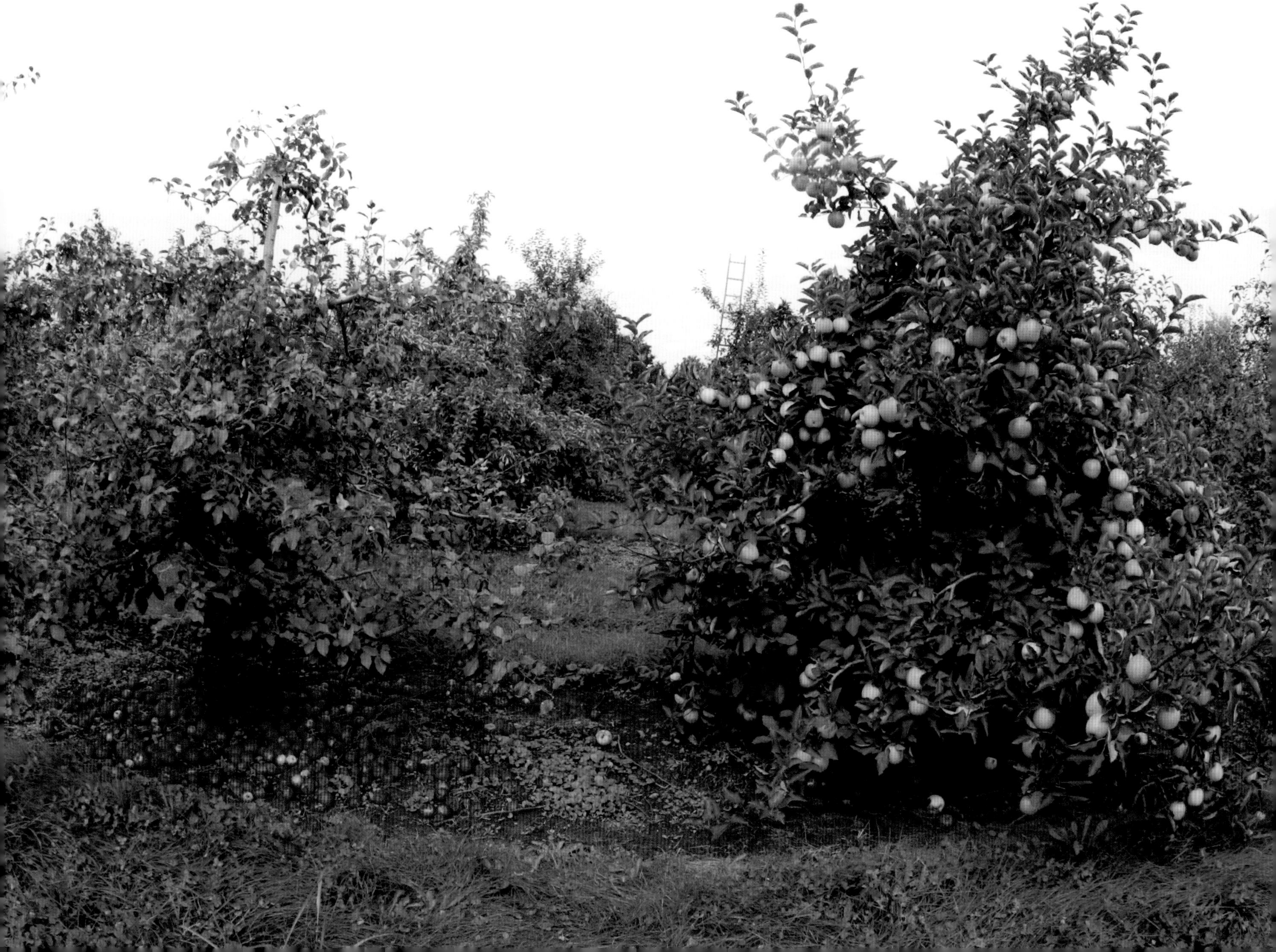

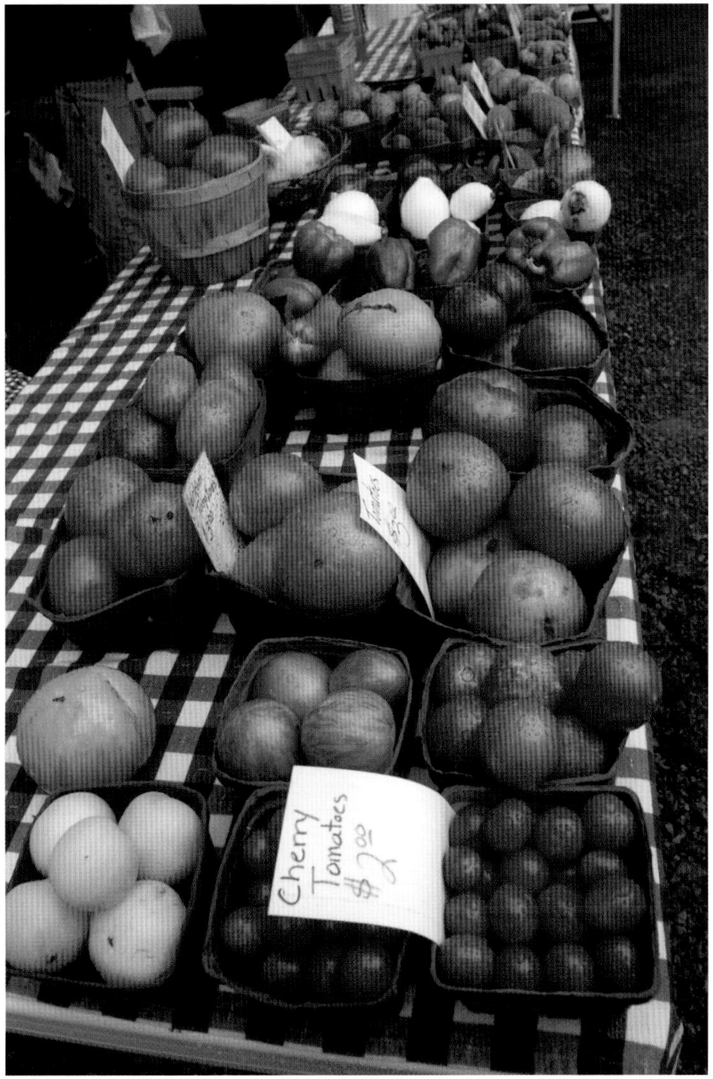

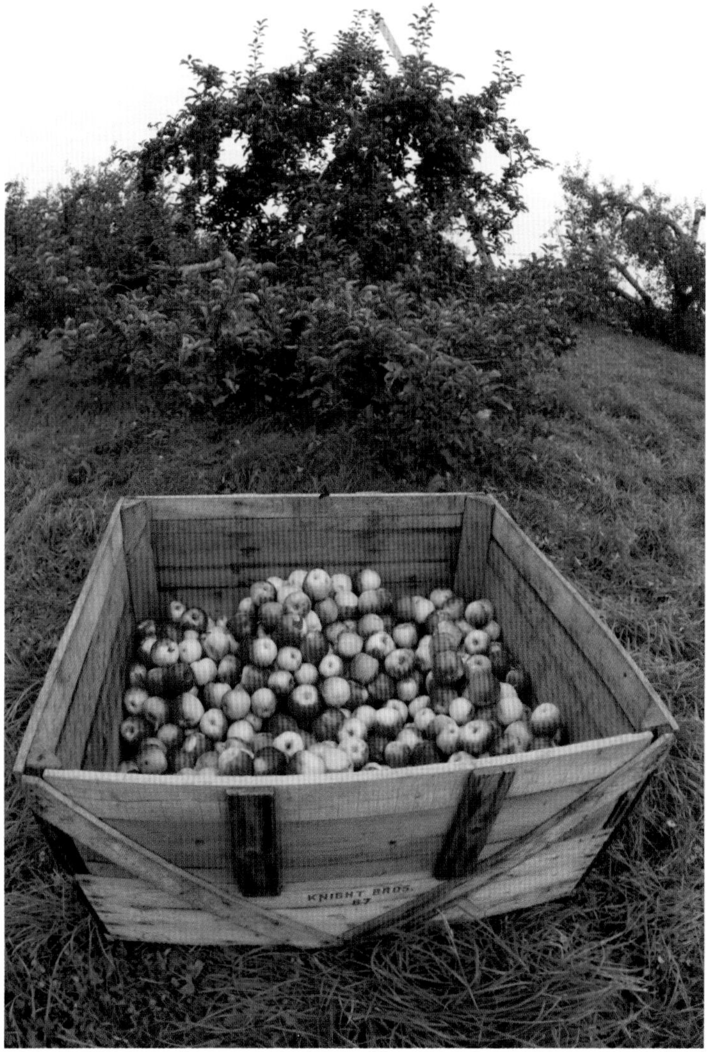

AUTUMN MEANS APPLE PICKING, and more fresh fruit and vegetables at the Farmer's Market.

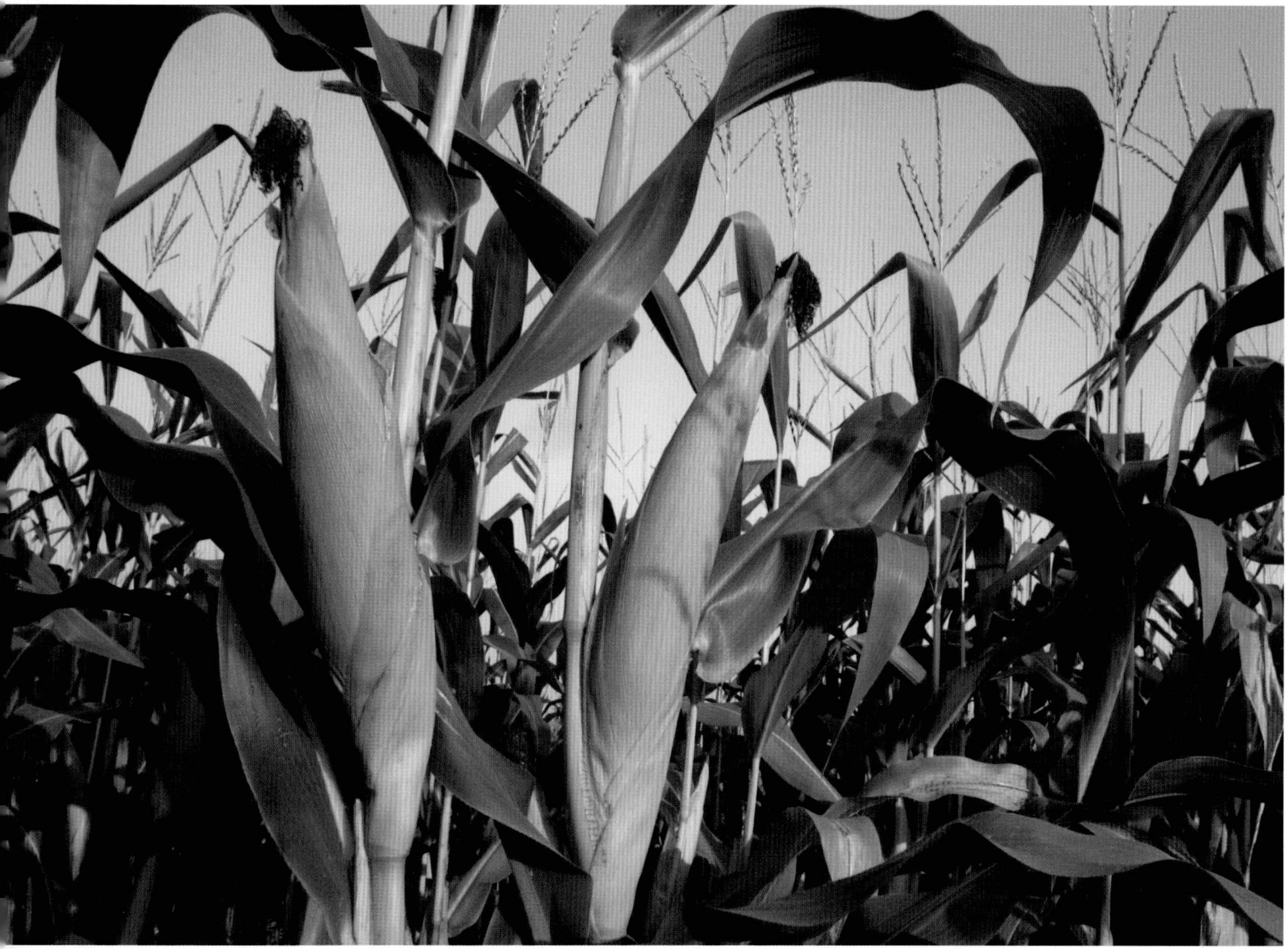

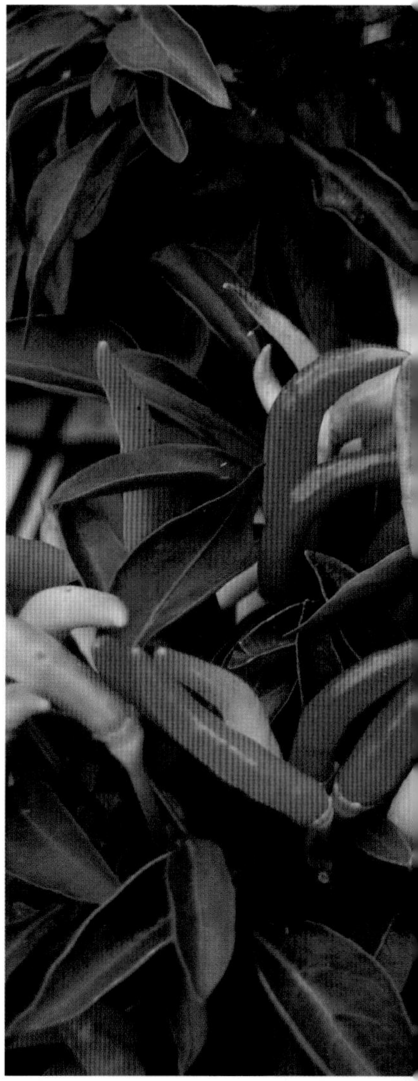

THE SEASON'S LAST CORN, brilliant peppers, and Hand melons, a Saratoga-area tradition.

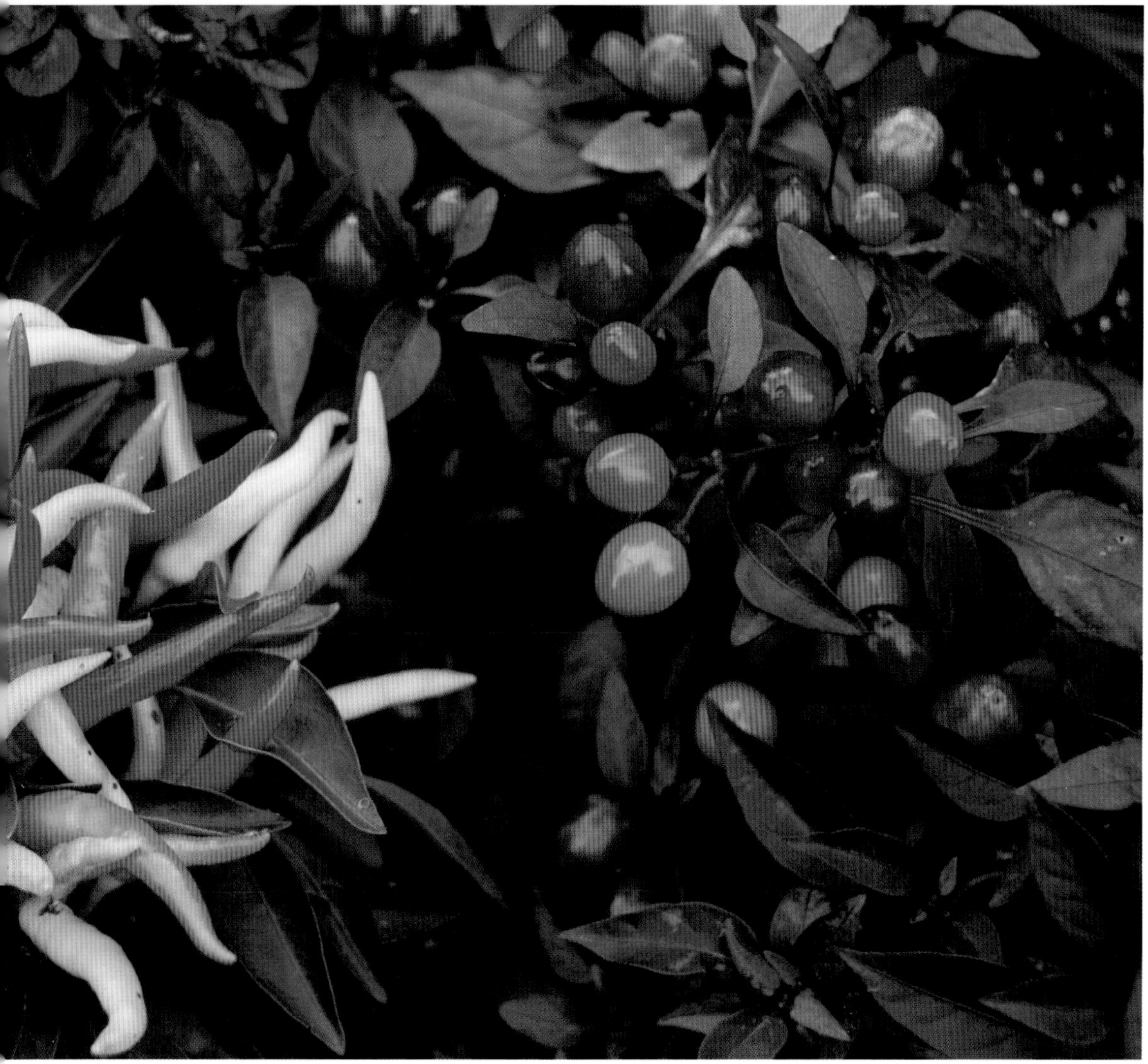

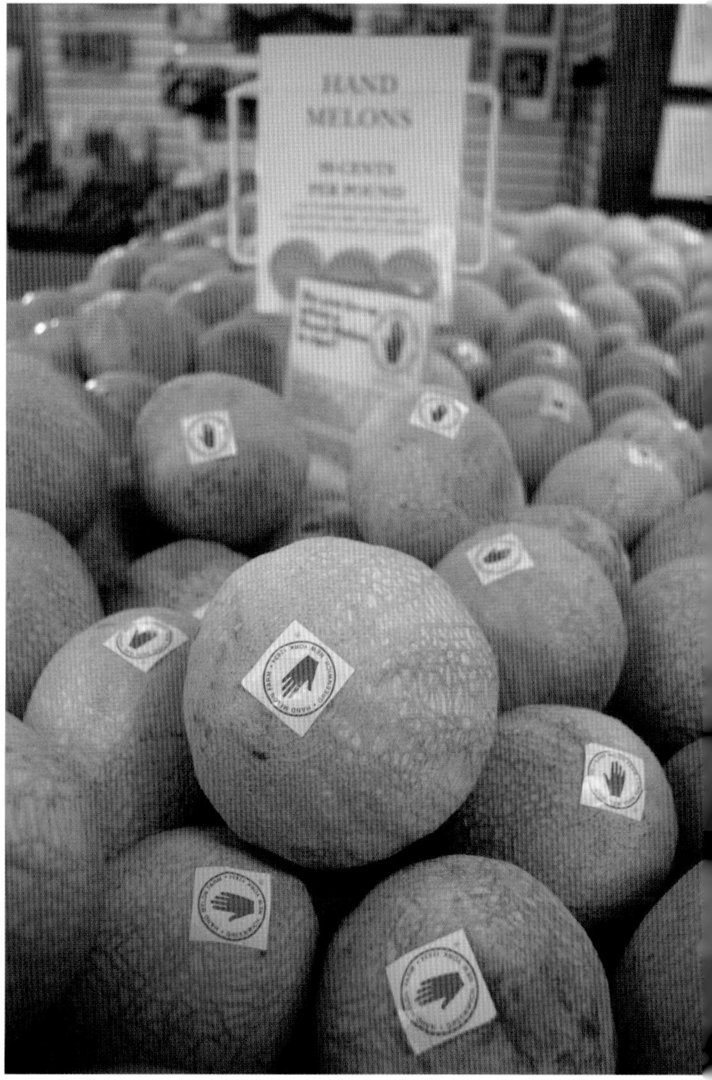
HAND
MELONS

HARVESTED APPLES at Knight Orchard of Saratoga Inc.

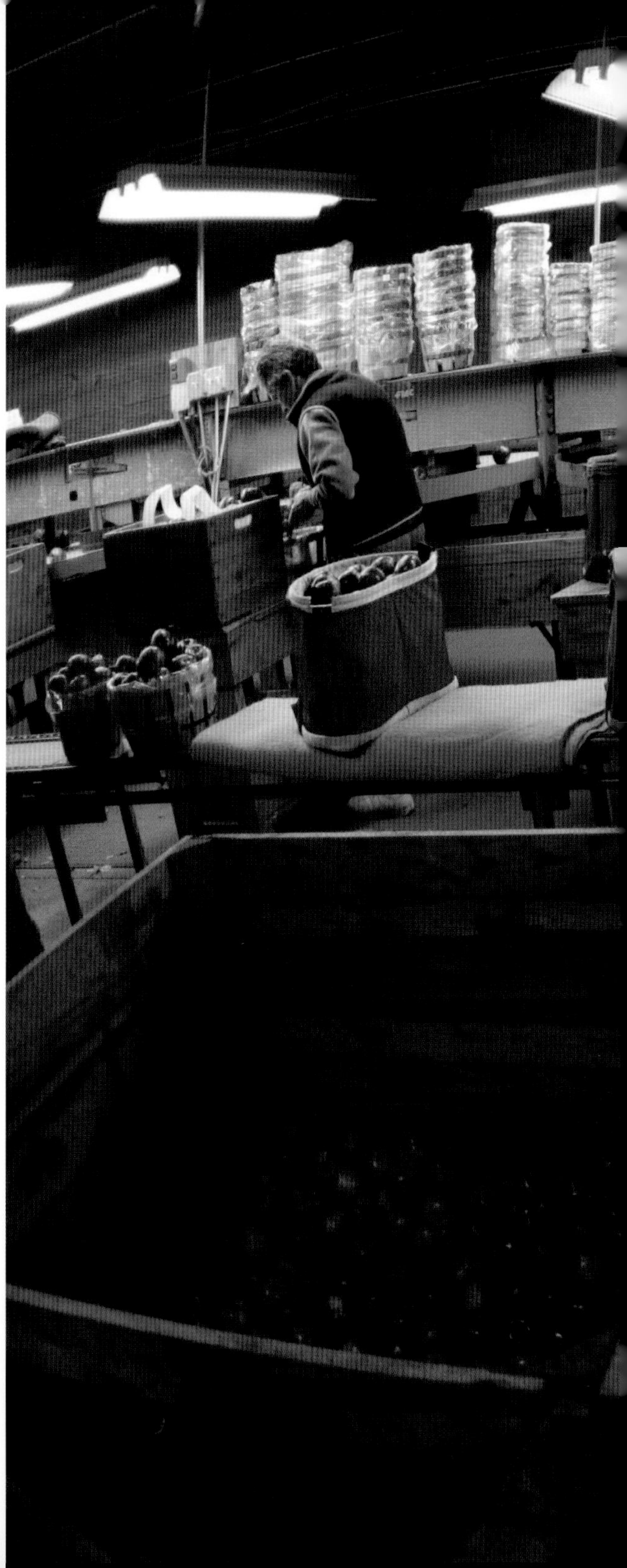

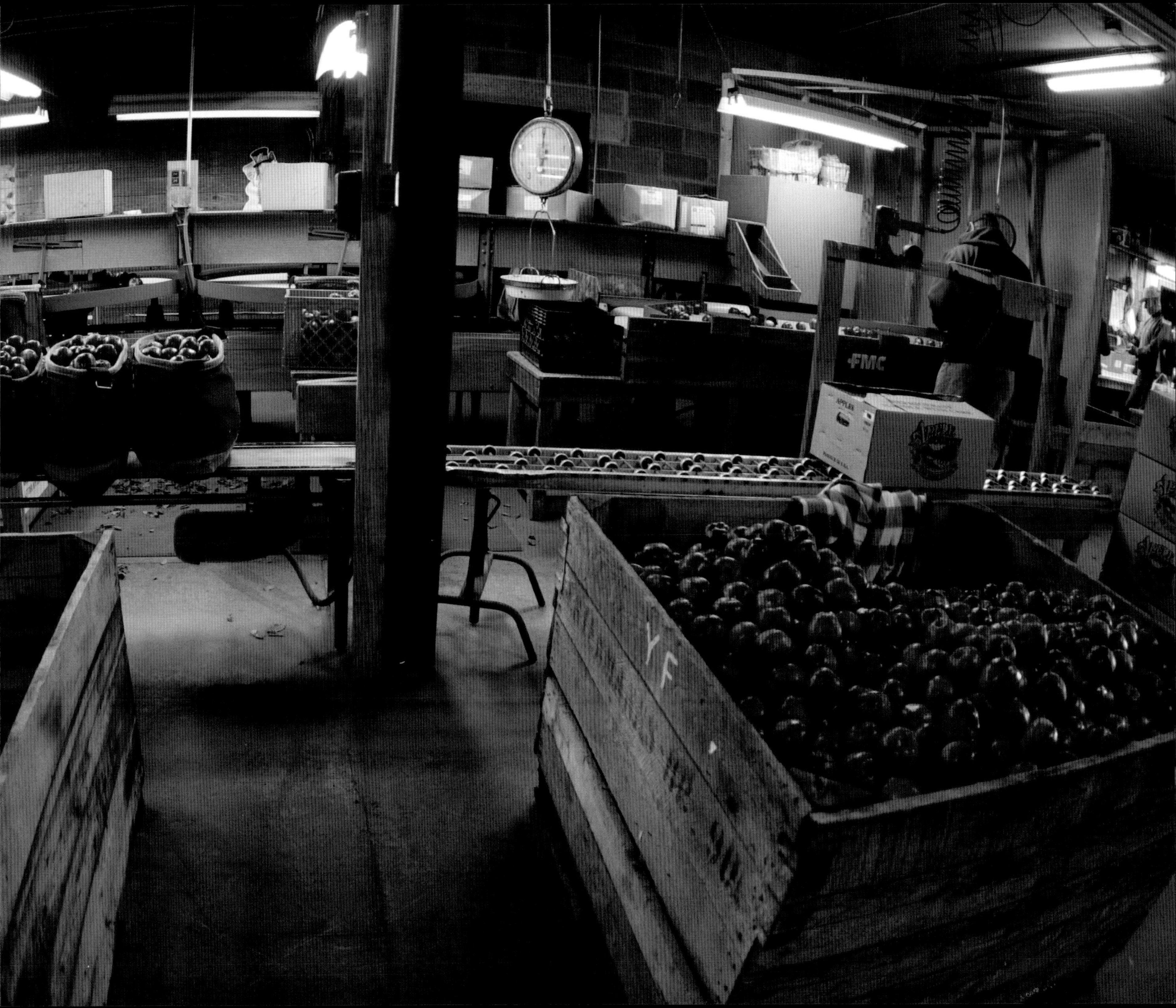
FMC
APPLES
YF

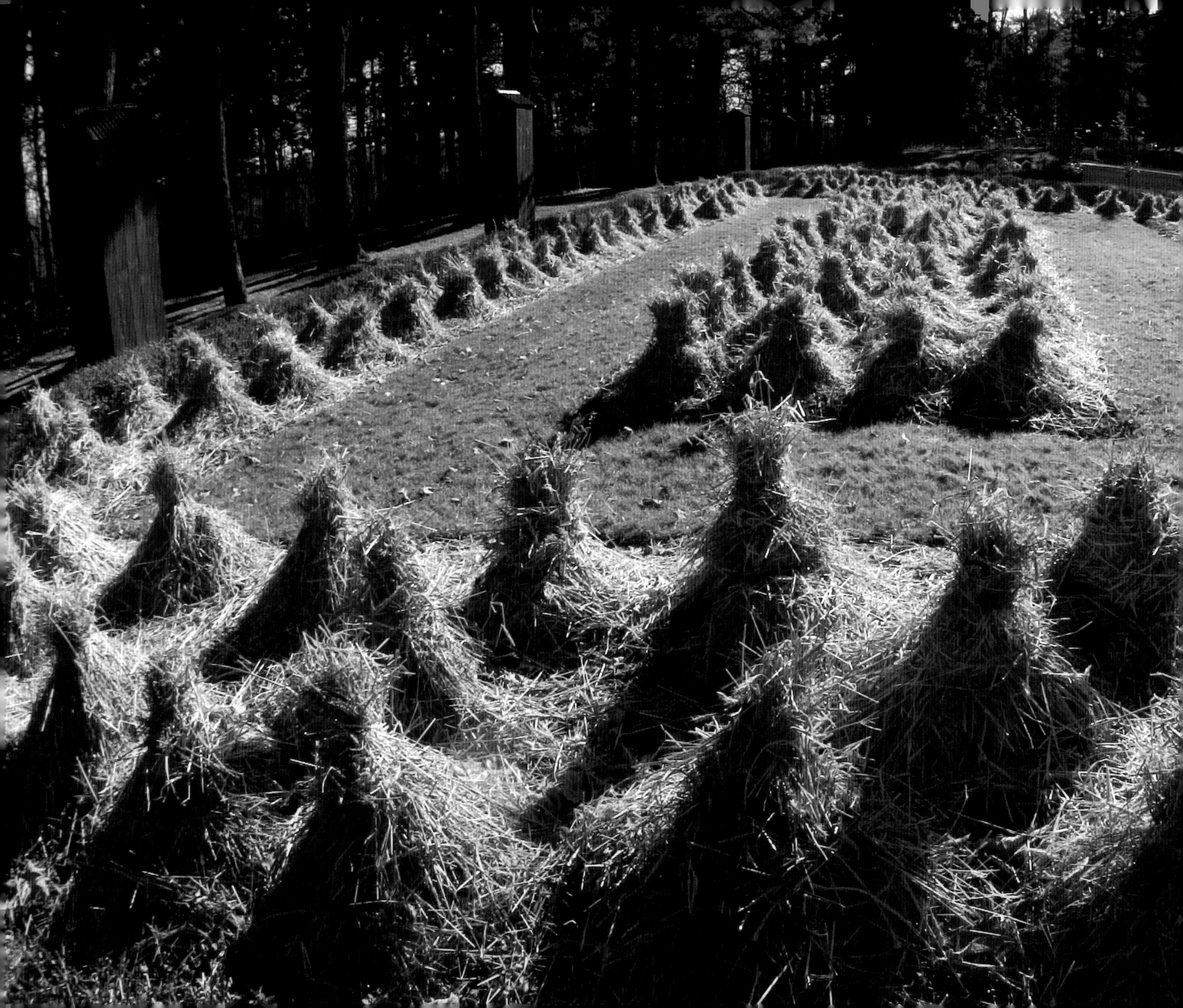

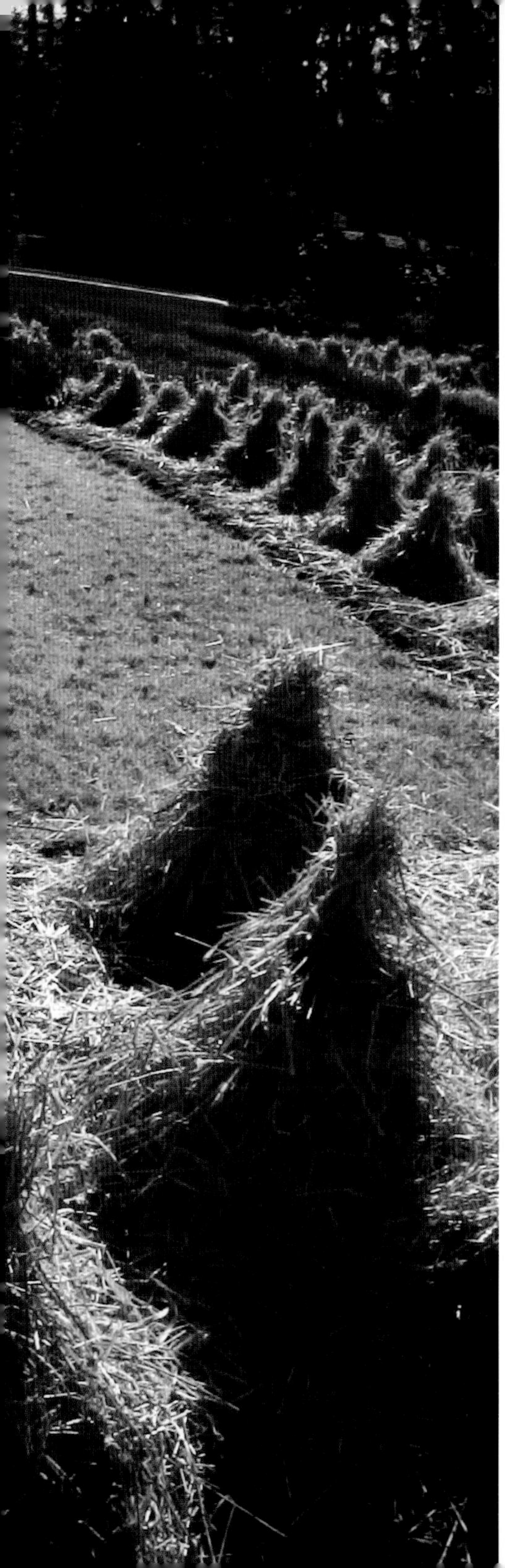

YADDO ROSE BUSHES are prepared each autumn for another cold Saratoga winter.

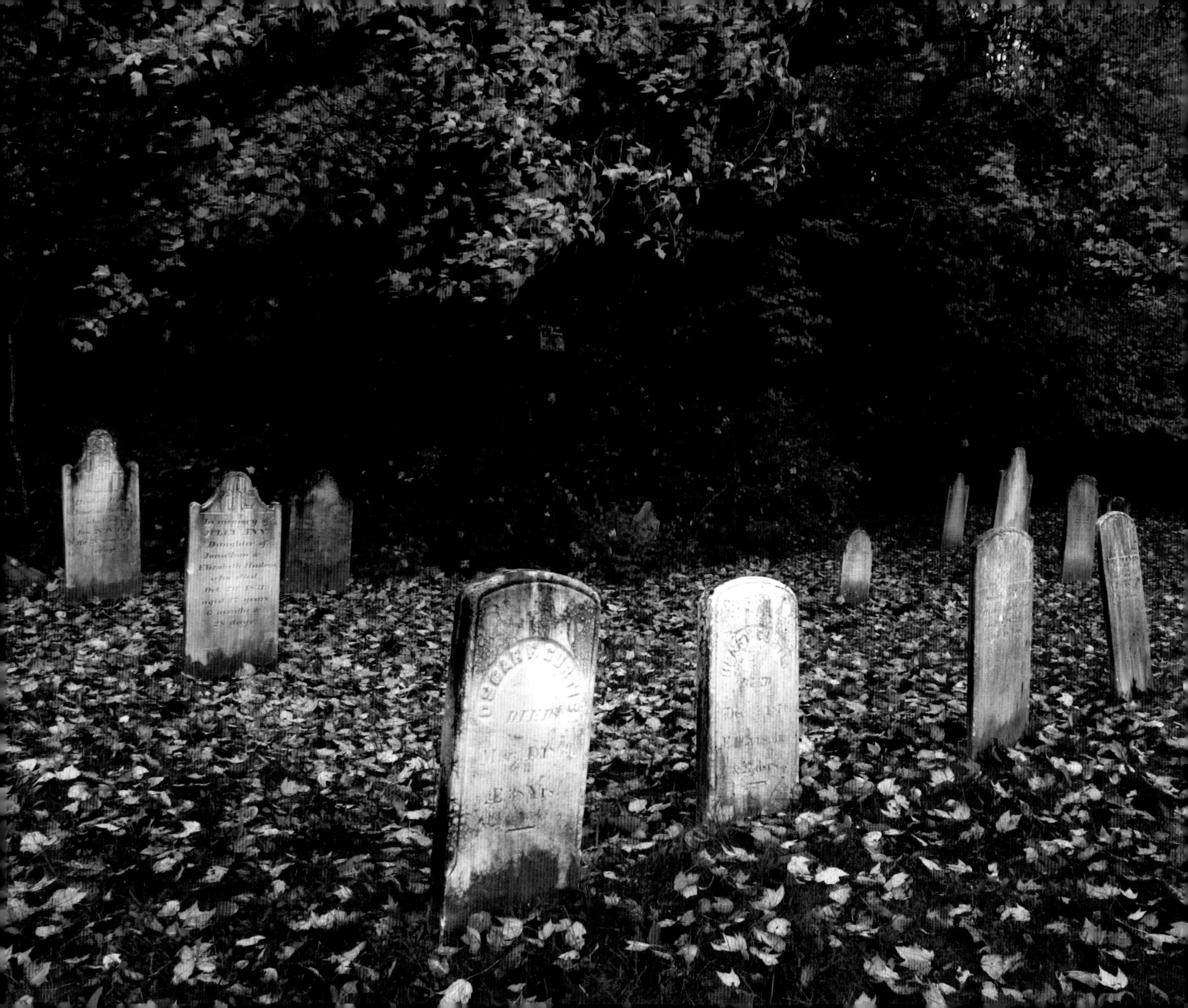

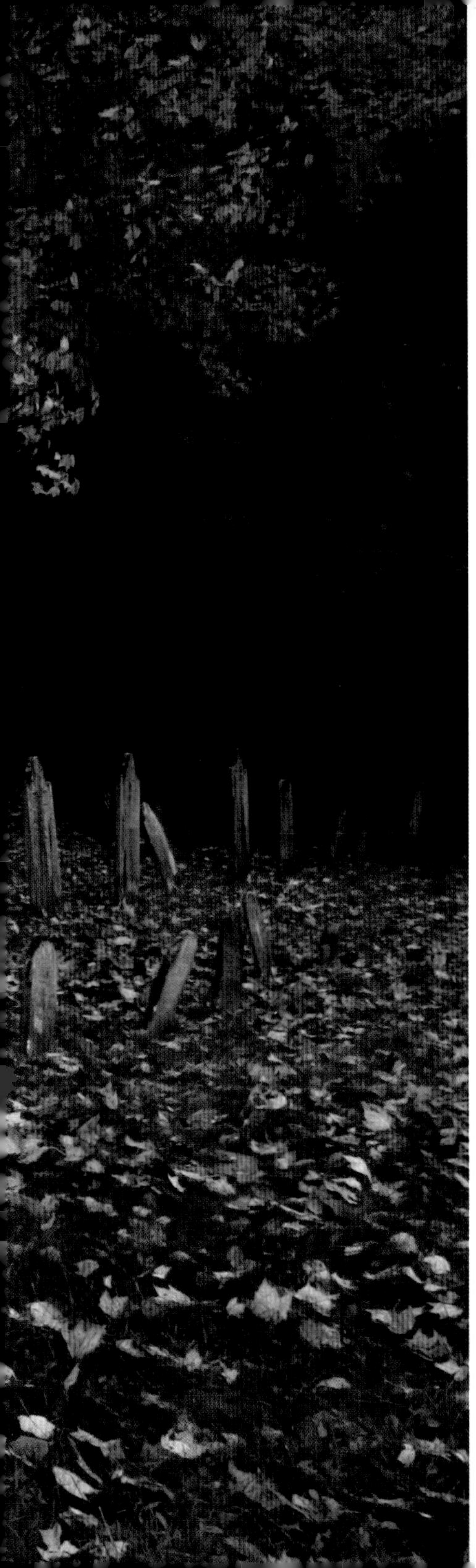

AREA CEMETERY WITH AUTUMN COLORS

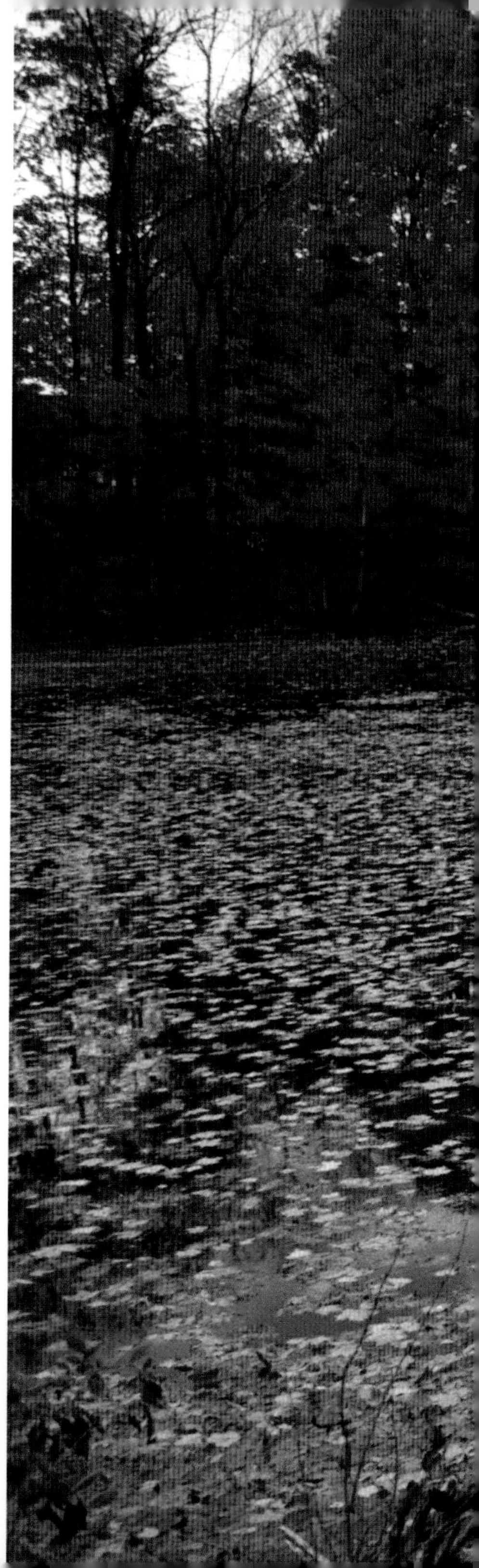

206 A SARATOGA COUNTY POND DECORATED IN AUTUMN FOLIAGE

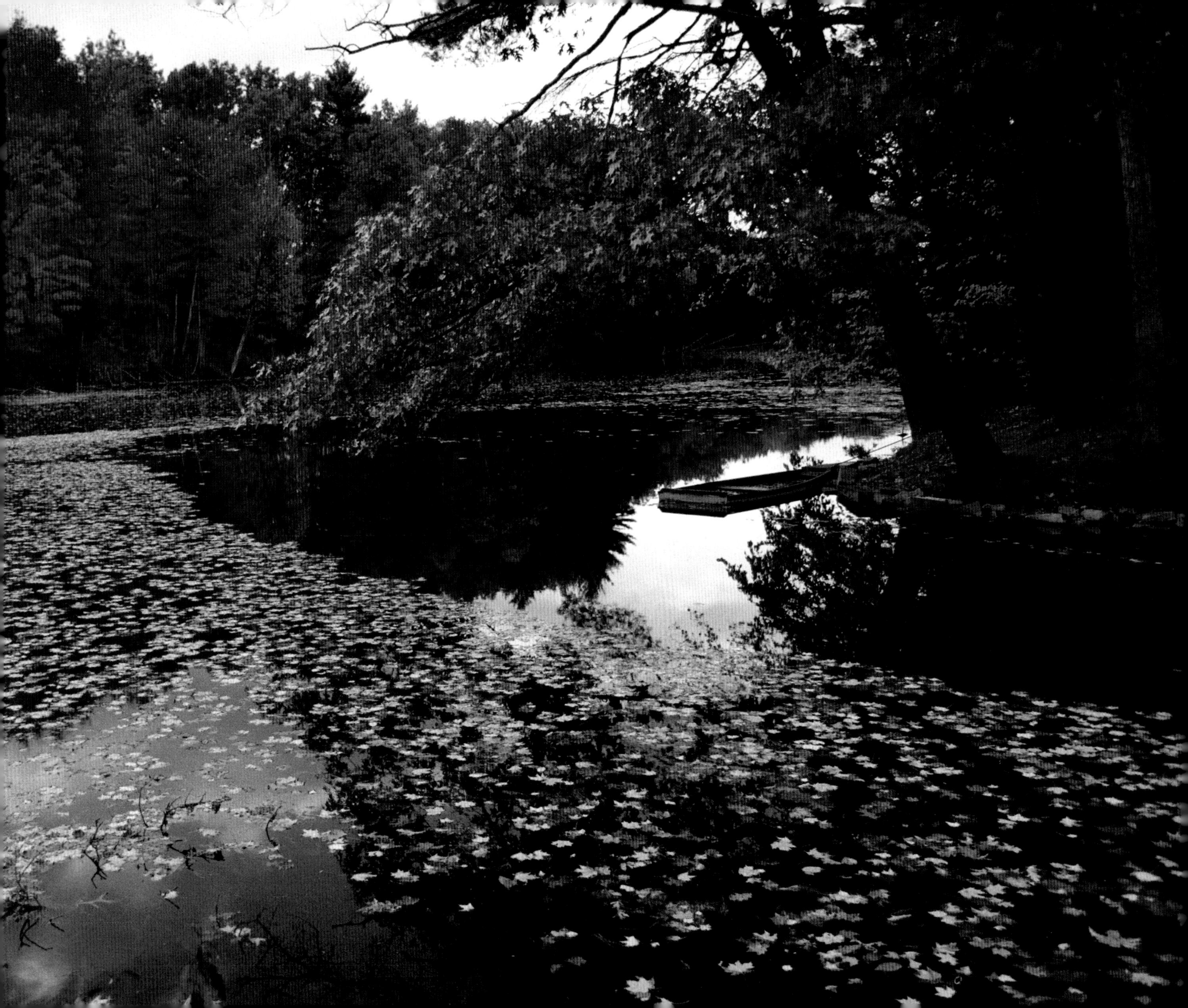

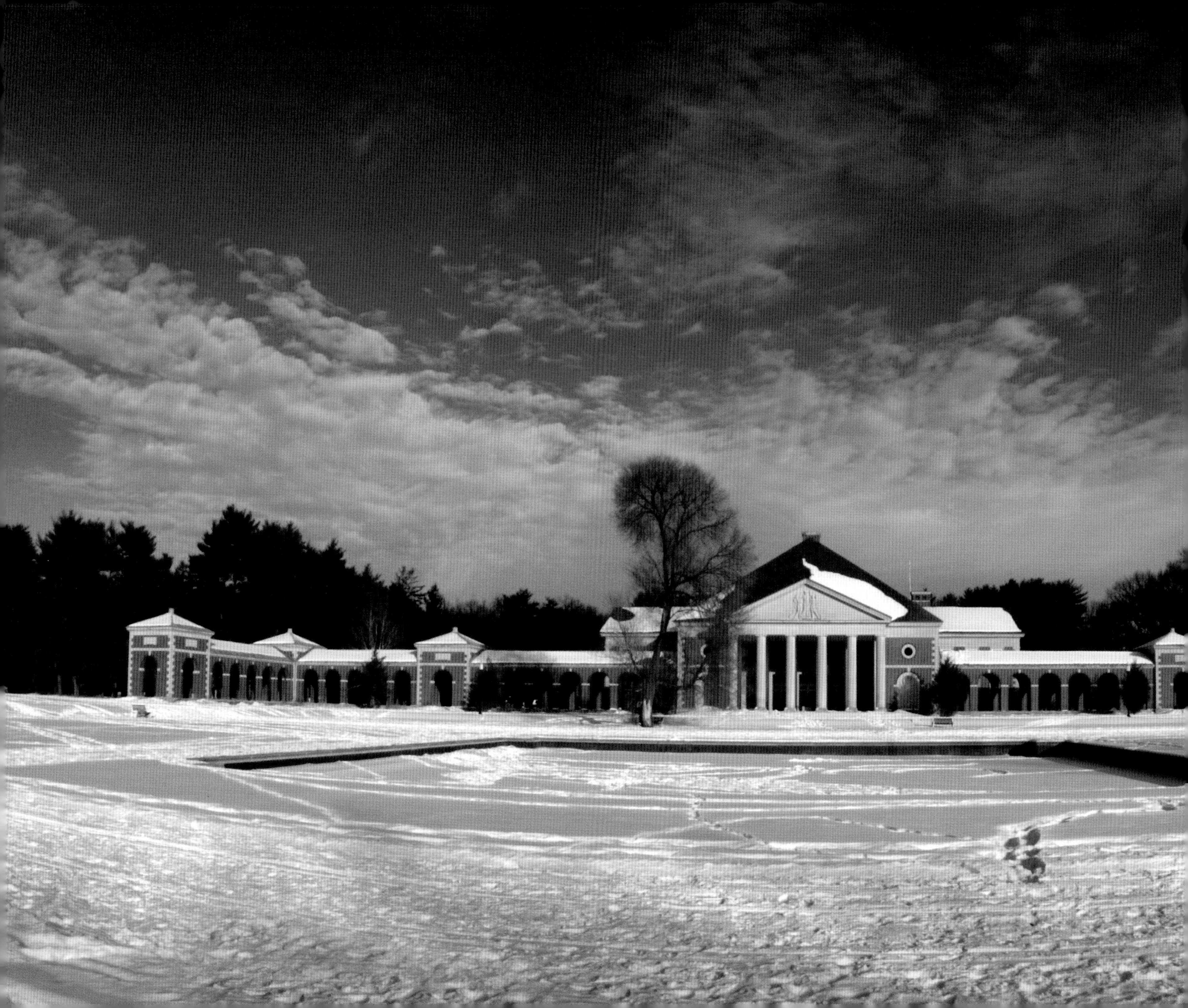

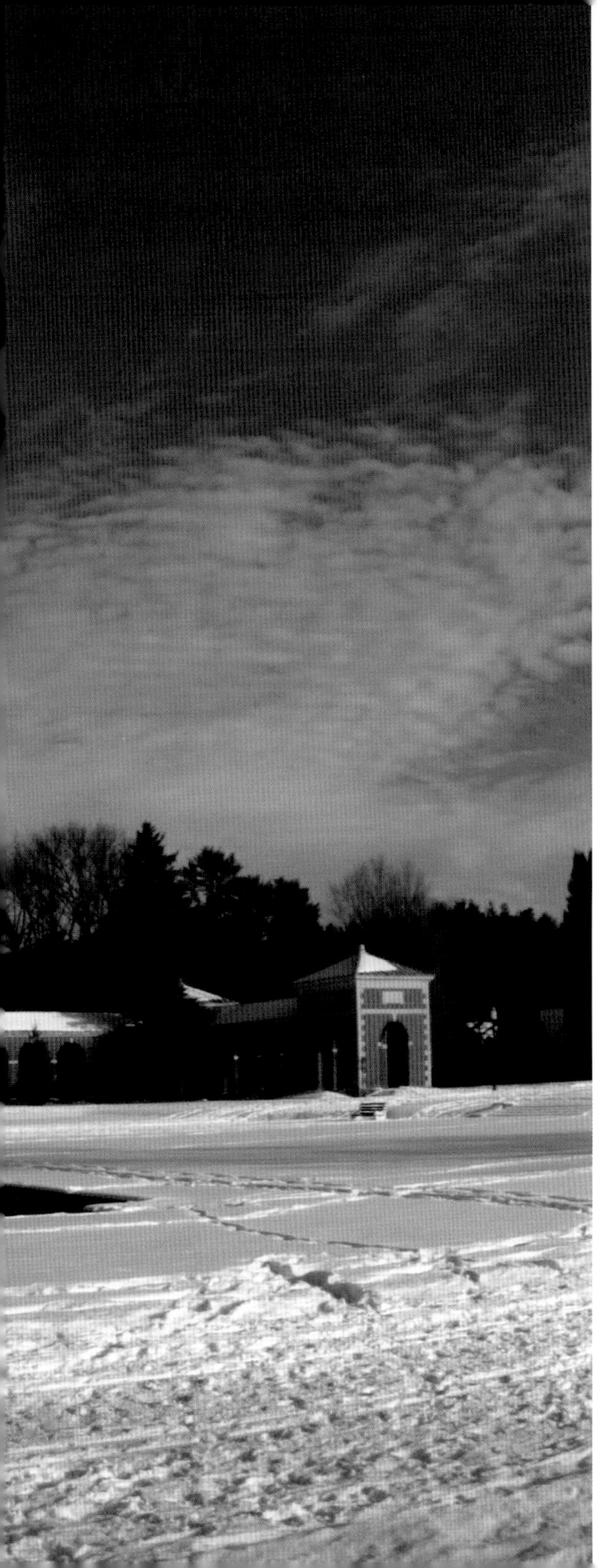

SARATOGA SPA STATE PARK IN A WINTER CHILL

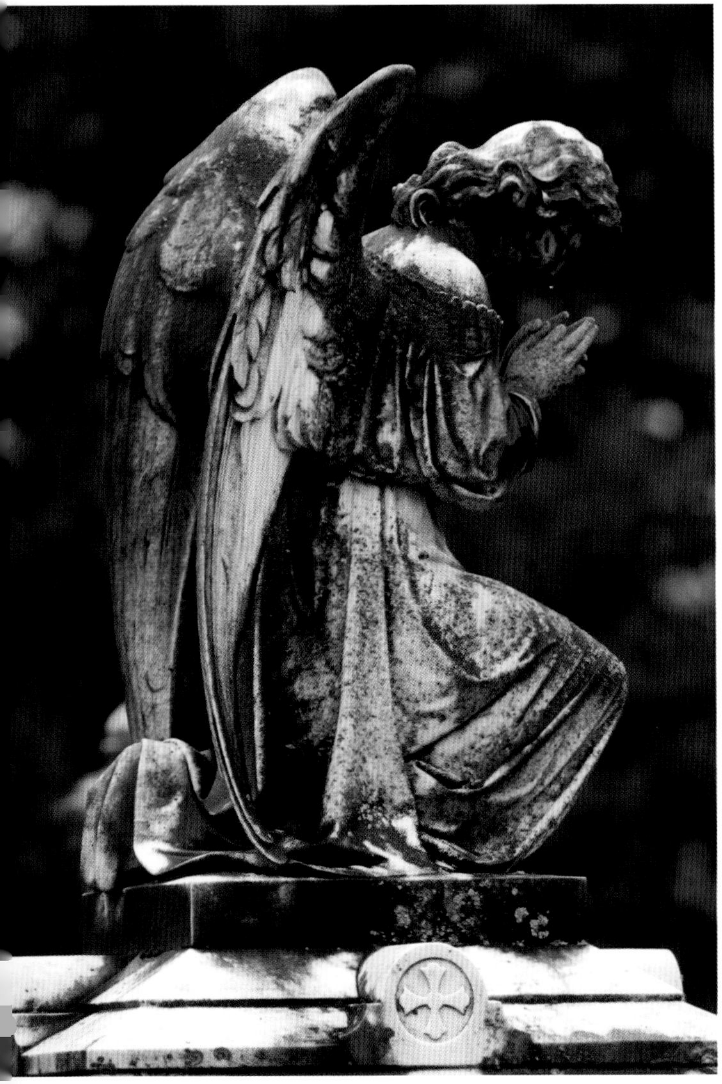

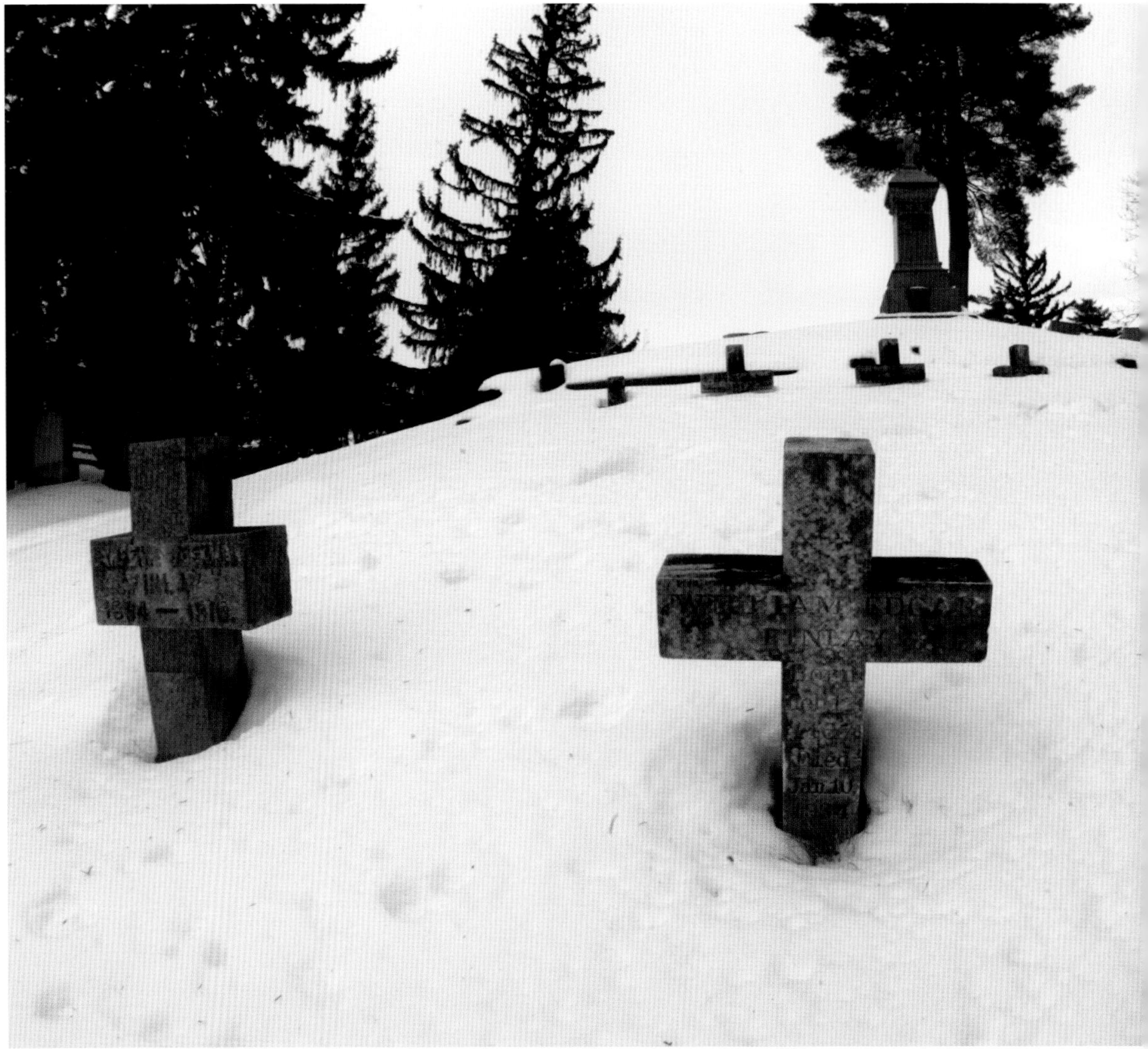

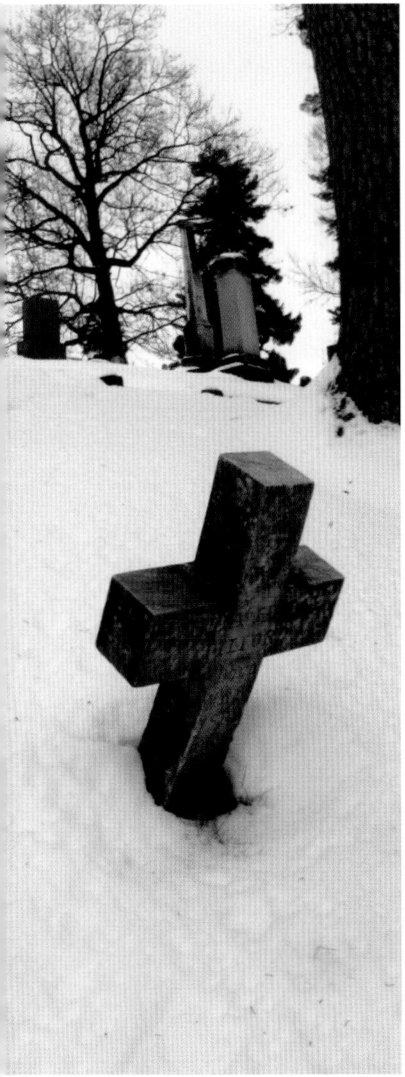
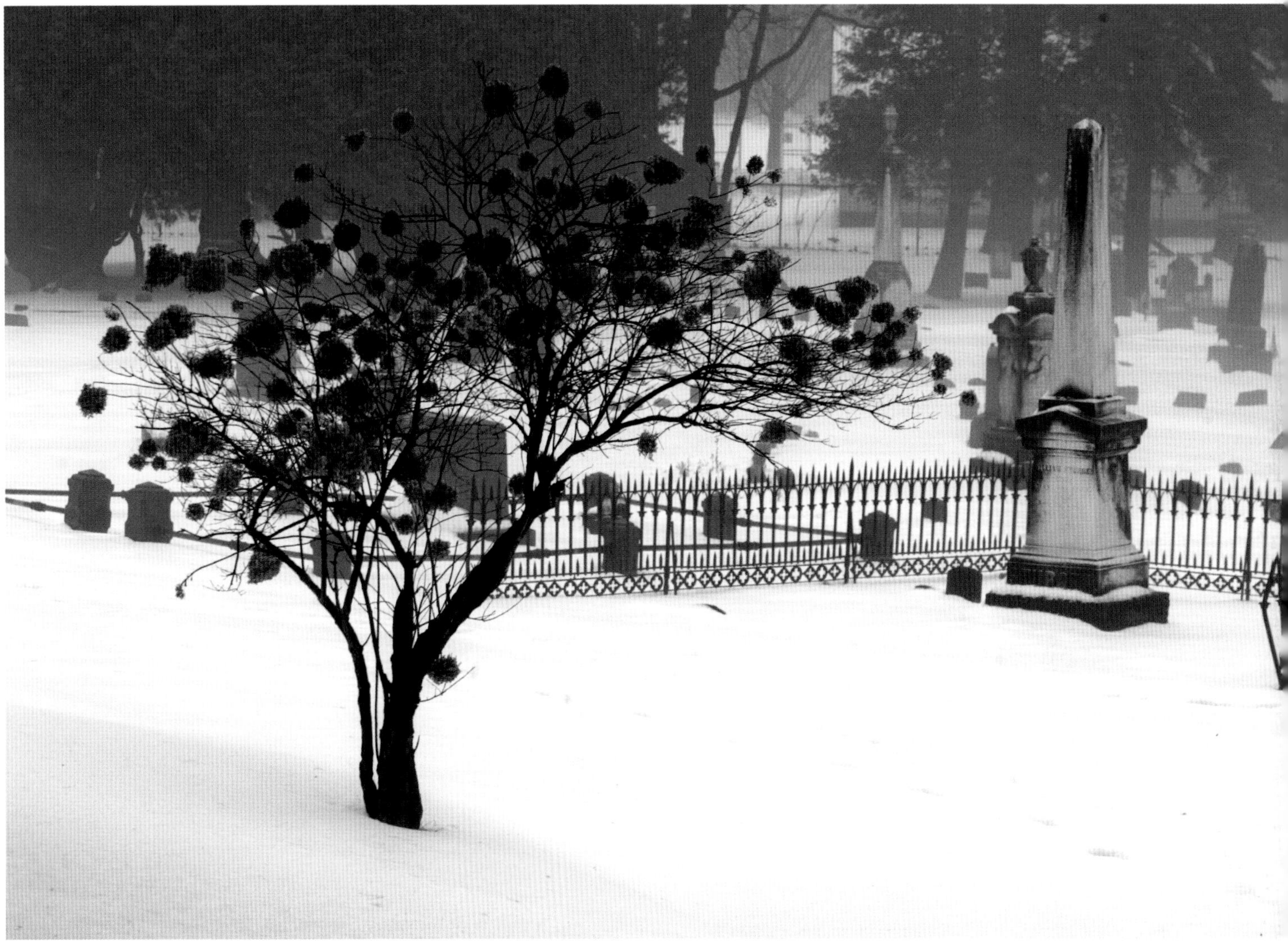

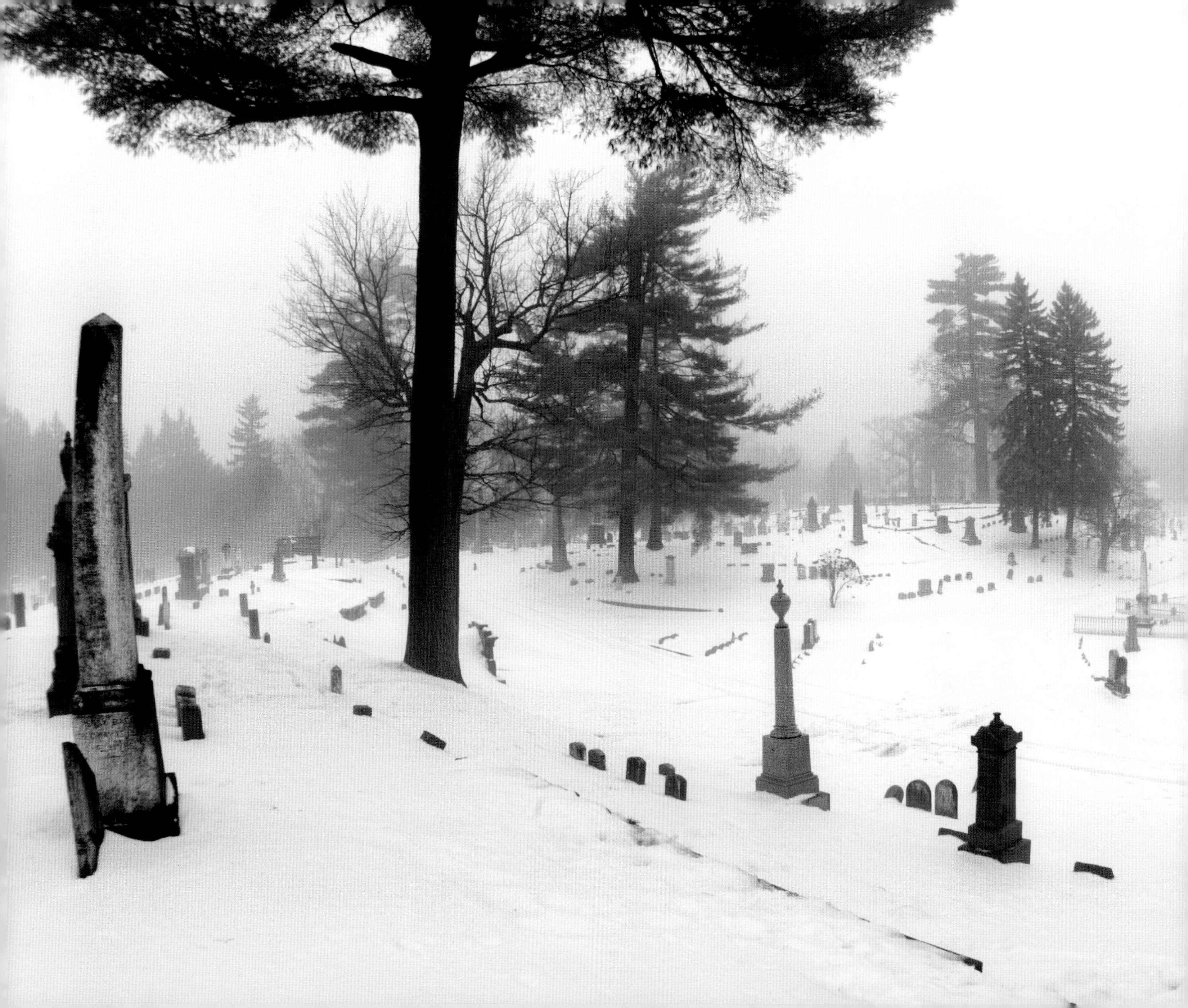

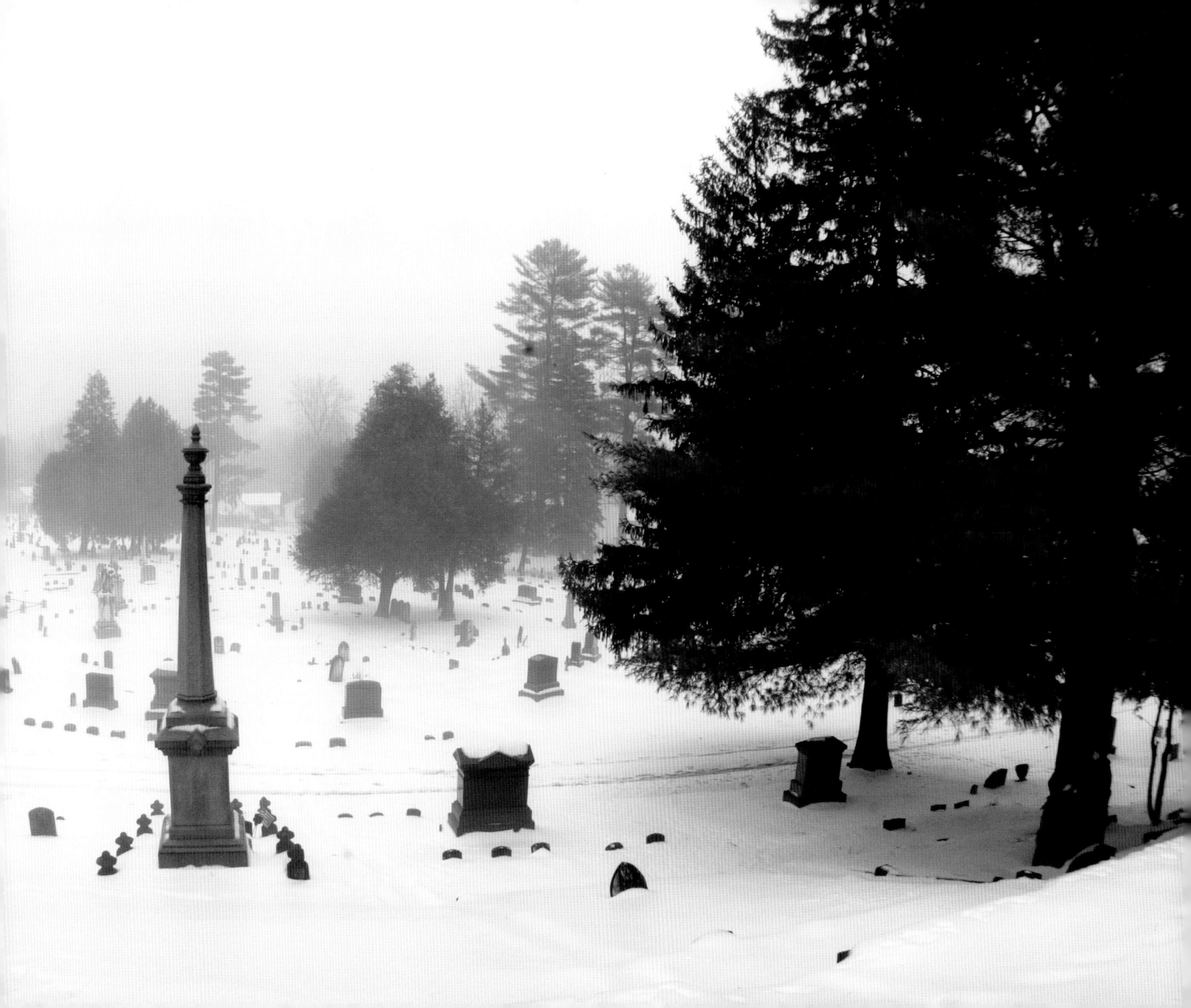

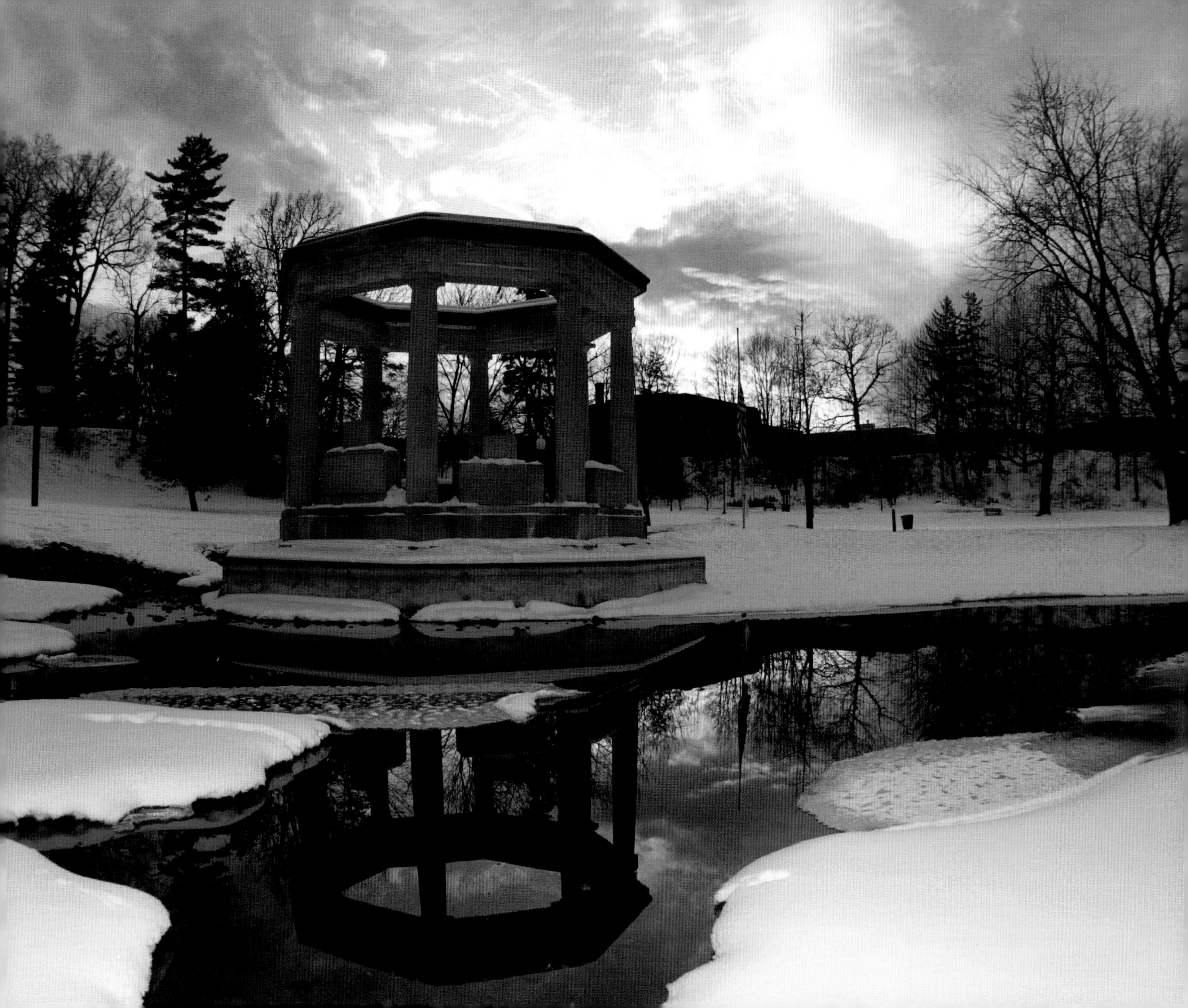

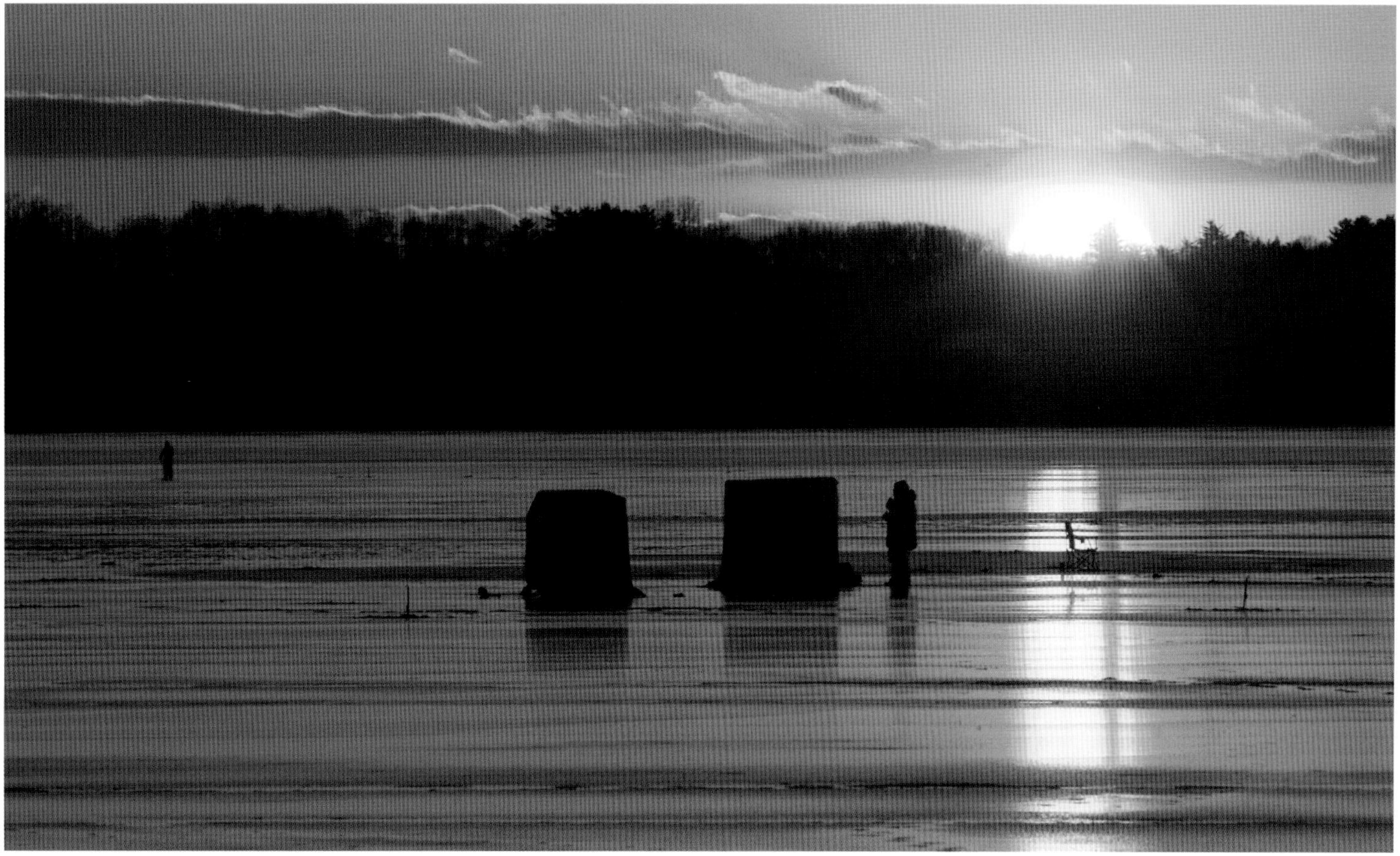

WINTER SUNSET AT CONGRESS PARK (LEFT)

ICE FISHERMEN ON SARATOGA LAKE (ABOVE)

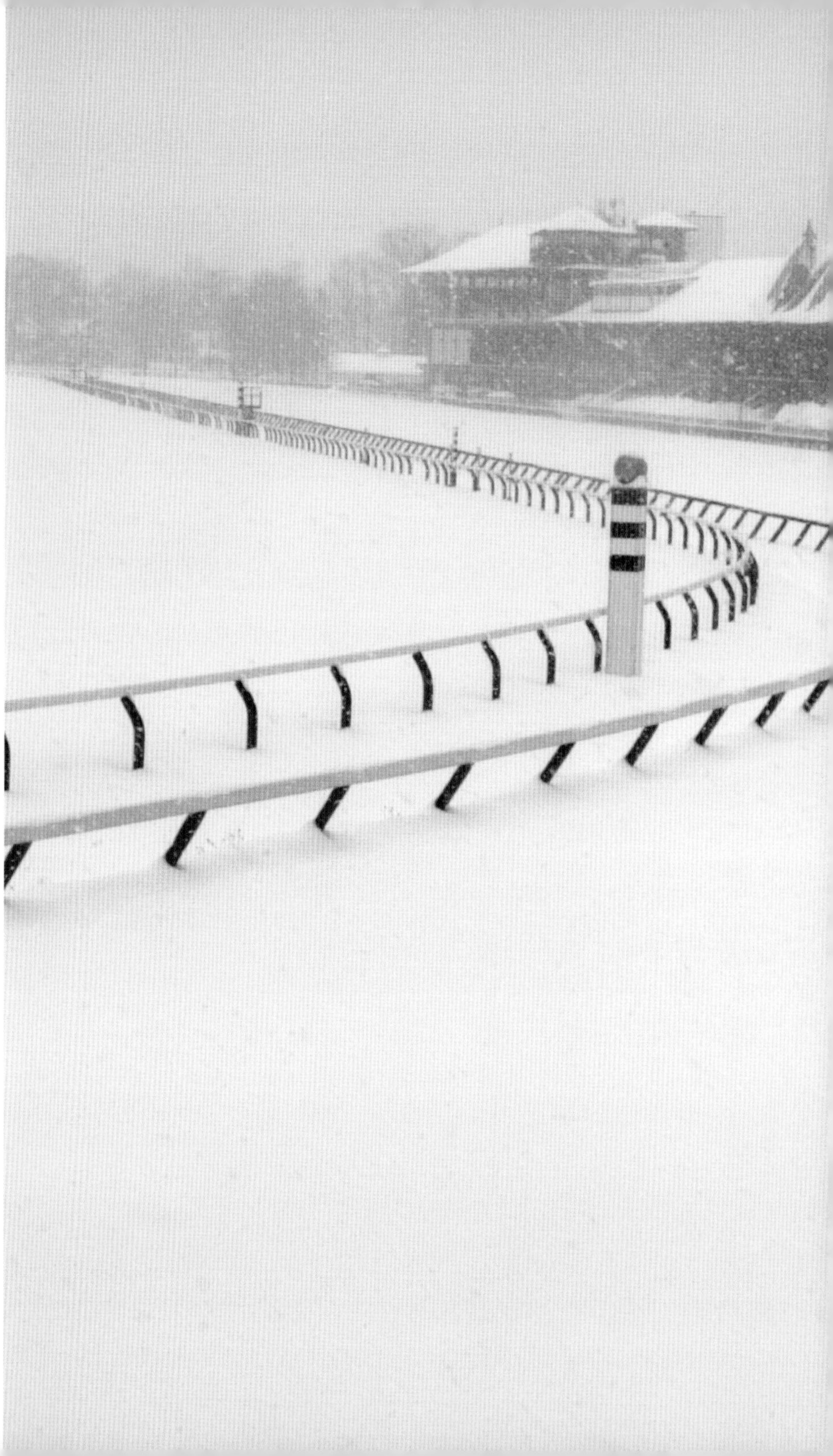

216 SARATOGA RACE COURSE IN THE SNOW

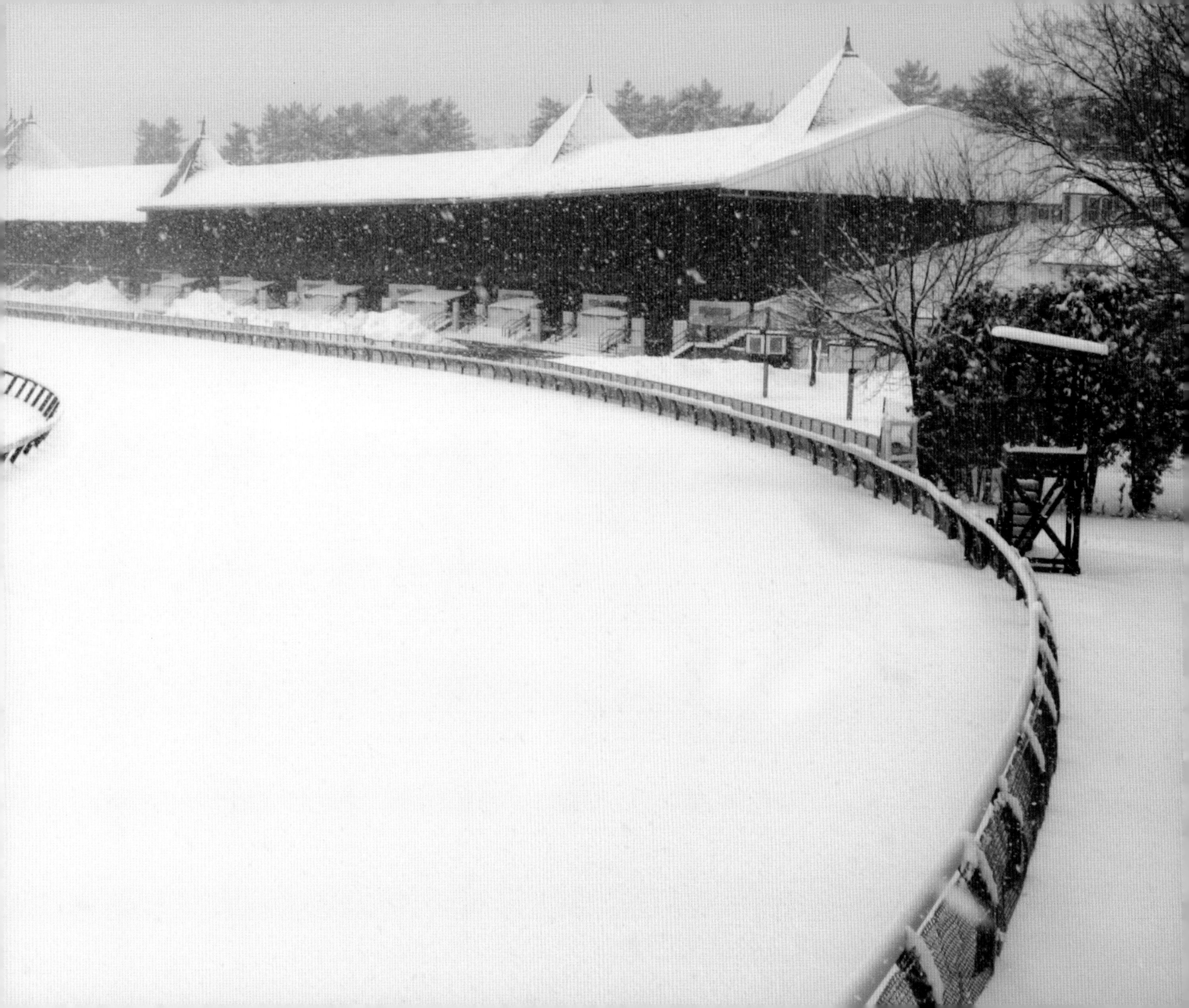

I would like to acknowledge the following for their assistance and/or inspiration: Nancy and Rolf Thorkildsen; Jim and Sherry Livingston; my sisters Joan and Susan Livingston; Saratoga Springs' city historian, Mary Ann Fitzgerald; the Saratoga Room of the Saratoga Springs Public Library; Yaddo's Public Affairs Coordinator, Lesley Leduc; Ray Paulick; Judy Marchman; Tom Hall; Rena Baer; Jackie Duke; Michael Tyner; Tom Keyser; David Young; Brian Turner; and George Hathaway.

Barbara Livingston's love affair with Saratoga Springs, New York, began when she first visited Saratoga Race Course as a horse-crazy adolescent. State-of-the-art camera equipment has replaced the Instamatic she once toted, but Livingston's passion for Thoroughbred racing and the environs of Saratoga Springs has remained constant during a highly lauded career.

Livingston has won two Eclipse Awards and numerous other awards for outstanding photography. Her romantic style and ability to capture the essence of the moment have made her a regular contributor to many publications, including *The Blood-Horse*. Her work also has appeared in Sports *Illustrated*, *Newsweek*, *People*, *Cigar Aficionado*, and *GQ* and on the cover of *TV Guide*. In addition, Livingston's work has appeared on many major book covers, including ones for Bantam; Doubleday; and Little, Brown.

Livingston also is the author of *Four Seasons of Racing* and *Old Friends: Visits with My Favorite Thoroughbreds*, both published by Eclipse Press.

A native of upstate New York, Livingston is a graduate of Syracuse University with a degree in fine arts.

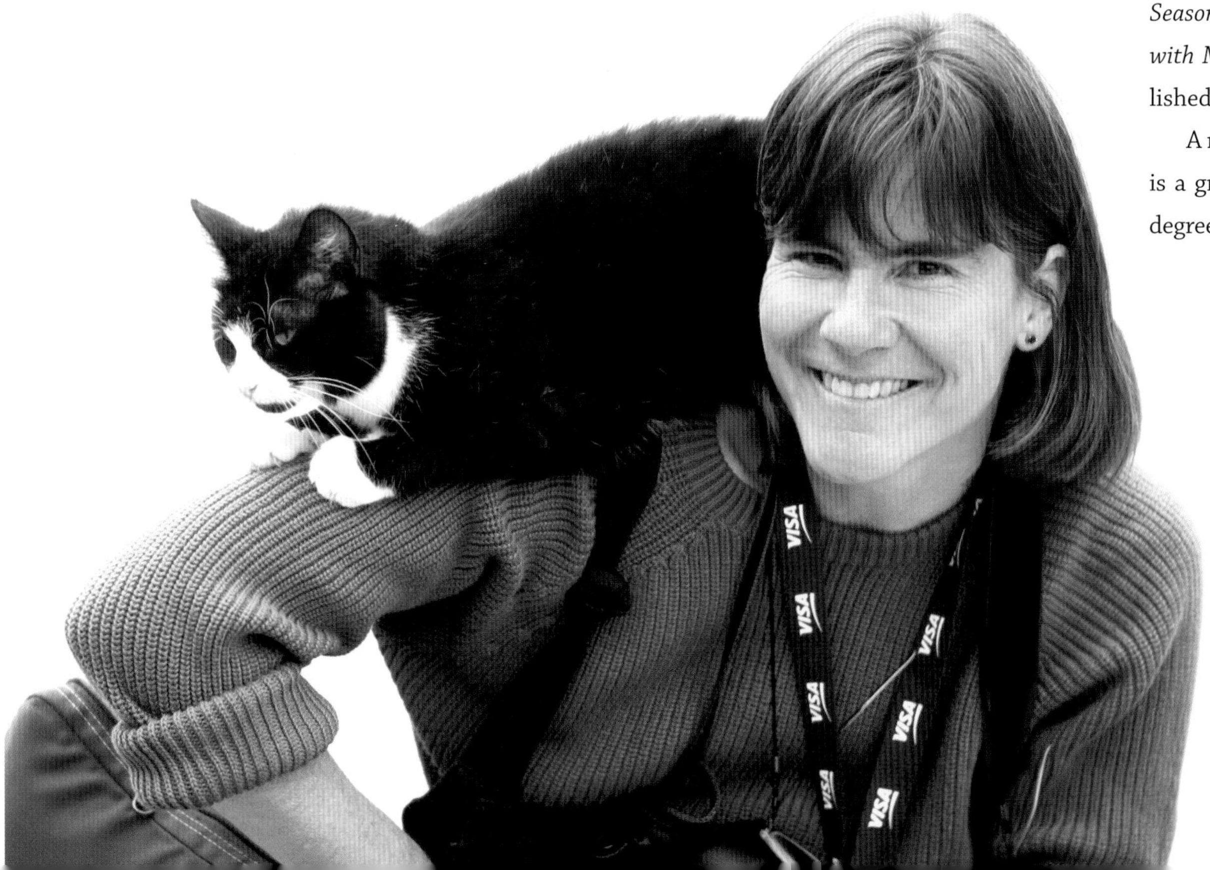

Photo courtesy of Patricia McQueen